18.00

INTERPRETATIONS OF CALAMITY

from the viewpoint of human ecology

Edited by **K. Hewitt**

Wilfrid Laurier University, Ontario

Boston
ALLEN & UNWIN INC.
London   Sydney

Allen & Unwin Inc.,
9 Winchester Terrace, Winchester, Mass 01890, USA

George Allen & Unwin (Publishers) Ltd,
40 Museum Street, London WC1A 1LU, UK

George Allen & Unwin (Publishers) Ltd,
Park Lane, Hemel Hempstead, Herts HP2 4TE, UK

George Allen & Unwin Australia Pty Ltd,
8 Napier Street, North Sydney, NSW 2060, Australia

First published in 1983

ISSN 0261-0507

Library of Congress Cataloging in Publication Data

Main entry under title:
   Interpretations of calamity from the viewpoint of
human ecology.
(The Risks & hazards series, ISSN 0261-0507; no. 1)
Includes bibliographies and index.
1. Natural disasters – Economic aspects.
2. Climatic changes – Economic aspects.   3. Crops and
climate – Economic aspects.   4. Meteorology,
Agricultural – Economic aspects.   5. Agriculture –
Economic aspects.   6. Food supply.   7. Man –
Influence of environment.   I. Hewitt, Kenneth.
II. Series.

HC79.D45I57   1983   304.4'85   83-2722
ISBN 0-04-301160-8
ISBN 0-04-301161-6 (pbk.)

British Library Cataloguing in Publication Data

   Interpretations of calamity.—(The Risks & hazards
series; no. I)
1. Hazardous geographic environments
2. Disasters—Human ecology
I. Hewitt, Kenneth
304.2   GF85

ISBN 0-04-301160-8
ISBN 0-04-301161-6 Pbk

Set in 10 on 12 point Times by Preface Ltd, Salisbury, Wilts
and printed in The United States of America

We only dimly realise how dependent we are in every way in all our decisions. There's some sort of link-up between it all, we feel, but we don't know what. That's why most people take the price of bread, the lack of work, the declaration of war as if they were phenomena of nature: earthquakes or floods. Phenomena like this seem at first only to affect certain sections of humanity, or to affect the individual only in certain sectors of his habits. It's only much later that normal everyday life turns out to have become abnormal in a way that affects us all. Something has been forgotten, something has gone wrong ... It's because people know so little about themselves that their knowledge of nature is so little use to them.

BERTOLT BRECHT (1965)
The Messingkauf dialogues

Foreword

The *Risks & Hazards Series* is designed to make available to a wider readership the research results and intellectual developments arising from current concerns with hazards in the environment, and the associated risks to human health and wellbeing. Scientific as well as public concern about hazards has reached a new peak but the changes occurring are more than a matter of degree.

There is in all Western industrial societies a new element of public anxiety about hazards, which threatens to erode the confidence and trust that people place in the most powerful institutions. Because of this anxiety and the common policy and management questions that arise, hazards are being studied for the first time as a set of related phenomena. This generic approach is leading to an erosion of the commonsense distinction between natural and man-made hazards. Across a wide spectrum of risks, many people are no longer content to accept the inevitability of adverse effects as being natural or to be expected. Each event requires an explanation, and often the search for explanation is linked to a search for the locus of responsibility – someone to blame. These new circumstances have been in part generated by intellectual enquiry, but in their turn they are now posing new questions for research and giving rise to a demand for more effective policies.

Two decades ago systematic enquiry into the causes and consequences of natural hazards was conducted in disciplines and professions that worked to a considerable degree in isolation from each other and from the public. Beginning in the 1960s a much broader interdisciplinary approach to hazards developed, strongly influenced by geographers (natural hazards research) and by sociologists (disaster research). This research has shown that the consequences of floods and droughts can no longer be explained away as 'Acts of God' but are often the result of the misapplication of technology. More recently the realisation is emerging that the technical shortcomings of particular human agencies are not the whole story either. To understand fully the problem of environmental hazards we must delve deeper into man's relationship with nature and the nature of human society.

The time seems opportune therefore to launch a new series that will provide more effectively for the substantial development and presentation of the empirical and conceptual advances that may be expected. In keeping with the nature of the subject matter, the series is planned to be international and interdisciplinary in scope and will deal with both natural and man-made hazards. As a vehicle for major contributions from scholars and practitioners the series is intended to meet needs in three directions: (a) professional managers, (b) research workers, and (c) students and teachers.

The social and scientific problems associated with environmental hazards now command the attention of a large group of management professionals in public and private organisations at local, national and international levels. The series is expected to help identify new directions in research and policy as the understanding of the causes and consequences of hazards deepens.

The interactions between hazard theory, research and management practice are now being incorporated into the content of university-level courses in the natural and social sciences as well as a number of interdisciplinary fields such as environmental studies and planning.

The common theme of the series is the concept of hazards and their management, and the orientation will be largely towards practice and policy. More theoretical works, and 'critical science' approaches are not excluded, and the series will be especially pleased to consider manuscripts that arise from interdisciplinary work; that consider more than one hazard; or that study hazards in a multinational or cross-cultural context; and present a broad human–ecological approach to environmental hazards.

In the first book in the series, Kenneth Hewitt has brought together contributions providing a critique of what he terms the 'dominant view', which has pervaded most of the thinking about hazards over the past two decades or more. Hewitt's own introductory chapter begins a critical examination of the 'dominant view', which is further supported directly and indirectly in the specific studies that follow. The three final chapters in the volume draw on discussions generated by these and other papers to propose some alternative ways of thinking about hazards. As Hewitt notes in his Preface, this collection represents a range of views that are designed to contribute to the intellectual debate about hazards. As such the book reflects a widespread feeling of discontent and dissatisfaction with the 'dominant view' in hazards research – the ship is leaking badly. But the function of this book is neither to repair the leaks nor to create a wholly new vessel. What it does is to sharpen our appreciation of the difficulties and to suggest some elements that will have to be incorporated into the eventual design of a new vessel. By this act Kenneth Hewitt and his colleagues have done an important service in stimulating us all to think afresh.

IAN BURTON
June 1982

Preface

In this book we consider risks to human communities from spontaneously occurring geophysical events such as storms, floods, and unseasonable cold or drought. A wide range of environments and cultural settings is involved. The geographical scales of analysis range from the small, local community to the global scene. Yet our main concern is with some issues we see as critical for the improvement of understanding and applications of natural hazards research. The material is primarily directed towards these critical issues. The subjects chosen therefore depend upon the way research has been developing, in an attempt to come to grips more adequately with events.

Constant reports of damages associated with geophysical extremes show them to be a continuing major problem for human communities. The chapters below discuss disasters in virtually every habitable region. The forms and human implications of these damages vary greatly, but one seems justified in recognising the generality of the problem. Moreover, several authors conclude that the global incidence of disaster and levels of damage have been increasing substantially in recent decades (see Ch. 14). The increase has occurred in spite of an enormous commitment to understanding and to manipulating the natural conditions involved. The nature of that effort, however, its assumptions and treatment of hazards, is as much a concern of the contributors to this book as is understanding natural disasters themselves. There is a sense of dissatisfaction with the state of hazards research. There is also the belief that the effectiveness of practices widely adopted has been undermined by rapid transformations of environment and society everywhere. How seriously the authors view the situation and how drastically they restate hazards problems varies. But the net result of their assessments is clear: without substantial changes of perspective and practice, the toll of damages is likely to get worse, however much wealth and expertise is applied.

In terms of context the material below deals mainly with agricultural and rural communities. In terms of problem framework we are especially concerned with the cross-cultural or comparative significance of the examples discussed, and their place within the international system. In the search for explanation, we enquire primarily about the role of sociocultural conditions in shaping the form and severity of damages from natural processes.

Such emphases undoubtedly reflect our backgrounds. The subject matter itself hardly departs from well entrenched interests of geographers and anthropologists. It owes much to a major research effort by resource geographers studying natural hazards in recent decades (White 1974, Burton & Hewitt 1974, Burton *et al*. 1978). This background partly explains the concentration on rural contexts and sociocultural variables. We do not imply that the environmental problems of urbanisation are less intractable or better understood. Indeed, several chapters identify increasing vulnerability to natural hazards everywhere as a direct consequence of the global impact of urban–industrial methods. But the study of environmental relations by geographers and anthropologists has tended to develop apart from urban geography and urban anthropology. So often it has concentrated upon societies stereotypically viewed as 'on the land', or outside the 'advanced economies'. This is probably a great failing. Yet it is in rural areas or non-industrial societies that we have lately encountered, or at least recognised, some of the more difficult and contentious problems of interpreting hazards (Vayda & McCay 1975, Waddell 1977, Torry 1978, Hewitt 1980). The problems that concern us have been further highlighted by efforts in hazards research to incorporate psychosocially grounded questions such as 'perception of environment', 'choice of adjustments' (Burton et al. 1967), and public policy issues. Most of us agree in principle with the attempt to incorporate sociocultural or human ecological concerns. But the chapters below adopt perspectives that depart more or less strongly from the bulk of the recent literature.

The book is organised into three sections, though the material in each is not exclusive of the others. In the first, the studies are preoccupied with the interpretation of major disasters. Apart from the intrinsic causes for concern here, it was felt that the course of recent hazards research and practice makes this an area where dissenting views must be proved effective.

The second section is devoted to case studies of a particular form of risk: that of climatic hazards in agricultural communities, agricultural development and food security. The subject is intrinsically important and in a more than academic sense. However, it seemed to us again to be the sort of area where our work has to be effective if it is to be useful at all. But there is a question of perspective involved in the choice too.

One of the main contentions of all the chapters is that a narrow focus upon 'the hazard' as an occasion of natural extremes, and upon the loss, crisis, relief and rehabilitation in disasters, can mislead us as to the decisive human ingredients of natural hazards. We easily come to ignore a range of other highly pertinent but ongoing relations to habitat. At most they are seen as conditions it is hoped to have restored, but not as important sources of vulnerability. Also, we tend to disregard important constraints upon effective social response to risks from nature that depend upon the 'normal' socioeconomic order. One obvious way to probe this is to take a community and an ongoing part of its material life as the focus, and ask where damaging natural events fit into that. Several of the studies of agricultural communities here did, in fact, arise tangentially from fieldwork or a long-term interest in an area that suffered natural disaster.

In the final section, several of the authors have undertaken to articulate a revised conception of natural hazards and disaster.

My general sense of this book is that it represents a range of interpretive responses, or styles of interpretation, relative to current hazards problems. It will serve its purpose if it contributes to debate and suggests the kinds of problem-formulation that social scientists might adopt. The chapters are, nevertheless, products of a period of retrenchment or new explorations in the field. My suspicion is that we are part of an 'interregnum' in hazards research, as much else. That involves the strengths and weaknesses that have become apparent to me in the period of preparing and editing the manuscript.

Some of the ideas and studies may well stand the test of time, others may not. Some of the authors contributed in a period of rapid change or recent excitement in their own views. That has not necessarily continued, or not in the same vein. Some chapters, for example those by Warrick, and Susman *et al.*, were very much part of continuing research that will hopefully have advanced and changed by the time this book reaches its readership. As interpretive formulation I feel they serve the purpose well here, but I hope the need to check later developments will be recognised. For the same reason, I have used a light editorial hand in substantive matters and style to avoid any sense of gratuitous unity, when it is the sense of a debate that is as important here as 'the findings'. In other words, the details of their position is for the authors to describe and the reader to judge. What I have done is to insert, before Parts I and II, introductory chapters designed to raise the sorts of concerns that were in my mind in bringing this group together and to outline something of the background to the more focused studies that follow.

KENNETH HEWITT
Elora, 1982

References

Burton, I. and K. Hewitt 1974. Ecological dimensions of environmental hazards. In *Human ecology*, F. Sargent (ed.), 253–83. Amsterdam: North-Holland.

Burton, I., R. W. Kates and G. F. White 1967. *The human ecology of extreme geophysical events*. Nat. Haz. Res., Work. Pap. no. 1 Dept of Geog., Univ. Toronto.

Burton, I., R. W. Kates and G. F. White 1978. *The environment as hazard*. New York: Oxford University Press.

Hewitt, K. 1980. The environment as hazard. A review. *Ann. Assoc. Amer. Geogs* **70** (2), 306–11.

Torry, W. I. 1978. Natural disasters, social structure and change in traditional societies. *J. Asian Afr. Studs* **13**, 167–83.

Vayda, A. P. and B. J. McCay 1975. New directions in ecology and ecological anthropology. *Ann. Rev. Anthropol.* **4**.

Waddell, E. 1977. The hazards of scientism: a review article. *Human Ecology* **5** (1), 69–76.

White, G. F. (ed.) 1974. *Natural hazards: local, national, global*. Oxford: Oxford University Press.

Acknowledgements

Generous help was received from Wilfrid Laurier University's Research Office for bringing the authors together for the seminar from which this book developed. In the preparation of the manuscript I have benefited from the comments and prodding of, especially, Ian Burton, Jerry Hall, George Morren and Michael Watts.

Thanks are due to Ms Lillian Peirce for unfailing support in preparing the manuscript, especially the numerous versions of my own chapters; and to Pam Coutts for preparing final versions of the diagrams. The subject index was prepared by Ms Farida Hewitt MA.

The following individuals and organisations are thanked for permission to reproduce copyright material. Numbers in parentheses refer to text figures unless otherwise stated:

Institute of Behavioral Science, University of Colorado (4.1, 2, 4 & 7); Association of American Geographers (4.6); Figure 8.5 adapted from W. H. Portig, *Geographical Review* **55**, 1965, with the permission of the American Geographical Society, and with the permission of Elsevier Scientific Publishing Company; Department of Geography, University of Chicago (9.3); the Food and Agriculture Organisation of the United Nations (Table 7.1).

Contents

List of tables

List of contributors

Jean Copans
Ecole des Hautes Etudes en Sciences Sociales, Centre d'Etudes Africaines, 54 bd Raspail, 75006 Paris, France

J. W. Fretz
Conrad Grebel College, University of Waterloo, Ontario, Canada N2L 3C5

Jerry A. Hall
Department of Geography, Wilfrid Laurier University, Waterloo, Ontario, Canada N2L 3C5

A. Hecht
Department of Geography, Wilfrid Laurier University, Waterloo, Ontario, Canada N2L 3C5

Kenneth Hewitt
Department of Geography, Wilfrid Laurier University, Waterloo, Ontario, Canada N2L 3C5

Gordon A. McKay
Atmospheric Environment Service, Meteorological Branch, 4905 Dufferin Street, Downsview, Ontario, Canada M3H 5T4

George E. B. Morren, Jr
Chairman, Cook College, Office Dean/Director, New Jersey Agricultural Experimental Station, PO Box 231, Rutgers University, New Brunswick, NJ 08903, USA

Phil O'Keefe
Department of Geography, Clark University, Worcester, MA 01610, USA

Colm Regan
Department of Geography, Maynooth College, Dublin, Ireland

Ihor Stebelsky
Department of Geography, University of Windsor, Windsor, Ontario, Canada N9B 3P4

Paul Susman
Assistant Professor, Department of Geography, Bucknell University, Lewisburg, PA 17837, USA

Eric Waddell
Department of Geography, Laval University, Quebec, Canada

Richard A. Warrick
Natural Hazards Information Center, Campus PO Box 482, University of Colorado, Boulder, CO 80309, USA

Michael Watts
501 Earth Sciences Building, University of California, Berkeley, CA 94720, USA

Ben Wisner
Cook College, Department of Human Ecology and Social Sciences, PO Box 231, Rutgers University, New Brunswick, NJ 08903, USA

Part I

NATURAL DISASTER: MISCHANCE OR MISNOMER?

1 *The idea of calamity in a technocratic age*

KENNETH HEWITT

I am compelled to fear that science will be used to promote
the power of dominant groups rather than to make men
happy.   Bertrand Russell (1925)

Human communities may have always suffered losses from flood, drought or
storm. The argument I wish to develop here, however, is that the prevailing
scientific view of these problems is a quite recent *invention*. And by that I
mean a partial and reconstructed view, carefully detached from almost all
previous ideas of calamity, and reflecting the singular social context of its
origins. That may not seem unusual. There is a widespread feeling that any
topic or view not actively developed in the most recent studies and literature
must be outmoded if not actually worthless. Equally, there is an assumption
that this development depends upon the initiatives of established researchers
and major institutions in, especially, the wealthiest industrial nations. Yet, for
the scientific community a consistent forward movement is supposed to rest
upon serious logical considerations rather than mere fashion. It presumes
more comprehensive and precise empirical bases, in turn co-ordinated with
increasingly powerful general concepts.

Contemporary natural disasters research is certainly rich in the results of
scientific enquiries, whether in geophysics or the psychology of stress. The
applications of scientific research are not, however, its definitive feature. It
may have internal coherence or at least conviction. That does not alter my
sense that it capitalises rather arbitrarily upon scientific discovery. Indeed it
accords with 'the facts' only insofar as they can be made to fit the assumptions, development and social predicaments of dominant institutions and
research that has grown up serving them. Moreover my assessment of it leads
me to believe that such developments have become the single greatest impediment to improvement in both the understanding of natural calamities and the
strategies to alleviate them. That is why I have felt justified in devoting most
of this chapter to a critique of the underpinnings of the prevailing views in
hazards research. As such, I may seem to stray far from the immediate interests of those concerned with flooding or earthquake disaster or weather-
damage to crops. However, the worth and message of subsequent chapters
that do focus on those phenomena depends not only upon their individual
merit but on what they imply collectively about the state of hazards research.
And essentially they go against the prevailing thrust of that research.

Looking across the range of studies and actions relating to natural hazards,

I am suggesting that one can recognise a convergence of opinion or approaches; a sufficient consensus to speak of a 'dominant view'. *Dominance* is evident in the resources allocated; in the numbers of highly trained personnel involved and the volume of their published works; in the public visibility and acceptance of these works; and perhaps most of all in the attachment of this view to the more powerful institutions of modern states. In the work of any subfield or study, the dominant view might be revealed by the literature quoted and emulated. It may appear in the terminology used or the audience anticipated. For example, the more visible work of geography or sociology seems to me largely to express such dependency even when making useful innovations.

What will be described as the dominant consensus has certainly not gone uncriticised, both within and from outside the various fields relating to natural hazards. Nor does it go unchanged. However, it seems that this consensus has gone forward resisting any fundamental criticism. Its changes have been chameleon-like exercises in superficial novelty – absorbing, co-opting or ignoring dissent at will. Of course, one must beware of giving it the attributes of a thing or actor. Rather, we have the convergence of a wide range of thinking upon a unified perspective that constitutes what Thomas Kuhn has called a 'paradigm' (Kuhn 1962), or more specifically what Edward Said calls 'an academic-research consensus' (1978, p. 275). For the dominant view of hazards is not merely enshrined in rarified language and technical apparatus, it is fully symptomatic of the social contexts in which it has arisen and that still form its main points of reference. Its strength depends less upon its logic and internal sophistications than on its being a convenient productive 'world view' for certain dominant institutions and academic spokesmen. In other words it is, above all, a construct reflecting the shaping hand of a contemporary social order. From a sociocultural perspective, it is itself a phenomenon requiring investigation as part of the so-called 'social construction of knowledge' (Mannheim 1952, Berger & Luckmann 1967).

The unease or outright criticism of accepted hazards interpretations in the chapters that follow seems to me to stem essentially from the struggle to articulate and to pursue intellectual and societal perspectives that the dominant view has served to stifle. Hence, behind the empirical and methodological detail looms the larger – and for social science the most fundamental of all research questions – self-conscious examination of the psychosocial underpinnings of thought, assumption and practice.

I shall not attempt here to review hazards research in a detailed fashion. In any case, there is no lack of reviews or lengthy studies of the various geophysical conditions involved. My purpose is rather to examine the styles of argument, the uses of information and managerial assumptions that *divide off* the dominant consensus not merely from other research, but from the variety of possible viewpoints and concerns of hazards research. I shall try to show the common ground that channels and reflects basic motivations and social contexts.

The dominant view in outline

The superficial features of the dominant view are not hard to discern, though it requires specialised, lengthy training to contribute to them. There is generally a straightforward acceptance of natural disaster as a result of 'extremes' in geophysical processes. The occurrence and essential features of calamity are seen to depend primarily upon the nature of storms, earthquakes, flood, drought. It may be accepted that 'hazard', strictly speaking, refers to the *potential* for damage that exists only in the presence of a *vulnerable* human community. Actual usage almost invariably refers to an objective geophysical process, such as a hurricane or frost, as 'the hazard'. In turn, damage and human actions are defined by, or as responses to, the type, magnitude, frequency, and other dimensions of these processes (e.g. Smith 1957, Part I; Hewitt & Burton 1971, White 1974, Unesco 1980, Burton *et al*, 1978, Ch. 2; Grayson & Sheets 1979).

Conceptual preambles and the development of a refined language of 'risk assessment' appear to have swept away the old unpalatable causality of environmental determinism seen in, say, Huntington's work on storms (1945, Ch. 21). The *sense* of causality or the direction of explanation still runs from the physical environment to its social impacts. The most expensive actions and the more formidable scientific literature recommending action are concerned mainly with geophysical monitoring, forecasting and direct engineering or land-use planning in relation to natural agents (NAS 1980a & b, Soloviev 1978, Ang 1978, Yoshino 1971).

Few researchers would deny that social and economic factors or habitat conditions other than geophysical extremes affect risk. The direction of argument in the dominant view relegates them to a dependent position. The initiative in calamity is seen to be with nature, which decides where and what social conditions or responses will become significant. Here is the geophysicist Bolt (1978, p. 156) discussing an especially 'bad year' for earthquake disasters: 'Paradoxically, despite these grim statistics, 1976 had slightly less than the average number of large earthquakes . . . [the] figures demonstrate that the misfortune of 1976 was not that more large earthquakes than normal occurred, but rather that more than usual occurred *by chance* in susceptible highly populated regions' [my italic]. The implication always seems to be that disaster occurs because of the chance recurrences of natural extremes, modified in detail but fortuitously by human circumstances.

Likewise, the geography of risk is usually treated as synonymous with the distribution of natural extremes such as large earthquakes, and with the natural features directly associated with them such as faults, flood plains, drought 'polygons' and avalanche tracks. To be sure, reference is made to past major disasters in assessing risk (Swiss Re 1978). Some account may be taken of population density, or national economic 'levels', themselves measured and treated so as to seem commensurate with geophysical parameters (see Kantarovitch *et al*. 1970, Burton *et al*. 1979). In such terms, the Soviet

geographers Gerasimov and Zvonova, for example, do speak of the difference between 'the intensity of a disaster' and the 'potential danger' which,
they say, 'remains the same' (White 1974, p. 243). However, even geographers have for the most part been content to treat the geography of hazards
as synonymous with the spatial distribution and frequencies of geophysical
extremes. The maps in Sections IV and V of White (1974) are examples. (See
also Strahler & Strahler 1973, pp. 218–25; Ayre 1975, Berlin 1980, vol. I.)

In the dominant view, then, disaster itself is attributed to nature. There is,
however, an equally strong conviction that something can be done about
disaster by society. But that something is viewed as strictly a matter of public
policy backed up by the most advanced geophysical, geotechnical and managerial capability. There is a strong sense, even among social scientists for
whom it is a major interest, that everyday or 'ordinary' human activity can do
little except make the problem worse by default. In other words, the structure
of the problem is seen to depend upon the ratios between given forces of
nature and 'advanced' institutional and technical counterforce.

One can summarise the bulk of the work and expenditures within the
dominant view as falling into three main areas:

(a)   An unprecedented commitment to the monitoring and scientific under-
      standing of geophysical processes – geologic, hydrologic, atmospheric –
      as the foundation for dealing with their human significance and impacts.
      Here the most immediate goal in relation to hazards is that of predic-
      tion.
(b)   Planning and managerial activities to contain those processes where
      possible, through flood control works, cloud seeding, or avalanche
      defences, and where it is not possible, physically to rearrange human
      activities in accordance with the objective geophysical patterns and
      probabilities. That involves zoning, building codes and 'fail-safe'
      artifacts. A remarkable unity of language has emerged here to discuss
      geophysical processes, physical planning and the assessment of risks.
(c)   Emergency measures, involving disaster plans and the establishment of
      organisations for relief and rehabilitation. The ability to put in place the
      insights developed by geophysical research and planning is important
      here. Study however is necessarily subordinate to action. Action is most
      commonly and directly put in the hands of military, or quasi-military
      organisations. (Since most of the world's people and land areas have
      little access normally to the products of modern geophysical science and
      management technology, it is through emergencies that they become
      involved in the perspectives of the dominant view.)

In terms of research, the main areas of expertise are those of the physical
sciences and engineering. However, social sciences play a substantial role,
notably in studying 'crisis behaviour' and emergency measures; or in focusing
upon places and groups singled out by the experience, expectation or exis-

tence of major natural disaster in their area (Disaster Research Group 1961, Baker & Chapman 1962, Grosser *et al*. 1964, Brictson 1966, Dynes & Quarantelli 1968, NAS 1976, Hewitt & Burton 1971, White 1974, Haas *et al*. 1977).

There have been important social analyses that disagree more or less profoundly with the dominant view (e.g. Walford 1878–9, Part II; Sorokin 1942, Kendrick 1956, Lifton 1970, Copans 1975, McNeill 1976, O'Keefe *et al*. 1976, Torry 1978). However, in recent decades, social scientists have tended to concentrate increasingly upon direct socioeconomic and behavioural relations of the three areas of the dominant view noted above. They ask how individuals or groups appraise the risks of occupying areas classified as typhoon coasts or flood plains. The results tend to be compared with geophysical knowledge of typhoons and floods. They ask how people respond to forecasts, requests to conserve water and hazard-zoning legislation. They examine how people and institutions 'cope' when the volcano erupts or a crop is destroyed.

These interests seem entirely reasonable in themselves. They become less so as they are tributary to supposedly more sophisticated geophysical and engineering knowledge. Moreover, by this narrow focus upon information that centres the problem upon natural extremes and damaging events, they easily miss the main sources of social influence over hazards. But the bulk of hazards work by social scientists is focused in that way and serves to reinforce the 'geophysicalist' and technological reductionism of the dominant view.

It is not unimportant how completely the funding and mobilisation of research depends upon the agencies of national governments or international organisations. A singular feature is the near universal adoption by them of the same concerns and supporting ideas. Some would say that the dominant view reflects particular ideological and group commitments. Yet the main concerns expressed in it are being pursued or sponsored by more or less identically named institutions in most states, universities and city administrations. The view appears at its sturdiest and is most forcefully sponsored in multinational co-operation and under the auspices of international agencies (cf. Eijkmann 1911, Armytage 1965, Ch. 21).

Burton *et al*. (1978, pp. 212 *et seq*.) have criticised the 'natural science' and technological preoccupations of relevant United Nations' studies. Nearly all the materials from Unesco's 'Disasters Division' illustrate precisely the concerns and research categories of the dominant view. The reader might consult a recent publication on earthquake risk as one of the more thorough, competent and convincing examples (Unesco 1980). Moreover, that book reveals a unity of language and mission in the work of participants from Turkey, Switzerland and Japan, no less than from the United States, Soviet Union and New Zealand. This might seem to be a tribute to the unity of science. In my opinion that is a secondary matter.

Rather, what these materials show is, first, that the dominant view constitutes a technocratic approach. That means, the work subordinates other modes and bases of understanding or action to those using technical procedures. More precisely, technocracy gives precedence in support and prestige to bureaucratically organised institutions, centrally controlled and staffed by or allocating funds to specialised professionals. For social scientists it is important to recognise that technocracy is not only or necessarily an obsession with technology in the narrow sense of engineering structures and machines (cf. Mumford 1967, 1970; Armytage 1965). Forthright critiques of the 'technological fix' approach can fall short of recognising the full scope of this phenomenon. The 'social, economic and political "people" factors involved in hazards reduction', that White and Haas (1975) emphasise, also can be and usually *are* approached technocratically. In fact, my own argument amounts to saying that the 'natural science–technological fix' approach to hazards is itself, essentially, a *sociocultural construct* reflecting a distinct, institution-centred and ethnocentric view of man and nature.

My sense of these developments as a socially constructed knowledge, is not, however, that commonly expressed in 'perception' studies of hazards and environment. I am not concerned to turn the tables on the experts and show that they are, in their way, as subjectively, attitudinally limited as the laymen in flood plains or people who buy homes astride an active fault. They surely are, but I do not find it useful to reduce the problem to the way individual perceptions are shaped at the interface of sense experience and personality. We are concerned with the way 'thought follows reality'. But the 'realities' here are not assumed universals of the empiricist's sense data and their psychological assimilation in acts of human perception and cognition. Rather we are looking at conditions that shape these pliable processes; the conditions that influence what facts we are likely to recognise and deem important; the acquired, accepted ways of interpreting them. These are matters of the social order. They relate to the societal means that shape learning and formal enquiry, that validate and communicate scientific discoveries, and especially that govern their implementation. As such, they are integral to Marxian notions of economic control and ideology. And we owe some of the most penetrating modern expressions of how 'thought follows reality' in this sense to Marx and Feuerbach (Marx 1964). Some of the more incisive criticism of hazards work in the dominant mode has also been Marxist (see Chs 5, 13 & 14). It seems to me, however, that like so much else in modern states, the dominant view of hazards differs little across the broadest spectrum of political affiliations. My own view of its social construction and implications is Weberian rather than Marxist. That is to say, I see here an expression of the way institutions – especially centralised, official and bureaucratically organised ones – route their human and material resources into particular styles of work and practice (see Weber 1947, Albrow 1970). We have to consider how far the dominant view in hazards research represents a continuing and deepening example of what Mills (1959) called 'the bureaucratic ethos'. That involves the channelling of scientists into a distinctive approach to 'facts', and a distinctive view of the nature of theory and practicality. Even in their most felicitous forms these tend to reflect mainly the organisation sponsoring the research or the researcher's image of what that organisation can and should do. Moreover, science and research themselves, however practical in orientation, tend to be determining factors only at certain levels in these institutions – rarely the highest – and only in the outlook of a certain class of persons within them – rarely those with the main powers of decision.

The dominant view suits very well institutions that carry out technical studies, develop technical plans, and train technical managers, or favour research oriented to such projects. Moreover, 'technical' invariably means wedding science to technology, preferably in what is considered the most 'advanced' form. Therefore it is a creature of the most powerful, wealthy and centralised institutions. Such, of course, is the style adopted most widely by dominant organisations of government, business and culture today (Habermas 1973, Ch. 7). There is little hope of doing much about that.

However, in drawing attention to this truism, I suggest first that natural calamity is one of the special and especially intractable problems for a technocracy. Secondly, many of those involved appear unaware that they are doing anything but pursuing an 'objective', scientific, and even a necessary, research strategy. Thirdly, we are in many ways stuck with a form of technocratic strategy that is peculiarly archaic and inflexible, at least from a sociocultural and geographical perspective. Fourthly, I suggest that the international system where the strategy is operating, and the social and intellectual debates raging in the most powerful states, themselves challenge the effectiveness as well as the truth of the dominant view. The chapters that follow reveal its many failings on the ground. Hence, it becomes a major issue to discover and describe the basis of the view's robustness within the technical context, as well as in relation to other, quite different approaches to natural calamity.

An 'enclosure system'

There is a close analogy between the dominant view of hazards and Michel Foucault's description of how 'madness' came to be treated, indeed invented, by the 'Age of Reason' (Foucault 1965). Natural calamity in a technocratic society is much the same sort of pivotal dilemma as insanity for the champions of reason. Disaster in the 20th-century international system involves comparable pressures upon dominant institutions and knowledge, as did the 'crazed poor' in the social and economic crises that formed the underbelly of the Enlightenment. Madness and calamity are very disturbing. They directly challenge our notions of order. Both threaten to be interpreted as 'a punishment for a disorderly and useless science' (ibid. p. 32). They can be seen as clear limits to knowledge and power, because they are initiated in a way that seems uncontrollable by society. However, there is also a long history of belief that both are 'judgements' upon human activity, a sentiment echoed in attitudes to environmental problems in the ecology movement today, for example.

In both cases, however, there has arisen a dominant view that counteracts these difficulties with a positive creed, an assertion of potency where the grounds for conviction seem the least. It is exactly here that we can see the benefits to a technocratic approach of dividing off hazards. It is very convenient to treat calamity as a special problem for advanced research in the areas noted above, and this outweighs other considerations. The problem is made manageable by an extreme narrowing of the range of interpretation and acceptable evidence. The resulting partial view has been achieved much as the 'great confinement' of the poverty-stricken and 'crazy' in the 18th century was to form the foundation for dominant perspectives on madness, crime and punishment – and the most severe criticism of them in our century (Rothman 1971, Cooper 1978). We are not only dealing with the substance of such questions, or with a particular philosophy and set of practical procedures. We are also dealing with a careful, pragmatic and disarming *placement* of the problem.

The language of discourse is often a good indicator of basic assumptions. In hazards work one can see how language is used to maintain a sense of *discontinuity* or *otherness*, which severs these problems from the rest of man–environment relations and social life. That is most obvious in the recurrent use of words stressing the 'un'-ness of the problem. Disasters are *un*managed phenomena. They are the *un*expected, the *un*precedented. They derive from natural processes or events that are highly *un*certain. *Un*awareness and *un*readiness are said to typify the condition of their human victims. Even the common use of the word [disaster] 'event' can reinforce the idea of a discrete unit in time and space. In the official-sounding euphemism for disasters in North America, they are '*un*scheduled events'.

What emerges is that 'hazards' are not viewed as integral parts of the spectrum of man–environment relations or as directly dependent upon those. We have abandoned that aspect of the earlier environmentalists from Strabo to Huntington. One does find philosophical introductions and conclusions locating 'hazards' within a panorama of human ecology and its diverse collections of adaptive problems. But they are described and dealt with as a separate problem.

We have noted the precedence given to specialised geophysical research and the geophysical processes its subfields concentrate upon. However, common features, found across the various specialisations, serve to reinforce the sense of separateness of disaster and its causes. In nearly all cases attention is directed towards the occurrence or likelihood of discrete, sharp bouts of damage. Natural hazards may be acknowledged to include a continuum of damages from ordinary wear and tear by sun or wind to major catastrophes. Human societies may be seen to exist in a continuous process of interaction with the habitat, and under conditions that ultimately link us to the entire system of relations in the biosphere. Yet, it is the temporally and spatially limited 'event' that is the specialty in hazards work – a Sahel drought, Hurricane Betsy, avalanches.

This geophysical approach is supported by a well entrenched logic. It identifies hazardous events in strong, step-like changes of geophysical measures that accompany disastrous damages. The changes may involve river levels, seismic shocks, wind gusts and so on. The picture of a pointer-reading swinging off the scale is one of science's contributions to the common stock of disaster imagery. Human vulnerability is, in turn, tied to these extreme 'pulses' in nature through such notions as 'damage thresholds'. My diagrams in Hewitt and Burton (1971, Figs 1 & 21) expressed this with forthrightness! (see also Haas *et al*. 1977, Ch. 1).

What we also find ourselves dealing with here are notions of stability and instability. In Scheidegger's words: 'evidently, if a prevailing status quo is preserved no catastrophe occurs. Therefore a catastrophe generally entails the *termination* of a stable state' [my italic] (1975, p 2), He also calls 'stable', the 'normal' state. Though he expressly refers to geophysical stability, the sense of a breakdown in a stable set of relations to the habitat is found equally in the social interpretations of these risks. Hazards are taken as natural events that destabilise or *violate* ordinary life and relations to the habitat. Research commonly takes the idea of failure in social systems as a fairly exact analogue of that in mechanical systems – the result of an (exceptional) force that exceeds the strength of the material or structure. Haas and Ayre (1969, p. 7) have expressed this more conscientiously than most:

'It does not seem unduly farfetched to think of a human community, in its response to dynamic input, as a second-order system described by the system of coupled nonlinear equations,

$[M]\{\bar{Y}\} + [D]\{Y\} + [R]\{Y\} = \{F\}$ where $\{Y\}$ is the response vector; $[M]$, $[D]$ and $[R]$ are matrices of "mass", "energy dissipation" and "restoration" . . .'

Given that the kind of mathematical model described here is virtually impossible to apply in practice, this statement expresses a metaphysical belief, not unlike the 'mumbo-jumbo' of numerologists. However, what is important is the further implication of a threshold, below which stable, 'normal', orderly activities and human competence apply; above it, disorder, the unexpected, the unplanned. This makes plain what is merely assumed in much of disaster research. J. W. Powell summed up the position by calling disaster 'the impinging upon a *structured* community of an *external* force on a scale wide enough to excite public alarm, and to disrupt *normal* patterns of behaviour' [my italic] (quoted Lemons 1957, p. 2).

The concern with rare, 'chance' events directs our attention in other ways. The more severe occurrences, the 'worst-case scenarios', tend to become definitive or at least symbolic of the whole problem (Barton 1969, Ch. 1; Bolt 1978, Ch. 2; Burton *et al*. 1978, Ch. 1). Certain kinds of disaster, especially those in major urban centres, or the very largest examples (i.e. those that are *least frequent* and most extraordinary of all disasters), come to represent the whole problem by a sort of historical–geographical compression. One sees this happening in the way the plight of San Francisco, the 1906 earthquake disaster, its anticipated recurrence and the San Andreas Fault, come to be touchstones of seismic risk problems, even as many other disasters occur and are forgotten. Furthermore, destruction, impairment, and what must be restored by *outside assistance* tend to form the entire concern in individual disasters. And these descriptions commonly deal only with the most severely damaging aspects. Patterns of survival and evidence of 'stability' in structures – which in most disaster zones could be seen to involve by far the larger fraction of people and property affected – are of little concern.

The disaster archipelago

In practice, then, natural hazards have been carefully roped off from the rest of man–environment relations. The enclosure where they reside is variously labelled 'unscheduled events', 'emergency social situations', 'negative resources' or simply 'hazards'. Not only do such acts of definition isolate them. Not only do such problem-formulations sever their explanation from supposedly 'normal' 'predictable' events. Major allocations of resources to manage 'risk' have involved, out of all possible 'alternative adjustments', attempts physically to wall in the places and occasions of disaster. Flood control work exemplifies this attempted enclosure system.* Meanwhile the dominant response to actual disaster is to invest and seal off the damage zone with military personnel and a network of officials, clearly demarcating it as a zone of exclusion from ongoing (peaceful?) life. In many examples we find the authorities making huge efforts to keep the people *in* the 'disaster zone' from moving out (see Waddell, Ch. 2), and others from moving in. Elsewhere, as in the 1980 Italian earthquake, we have a tremendous struggle to relocate people against their will (cf. Oliver-Smith 1974, Torry 1978). When there is a forecast, we see in industrial states the growing civil defence strategy of massive total evacuation that leaves 'the hazard' in a no-man's land. These may well be fair and desirable responses in some cases and within the possible options of given communities. They nevertheless serve to reinforce the 'otherness' of the source of disaster, and also to emphasise the blanket classifying of entire areas as disaster zones.

By these and other means, natural disaster is quarantined in thought as well as practice. The geography of disaster is an *archipelago* of isolated misfortunes. Each is seen as a localised *dis*organisation of space, projected upon the

* Though the language is different, I do not see this as unlike Gilbert White's much earlier formulation of the problem in flood responses, as being to counter narrow, confining emphases upon 'technological' solutions with a sense of a 'range of possible adjustments' (White 1961). However, two decades or more later, the problem looms as less one of 'choice of use', and more one of intellectual and institutional frameworks that circumscribe (technical) choice in general.

extensive map of human geography in a more or less random way due to independent events in the geophysical realms of atmosphere, hydrosphere and lithosphere. More specifically, each disaster is an unplanned hole or rupture in the fabric of *productive* and orderly human relations with the habitat or 'natural resources'.

The importance of isolating the problem in this way may not seem as necessary as in disease control, in the asylums or lazar houses Foucault tells us they replaced in the 18th century. There may not seem a logic to it like the 'Gulag Archipelago' of Soviet labour camps, and similar mechanisms devised to remove 'undesirable' elements from intercourse with the rest of society. But the analogy and convenience of this isolation is there, deep in the structure of technocratic thought and its precursors.

In each field that has entered into hazards research it seems that, sooner or later, great excitement develops about how to classify and partition off the issues involved in the subject. However, this is rarely done in an open-ended, philosophical and curious way. Rather, it becomes a 'territoriality' question, a zoning regulation for these sorts of studies. Nowadays, to judge from our efforts in geography, it most often takes the form of plausibly locating the hazards 'box' within a model or diagram of the components and lines of interaction in man–environment studies (Kates 1971, Burton & Hewitt 1974, Fig. 12.2; Ayre 1975, p. 12). A moment's reflection usually shows that these are not 'models' of reality at all, but *managerial devices* to show the relations among the study areas or dimensions currently fashionable in the discipline and related fields.

The diagrams themselves tend to resemble nothing so much as an 'organisation chart' of a large bureaucracy. They often bear little or no relation to actual places or conditions, the material interactions or human experience involved. They are prescriptions for showing where academic and managerial categories fit together. However, it is not merely that reputations are made by this sort of activity. The placement of the problem is a necessary founding act whereby each specialty field demonstrates its coherence with the whole dominant view. It is an act that will be paid homage to as an intellectual demonstration at the start of each new study. This is important because hazards studies have rarely been research in the full sense. Most are seen in terms of 'applications', commonly on behalf of or as an assessment of public policy and the performance of particular agencies. The 'expertise', therefore, is invariably that of a discipline such as seismology or cognitive psychology, or a technique in, say, statistics or remote sensing. The 'research' is essentially an empirical study of questions specified by an agency's responsibility or a critique intended to contribute to management within such institutional frameworks. These considerations encourage the encapsulating of the problem in an official-looking diagram or 'model' of man–nature relationships.

Once we have located the hazards 'box', however impulsively, we can then concentrate upon it. We are at liberty to define parameters, revalidate properties, gather expensive data and seek cures or restraining devices, all within a technical *monologue*. Thus encapsulated, the problem appears neutralised, objectified. Past and present notions that seem technically obscure or unpalatable are defused. Most comforting of all, the forces involved, so charged with drama, emotion and blame in the everyday world, become subordinate to objective dimensions and impersonal dynamics. We and the agency are simply doing a job. The work can then develop as a *well crafted* monologue. That is not only because the language is so specialised. We are now free to speak of hazards *alone*, as if all these 'events' and all that happens within each one belong not only to a separate domain, but to a single, albeit 'multivariate' reality.

'Monologue' is Foucault's word to express how society and its instrument psychiatry closed themselves off from a *dialogue* with madness and its sources in the everyday world. The psychiatrist was to be reason's priest, and not obliged to contemplate his own madness, nor his part in the social conditions that might drive others over those bounds where abnormality or passion were to be confined. So it is with hazards research in its main stream. It has invented its problem field to suit its convenience. It does not reflect upon the extent to which the institutions it serves – the societies that have made such technocratic authority possible – could be part of the problem. It does not reflect upon the flaws in itself, except in relation to what is deemed sophisticated in the current fashions of the scientific community. It gathers data about people at risk, but may not engage in dialogue with them. Most disaster reports in the so-called Third World are by persons who cannot speak the language of the area affected, or have no background in its sociocultural composition (see Chs 2, 5, 13).

However, none of this could alone sustain the dominant consensus. It could not leave so many feeling satisfied to treat hazards as a separate set of problems if there were not a deeper level of scientific, or supposedly scientific, understanding implicit in it. That underpinning of the justification for keeping hazards separate, of paying lip service only to their place in other man–environment relations, brings us back to the sense in which disaster is a specially intractable problem for scientific rationalism and technocracy. We cannot, in fact, divorce the development of the dominant view from the entire perspective of materialism and the social pressures upon materialist and secular institutions required to interpret and deal with unpalatable or apparently unmanageable material events. The formulations of the dominant view must be seen against the background of what can serve as acceptable explanations of natural disaster in a technocratic framework; as a strategy that allows us to 'save the facts' and ourselves!

The convenience of accidents

Conceptually and analytically, what the dominant view (the perspective that all the related hazards work has converged upon) does is to define the distinctive features of the problem through the language and apparatus of 'the accident'. Natural 'calamities' are, before anything else, severed from the rest of material life by being what the *Oxford English Dictionary* calls 'unforeseen contingencies'.

Toblin (1977) states that '[disaster] implies the occurrence of an *unusual* event which was *not* adquately *predicted* in time or place to allow measures to be taken for the protection of the threatened people and property' [my italic] (p. 13). The Soviet geographers Gerasimov and Zvonkova (1974) note that 'Natural hazards derive from highly dynamic processes whose elemental essence consists in their *indefinite* and *equivocal* manifestations' [my italic] (p. 243). We will not enquire here why Lenin, and from a quite different ideological perspective Sorokin, emphasised other socioeconomic or sociocultural interpretations, for this is the language of detente! White (1974) is quite firm about it and also states clearly its other implication that 'were there perfectly accurate predictions of what would occur and when it would occur in the intricate web of atmospheric, hydrologic and biological systems, there would be no hazard' (p. 3).

In such a view, the human ingredients are necessarily of a dependent or tangential nature, being responses and contingencies that stem from *un*antici-pated damage by nature. To the extent that there are human conditions specifically affecting hazard, they are found to lie in the category so com-monly invoked in accidents – 'human error'. The literature is full of reactions or conditions described as *un*informed, *un*sound, *un*planned, or impaired, irrational or arational.

Again, natural disasters are 'accidents' only in the sociocultural implica-tions of the dominant view, not for its geophysical focus or the technologies it would bring to bear on the problem. There is an important contrast brought out between these 'accidents' and the scientific possibilities for handling them. Once research is under way, then indeed the 'controls', mechanisms and models take over the discussion. For it is refined statistical and geophysi-cal techniques that alone are thought able to reduce these rare, high-magnitude, uncertain events to some sort of rational description. The com-mon run of humanity is considered to have poor or 'subjective' impressions of 'the hazard' and its occurrence. Likewise, their ability to survive it at all seems puzzling. As one recent official document put it, 'Although human beings, unlike other animals, can project themselves into the future and make plans to deal with future *uncertainties*, they are more apt to be oriented to the "here and now". Present satisfactions, pleasures and rewards far outweigh their future counterparts and particularly their *indefinite* or *uncertain* counterparts' [my italic] (Working Group of Earthquake Hazards Reduction 1980).

Never mind the Saruman-like tone, the unsupported (unsupportable?) assumptions and an omniscience that would attribute such banalities to 'human beings', this is a genuine, concerned (but technocratic) expression of what hazards are about and how people fit into them. The role of research is also placed carefully. We are apparently in the presence of a new kind of 'white-man's burden'! There is little evidence that it is taken to apply only to North American or urban societies (cf. Waddell below).

For a variety of reasons, the research literature strives to dissociate itself from the full implications of these emphases and some will no doubt feel I am developing an unfair caricature of it. 'Accident research' has been at pains to rid itself of the view of accidents as 'accidental' (Haddon *et al.* 1964). The sociologists Quarantelli and Dynes (1972) have voiced the need for a 'principle of continuity' built into disaster research, to avoid the sense of the bizarre, or the impression that crisis behaviour bears little relation to pre-existing conditions and human roles. North American hazards work has continued to shift its language towards more neutral terms, preferring to speak now of 'risk assessment' or 'probabilistic consequences' (Whyte & Burton 1980), and to set research in ever more refined statistical and global 'systems' models.

Such developments reflect genuine unease. I suggest, however, that the sense of, indeed, the fundamental metaphysic of accident is so entrenched in the dominant view that these efforts are largely window dressing, dealing with issues that do not penetrate beyond conceptual preambles. In the technocratic style of work there is a structure of assumptions, and a use of science and management that always situates natural calamity beyond an assumed order of definite knowledge, and of reasonable expectation. More importantly it places disaster outside the realm of everyday responsibility both of society and individual. More important still, it makes assumptions about everyday life – about its being 'normal', 'stable', 'predictable' – that are in turn debatable. We shall return to that.

What we must now ask is how this accidentalism operates as a solution to the problem of explanation in a technocratic context. How have we, as scientists, managed to inform it with the appearance of logical necessity and technical sophistication?

Problems of explanation

The break with the past   Viewed historically, and perhaps in relation to the sense of disaster among the vast majority of people who are today excluded from its monologues, the dominant view of hazards is decidedly odd. But the source of its oddness lies deeper than the expediency of a technocratic 'package'. Unlike virtually all past views of calamity, materialism, especially in its technocratic form, cannot readily attribute disaster to 'acts of God' *or* to 'Acts of Man'!

The former is inadmissable in scientific, utilitarian thought. However, it is the question of 'Acts of Man' that is more problematic. Obviously humans are involved. It is their vulnerability and misfortune that are the central concern. But the question of human *action* is the difficulty here. Action is not mere process. Properly defined, it refers to organised, deliberate attempts to bring about change or maintain a certain status (cf. Arendt 1958). It is not a matter of spontaneous, impersonal, unmanaged change such as physical science sees in the workings of the atmosphere or lithosphere. Action constitutes the very domain of management and planning. Thus, action is comfortably spoken of in the exploitation of natural resources or government response to an actual disaster. But the utilitarian assumptions of the dominant view cannot contemplate human *action* as leading to destruction, to the collapse of institutions or disorganisation of the space economy. Materialism assumes that human activity derives from 'self-interest', whose first rule is 'survival', or at least belongs to an underlying principle of adaptation. An activity that directly invites catastrophe would not be wilfully put in place, *except* 'by accident'. To orchestrate devastation in a rational, materialist world is to be criminal or mad. War for some people is an exception, the domain of human action *par excellence*. Beyond that however, to argue that government, business, science or other institutions create disaster has been in a sense outlawed from rational discourse. It is portrayed as possible only by invoking 'conspiracy theories', and conspiracies again are supposed to be practised by criminals and imagined by the paranoid. I would just note here that the chapters that follow seem to me to give the lie to the idea that 'Acts of Man' do not bear a large responsibility for recent disasters, although few of the authors have found it necessary to talk of conspiracies.

It is also worth pausing to note how great is the assurance of the dominant view's proponents not merely of its superiority but that it has totally discredited views that prevailed in the past. The latter are generally labelled as religious, cosmological, magical or fatalistic. They are views that do not find the source or explanation of calamity to lie in an inherent potentiality of brute matter or its physical processes. They generally appear to us to depend upon non-material, magical and ethical imagery or direct human agency to interpret disaster (see Eliade 1954, Ch. 3; Blum & Blum 1963, Tuan 1980). 'God' is invoked, but rarely as an arbitrary actor with respect to man. Even when speaking of divine wrath as the immediate source of destruction, past societies invariably attribute this in turn to human responsibility. This may be expressed as competition between religio-magical communities and the strength of their divine sponsors or their faith. More often, calamities are ascribed to the workings of a moral *calculus* in human affairs. The ethical and societal aspects of human behaviour are central. In the West and Islamic lands until recently, the dominant view had been essentially that represented by the Old Testament prophets. For them, the message behind calamity or its threat is a people become immoral, idolatrous or vain (Heschel 1962, Ch. 9; Scott 1968, Ch. 6).

I need hardly review the sorts of developments that lead us to neglect and demean this enormous part of the human experience. For even sympathetic studies tend to present it as, at best, archaic. This entire cultural past is laid aside as a tissue of what John Brill calls 'original, childlike and primitive concepts' (1956, p. 6). And the further removed historically or geographically is a society from urban–industrialism, the surer studies of disaster are to find its people to be 'fatalistic', 'subjective', and in the thrall of 'mystical', 'arational' or at least 'pre-scientific' notions (e.g. Kates 1971, cf. Torry 1978). But it is also an article of faith in the dominant view that by a sort of reverse logic the further removed people are from urban–industrialism and its technocratic forms, the more completely they are at the mercy of an elementary biophysical struggle with the habitat. Part of the justification for the technocratic monologue is, of course, that the vast majority of these societies seem not to have the faintest idea of their thoroughly Malthusian condition and the natural selection that arbitrates it! Necessarily therefore, the technocrat may presume to speak *for* these people, but can find little value in dialogue *with* them or learning from them.

The dominant view then, belongs to an historically special culture that seeks to interpret the world through its underpinnings in material phenomena and mechanism. Yet, disaster remains a difficult, perhaps a decisive, test of such explanations. It is a delicate problem for the prevailing interpretations of nature and human development and the way they are appropriated by technocratic institutions. These interpretations tend to be uniformitarian, evolutionary and normative. They articulate with a view of human life as essentially progressive. Disaster, taken literally, however, suggests revolutionary change. Flood, famine, pestilence suggest retrogression rather than progress. Severe degradation of the habitat suggests devolution, even the threat of extinction.

These would not be such problematic questions, but for the recent history of the sciences that has propelled them from the dispassionate realm of natural philosophy into the main street and market places of modern states. The sciences are identified with, and most of their more visible public figures *want* to be identified with, predicting, controlling and reproducing natural forces at will, rather than merely understanding them. In the process the sciences have become integral to the power and authority of leading institutions.

Disaster interpretations in the past were set within landscapes ascribed to the works of the Almighty, the labour of men's bodies and work of their hands. Today's landscapes show the most striking changes through technocratic initiative. In the minds of those who promote and resist such changes, applied science is made firmly responsible for them. If blame in damaging events (the still widespread world of moral rather than material calculation) were to be ascribed to a particular source, then it could very well be turned upon the technocratic ethos. Moreover when knowledge is mobilised for purposes of control, its failures and limits, especially if they result in human misery and disarray, become a threat not merely to its credibility as knowledge, but also as power.

Surely these are major considerations in the thrust to make natural extremes the cause, and accidents the human framework of, disaster? The 'space of the accident' emerges as an expedient if not a 'face-saving formula' (cf. Hawkins 1964).

On remaining calm Appeal to natural processes as cause is, however, a convenient scientific rationalisation too. The processes involved can readily be set within scales of space and time that dwarf them into normalcy. Globally, or over short spans of 'geological time', the conditions in natural disasters come to appear commonplace. Catastrophist notions – the idea that rare, extremely violent or unique events have shaped past and future – have met with solid and apparently secure resistance in the geophysical and biological sciences. Neocatastrophism, except in events as remote as the 'Big Bang', meets with even less favour than Cuvier's ideas. Though their expertise may be *applied* to sets of extreme events, geophysicists can feel that the extremes are part of measurement continua, and that such events as earthquake or volcanic eruption are, in the end, part of the inexorable development of the solid Earth. The power of scientific thought has derived especially from discovering scales and perspectives where phenomena seem to fall into elegant and parsimonious forms, regardless of how far these scales and perspectives diverge from the compass of everyday human experience.

The pressures to concentrate upon the geophysical conditions in disaster is great when we consider how much more difficult such detachment is from their sociocultural significance. When our concern is with people, the sense of disorder, of 'worlds' threatened if not destroyed, of meaningless and arbitrary death, is less easily dispelled from disaster. It challenges the belief in coherent development through conservative and lawful processes. Albeit emotional or subjective, disaster leaves its victims feeling their world will never be the same again; that an unprecedented revolutionary change took place – or ought to have taken place! Catastrophism has a strong psychosocial appeal as explanation for the powerless and victims of great distress. The dominant views of disaster in the past dealt with all of this by firmly locating *blame*. Calamity was not divided off in its *meaning* from the rest of life. The destruction was not therefore meaningless or *absurd* in Camus' sense, as it tends to appear in the materialist universe of the dominant view. It would be quite naïve to imagine that the legacy of such ways of thinking does not still exert an enormous pressure upon our dominant institutions and the scientific ethos.

While I cannot say this 'space of the accident' is the only one where technocratic thought could place natural calamities, and while it has not been the only scientific view, it is a persuasive one for science and technology. It makes of disasters not a 'judgement' but an 'unplanned side-effect'. They become not a limit but merely a 'frontier' of knowledge between the tamed and the wild, the controlled and the as-yet uncontrolled. Natural hazards, like disease, poverty, even death, become simply the unfinished business of our endeavours. We can then focus daunting technical equipment and expertise upon tasks technocracy understands: forecasting physical conditions; ever more complete containment of natural processes; educating government and the public; devising general, centrally controlled systems to protect those at risk; to zone 'high hazard' areas; redesigning installations; and if all else fails, organising relief on a grand scale. The hierarchy of expertise is thus preserved. The wealthiest, best-equipped institutions can help and lead the less sophisticated or fortunate. Of course, whatever else may be done, there is no place for any sort of 'grass roots' input; no way for any but the 'experts' to break into the technical monologue. A 'citadel of expertise' has indeed been created here (cf. Roszak 1973).

Uncertainty and prediction

We have been discussing this 'citadel', as it were, from the outside looking in. We have asked about the interface between society and science, as it influences the kinds of questions we are obliged to consider and the sorts of answers that will satisfy us. But these are considerations often far removed from the everyday preoccupations of science and technology. Few scientists would feel commitment to the dominant view were it not also informed with logical and technical features of some sophistication and intrinsic interest. This, from the inside looking out, comes first. That it touches base in plausible ways with human need, managerial concerns and the politics of support for scientific activity is, for most of us, someone else's work.

The scientific ingredient that most helps to maintain the dominant view is the thoroughly respectable notion of *uncertainty* and related ideas. Uncertainty is the umbilical cord that grounds the otherwise gratuitous notion of the accident, the separate assessment of 'extremes', in a challenging and refined language. Elsewhere this ground involves the very frontiers of physical science. And it is a form of reasoning that has done more than anything else to transform social science, environmental science and most applications of scientific work in recent decades; namely through the use of statistical techniques and inference. Universally the hazards literature states that the fundamental problem with hazards, the ultimate reason why disasters occur, is that people have little or no way of telling when, where or to whom they may happen. The quotation from White (p. 44) represents this in its purest form. The uncertainty thus identified is not just intrinsically important. It is used to specify what is and is not likely to improve our grasp of the problem. And it provides scientific credibility for the treatment of natural disasters as 'accidents'.

Uncertainty then, in the form of probabilistic reasoning about threatening natural processes and the occasions of major damages, defines the technical logic and challenge of the dominant view. Herein lies its concern not merely with natural extremes, stochastic forecasting models and actuarial types of risk assessment. We are also led to flirt with the fashionable spin-off of the enormous statistics and probability industry. Examples exploited by geographers include aspects of the theory of games, Bayesian decision making, and various cognitive models designed to deal with uncertainty or imprecision in the 'perception of hazard'. The idea of 'bounded rationality' is an example currently in vogue (Gould 1963, Gibson 1976, Kates 1978, Burton *et al*. 1978, Whyte & Burton 1980).

Statisticians, whose job it is to recognise the basic nature of the data with which a field works, have been serving all areas of hazards research through similar styles of analysis and probability models. The widespread application of 'extreme value statistics' is a case in point (Gumbel 1958). A statistician has described what is at issue in much hazards work with respect to seismic risk (Vere-Jones 1973). He recognises three categories of risk: 'geophysical risk', meaning the probability of an earthquake of a given magnitude in a given location; 'engineering risk', the probability that a given structure will fail; and, thirdly, 'insurance risk', meaning the probability that clients will make claims against a given policy. This nicely catches the flavour of hazards research as a concern with rare, stochastically governed events. This also defines how they are 'accidents' in a seemingly rational sense. The realm of accidents has long been a specialty of statisticians (Maguire *et al*. 1952, Haddon *et al*. 1964, Gibson 1976). There is a substantial body of work, often not with applications in mind, that examines large-magnitude natural events as separate phenomena, using the same or similar probability models as in accident research (Hewitt 1970, Scheidegger 1975). It shows them often to appear as random or nearly random points in time and space, or to be separated by 'recurrence intervals' of nearly random length. Evidently, if it is these events that are 'the hazard', a probabilistic definition of the problem seems unavoidable. If human societies are unprepared or ill prepared for these events mainly because of their rare and uncertain occurrence, then predictability has to be the essence of the problem of management. In the end, only improved knowledge of when natural extremes occur, a chipping away at the degrees of uncertainty, are offered as a rational solution. Hence, the colossal commitment to means of improved forecasting.

We need to pursue the scientific and technical basis of this reasoning no further here. The logic of using statistical models to describe larger-magnitude geophysical events or sets of disasters is not in question. It is the transference of that logic, and the reduction of the interpretation of hazards largely to it, that I would call a face-saving and misleading formula. Impressive as the techniques may be in their home disciplines of statistical hydrology or seismology or actuarial science, they serve to misrepresent the sources and significances of natural disaster except in very narrow technical contexts. My argument is not that uncertainty, in a general sense, has no meaning here. It can reasonably be seen as a major ingredient of these as of most human affairs today. Nor am I suggesting there is no value in striving to foresee future developments and risks. The problem is with the way the *source* of the uncertainties involved is described; with that, the *kind* of prediction championed, and hence the severance of the interpretation of disaster from the rest of material life through these devices.

The myth of 'ordinary life'

Ultimately, the inadequacies of the dominant view arise less from what it says about disaster, than what it chooses to infer about the rest of human activity and its environmental relations. It is here that the whole fabric of the view and its foundation in the ideas of geophysical uncertainty and social accident take on the character of *myth*. As we have seen, its essential interpretive structure involves treating everyday life and disaster as opposites. The ongoing conditions that provide the setting for disaster are inferred to be 'stable', 'orderly' and 'predictable', or at least sufficiently so to be called 'managed' and even 'planned'. In the language of Burton *et al.* (1978) this is the 'human-use-system', typified by patterns of settlement and activity permitting effective and controlled use of natural resources. 'Hazard' arises from the intrusion into this activity of unforeseen, essentially independent natural processes of extreme and rare occurrence. The only ongoing manifestation of hazard is incautious settlement on natural features or in zones where those extreme events recur. Thus is the meaning of everyday life severed from that of disaster. Man's relations to nature are given two modes – one normal, secure, *productive* and the other abnormal, insecure and the occasion of losses. The dominant view pursues its analyses as though the continuities and discontinuities, the sources of stability and instability in human affairs, are uniquely defined at the times and for the places where damaging extremes terminate ordinary life.

Few things have done more to furbish the imagery of everyday life with the epithets 'normal', 'ordinary', 'scheduled', than the statistical treatment of social and natural conditions. Increasingly, social and environmental scientists work with data of the kinds defined, standardised and gathered by government and other centralised institutions. Statisticians know well that 'normal' social conditions are as much a fiction as the 'average man'. That does not prevent such constructs becoming the cornerstones of technocratic ideas of 'reality'.

Together, these notions of 'normal life' on the one hand and statistical uncertainty of natural extremes on the other form the rationalising of the 'accidentalism' of the dominant view. Everyday life appears therefore to affect disaster only fortuitously or by default.

The type of prediction being discussed in the dominant view is in turn of an official, technological and centralised sort. Even when asking about frost in New Guinea, drought in the Sahel, or earthquakes in remote Himalayan valleys, 'prediction' for the dominant view means that sort of forecasting served by the monitoring, data processing and mathematical expression that technocratic agencies provide. Such prediction is, in its turn, modelled from the sort of forecasting required in the day-to-day, clock-time regulation of industrial economies, machine technology and mass institutions. It is associated with those forms of social control peculiar to the productive and institutional forms of urban–industrialism. What appears as uncertainty in *that* context is taken to hold sway everywhere. Yet, with respect to rare, extreme fluctuations on nature, this sort of prediction encounters the same difficulties and failures as in its forecasting of the extreme swings and dislocations of economic and political kinds.

One might begin by pointing to the well known difficulties of preparing, communicating and getting appropriate responses to technocratic forecasting. Far more critical, however, is what is implied by making technical prediction the essence of the problem. What does it imply about 'ordinary life' and the means to encompass and defuse hazard within it?

First we can agree with Burton *et al*. (1978, p. 19) that hazard arises from the interaction of 'natural and social systems'. And suppose for the moment we agree that there would be no hazard if geophysical events were wholly predictable. That must surely mean, first, that all aspects of the natural environment are predictable or benign *except* the 'extremes'; but, secondly, that *all other aspects of human life are themselves either predictable or irrelevant*. It also implies that, if prediction of nature improves, society automatically follows with adjustments that remove risk to that level. Everyday life thus comes to appear as a 'frictionless' process, readily poured into whatever mould technology and the certainties of nature require. It is not difficult to see why some accuse this approach of a covert environmental determinism (Waddell 1977).

This approach also infers that persons and institutions are uniformly and unambiguously committed to removing known, manageable risks from everyone's life, failing to do so only where the risk is highly uncertain. There is a lot of evidence that human groups and institutions are rather less fervent about equity and social justice than that. In any case, it is an odd view, given the evidence that improved prediction and control of natural processes can have the effect of making people more careless, acting on a false sense that 'risks from nature' have been dealt with.

Even were human affairs in no way responsible for disaster or its forms, except by default, these assumptions about predictability would be debatable. Moreover, they lead us swiftly from the complex realm of human ecology to the inner sanctum of that 'new, illiberal practicality' that Mills (1959) described as characteristic of this sort of technocratic applied science. Specifically it leads to that dangerous transfer of the notion of 'predictability' as a feature of scientific method, to the partial and scientistic notion of *predicting society*, which is tantamount to controlling it. This is not the stuff of scientific enquiry but technocratic wishful thinking, a rhetoric that sees society as running smoothly only when fully predicted and managed by its 'experts'.

Moreover, what of that other, even larger body of thought and literature, much of it also technocratic, that describes *everyday life* in the 20th century as something *extra*ordinary? Technological innovation and risks, 'future shock' and unprecedented human powers are some of the main stresses said to be involved. From that view, it is natural disasters that are in some ways 'ordinary', the age-old scourges of civil societies signifying a kind of continuity in human experience and predicaments. Here one might explore Robert W. Kates' suggestion that, after all, perhaps risk or hazard is conserved, merely being shifted around by socioeconomic change.

In such terms, the prevailing interpretation of disasters described above takes on the quality of myth. Of course, in a sociocultural framework that is not the condemnation it may appear. Careful examination of the mythologies of the past shows them to express and have been grounded in definite psychosocial contexts and predicaments. They are important evidence of the way knowledge is a social construct, although it is true we usually call an example 'myth' when its relevance has gone or it appears anachronistic in the context being discussed. I am calling the dominant view of hazards a myth in that sense too.

In the past, most myths actually reflected the views and problems of particular classes or activities; of princes or priests, farming or childbirth. I have described the dominant view of hazards in such a limited perspective of technocracy. Nevertheless, mythologies are generally grounded in a cosmic or genesis-type of myth that supposedly gives the others overall coherence. The dominant view of hazards masquerades as though it were the equivalent of a cosmic myth, subsuming all other approaches in an objective and fundamental ground. I find that unacceptable at least for social science, even if one believes in scientific materialism and promotes the technocratic organisation of human affairs.

For all that, one does not readily or lightly abandon a dominant view, whether myth, theory, paradigm or 'academic-research consensus'. This is not accomplished on mere grounds of logic or demonstration (cf. Kuhn 1962, Polanyi 1958, Ch. 1). Such procedures may help the scholar to modify a view or convince those involved to modify it. Geographers and other social scientists have been trying to do that in the hazards field for several decades. Indeed, I think the dominant view of hazards has arisen out of sufficiently rich founding statements by scientists to embrace all but the most radical proposals. But, as Whitehead said of 'the philosophy of organism', these rich grounds are lost in aspects that 'subsequent systematizations have put aside' (1929, p. v). For instance, as the hazards work of geographers has been gradually adsorbed into the dominant view, the rich possibilities deriving from the ideas of human ecology and geographic diversity have also been lost.

Alternative viewpoints

In contrast to the three features of the dominant view singled out earlier, it seems to me the chapters that follow tend to demonstrate:

(a)   The important degree to which natural hazard is *not* explained by, nor uniquely dependent upon the geophysical processes that may initiate damage.

(b)   The important degree to which human awareness of and responses to
       natural hazards are *not* dependent upon the geophysical conditions,
       whether their mechanisms, frequency or past experience of them.
       Rather hazard is seen to depend more upon concerns, pressures, goals,
       risks and, above all, orchestrated social changes that are tangential to, if
       not wholly indifferent to the particular society–environment relations
       where disaster has occurred. Perhaps more crucial still, effective or inef-
       fective means to avoid or reduce risk are found to depend upon the
       ongoing organisation and values of society and its institutions.
(c)   The important extent to which natural disaster, its causes, internal fea-
       tures and consequences are *not* explained by conditions or behaviour
       peculiar to calamitous events. Rather they are seen to depend upon the
       ongoing social order, its everyday relations to the habitat and the larger
       historical circumstances that shape or frustrate these matters.

These emphases do not arise from trivial or minor aspects of hazards and
their human contexts. If they have validity, it has a profound bearing not just
on the kind of social and environmental understanding geographers or anthropologists might contribute, but also on the general significance to be
placed upon these problems.

In isolation, of course, in the absence of the dominant view described, our
emphases would also add up to an unbalanced view. It would be wrong to
suggest that events associated with flood or earthquake in no way reflect the
nature of these geophysical processes. It would be indefensible to argue that
the disruptions occasioned by disaster produce no distinctive, even unique,
crisis phenomena. There are particular aspects of hazard that can be helped
by improved geophysical forecasting. Nor are any foreseeable human actions
going to remove the need to bring emergency assistance to ill equipped victims of natural calamities.

However, the burden of what follows requires the social scientist to consider seriously whether the dominant view has not got the whole problem of
disaster back-to-front. My own view, and the one I see supported by what
follows, is that:

(a)   Most natural disasters, or most damages in them, are *characteristic*
       rather than accidental features of the places and societies where they
       occur.
(b)   The risks, pressures, uncertainties that bear upon awareness of and
       preparedness for natural fluctuations flow mainly from what is called
       'ordinary life', rather than from the rareness and scale of those fluctua-
       tions (see Ch. 14).
(c)   The natural extremes involved are, in a human ecological sense, more
       expected and knowable than many of the contemporary social develop-
       ments that pervade everyday life.

There is a good deal of evidence that the settings, where recent disasters have occurred, are suffering extraordinary sociocultural change and environmental impacts in an ongoing way (e.g. Hewitt 1970, 1976, 1980). Are these transformations, in and due to social circumstances, more manageable, expected, or certain for the victims of disaster than natural extremes? What is more characteristic of the Sahel, and to be expected by its long-time inhabitants: recurrent droughts or the recent history of political, economic and social change? What are more certain along the San Andreas Fault: occasional large earthquakes, or the sprawling developments of its so-called, 'post-industrial' society?

A careful look at a century or two of history in the 'hazard-prone' regions of today generally shows the sorts of geophysical processes associated with disaster to be entirely likely, even inevitable. In any group of inhabitants there are those who know the processes have occurred and can occur again. However, I am using certainty and uncertainty here in a broad biosocial sense, in terms of cultural reproduction, rather than the technological prediction discussed above. In most places and segments of society where calamities are occurring, the natural events are about as certain as anything within a person's lifetime, or at least that of himself, his children and grandchildren. One of the few real *advantages* we have with these risks is that the large task of being ready for them can be accomplished incrementally, *because* they are relatively rare events! Or should a sane social order disregard the likelihood of massive destruction, simply because it is not quite sure on which day of which year in the next decade or two it will occur? Is it, as Brecht's philosopher suggests, 'because people know so little about themselves that their knowledge of nature is so little use to them. [They] can cope with earthquakes, but not with their fellows' (Brecht 1965, p. 31). In hazards research, at least by social scientists, even for earthquakes it is our 'fellows' with whom we are required to cope first, and earthquake processes second. Here again one must resist a technocratic fiction.

Are people unaware and poorly prepared because natural extremes are rare and unpredictable? Are they indifferent to the possibility of flood or earthquake because preoccupied with 'present gratifications'? Or is it because the everyday conditions of work, life support, social and mental security or the artificial environment require *all* of their risk-avoiding and risk-taking energies? Do 'laymen' appear 'poorly adapted' to us because the socially narrowed world of technocratic or academic specialists leave us incapable of recognising the realities with which other persons and groups must deal?

Surely, in the urban–industrial, commercial societies for which the dominant view is tailored, most people simply have not the time or means to prepare for and recover from natural disaster. It has become as difficult for individuals and families to set aside time, resources and worry to guard against these things as to care for their aged parents, the chronically sick, the handicapped, mentally deranged, and all the other 'abnormal' and *especially* 'unproductive' elements of the human condition. Moreover, one of the characteristic impacts of modernisation is to weaken and eventually destroy the traditional arrangements whereby extended family, village, 'tribe', reciprocal duties of lord and people, absorbed and dealt with such problems. This is surely a major aspect of the process that puts the poverty-stricken, the beggars, orphans, amputees, victims of famine and flood on the streets of cities in 'developing countries', as it did in Europe and North America until 'institutions' were created to hide them in. Such social developments, flowing from that most fundamental of all geographical and human ecological processes of modernisation – *alienation from the land** – are integral to the unavoidable vulnerability of 'ordinary' folk to natural calamity; to the futility of their developing a sophisticated knowledge of the risks even if they had the leisure for it; and, in the end, of the responsibility that indeed rests firmly upon centralised, technocratic institutions and hazards research.

There are natural forces and some damages in most disasters that lie beyond all reasonable measures any society could make to avoid them. What I believe to be definitive of the disasters I have examined is, however, that most of them would not be disasters, and many of the damages would not (indeed *do not*) occur except as a direct result of characteristic and vulnerable human developments (e.g. Hewitt 1976). These developments record mainly the mismatch between the requirements of sensitive, secure environmental relations at the local or regional levels – more exactly in certain segments of society and activity at these levels – and the demands of those extensive geographies of power and economy with which technocratic strategies have grown up, and mainly serve.

What is being explored in the chapters below is firstly a revised vision of how and why disaster occurs, giving full credit to the ongoing societal and man–environment relations that prefigure it. This immediately makes the range of phenomena that form the main stream of the social sciences of direct interest. It means that the common concerns and competence of human geography, human ecology and anthropology are of intrinsic interest to the understanding of hazard, rather than fortuitous matters arising only, and in special ways, when there is the impact of natural extremes or their threat. If society in its everyday development is integral to 'risks from nature', then questions of social order become central matters of research and discussion. That includes the exercise of political and economic power, as integral to vulnerability and management and the redistribution of risk by institutional means. If and where social scientists prefer to treat these matters in terms of 'impersonal, objective' forces, of natural extremes and crisis responses, then their social science itself is, as Copans points out below (Ch. 5), a major part of the problem.

There are also serious implications for the evaluation of crisis management too. The dominant view serves to justify the channelling of a disproportionate share of resources and expertise into projects that are only indirectly or not at

* And therefore from nature and the 'man–environment relations' that must develop to deal with natural extremes.

all concerned with the human misfortunes involved. Whatever its intrinsic interest, the enormous commitment to geophysical monitoring and prediction deals with a peripheral rather than a central ingredient of disaster. The evidence assembled below and elsewhere serves to suggest that the dominant view supports forms of official response to disaster that are almost guaranteed to see that those whose need is greatest will be heard, understood and helped the least. Relief and reconstruction are shown to be often disproportionately focused upon restoring, and *more* than restoring, the infrastructural arrangements of the more powerful institutions of the economy, the state and international system, rather than direct responses to the needs of victims.

Nevertheless, the chapters in this book do not suggest radical abandonments of the technocratic approach. Like most contemporary scholarship they are more or less powerfully influenced by technocratic ways of working. They might even be subsumed under a technocratic framework – *if* it were not of the sort described above. Most of us utilise the same sorts of data and methods found in the dominant view. However, the perspectives brought to bear and the evidence that influences us most do not square with the dominant view. We need a new consensus. That consensus is unlikely to do much about the grosser misconceptions of the dominant view or to be intellectually honest and scientific unless enquiry is much more independent of the pressures and interests of technocratic institutions. It is also unlikely to improve matters unless, in due course, it can influence these institutions at least to adopt frames of reference that are more aware of their own serious limitations in face of these problems and of the predicaments of those who most often suffer disaster and are least equipped to deal with it.

Of singular importance for geographers and anthropologists is the sense in which the dominant view is unashamedly indifferent to history and to human and environmental diversity; the way it becomes more abstracted and irrelevant to human predicaments the farther removed they are from urban–industrial centres and processes. When looking at hazards in a cross-cultural context, and disasters in non-Western, non-industrial contexts, one begins to have the suspicion that the authority of the dominant view derives from much the same source as Said (1978) sees in the European view of 'The Orient'. It involves an invented geographical vision that is powerful 'a) because a white [*sic*] specialist with highly refined scientific techniques could do the sifting and restructuring, and b) because a vocabulary of sweeping generalities . . . referred not to a set of fictions but rather . . . [in classical empiricist terms] . . . to a whole array of seemingly objective and agreed upon distinctions' (p. 233).

Concluding remarks

To summarise, I find much that is fascinating and useful in work that falls within the dominant view. In criticising it, I have criticised most of my own past work which largely pursued the dominant perspective. Yet, I believe that this perspective, which pervades natural disasters research, is the single great- est impediment to improvement in its quality and effectiveness. The perspec- tive functions as though 'objective', 'general' and rigorous, but its rigour and generality are achieved through an extreme, opportunistic narrowing of interpretation and empirical interest. This involves a covert environmental determinism and the language of the accident. Yet it serves to conceal both a particular *metaphysic of enquiry* and *politics of management*. The former involves the face-saving formula of a 'natural sciences' style of analysis. The latter relies on a sort of *habeas corpus*, whereby disaster is appropriated and severed from its roots in the rest of material life. Behind that is a view of management whose obsession is with 'normality' in the productive functions of society. Moreover, technocratic thought never for a moment pauses to question how those functions require and depend upon a centrally planned socioeconomic order or whether that is always or necessarily more reliable and sophisticated. Hence, to that order goes precedence in the treatment of disaster. The point is most obvious in so-called Third World, 'peripheral' areas, as can be seen in the descriptions of Waddell, Morren, Copans, Hall, and Watts below. Regan's discussion of the Irish 'potato famine' reminds one that there is a certain structural recurrence in these relationships of develop- ment, dependency and centralised power. But the obtuseness of the dominant view is no less evident in the socioeconomic ramifications of natural hazards in the so-called First World, 'affluent', or central states (see Chs 3, 4, 11 & 12).

In sum, the geophysicalism of the dominant view hides within the assump- tions that natural calamity is essentially the breakdown of the productive functions of society and, as crisis, is essentially an infringement upon the centralised ordering of space – or in remoter areas, an indicator of what happens when you lack the benefits of this order. The restorations of produc- tivity and reimposing of 'normal' relations become the main prescriptions of crisis management, relief and reconstruction. The ability to predict or contain natural processes in a technocratic framework becomes the main goal for disaster prevention. Now, I question whether this recognises some major, indeed *the* major, ingredients of disaster. Because it fails to do so I think it fails to effectively deal with hazards problems. I think, in particular that it fails to recognise how the roots and occurrence of contemporary disasters depend upon the way 'normal everyday life turns out to have become abnormal, in a way that affects us all' (Brecht 1965). The chapters below show the assump- tion that what is best in dominant view may not be best for the victims of disaster. Meanwhile the continuing burden and changing forms of damage from natural processes create a growing sense that the management strategies supported by the dominant view become more and more like King Canute commanding the waves.

References

Albrow, M. 1970. *Bureaucracy*. New York: Macmillan.

Ang, A. H-S. 1978. *US–Southeast Asia Symposium on Engineering for Natural Hazards Protection*. Rep. Nat. Sci. Foundation Univ. Illinois, Urbana.

Arendt, H. 1958. *The human condition*. Chicago: University of Chicago Press.

Armytage, W. H. G. 1965. *The rise of the technocrats: a social history*. London: Routledge & Kegan Paul.

Ayre, R. S. 1975. *Earthquake and tsunami hazards in the United States: a research assessment*. Inst. Behavioural Science, Univ. Boulder, Colorado.

Baker, G. W. and D. W. Chapman (eds) 1962. *Man and society in disaster*. New York: Basic Books.

Barton, A. H. 1969. *Communities in disaster: a sociological analysis of collective stress situations*. New York: Doubleday.

Berger, P. and T. Luckmann 1967. *The social construction of reality*. Garden City: Doubleday.

Berlin, G. L. 1980. *Earthquakes and the urban environment*. Boca Raton, Florida: CRC Press.

Blum, R. and E. Blum 1963. *The dangerous hour: the lore and culture of crisis and mystery in rural Greece*. London: Chatto & Windus.

Bolt, B. A. 1978. *Earthquakes: a primer*. San Francisco: W. H. Freeman.

Brecht, B. 1965. *The Messingkauf dialogues*, (transl. J. Willet). London: Methuen.

Brictson, R. C. (ed.) 1966. *Symposium on emergency operations*. System Dev. Corp. Santa Monica, California.

Brill, J. 1956. *The chance character of human existence*. New York: Philosophical Library.

Burton, I. and K. Hewitt 1974. Ecological dimensions of environmental hazards. In *Human ecology*, F. Sargeant (ed.), II, 253–84. Amsterdam: North-Holland.

Burton, I., R. W. Kates and G. F. White 1978. *The environment as hazard*. New York: Oxford University Press.

Cooper, D. 1978. *The language of madness*. Harmondsworth: Penguin.

Copans, J. (ed.) 1975. *Sécheresses et famines du Sahel*. Paris: Maspero.

Curry, L. 1964. The random spatial economy: an exploration in settlement theory. *Ann. Assoc. Am. Geogs* **54**, 138–46.

Disaster Research Group 1961. *Field studies of disaster behaviour*. National Academy of Sciences–National Research Council, Washington, DC.

Dynes, R. R. and E. L. Quarantelli 1968. Group behaviour under stress. *Society and Social Research* **52**, 416–29.

Eijkman, P. H. 1911. *L'internationalisme scientifique*. The Hague: W. P. van Stockum.

Eliade, M. 1954. *Cosmos and history: the myth of the eternal return*, (transl. W. R. Trask). New York: Harper.

Foucault, M. 1965. *Madness and civilisation*, (transl. R. Howard). New York: Mentor Books.

Gerasimov, I. P. and T. V. Zvonkova 1974. Natural hazards in the territory of the USSR: study, control and warning. In White (1974, pp. 243–53).

Gibson, S. B. 1976. The use of quantitative risk criteria in hazard analysis. *J. Occup. Accidents* **1**, 85–94.

Gould, P. R. 1963. Man against his environment: a game theoretic framework. *Ann. Assoc. Am. Geogs* **53**, 290–7.

Grayson, P. K. and P. Sheets (eds) 1979. *Volcanic activity and human ecology*. New York: Academic Press.

Grosser, G. H., H. Wechsler and M. Greenblatt (eds) 1964. *The threat of impending disaster: contributions to the psychology of stress*. Cambridge, Mass.: MIT Press.

Gumbel, E. J. 1958. *Statistics of extremes*. New York: Columbia University Press.

Habermas, J. 1973. *Theory and practice*, (transl. J. Viertel). *New York: Beacon Press.*

Haas, J. E. and R. S. Ayre 1969. *The western Sicily earthquake of 1968.* Washington, DC: National Academy of Sciences.

Haas, J. E., R. W. Kates and M. J. Bowden (eds) 1977. *Reconstruction following disaster.* Cambridge, Mass.: MIT Press.

Haddon, W., E. A. Suchman and D. Klein 1964. *Accident research: methods and approaches.* New York: Harper & Row.

Hawkins, D. 1964. *The language of nature: an essay in philosophy of science.* San Francisco: W. H. Freeman.

Heschel, A. J. 1962. *The prophets: an introduction.* New York: Harper & Row.

Hewitt, K. 1970. Probabilistic approaches to discrete natural events: review and theory. *Econ. Geog.* **46** (2), 332–49.

Hewitt, K. 1976. Earthquake hazards in the mountains. *Natural History* **LXXXV**, 30–7.

Hewitt, K. 1980. Review: 'the environment as hazard'. *Ann. Assoc. Am. Geogs* **70** (2), 306–311.

Hewitt, K. and I. Burton 1971. *The hazardousness of a place: a regional ecology of damaging events.* Univ. Toronto, Dept of Geog. Res., Publn no. 6.

Huntington, E. 1945. *Mainsprings of civilisation.* New York: Wiley.

Kantarovich, L. V., G. M. Molchan, V. I. Keilis-Borok and E. V. Vilkovich 1970. *A statistical model of seismicity and an estimate of the basic seismic effects*, (transl. J. Findlay). Izvestia Earth Physics, no. 5, 85–102.

Kates, R. W. 1971. Natural hazard in human ecological perspective: hypotheses and models. *Econ. Geog.* **47**, 438–51.

Kates, R. W. 1978. *Risk assessment and environment hazard.* Scientific Committee on Problems of the Environment (SCOPE), Rep. no. 8. Chichester: Wiley.

Kendrick, T. D. 1956. *The Lisbon earthquake.* London: Methuen.

Kuhn, T. 1962. *The structure of scientific revolutions.* Chicago: University of Chicago Press.

Lemons, H. 1957. Physical characteristics of disasters: historical and statistical review. *Ann. Am. Acad. Pol. and Soc. Sci.* **309**, January, 1–14.

Lifton, R. J. 1970. *History and human survival.* New York: Random House.

Maguire, B. A., E. S. Pearson and A. H. A. Wynn 1952. The time intervals between industrial accidents. *Biometrika* **39**, 168–80.

Mannheim, K. 1952. *Essays on the sociology of knowledge*, P. Keskemeti (ed.). London: Routledge & Kegan Paul.

Marx, K. 1964. *The economic and philosophical manuscripts of 1844*, transl. M. Milligan, D. J. Struik (ed). New York: International Publishers.

McNeill, W. H. 1976. *Plagues and peoples.* Garden City, New York: Doubleday.

Mills, C. W. 1959. *The sociological imagination.* Oxford: Oxford University Press.

Mitchell, K. 1974. Natural hazards research. In *Perspectives on environment*, I. Mannors and M. Mikesell (eds). Commission on College Geography, Assoc. Am. Geogs Publn 13.

Mumford, L. 1967 and 1970. *The myth of the machine.* New York: Harcourt, Brace & World.

NAS (National Academy of Sciences, US) 1976. *Earthquake prediction and mitigation options for USGS and NSF programs* (Newmark report). Washington, DC.

NAS 1980a. *The atmospheric sciences: national objectives for the 1980s.* Steering Committee for the Atmos. Res. Rev., Comm. Atmos. Sci.; Ass. Math. Phys. Sci., Nat. Res. Council, Washington, DC.

NAS 1980b. *US Earthquake observations: recommendations for a new national network.* Comm. Seismol. Nat. Res. Council, Washington, DC.

O'Keefe, P., K. Westgate and B. Wisner 1976. Taking the naturalness out of natural disaster. *Nature* **260**, 15 April.

Oliver-Smith, A. 1977. Disaster rehabilitation and social change in Yungay, Peru. *Human Organization* **36**, 5–13.

Polanyi, M. 1958. *Personal knowledge: towards a post-critical philosophy*. New York: Harper & Row.

Quarantelli, E. L. (ed.) 1978. *Disasters: theory and research*. London: Sage.

Quarantelli, E. L. and R. R. Dynes 1972. When disaster strikes. *Psychology Today* **5**, 66–70.

Roszak, T. 1973. *Where the wasteland ends*. Garden City, New York: Doubleday.

Rothman, D. J. 1971. *The discovery of the asylum: social order and disorder in the New Republic*. Boston: Little, Brown.

Said, E. 1978. *Orientalism*. New York: Random House.

Scheidegger, E. 1975. *Physical aspects of natural catastrophes*. New York: Elsevier.

Scott, R. B. Y. 1968. *The relevance of the prophets*, (revised edn). New York: Macmillan.

Smith, de W. (ed.) 1957. Disasters and disaster relief. *Ann. Am. Acad. Pol Soc. Sci.* **309**.

Soloviev, S. L. 1978. Tsunamis. In Unesco (1980, pp. 118–39).

Sorokin, P. A. 1942. *Man and society in calamity*. New York: Dutton.

Strahler, A. N. and A. H. Strahler 1973. *Environmental geoscience: the interaction of natural systems and man*. Santa Barbara, California: Hamilton.

Swiss, Re. 1978. *Atlas of seismicity and volcanism*. Kummerly-Frey, Switzerland: Swiss Reinsurance Company.

Toblin, J. 1977. Disaster prevention and control in the earth sciences. *Impact of Science on Society* **27**, 131–9.

Torry, W. I. 1978. Natural disasters, social structure and change in traditional societies. *J. Asian Afr. Studs* **13**, 167–83.

Tuan, Yi-Fu 1980. *Landscapes of fear*. New York: Pantheon Books.

Unesco 1980. *The assessment and mitigation of earthquake risk*. Paris: Unesco.

Vere-Jones, D. 1973. The statistical estimation of earthquake risk. *Bull. NZ Soc. Earthquake Engng*, September, 122–7.

Waddell, E. 1977. The hazards of scientism: a review article. *Human Ecology* **5**(1), 69–76.

Walford, C. 1878–9. *Famines of the world, past and present*. New York: Burt Franklin.

Weber, M. 1947. *The theory of social and economic organizations*. Oxford: Oxford University Press.

White, G. F. 1961. The choice of use in resource management. *Natural Resources J.*, 23–40.

White, G. F. (ed.) 1974. *Natural hazards: local, national, global*. Oxford: Oxford University Press.

White, G. F. and J. E. Haas 1975. *Assessment of research on natural hazards*. Cambridge, Mass.: MIT Press.

Whitehead, A. N. 1929. *Process and reality: an essay in cosmology*. New York: Free Press.

Whyte, A. V. and I. Burton (eds) 1980. *Environmental risk assessment*. SCOPE, Report no. 15. Chichester: Wiley.

Working Group on Earthquake Hazards Reduction 1980. *Earthquake hazards reduction: issues for an implementation plan*. Office of Sci. and Technol. Policy, Executive Office of the President, Washington, DC.

Yoshino, M. M. (ed.) 1971. *The water balance of monsoon Asia*. Honolulu: University of Hawaii Press.

2 Coping with frosts, governments and disaster experts: some reflections based on a New Guinea experience and a perusal of the relevant literature

ERIC WADDELL

'Disaster' in the New Guinea Highlands

In 1972 there was a prolonged drought in much of New Guinea.* Above 2300 m it gave rise to some 30 nights of ground frost over a four-month period. The frosts did considerable damage to the natural vegetation and to the food gardens of the subsistence agriculturalists living there. This damage is to be explained by the fact that they have a largely tropical lowland (and therefore non-frost resistant) domesticated food complex. The immediate reaction of local expatriate observers was to interpret this 'extreme geophysical event' as being of 'disaster' proportions. Following representations to the central government a massive famine relief programme was mounted.

The programme had two stated objectives: first, to maintain the existing nutritional status of the population, and, secondly, to ensure a rapid return to normalcy. It lasted 8 months, involved feeding up to 150 000 people using Australian rice and Japanese tinned fish that had probably been caught off the coast of New Guinea. It dictated the co-operation of the Royal Australian Air Force, plus the co-opting of Papua–New Guinea Administration and local missionary personnel. In direct costs, $(Aust.) 3.0–4.5 million were spent on the exercise. As a relief operation it was a *total* success. No one died, the nutritional status of the population actually increased (mortality rates dropping to two-thirds the normal figure), and the return to 'normalcy' occurred much faster than expected. It became 'a famine that never was'.

Why was the programme mounted in the first place among a population where the level of 'dependency' was extremely low? Through most of the area 'contact' had been established by the colonial government only in the 1950s. The production of commercial crops (pyrethrum and temperate vegetables) had only commenced a few years before, with total annual sales not above $(Aust.) 250 000.

* This summary is based on Waddell (1975).

The basic assumption of expatriate observers was that a disaster of 'unprecedented proportions' had occurred and that therefore the local population would be unable to cope. In particular a variety of disruptive effects were anticipated, notably 'fleeing' and 'forced migration', which would in turn create a series of secondary effects such as 'social disorganisation, disruption of sanitation, and the spread of infectious diseases'. In the circumstances outside help was necessary. This was a crucial judgement. It was inspired by a missionary relief expert with Biafran experience (!). That it was accepted in its totality can only be understood with reference to the context of those who were party to the decision:

(a)   Those evaluating the situation (American missionaries and Australian administrators) had no previous experience of the hazard, previous major frosts having occurred prior to contact. Hence they assumed the event to be a novel one, to which the local population could not be expected to respond.

(b)   This judgement was reinforced by the kind of paternalism typical of a colonial situation: it was assumed the expatriates had superior knowledge and judgement to the local population. They, therefore, did not bother to consult the latter.

(c)   Expatriate ignorance, that was the product of a lack of historical perspective, was reinforced by lack of knowledge of the subsistence economy. This is again a typical feature of colonial regimes. 'Experts' sent to evaluate the situation were unable to assess the effect of the frosts even on the sweet potato staple and they had no idea what local food resources were available at the time.

(d)   The event occurred at a critical time in the history of the nation – the transition from colony to independent state. The Australian *administration* and the Christian missions were both involved in a process of disengagement. The new *government* was concerned to strengthen the very fragile (and artificial) sense of national unity that is characteristic of most ex-colonial territories. Hence the former were concerned to assume a strong interventionist role as was their custom, thereby countering possible criticism and suspicion. Decisions that were based on ignorance became enveloped in a sense of urgency and were further reinforced by over-riding humanitarian preoccupations. As one observer noted, 'Any suggestions that caution and more accurate assessment ought to characterise our response, were met with cold, less-than-humanitarian reaction' (Brennan 1974). Insofar as the new government was concerned it immediately supported the initiative to set up a relief programme, seeing it as a vehicle for affirming its leadship and demonstrating the solidarity of all New Guineans. Soliciting aid throughout the country was seen as a confirmation of the setting aside of tribal and regional loyalties. (However, people were only invited to contribute cash ... to buy imported goods!) Local politicians also favoured intervention because, as members of new and alien institutions, they viewed an ability to attract central government largesse as an excellent means of legitimising their status.

In sum, political considerations plus ignorance and a basic humanitarian instinct were all critical factors in determining intervention. Further, once the famine relief programme was established, initial objectives (and misconceptions) were reinforced, this by virtue of the centralisation of decision making away from the disaster area and hence the systematic bypassing of local officials and expertise.

What about the local population? All the available evidence indicates that they knew quite well how to deal with a familiar hazard; it was the third in living memory. According to Wohlt (1973) 'Even the young men and women are conversant with *hungri* lore and what one does in response to famine'. Essentially, their normal response is characterised by a high degree of flexibility, with an escalating set of strategies according to the gravity of the hazard. At the *local* level the frost-vulnerable food crops are cultivated in small amounts, which modify the microclimatic regime by promoting the drainage of cold air away from the plants. In addition, gardens are maintained in two ecological niches within each territory, one, in the valley bottoms, of relatively high fertility and frost vulnerability, and the other, on the adjacent slopes, of lower fertility but also lower vulnerability. At an *intraregional* level (normally within a single valley) gardens are more or less constantly maintained in two separate areas up to 2 days walk apart. Although at roughly the same altitude they protect against frost variability due to such considerations as aspect and major patterns of air drainage. Finally, at the *extraregional* level and in the event of extreme frosts, migration occurs to frost-free areas up to 7 days walk away, to stay with customary hosts and establish food gardens.

Such a set of responses is characterised by a high degree of mobility articulated on a clearly defined social fabric of wide-ranging agnatic and affinal ties plus exchange partners. It involves the maintaining of outright and usufruct rights to land outside the local group territory that serve as sources of both food and planting materials, plus, in extreme circumstances, temporary resettlement elsewhere. The responses are carefully structured and they accommodate virtually all residents of the frost hazard region, with the notable exception of the old and infirm who are not mobile. Wohlt (1973), who was resident in the area throughout the disaster period, points out that in his local group only one of the 61 families who migrated out in 1972 returned because it was unable to find refuge. Further, 50% of those who migrated went to the same place they or their fathers had gone to on the occasion of the previous disaster (in 1941). Also, significantly, 'During a one month tour of the Lagaip and Porgera areas [two major refuges] no significant troubles between hosts and guests were encountered or elicited . . . It was a time of increased socialisation' (ibid.).

The famine relief programme was, of course, incompatible with such an adaptive response. In particular it sought actively to discourage outmigration from the disaster area. In fact the basic strategy adopted by the population in the circumstances was one of attempting to exploit both options. Some moved out, others stayed, and yet others moved backwards and forwards, collecting relief and establishing gardens in frost-free areas. Through the experience certain distinct trends were noted that are probably of some significance for the future. First, customary hosts indicated an unwillingness to receive frost victims in future, responsibility being displaced towards the government and relief organisations. The codified response was being undermined and a process of fragmentation initiated. Secondly, the relief itself provided a stimulus for the development of new consumption patterns, notably an acquired taste for imported foodstuffs and increased protein intakes. In sum there were signs of local and regional autonomy being undermined and institutional dependence encouraged as a result of the venture. To cite one discordant voice among missionary observers, 'We have now begun to reap a parasitic mentality and, if unchecked, the expatriate community can expect to see a fractured confidence in traditional strengths and self-esteem and, of course, a reactionary hostility for having contributed to the problem' (Brennan 1974). He is, of course, referring to all the tensions and ambivalence associated with dependency where relief becomes the guarantee of a continuing commitment to a basically unsatisfactory and deteriorating arrangement.

Strategies and implications of relief programmes in the Third World

The continuities that exist between the New Guinea disaster and those experienced elsewhere in the Third World are significant in spite of the profound differences existing in the scale and duration of colonial penetration. In terms of the strategies of intervention, mobility is always opposed as a solution – ignoring the ancient Chinese proverb reminding us that 'Of 30 ways to escape danger . . . running away is best'! Invariably, too, the responsibility for defining the strategy and for managing intervention is removed from the local to the national and international levels. With respect to the consequences of intervention, they are typically characterised by increasing dependency of victims vis-à-vis their central government. This arises out of an undermining of traditional coping mechanisms through victims having been brought more within the orbit of modern medical facilities, and their nutritional patterns having been modified. The motives are, of course, formulated in humanitarian terms and stress the return to 'normalcy' as soon as possible, normalcy being construed as the pre-disaster order of political, social and economic life. Such order means, specifically, the prosecution of state-regulated administrative functions and religious activities, and the continued operation and development of the commercial economy.

However, the New Guinea experience indicates it would be wrong to view such intervention in strictly conspiratorial or imperialistic terms, at least at the level of the individuals concerned. If relief has a long-run disabling effect, it is largely because of constraints imposed by the institutional arrangements that characterise a colonial situation, notably a state and a church both of whose legitimacy and authority are uncertain. Thus mobility in any form is disapproved of because such people are viewed as being 'elusive', 'undisciplined' and 'poor citizens'. A disaster serves as an excellent opportunity for reinforcing institutional control over them. At the same time the means for doing it are enhanced because of the opportunity of receiving material support from the metropolitan powers and the international community. A whole chain of dependency is thereby set up whereby the disaster victims become the focus of attention, but actions originate elsewhere and these actions are influenced by other than strictly humanitarian considerations. Such is the case even with the international relief agencies, they being creatures of the developed nations that inevitably tend to reinforce metropolitan dominance. At the most basic level, as Quarantelli and Dynes (1973) have indicated, their very *raison d'etre* is not infrequently to provide relief, and they inevitably seek out all opportunities to do this in order to justify their existence, organising such operations along military lines. As such, 'These agencies are themselves extensions of the international system and, in most cases, have been created by the major industrialised countries to serve their interests. This is as true of UN agencies as of national development agencies like USAID. The framework within which these organisations operate, makes it unlikely that suggestions for significant changes in the *status quo* will derive from them' (Ball 1975, p. 370).

The ultimate irony of this displacement of responsibility for dealing with disasters is that power becomes vested in the hands of people and nations that are environmentally extremely unsophisticated. The professional products of a highly mobile, urban–industrial civilisation thereby acquire the means of imposing their will on rooted peasant populations that have a strong sense of place and considerable accumulated knowledge and wisdom regarding local environmental conditions.

Nutritional dependence is perhaps the most frightening form of Third World dependency in this respect. It can be converted into a most effective political weapon, as illustrated in recent years in the strategies of US opposition to the Cambodian revolution (Hildebrand & Porter 1976) and Ethiopian central government opposition to regional liberation movements (Shepherd 1975).* In spite of this fact approved strategies of disaster relief and prevention invariably complement and reinforce economic development strategies in the Third World in their encouraging a reliance on external food sources, so rendering all hazard-prone populations ultimately vulnerable to this kind of manipulation. Indeed, regrettable as it may be, much of the natural hazards

* North American farmers are also beginning to appreciate the potential leverage they have on the OPEC nations in the context of the present energy crisis, as is clearly evoked by the bumper sticker popular in the mid-west, 'Cheaper Crude or no more Food!'.

literature provides a scientific caution for this strategy of intervention, going so far as to propose an actual reinforcement of the 'chain of dependency' between the developed and underdeveloped nations as a means of minimising the risk of disasters in the latter! Thus, in one of the major publications of the Gilbert White school of hazard researchers (White 1974) both Heijnan & Kates (p. 114) and Dupree & Roder (p. 119) assert that Third World capacity to withstand drought can be increased by more effectively linking local into national and international economies.

Natural hazards research

Until four or five years ago natural hazards research was more or less the preserve of a small group of geographers centring on White. He, together with Burton and Kates, had succeeded over the years in building an empire of no mean dimensions out of convincing the United Nations and its specialised agencies (Office of Disaster Relief Co-ordination, Desertification Prog-ramme, etc.) that 'not only the cause of . . . [natural] disasters fall within the province of science and technology, but also, in some cases their prevention, as well as the organizational arrangements made for forecasting them and reducing their impact when they occur' (Kates 1975, p. 16). Since then the subject has entered a period of exponential growth, with most of the social and environmental sciences joining the band wagon, and it has at the same time become something of an ideological battleground. The naïve determin-ism and technocratic optimism of Burton, Kates and White is now challenged by the revolutionary zeal of O'Keefe, Westgate and Wisner (see Ch. 14) who account for the incidence of disasters in the Third World in terms of political economy – the penetration of capital and the marginalisation of entire popu-lations. The analysis is Marxist, the causes are structural and the solution is one of 'guerilla warfare'. Acts of God become Acts of Capital and the disaster that struck the highlands of Guatemala in February 1976 is characterised by one as an earthquake and by the other as a classquake. One school is centred on the Programme on Environment, Technology and Man at the Institute of Behavioural Science, Boulder, USA and the other was on the now defunct Disaster Research Unit, University of Bradford, England. Both are prolific publishers. Wisner is a transfuge.

The logic underlying the evolution from one position to another is readily explicable – the necessity for establishing a clear distinction between a *natural* or *geophysical* event and its *human* consequences (cf. Ch. 1). In the case of the Sahel experience this dictates isolating *drought* as a *climatic* phenomenon from famine as a *social* phenomenon, where the mediating variable is, fol-lowing Lofchie (1975, p. 553), 'the political and economic arrangements of a society'. Although White *et al.* do make this distinction in their work, they nevertheless interpret crises as being a function of the 'imperfect knowledge' of the victims, which problem can be resolved by the transmission of knowledge and technology from the developed nations. The essential shortcomings of their analysis lie in their positing a simple causality that ignores the political and economic conditions that prevail in the Third World, and that intimates ignorance on the part of such populations of their immediate environmental conditions and of their capacity to furnish effective responses to environmentally induced stress. Their radical critics point to the structural imbalances which characterise the relationships between the developed and underdeveloped nations, which conditions create dependency and dislocate populations, economies and societies. These transformations not only render people more vulnerable to 'extreme geophysical events' but they even serve to intensify the events themselves through systematic modification of the environment (e.g. deforestation).

The White school has produced a substantial literature that includes many Natural Hazard Working Papers published by the universities of Chicago, Colorado and Toronto and books such as Burton *et al*. (1969), Hewitt and Burton (1971), White (1974), and White and Haas (1975). Ready reinforcement of their position has been furnished by the plethora of relief organisations and experts, White's models serving to legitimise their existence and comfortably to validate their 'instrumentalist' approach to disasters. They too are generating their own literature, as for instance Skeet (1977). Chapter 1 of that text, 'The ecology of disasters', draws a clear distinction between 'disasters caused by natural phenomena' (meteorological, telluric and tectonic, biological) and 'man-made disasters' (civil disturbance, warfare, refugees, accidents) while noting that 'development conditions exacerbate the destructive potential of disasters'. A specialised journal even appeared on the market in 1977, *Disasters: The International Journal of Disaster Studies and Practice*. Edited by a member of the London Technical Group (!), its first issues include an article of 'Disaster equipment – from a vitamin deficiency viewer to hovercraft'. We are, unquestionably, in the midst of a hazards and disasters bonanza.

As implied above, the developing opposition to this simple but powerful environmentalist credo has taken the form of, (a) its demystification and, (b) the elaboration of alternate models. Demystification emphasises the dubious assumptions and methodological weaknesses of the White school, and it urges that disasters cease to be automatically qualified as 'natural'. See, for instance, Ball (1975), O'Keefe *et al*. (1976), Tiranti (1977) introducing a special issue of *New Internationalist* entitled 'Disasters – Acts of God and Man: an enquiry into the causes of Third World tragedies', and Waddell (1977). All point to the ethnocentrism and inadequacy of White's initial assumptions. The most significant evidence to support this criticism is being provided, for example, by O'Keefe *et al*. (1976) and by Watts (see Ch. 13). O'Keefe *et al*. stress that there has been an important tendency for disasters to increase in occurrence and gravity over the past 50 years and that they are becoming increasingly focused in the Third World, where nearly all the major tragedies now occur. They further point out that there is no clear evidence to indicate climatic change being the cause of this trend.

The alternative, Marxist, model that is most clearly formulated in the English language literature in Chapter 14 stresses the close relationship that exists between dependency and disaster, which condition is the product of a global economic order that promotes underdevelopment. Concentrating the urban proletariat in *favelas* and obliging the rural peasantry to develop cash crop production for export are but two illustrations of this process which intensifies disaster proneness. Solutions, then, must of necessity involve structural changes. Technological 'solutions' and relief, all originating in the developed nations, can only exacerbate the condition of dependency, thereby reinforcing vulnerability.

That there should be this growth and ferment in disaster research is not surprising. An increasing number of social scientists are eager to market their 'expertise' as the academic job market tightens and the urge to demonstrate one's 'relevance' grows. At about the same time as this surge occurred the Sahel drought broke upon us. The conjuncture was a 'fortunate' one. It provoked a

'profusion of research activities in the Sahel which is now almost a corporate bandwagon (Drought Inc.?). The number of organizations that have had projects or are now currently engaged in research in the area is quite staggering (ENDA, IDRC, IRSH, ORSTOM, UNEP, DRODAT, IDEP, CILSS, OCLALAV, LEMFT, MUSAT and a bewildering array of AID sponsored University projects plus, of course, the ever present plethora of Conferences, workshops and symposia). The general impression is that coordination has been at a minimum and replication at a maximum. My own experience with a variety of Sahelian projects in the States has been that they have been little more than report writing machinery for AID, employing personnel who have little working knowledge of the Sahel and the quality of whose product is, at best, academic kitsch' (Watts, 1977a, p. 20).

As the same author said in a personal communication to me, 'The Sahel is crawling with AID type mega-projects (the Kissinger pledge) most of which are run by people who didn't know where the Sahel was until the money came their way' (Watts 1977b). But the Sahel is also part of francophone Africa and this fact forcibly brought some of the researchers into contact for the first time with a much more critical and scientifically rigorous literature dealing initially with underdevelopment in West Africa and subsequently the conditions surrounding the Sahel drought and famine itself. This was the work of the French neo-Marxist school of economic anthropologists best represented in the writings of Meillassoux (especially 1974 and 1975, and the collection of major articles in 1977). Their analysis of the Sahel question is formulated in the Comité Information Sahel's *Qui se nourrit de la famine en Afrique?*

(1974) and Copan's collection on *Sécheresses et famines du Sahel* (1975). This literature is notable for its explicit historicism with respect to both external economic relations (production of commercial crops for export, and its implications for domination and dependency) and local ecological conditions (the progressive destruction of the local ecosystem through population growth, expansion of the area under cultivation, intensification and poverty). Against this perspective, development and relief experts of the 1970s assume exactly the same functions as the colonial administrators of earlier decades. But what is perhaps more important from an academic viewpoint is that it effectively integrates cultural ecological models into economic anthropology and underdevelopment theory.*

In light of this analysis the contribution that social scientists can make to disaster research becomes evident, if not indeed urgent, for one of the 'instrumentalist' school's myths still remains prevalent – that of peasant ignorance. In laying this myth to rest once and for all, models of adaptive strategies that are more sophisticated than the simple equilibrium ones of the 1960s, such as Rappaport's (1967), need to be developed. These must elaborate on strategies of response to periodic environmental stress. Some progress is, I think, being made in this direction. At the same time, in conducting disaster research, it is necessary to review critically the radical analyses that have been formulated by Copans and Meillassoux in particular (see Ch. 5). They are, after all, based on a region where the disruptive effects of capitalism have a very long history. In such circumstances it is highly unlikely that any disaster relief strategy, however well conceived, can modify the structure of the economy or concomitant social order. What we need to establish is whether, in situations where structural dependency does not exist or is only poorly developed, relief operations create and encourage such dependency. Torry (nd) addresses himself to this question in his paper on *The impact of natural disaster aid on traditional societies* and answers it in the affirmative (see Torry 1978). The events that occurred in the New Guinea highlands in 1972–3 and that are described in the first half of this chapter confirm Torry's analysis. Indeed, with regard to the issues in question, the New Guinea experience is of considerable diagnostic value. Its limited dimensions and location, plus the fact of it being 'an early colonial situation', make it possible to identify most of the dimensions of the crisis and to determine the conditions and mechanisms by which relief serves to create and reinforce a state of disequilibrium and dependency.

Conclusion

Given this reality it is scarcely possible to adopt even a *laissez-faire* attitude to disaster relief – that it serves as a 'limited kind of wealth redistribution at the

---

* Godelier (1974) has, of course, been exploring this relationship in general theoretical terms.

periphery' (Brookfield 1975). Since it is the institutional and structural order which is at fault disaster research and relief should formulate models and strategies which challenge this order. These should be based on the preservation and reinforcement of indigenous responses and involve a minimum of external intervention (national or international). A wealth of local knowledge exists, even if it is not entirely appropriate to the changing material conditions in which the population finds itself. Anthropologists, geographers and other social scientists can make available this knowledge. Finally, such a *decentralised* response can also serve to keep at distance yet another breed of those disabling but well meaning experts of which the Third World is chronically victim – René Dumont's sorcerer's apprentices: 'Au milieu de tout cela, l'humanité dite 'développée', issue de la révolution industrielle, *joue à l'apprenti sorcier*, sans aucun souci des générations qui nous suivront. La nature d'avant homme pouvait être comparée a un magnifique magasin de vieilles porcelaines chinoises, et nous y lachons inconsidérément le troupeau d'éléphants des hommes de feu . . .' (Dumont 1975, pp. 64–5). Areas where the incidence of natural hazards is high are, of course, especially fragile . . .

References

Ball, N. 1975. The myth of the natural disaster. *The Ecologist* **5**, 368–71.
Brennan, P. W. 1974. Personal communication. 22 April.
Brookfield, H. C. 1975. Personal communication. August.
Burton, I., R. W. Kates and R. E. Snead 1969. *The human ecology of coastal flood hazard in megalopolis*. Dept Geog. Res. Pap. no. 115, Univ. Chicago.
Comité Information Sahel 1974. *Qui se nourrit de la famine en Afrique?* Paris: Maspero.
Copans, J. (ed.) 1975. *Sécheresses et famines du Sahel*. Vol. I: *Ecologie, denutrition, assistance*. Vol. II: *Paysans et nomades*. Paris: Maspero.
Disasters: The International Journal of Disaster Studies and Practice. New York: Pergamon.
Dumont, R. 1975. *La croissance de la famine*. Paris: Seuil.
Dupree, H. and W. Roder 1974. Coping with drought in a preindustrial, preliterate farming society. In White (1974, pp. 115–19).
Godelier, M. 1974. Considérations théoriques et critiques sur le problème des rapports entre l'homme et son environnement. *Inform. Sciences Sociales* **13**(6), 31–60.
Heijnen, J. and R. W. Kates 1974. Northeastern Tanzania: comparative observations along a moisture gradient. In White (1974, pp. 105–14).
Hewitt, K. and I. Burton 1971. *The hazardousness of a place*. Toronto: Toronto University Press.
Hildebrand, G. C. and G. Porter 1976. *Cambodia: starvation and revolution*. New York: Monthly Review Press.
Kates, R. W. 1975. *Natural disasters and development*. Wingspread Conf. Backgrd Pap. Centre for the Study of Democratic Institutions/Fund for the Republic Inc., Racine, Wisconsin.
Lofchie, M. 1975. Political and economic origins of African hunger. *J. Mod. Afr. Studs* **13**(4), 551–67.

Meillassoux, C. 1974. *Anthropologie economique des Gouro de Cote d'Ivoire: de l'économie de subsistance a l'agriculture commerciale*. Paris: Mouton.

Meillassoux, C. 1975. *Femmes, greniers et Capitaux*. Paris: Maspero.

Meillassoux, C. 1977. *Terrains et theories*. Paris: Editions Anthropos.

O'Keefe, P., K. Westgate and B. Wisner 1976. Taking the naturalness out of natural disasters. *Nature* **260**, 15 April, 566–7.

Quarantelli, E. L. and R. R. Dynes 1973. When disaster strikes. *New Society* **23** (535), 5–9.

Rappaport, R. 1967. *Pigs for the ancestors: ritual in the ecology of a New Guinea people*. New Haven: Yale University Press.

Shepherd, J. 1975. *The politics of starvation*. New York: Carnegie Endowment for International Peace.

Skeet, M. 1977. *Manual for disaster relief work*. Edinburgh: Livingstone.

Susman, P., P. O'Keefe and B. Wisner nd. *Global disasters. A radical interpretation*. Multicopied.

Tiranti, D. 1977. The un-natural disasters. *New Internationalist* **53**, 5–6.

Torry, W. I. nd. *The Impact of natural disaster aid on traditional societies*. Multicopied.

Torry, W. I. 1978. Natural disasters and social structure and change in traditional society. *J. Asian Afr. Studs* **13**, 167–83.

Waddell, E. 1975. How the Enga cope with frost: responses to climatic perturbations in the Central Highlands of New Guinea. *Human Ecology* **3**(4), 249–73.

Waddell, E. 1977. The hazards of scientism: a review article. *Human Ecology* **5**(1), 69–76.

Watts, M. J. 1977a. *Pre-disaster planning and the Nigerian drought*. Conf. on the aftermath of drought in Nigeria. Federal Ministry of Water Resources and Centre for Social and Economic Research, Ahmadu Bello University, Nigeria. Multicopied.

Watts, M. J. 1977b. Personal communication. 1 June.

White, G. F. (ed.) 1974. *Natural hazards: local, national, global*. New York: Oxford University Press.

White, G. and J. Haas 1975. *Assessment of research on natural hazards*. Cambridge, Mass.: MIT Press.

Wohlt, P. B. 1973. *Migration from Yumbisa: traditional response to 'taim hungri'*. Multicopied.

3 *The Bushmen and the British: problems of the identification of drought and responses to drought*

GEORGE E. B. MORREN, Jr

Introduction

This chapter discusses two cases involving apparent drought and responses to drought, that of the !Kung Bushmen, a hunter–gatherer population inhabiting the Kalahari Desert of Botswana, and that of the British, an urban–industrial population inhabiting a normally well watered island in north-west Europe.

The first concern was to develop a way to identify realistically and describe the environmental problems involved. Economic and political 'causes' of environmental problems, so frequently overlooked in natural hazards studies, were to be included. A second feature of the approach here is more clearly anthropological. It involves a naturalistic account of the range of human responses and coping devices, including those of ordinary people (left to their own devices or not) and those of groups. A third feature is to use the notion of a 'process of response' to conceptualise the relationships of human responses and their properties to environmental problems and their properties, with particular attention to the temporal dimensions of each (see Ch. 15).

The Bushmen case involves people that, for the purposes of this chapter, are assumed to be more or less well adapted to the problems of survival in dry lands. Accordingly, the discussion of this case begins with an attempt to describe a 'traditional' response process consisting of ways of coping with seasonality and other forms of environmental variability, including extreme drought. This model is then used to examine Bushmen responses to what appears to be as major a factor as water scarcity, namely the invasion of their range by herding populations.

The British case involves a people who, according to a well established stereotype are adapted to high levels of precipitation, as well as veterans of the struggle to survive the hazards of industrialisation. It was found that an extended period of low rainfall transferred some of the burdens of urban–industrial life to rural people, even those in areas with adequate local water resources, and to agriculture, with direct effects on food production. This situation was also strongly influenced by government policy, the state of the national economy, and relations with the European Common Market. Despite the huge differences between the two societies, the structure of the British situation can be likened to that of the Bushmen. Furthermore, the fact that water supply and associated secondary problems turn out to be no more novel in Great Britain than in the Kalahari is profoundly important to our understanding of responses to drought.

!Kung Bushmen: a seasonal response process

The !Kung are a loosely organised population of hunter–gatherers and part-time farmers and herders. They live in the semi-arid Kalahari desert area in the Republic of Botswana and the Territory of Namibia (South West Africa). The account that follows is based primarily on the research, centred in the Dobe area of northwestern Botswana, by Richard Lee and associates (Lee 1969, 1972a–e; Lee & Devore 1968, 1976; Guenther 1976, Howell 1976). This area, according to Lee's 1964 census, contains a total effective population of 676, including 336 !Kung Bushmen. It is characterised climatically by hot summers which include a five-month rainy season from November to March, cool dry winters which run from April to August, and hot dry springs in September and October. In the spring and summer periods the daily temperature range is from 15.6°C to 37.8°C, with maxima as great as 42.2°C recorded. In winter the daily range is from −1.1°C to 25.6°C. 'Normal' rainfall for the year is in the 150–250 mm range. According to Lee (1972b), 'average annual rainfall has little meaning in an environment in which rainfall may vary by as much as 300% from year to year'. Lee measured rainfall during the various years spent in the field. During the rainy season of 1963–4 239 mm of rainfall were recorded. During 1967–8, in the same season, 597 mm were recorded.

Lee also reproduced 46 years of rainfall records from a government weather station located at Maur some 300 km south-east of the Dobe area. This permitted him to talk about the extremes of rainfall variability, a subject which is particularly relevant to the present discussion. During the 46-year period for which data were available, drought occurred in 17 years (37% of the years), and of these drought years, 12 (26% of 46) could be classified as severe drought with less than 70% of the average rainfall occurring. Put another way, the probability of drought occurring (at Maur at least) is 2 years in 5, and of severe drought 1 year in 4. Lee felt that the situation might be even more serious at Dobe where the average annual rainfall appeared lower (350 mm at Dobe v. 462 mm at Maur), but the quality of the data does not really permit such a comparison. In any event, Lee (1972b) concluded that, based on his experience in the Dobe area from 1963 to 1969 and the experience of the Marshall family in another area of the Kalahari occupied by Bushmen, 'drought conditions probably characterize about half the years'. Further, he states that 'the northern Kalahari appears to experience alternating *runs* of good years and bad years of varying length' [my italic]. We may conclude that drought conditions are 'normal' (occurring half of the time) and that a possible extreme perturbation of 'severe drought' is presented in 2 or 3 years out of every 10.

Lee (1972b) reports a second kind of rainfall variability: the difference in rainfall between places for any time period. Long-term records from five weather stations along a 200 km transect some 300 km south of Dobe, though having comparable average annual rainfall, showed as much as 10-fold monthly variability between them. This local variation is particularly critical in the October to December period, since these *early rains* strongly influence the productivity of wild food plants harvested later on. With such local variation, Lee notes that 'the desert may be blooming in one area while a few hours walk away it will still be parched' (ibid.). The Bushmen, and other people living in the area, must cope with such variations, whether regular and more or less predictable, or irregular and more or less unpredictable, if extreme physiological stresses are to be avoided.

The distribution of surface waters upon which the !Kung depend reflects the variability of rainfall. It is a seasonal phenomenon and variable within the seasonal framework from year to year and from place to place. The availability of certain faunal resources and the occurrence of other problems are also likely to be influenced by these variations (see below).

It should be noted that, although based exclusively upon Richard Lee's reports (particularly Lee 1969, 1972a–c), the present analysis deviates from Lee in certain important respects. This is particularly true of its treatment of Bushmen responses to the activities of Bantu pastoralists, important matters on which Lee has not reported. This is because my approach has generated new questions about the situation. The part dealing with 'traditional' responses to 'normal' seasonal variability is similar to Lee's view, if organised somewhat differently and bringing together information from several of his reports.

The pattern of !Kung responses to water supply and other problems is outlined in Figure 3.1 and will be described in detail immediately hereafter. I have provisionally assigned !Kung 'traditional' responses to five levels, four of which are seasonal, with the fifth representing responses to extreme conditions. In describing such a cyclical pattern, the choice of where to start may appear to be arbitrary. However, taking the characteristics of the seasons in the Dobe area as a guide, the description begins with the situation pertaining to the most benign time of the year. This is reflected in the Bushman response process, at a relatively flexible time.

(1)   With the onset of the spring rains sometime in October or November – which season the !Kung label *!huma* – they disperse in small groups, moving away from permanent water wells, and shifting to the vicinity of mongongo, baobab, and *Terminalia* trees. These trees possess small water reservoirs in their hollow boles. Lee estimates there to be approximately 100 such water points within a sample area of 6400 km². In

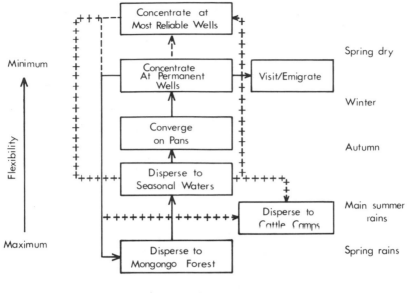

Minimum

Flexibility

Maximum

Spring dry

Winter

Autumn

Main summer rains

Spring rains

⟶ response pathways under 'normal' conditions

--⟶ response to extreme drought

+++⟶ response path under pressure from pastoralists

Figure 3.1 !Kung 'traditional' seasonal response process and its disruption.

1964 Lee found that 248 !Kung were distributed in 14 separate temporary camps associated with such sites, an average of 18 per camp. This is a period when the !Kung diet noticeably improves, both in quantity and in the ease with which it is obtained. This is the period of plant growth and animal reproduction. As noted, the onset and quantity of spring rains is critical because it determines the quality of the vegetable harvest eaten in the cycle.

(2) With the onset of the main summer rains in December to March, the season the !Kung call *bara*, they continue the dispersal, moving up-country to camp near seasonal water points. These consist of standing water and numbered approximately 50 in Lee's sample area referred to above. Camp size varies from 7 to 50 people.

This is a season of plenty, with !Kung benefiting from a variety of vegetable foods including fruits, berries, melons and leafy vegetables, and, if the rainfall has been particularly abundant, wet-country fauna such as ducks, geese, elephants and buffalo, which would flock to the Dobe area. It is the period when the largest amounts of game are taken.

(3) With the cessation of the rains and a progressive drop in temperature, winter approaches. In the seasons the !Kung call *≠obe* (autumn) and *!gum* (winter) between April and August, the bushmen fall back on the main summer pans and, or the permanent wells. It is also a period in

which more long-range visiting and emigration occur between main groups and out of the area. In particularly good years the largest pans may contain water far into winter and thus provide a base for bushman camps. In Lee's sample area there were, in addition, five permanent wells that would otherwise attract large numbers of !Kung. In this period groups range from 100 to 200 people. At the beginning the nut harvest matures and summer fruits are still abundant, but the diet becomes increasingly heterogeneous, scarce and difficult to obtain. Food plants exploited later in this period include mongongo nuts, roots and tubers along with a wide variety of other plant species. Much time is spent in hunting and snaring. The main food problem is the distance which must be travelled to obtain it. A much higher level of co-operation and public living is demanded of individual !Kung than is otherwise characteristic, hence a greater probability of conflict exists. This motivates some of the visiting and emigration referred to above.

(4)   Under very severe winter conditions and, or with the onset of the spring dry season, in the August to October period, the people may concentrate at the two very reliable water holes that exist in their range. These have never been known to fail. This season which the !Kung call *!qua*, is a hot and dry period when people are even more concentrated and restricted. Good food is available only at great distance from the camp. Hunting is difficult but undertaken frequently with only indifferent success. With the onset of spring rains, the !Kung are once again able (happily) to disperse into isolation in very small groups.

As Lee notes, the pattern of responses is very similar in outline to the seasonal responses of other modern hunter–gatherers including Eskimos, Australian Aborigines, Sub-Arctic Indians, Great Basin Indians and Congo Pygmies. However, contrary to Lee's interpretation, the significance of the claimed 'worldwide' occurrence of the pattern lies not in what it says about basic hunter–gatherer adaptation (Lee 1972b, Lee & DeVore 1968), but rather in the fact that it *is not world wide*! Its documented occurrence is indeed limited to the hunter–gatherers who survived long enough for us to study them. These are relict populations living on lands that until recently have been marginal to the exploitative patterns of other, expanding human populations. In most instances such marginal lands are subject to unbuffered extremes of seasonality. We can only speculate about the details of the way of life of hunter–gatherers living in more favourable habitats in the past. I would, however, assert my belief that basic hunter–gatherer adaptation in a less stressful environment included not only seasonal movements but other kinds of movement responses not strictly keyed to an annual cycle. Here I draw upon my own research among the Miyanmin of New Guinea (Morren 1974) who, although not hunter–gatherers in the strictest sense of the term, not only depend on wildfoods for a significant portion of their diet but also move around a lot. It is not appropriate to elaborate these assertions here. It does, however, suggest one possible qualification of our understanding of the 'traditional' nature of the Bushman pattern of responses. That pattern can be viewed as traditional only to the extent that the !Kung, and similar Bushmen groups, have been confined to their marginal habitats and forced to eschew other kinds of movement responses for an extended period of time.*

Disruption of the process These considerations lead me to look more closely at the interaction of Bushmen with Bantu pastoralists, who have been a problem for the Bushmen and similar hunter–gatherer groups for a long time. According to Lee, Tswana cattle herders appeared in the Dobe area in the 1880s, 'and from the 1890s onwards the area was used as a regular summer grazing ground by these pastoralists' (1969a, p. 51). The first year-round residence by outsiders began in 1925 when two Herero families set up a cattle post at !Aŋqwa. Provoked by the murder of a Bantu colonist by a !Kung, the British colonial administration legitimised the appointment of a Tswana headman in 1948, thus recognising the Bantu to be the dominant group in the area. Since then conflicts, including those of Bantu–!Kung labour relations, are settled by him. The character of the situation changed further, starting in 1954, when there was a large influx of Hereros and several thousand cattle into the Dobe area on the Bechuanaland (now Botswana) side of the border (Lee 1969, p. 51). Clearly the Bantu pastoralists have been experiencing problems too, probably of a long-standing nature. The influx of Hereros from the Okavangi Swamps in 1954 was driven by an outbreak of tsetse fly, a disease vector whose range has been extending southward in historic times.

By 1964 the non-Bushman population consisted of 340 Herero and Tswana and several thousand head of cattle, goats, donkeys and horses. At the same time, the Bushman population was 336. A further 89 Bushmen with some affinity with the Dobe area were no longer full-time residents; 55 alternated in and out of the area, and 34 had emigrated to more distantly located clusters of Bushmen.

To summarise, Lee was able to enumerate some 765 people living in the Dobe area or affiliated with it. Of these, 340 were Bantu and 425 were Bushmen. Of the Bushmen, only 336 were full-time residents of the area. Of these Bushman residents, 88 (36%) were associated with Bantu cattle camps, employed as 'cowboys' and 'milk maids'. At this time, in addition, 7% of Bushman women in the area were married to Bantu. During a later field period, in 1968–9, Lee observed 150 Bushmen residing with 70 Herero and 500 cattle around one reliable water well. The subsistence side of this Bantu–Bushman interaction can be briefly characterised. In exchange for their labour, the !Kung Bushmen receive a 'generous' daily ration of sour milk, agricultural produce and occasional meat, some of which food may be shared among a larger circle of Bushmen.

* Actually, one statement of Lee's has the !Kung in the Dobe area for at least 100 years (1969, p. 50–1). C. Schrire claims that the Bushmen have been part-time farmers for at least 400 years (unpublished MS).

In the face of his own observations, Lee nevertheless asserts that 'the Dobe area has maintained its character as a hunting and gathering stronghold' (1972a, p. 330) and, as noted he takes it to be a model of hunter–gatherer adaptation. He feels he can justify this on the basis of the fact that 'wild vegetable food and game still provide over half of the total subsistence in calories' (1972d, p. 348). But I think he paints an overly benign and distorted picture of contemporary Bushmen–Bantu pastoralist relations. He refers to this situation as a 'happy state of affairs' (ibid.). He further states that 'without Herero food, the /ai/ai/ (permanent water hole) aggregation would not be possible' (1972d, p. 349). What he does not seem to realize, however, is that without the Herero, the /ai/ai/ aggregation would not be necessary. And, in any case, if *almost* half of Bushman subsistence comes from the pastoralists, how can they be called 'hunter–gatherers'?

If we turn once again to the outline of !Kung responses (Fig. 3.1), a very different picture emerges. It is characterised by the serious, and in the long run perhaps fatal, disruption of an already stressed response process. Actually, the !Kung have responded to the Herero problem *as if to a severe, perhaps permanent, drought*! How could it be otherwise? Even without the Herero and Tswana, the Bushmen had a water problem of moderate to severe intensity. The presence of these outsiders has the effect of trebling (at least) the effective population in the area – twice as many people and a great number of large, domesticated (thirsty!) animals.

The resulting response on the part of the Bushmen has entailed a major loss of flexibility and self-sufficiency. They now occupy camps around a perennial water well, not *three months* of the year, but *eight or nine*. They are able to disperse in small groups into the countryside for three or four months. Even the possibility of emigrating away from this zone of disruption, while apparently elected by some, has been interfered with. Those !Kung who may have preferred to move back with the Nyae Nyae Bushmen (whence they came, apparently, over 100 years ago), perhaps to become farmers under South African tutelage, have been prevented from doing so by the (illegitimate) South African administration of Namibia. It is also likely that other areas of possible emigration have been disrupted by Bantu pastoralists. Now a major consequence of these stresses is that the range of environmental variability the !Kung can cope with has narrowed significantly.

Meanwhile, the Bantu have gained at least a partial solution to *their* problems. As a matter of fact, they employ a device well known everywhere: they transfer some of their problems to a minority or relatively less powerful population, in this case to the Bushmen. The !Kung may indeed be fortunate that the pastoralists have some use for the ex-hunter–gatherers as cheap labour! One can only speculate concerning the precise details involved, and this speculation focuses on the apparent need for 'cowboys'. In a wetter habitat the need to divide herds in the search for watering places and accessible forage is minimal. The herd could be easily managed with available manpower. In the semi-arid Dobe area, even in the better seasons of the year, the cattle and other livestock must be divided, hence the need for Bushman 'cowboys'. One must anticipate very hard times for the !Kung Bushmen in a future run of 'good' years since then the pastoralists will have less use for them.

The Bushman case may be intrinsically interesting to anthropologists and Africanists, but is offered here primarily as a 'cautionary tale', about the problems of disentangling and interpreting multiple environmental problems and responses.

Implicit in the argument so far is the basic question, 'When is a drought not a drought?', or more properly speaking, 'When is a problem "perceived" as drought, not a drought?' The Bushman case shows the ambiguity of the question. They respond *as though* there were a drought when, in our common understanding of that term, drought is not the problem. Indeed, all else being equal, they seem very well able to cope with rainfall scarcity. In ecological studies 'all else' is rarely equal. The Bushmen, like other organisms and peoples, have multiple problems. Responding to one problem reduces their ability to respond to other problems. The British case which follows, though more complex, seems to reinforce a similar sense of universal features of adaptation and survival.

The British

Beginning in the summer of 1975, news media took notice of the remarkable spell of sunny weather that had settled on northern Europe. As is often the case in such slow-onset disaster situations, possible long-term implications were not contemplated by reporters. Rather, it was reported to be a boon to tourism and a spur to local people enjoying the great out-of-doors in ways which were to them unusual.

By late spring of 1976 the potential seriousness of the situation had become apparent to people in Great Britain, particularly farmers, and the developing problem was noted in the British press. In North America where I was at that time, newspaper response was at least partly based on stereotypes: that of the dignified, freedom-loving, stiff-upper-lipped British, and the one that describes the United Kingdom as foggy and rainy. As with all accounts based on stereotypes, there were several grains of truth to all of this, but realism about individual hardship, political obfuscation and historical truth was generally lacking.

In any event, I began to look at the British situation in a manner not unlike that of the American journalists described, involving the same umbrella-wielding stereotypes of Britain and its people. After all, under normal conditions the British climate does assure adequate rainfall over most of the land. For most of Britain, wetness is more of a problem than drought (Hanna 1973,

p. 180). And, during those two exceedingly dry years, according to press reports, the British umbrella industry collapsed!

The picture of rainfall and water availability is, however, much more complicated than the stereotype allows. For one thing, England and Wales have significantly *smaller* resources of water in relation to population than any other country in Europe. Some rainfall estimates are available for England and Wales from 1727 onwards. Fairly reliable data based on an adequate number of stations, are available from 1916. Discussion of the unprecedented magnitude of the recent drought – said to be the worst in 250 years – is apparently based on the former. But the notion of 'rainfall deficits' – used in government press releases explicitly to convince the populace of the seriousness of the problem – were based largely on the latter. The data show the average annual rainfall for England & Wales to be approximately 900 mm, but with much variability from year to year and from place to place. Moreover, the very areas reported to have been hit hardest by the 1975–6 drought (Devon and the south generally) are always subject to a potential soil moisture deficit between (roughly) April and October (Hogg 1969). Of course, most of the rainfall evaporates or ends up in the sea. Only 3% actually enters controlled water supply systems in normal times, although agriculture depends upon a much larger fraction as 'uncontrolled' supply.

During the course of the drought in 1976 the UK Department of the Environment chose to publish rainfall summaries showing the cumulative rainfall deficit from month to month. For the 16-month period ending in August 1976 it amounted to 330 mm. Although meteorologists questioned the usefulness of this measurement, correctly claiming that the soil moisture deficit was a more accurate way of informing the public, the cumulative rainfall deficit was defended as a public relations tool needed to prevent complacency. However, one also suspects that policy makers themselves were influenced by the built-in exaggeration of the magnitude of the drought, while an accumulated exaggeration promoted some over-reaction. Clearly, the amount of rainfall required to bring the drought to an end was much less than 330 mm. No one denied that, by any measure, water stocks were seriously low by August and early September of 1976. Yet, there were growing claims of unnecessary exaggeration and, by October, calls for investigations of the management of the drought response itself.

Without attempting to minimise the reality of an extended period of low rainfall, I would like to turn the argument away from earth and atmospheric facts and look instead at some of the other causes of the problems and discomfitures to which the people of Britain were being subjected in connection with the drought.

Some historical background   The British have had a water problem for a long time, a problem directly and obviously related to increasing demand over the past 200 years. Throughout this period, embracing the industrial revolution, rapid population growth, the founding and loss of an empire, per-capita water consumption has closely followed the rise in energy consumption.

The history of national water legislation is particularly informative. It shows that the primary concern of public policy has always been to ensure adequate water supplies to cities and to industry. Though the object of one early piece of legislation in 1848 was improved water quality and public health, it laid the basis for a number of chartered commercial water projects aimed directly at serving the expanding cities of the period. An 1875 law empowered local authorities to supply water where no commercial water companies were willing to operate.

During the 19th century a number of basic patterns of water resource exploitation were established. The most common involved artesian or drilled wells centred in the upper parts of river valleys, a pattern which still provides most of the water consumed in Britain. The direct exploitation of rivers and the creation of large reservoirs in mainly a 20th-century pattern initiated when demand exceeded the capacity of well-pumping. Meanwhile, the continued exploitation of the wells has led to wholesale disappearance of small rivers and spring-fed chalk streams around large cities such as London within the past 15 years.

Again, the pace of legislative responses alone suggests that World War II and the post-war period saw a spurt in consumption. Wartime rationing and other 'emergency' conservation measures were consolidated in the Water Act of 1945. This Act fostered mergers of local authorities and the acquisition of private water companies by public authorities. A severe drought in 1959 led to the Water Resources Act of 1963 which established river authorities to administer national water resources, and a Water Resources Board to act at the national level. At this time responsibility for water supply still resided in some 180 separate companies and authorities in England & Wales. Finally, the Water Act of 1973 set up 10 regional water authorities in England & Wales, consolidating in these bodies responsibility for supply, conservation, sewerage, water quality, inland fisheries, land drainage and recreation. The Act also created a centralised planning unit and research centre with responsibility for national policy but with control otherwise divided between various ministries. In sum, this legislative history suggests, at least indirectly, a continuing water problem during the period considered.

Another important matter is the uneven distribution of and unequal relations between rainfall, water resources and population in England & Wales. Roughly speaking, rainfall and quantity of water resources increase from the south and east towards the north and west of the British Isles (see Mackinder 1925). Scotland, North Wales and the northern districts of England are extremely well watered (2500–3800 mm annually). The south and south-east are the driest parts (c. 500 mm annually). Population and demand for water (including industry) have been centred in cities since the 19th century. Although the cities are widely distributed within England at least, population and urban–industrial growth in England and Wales have become progressively more concentrated in the south and south-east, aggravating problems of the unequal geographical distribution of water resources.

Demand itself has been expanding very rapidly in recent years in all sectors. Domestic demand in the early 1970s in England & Wales amounted to 168 1 per capita per day and is expected to rise to 273 1 per capita per day by the 21st century. Much of the expansion of demand in this sector over the past two decades can be related to new housing (possessing modern plumbing), the addition of modern plumbing to existing housing, lawn watering, car washing and wider use of appliances such as washing machines. As noted, industrial demand has also been growing, accounting for 23% of all abstraction. The nationalised electrical utilities use 51% of that for cooling, much of which can be returned and re-used. Demand in the agricultural sector has also been growing mainly due to the extension of water mains into rural and suburbanising areas and greater supplementary irrigation, notably again in the market garden areas of the south and south-east.

Finally, responses to the drought (and the problems *these* cause) cannot be understood without reference to the state of the British economy in recent years. One summary of the state of the British economy describes it as 'hopeless but not serious!'. The general picture has been one of falling industrial output, falling gross national product (GNP), rising unemployment, rising imports of industrial goods, inflation, continuing unfavourable balance of international payments, the shrinking pound, rising consumer prices, the 'brain drain' of scientists, professionals and managers, and so on. On the very day which I mark as the 'height' of the drought crisis (because 10 drought stories appeared in a single issue of *The Times* of London), 25 August 1976, the *Wall Street Journal* reported that unemployment in Britain had hit its highest point since World War II. Factors operating to mitigate some of this gloom include the willingness of governments and central bankers of other Western countries to prop up sterling, the influx of US and Middle Eastern capital, and the prospective benefits of North Sea oil. Meanwhile, the government's policy of promoting the expansion of agriculture appears to have made it the best performing sector of the economy despite the low food prices.

Governmental responses   These background features take on special meaning in relation to the actual course of national government actions during the drought. In fact, the drought and heat wave were not directly much of a problem for most people in Britain until the late summer of 1976. There had been a growing problem for farmers, graziers and stockmen in a number of districts, as well as for some other rural functions, such as firefighting, throughout 1975 and 1976. But the drought became a problem for the general population when the national government made it a problem in August 1976.

Until that time regional water authorities had at their disposal a crude and ungraduated array of conservation measures and restrictions, which they might legally impose. As some water authorities had previously complained (in June), their powers to act were either too limited or too extreme. On the one hand, they could ban the use of hoses, car washing and other non-essential uses of water by ordinary citizens; on the other, they could escalate to supplying domestic water only from hydrants in the streets. Water authorities were, in effect, requesting that a more graduated set of responses be put at their disposal, including the ability to implement quickly measures aimed at end users and not just including industry and agriculture. Proposals to establish a National Water Authority and construct a national water 'grid' also resurfaced at this time. Moreover, the claims of some activist critics of the government and water authorities notwithstanding, some regional authorities *did* implement lower-level restrictions as early as February 1976. According to the chairman of the Wessex Area Authority (London, *The Times* 26 Aug. 76) planning and the acquisition of hardware (hydrants and pipe) for future contingencies had commenced much earlier.

Early in August the national government finally moved to establish a policy in relation to the drought and to press legislation through Parliament granting new powers to regional water authorities. A minister ostensibly with special co-ordinating responsibilities was named.* Supply priorities were established, and a more graduated set of responses were defined providing for the granting of various powers to water authorities on a case by case basis.

In effect, the new legislation enacted in August involved the expansion of the list of non-essential uses which might be banned and the insertion of another mechanism of only moderate severity between the existing graduated responses. Thus in addition to being able to plead for voluntary savings and to apply to the Department of the Environment for power to ban a wide range of domestic and commercial uses (section 1 of the law), water authorities could now also apply to impose specific restrictions on industry and/or agriculture (section 2 of the law) before having to resort to the use of hydrants in the streets. In addition, water authorities were given discretion concerning the specific uses and restrictions which they might seek power to impose so that orders could be adapted to conditions in particular areas. They were also enabled to impose restrictions on small districts as necessary rather than on the entire area covered by their individual charters.

In the meantime, a number of water authorities in the south and south-west, who obviously were better prepared than critics might have thought, had already started to install special water mains to serve hydrants in the streets.

As described in a Department of the Environment press release (no. 765) of 24 August 1976, the government's policy and legislative programme was based on what were described as 'four equal priorities':

(a)   industry – and within industry – the need to discriminate in favour of industries which are crucial to the national life of the country and the locality concerned;

* He was previously the Minister for Sport!

(b)   agriculture;
(c)   health and safety;
(d)   essential domestic supplies.

The use of the word 'equal' was misleading. In practice, end users of water were more likely to feel the bite of restrictions the further down the list they appeared. Special efforts were directed at minimising problems for industry. It was enjoined to conserve, but shutdowns or partial shutdowns were merely threatened. South Wales was an exception, the work week being curtailed there. Of course, industrial consumption of water had already been reduced by the slump in the economy.

The health and safety area was particularly sensitive. This, however, had more to do with the secondary problems or 'side effects' of the restrictions or other emergency measures. For example, in areas where mains were closed, special squads of water-authority employees would be in readiness to respond to fire alarms in order to open the mains. When the Anglian Water Authority increased the amount of water abstracted from canals, high nitrate levels were discovered. The authority responded to this secondary problem by supplying bottled water to households with babies.

The more stringent restrictions were directed at the end user who used the least water, individual citizens in their homes.* Agricultural users were severely restricted in some areas (see below).

Some specific responses   Throughout the hot dry summer various water authorities were prepared to take extraordinary measures. Supplies were shifted from place to place and, in a few cases, new pipelines were laid for the purpose. An instance widely reported in the world press late in August was the 'stopping' of the River Thames, when the Thames Water Authority was pumping water back over a series of dams and, in effect, reversing stream flow. One consequence of such practices was, however, that farmers and others on the lower reaches of such rivers were threatened by rising pollution and salinity.

Throughout September all but two of the ten regional water authorities in England & Wales petitioned the national government for special powers. Domestic users in South Wales were placed on 'water hours' in early September. Industrial users there had their water allotments halved. Hydrants were brought into use in quantity for the first time on 15 September in north Devon (South-West Water Authority) affecting some 80 000 people who were then restricted to the amount they could carry from the street to their homes. It should be noted, however, that this conservation measure was implemented despite the fact that 70 mm of rain had already fallen on Devon in that month. Plans to bring hydrants into operation around Halifax and Huddersfield (potentially affecting 750 000 people) and Leeds and Harro-

---

* Although official figures claim that the domestic sector consumes 40% of water supplies, this includes commercial users such as fish stores and bars, and other community facilities such as hospitals and golf courses, and is therefore grossly misleading.

gate (600 000) at the same time were deferred due to significant rainfall. The cities of Exeter and Plymouth were scheduled to be so restricted on 15 October. Reviewing this evidence, only villages, suburban areas and smaller cities seemed possible candidates for turn-offs and hydrant operations, this being considered impractical for larger industrial cities such as London. In some large cities water pressure was reduced 20% or so.

Twice the normal rainfall fell over most of Britain during the month of September, touching off flash floods in some areas. In October the most stringent restrictions on water use were relaxed in South Wales and other areas as rivers and reservoirs approached normal levels. By mid-November, press coverage had petered out, and all but the lowest class of restrictions covering 'non-essential uses' of water had been removed. The government was apparently reluctant to completely de-escalate because of uncertainty about the state of the aquifers. But proposals made at the height of the drought to create a National Water Authority, a national water grid, and to nationalise 28 privately owned water companies have been opposed by the National Water Council.

By May of 1977 a droughtless summer could be confidently predicted (according to *The Economist* 21 May 1977, p. 26).

In summary the evidence suggests that government response to the drought was almost a 'non-response', or alternatively, was a response to the state of the industrial economy rather than to the drought. Heavy industry has been the weakest sector of the economy for some time and the heaviest consumer of water. Perhaps one should combine the two foregoing, and say that Britain's ability to respond to the drought had been compounded if not determined by continuing efforts to cope with the economic difficulties described. Meanwhile, the sector most directly vulnerable to drought, agriculture, was subject to special and highly anomalous treatment.

British agriculture in the drought   British agriculture had also participated in the long-run trends involving energy and water intensification. It did, however, lag well behind. Up until World War II British agriculture was almost exclusively rain-fed agriculture. Most of the effort involving water control in the past was devoted to drainage. The War provided the impetus in Britain as elsewhere for the expansion of agriculture into less well watered lands and the development of irrigation schemes. Rural Water Supplies and Sewerage Acts of 1944 to 1971, first enacted at the height of the War, were aimed partly at this situation. I have not yet found a compilation of longitudinal data on the growth of irrigation agriculture in Britain, but it has obviously become of major proportions in some sectors. Thus for vegetable farmers practising irrigation the onset of the drought was rather sudden, when, in the summer of 1976, water alloted to irrigation by regional water authorities was halved. By then, grain farmers and those involved with livestock, dependent almost completely on rainfall, were in their second year of drought but received little government help.

One concomitant of the 'industrialisation' of agriculture in Britain (as in the US and Canada) has been diminished ability on the part of farmers to cope with *normal* climatic variation.* Every dry year since the 1940s has stimulated the expansion of irrigation (Prickett 1969, p. 199), presently the single largest agricultural use of water. Moreover, because water control by public authorities has increased, the difficulties of farmers needing water have also increased. At first only those farmers drawing water from public mains were affected. But, by the 1960s all abstractions of water, including those from rivers and other watercourses and even from farmers' own private reservoirs, required licences. By 1967 two-thirds of all farms in England & Wales were connected to public mains. Hence the expansion of the water system, while stimulating agricultural consumption of water, has increased its dependency on non-agricultural institutions. It is as if British agriculture (along with intensive agriculture elsewhere) had its own 'industrial revolution' starting in the 1940s.

Nevertheless, in late 1976 agriculture was in many respects the strongest sector of the British economy able to cope even with such 'man-made hazards' as the national policy affecting the expansion of agriculture, price controls and accommodations to the European Common Market. This is not to say, that there have been no farm failures over the past few years!

One major and invariable effect of socioeconomic or environmental change is to give new definition to the nature of the marginal unit. Rather like the situation of US farmers in the 1920s and 1930s, throughout 1976, brokerage houses were launching farmland investment schemes to take advantage of the displacements caused by the drought. Some observers related this phenomenon to the dearth of *other* investments. But, here again, agriculture was undoubtedly a good investment as long as you were not a farmer.

The farmer's year did not start auspiciously in 1976. Although winter cereals were in good condition, the second successive dry winter left farmers in a state of uncertainty. Some responded by planting more land, with record increases in area sown in oats, wheat and potatoes. April frost and cold wind in many districts had affected some newly planted crops including potatoes, sugar beets and some pasturage, slowing growth and damaging leaves, but the situation was not as severe as in May 1975. Vegetable farmers who usually sold to food processors were in a quandary, too. These users of very large quantities of water had been warned by water authorities in May to expect cutbacks. As a consequence, many pea growers did not plant at all. There are also reports indicating that at the same time many food processors had large inventories of frozen peas left over from 1975! Farmers gamble, industries speculate and financiers invest!

By June, non-irrigated vegetable crops were beginning to wilt, especially in the south and east. The government, however, was still expressing strong optimism for potatoes, forage crops and sugar beets. Simultaneously, the National Farmers Union was pessimistic, lobbying for government action on

* See the Institute of Ecology study cited in *Nature* **262**, 1976, 530.

the drought and on price structure, too. Yet by late June the supply of potatoes was so high that the market price was halved. Lettuce was being ploughed under due to low prices. In some areas such as Essex, however, pasturage was deteriorating, and livestock were already being fed winter rations, with yields of hay and silage half normal levels. Stories of panic selling of cattle on the continent of Europe were not yet echoed in Britain. Other farmers were irrigating heavily, but by mid-June water authorities were rejecting applications from tomato growers for more water, and by the end of June normal allotments were being cut in half in some districts (e.g. Bedfordshire and Cambridgeshire). Spray irrigation was banned completely in other places (e.g. Somerset). There were wide reports of damage to winter and spring cereal crops in the south and east, and milk output was beginning to suffer. In fact, in early August, it was reported that the budget of the Common Market was expected to *benefit* from a projected 10% fall in dairy production – some £110 million which would not have to be spent to buy and store surplus dairy products. Other projected beneficiaries of the drought included oil seed and grain exporters in the United States, English and continental vineyards, 'hot house' tomato growers, onion growers, and farmers throughout Scotland who were enjoying the best of all possible (climatic) worlds.

Secondary problems associated with the drought in rural areas included increased incidence of forest and brush fires, the build-up of oil and grease on roads contributing to accidents and an increase in certain agricultural pests due to very dry conditions. Pests reportedly fostered by the drought in Britain included rabbits, aphids in cereal grains, cutworms in potatoes and onions (in addition to the more usual infestation of lettuce) and the Colorado beetle surfacing in some potato fields in Kent.

August appears to have been the crisis month for farmers as well as for other Britons. Most grain crops harvested from mid-July into early August were below average; in the driest areas half the normal yields were experienced. In Lincolnshire, farmers were 'voluntarily' refraining from irrigating crops because the rivers in the area had stopped flowing and were contaminated with salt and pollutants. Even those root crops which were later to produce good harvests, such as potato and sugar beet, were reported to have 'stopped growing'. The future cultivation of more maize and oil seed, presently rare in Britain, was being touted as a possible solution if dry conditions proved to be the norm in succeeding years. Price increases were being predicted for all major agricultural commodities grown in Britain. In mid-August, the government was advising stockmen to begin stringent rationing of hay and silage. At the same time, farmers were demanding the enactment of a ban on export of hay – an extreme measure considering that Britain shares with Denmark the status of top hay exporter in Europe in normal times. By 19 August, farmers were being told to abandon any hope of obtaining feed from autumn catch crops. It was on 16 August that the Minister of Agriculture, Fisheries & Food, Mr Peart, began a nationwide tour of farms to show the governmental pennant and offer advice. (During this same period the more fractious farmers of France and Germany were receiving more practical assistance in the form of grants, subsidies and cheap loans as drought aid.)

Slowly but surely British food prices began to rise in the second half of August. Potato prices had recovered a third to a half of the declines experienced in June. Processors and wholesalers were calling on the government to lift the traditional seasonal ban on importation of vegetables normally produced in Britain. There were also reports of consumers hoarding frozen vegetables stimulated by the same forecasts of shortages and price rises. In addition to requesting direct financial assistance (such as farmers on the continent were receiving) farmers began to campaign for the devaluation of the so-called 'Green Pound', a device whereby trade in agricultural commodities between Common Market countries where food prices are high, and Britain where food prices are low, is subsidised by the EEC. The effect of devaluing the Green Pound would be to give more money to those British farmers with produce to sell, perhaps partially compensating some farmers for drought losses and rising costs, and raising the incomes of those not injured by the drought at all (as in Scotland and Northern Ireland). British food processors were against this devaluation and, along with consumer groups, accused the farmers of using the drought as a pretext for pressing this and other demands on the government. Late in August the government responded by announcing that it had postponed making a decision on devaluation, and had little aid to offer to various supplicants, except advice and bureaucratic sleight-of-hand. The government put into operation a livestock food planning service and suggested that farmers start buying food now rather than later. Also late in August it offered stock breeders the opportunity to eliminate marginal animals for compensation, thus saving fodder, under the guise of a brucellosis eradication programme which would otherwise have begun in November. Around the same time food processors were offered relief from a rule requiring a 1-month delay before implementing a justified price increase. Potato imports were also allowed and a ban on potato exports extended. During the month of September butter production was banned by the Milk Marketing Board in order to maintain supplies of liquid milk. In addition, there were accusations from opposition parliamentarians that the government was using the drought to disguise the real reasons for the prospective steep rise in food prices – inflation and general economic policy.

As noted earlier, with the onset of heavy rainfall over much of Britain in early September, the government commenced its battle against complacency. The Ministry of Agriculture, Fisheries & Food, which had been complacent in August, was now gloomy, as were food processors. The leaders of the National Farmers Union were now aiming their demands more narrowly at aid to the hard-hit livestock and cereal farmers. While labour economists were claiming that 'discounting the drought, there is a clearly strong underlying improvement in farmer incomes' (N. Bedoc, Trades Union Research Unit, Ruskin College, Oxford, in a letter to *The Times*, 26 August 1976). An agricultural economist employed by the National Farmers Union was claiming that farm income would be down by £3–4 million. The latter figure was apparently accepted by opposition politicians and repeated in the European Parliament's discussion of food pricing policy. By late September and early October spokesmen for the wholesalers, perhaps reflecting the complacency of victors, offered the good news that meat prices would hold steady and that no shortage of potatoes was expected. The latter fact was attributed by authorities variously to the planting of 49 000 hectares above 1975 plantings and a drop in potato consumption, as well as to the recovery of the crop promoted by heavy rainfall in September and October. The sugar beet crop was apparently also helped by the latter. According to some reports the harvest of potatoes was actually impeded by waterlogged fields.

Also in early October the government proposed to raise the supported price of milk 0.4p per litre (worth £30 million to dairy farmers), and the supported price for sheep by 6.6p per kilo. It also increased temporarily the levels of grant aid available to farmers to install reservoirs on their land by £1.5 million.

Conclusion The foregoing narrative of the context and events occurring during the British Drought 1975–6 takes on more meaning when interpreted in light of the 'principles' or features of response processes described elsewhere (see Ch. 15). The context of the drought and responses to drought when viewed at the national level in Britain is exceedingly complex. It involves not just the history of 'water problems', but also of industrialisation, urbanisation and other related factors. These are not just responses to problems identified with water scarcity, but also those related to the state of the industrial economy, the influence of the European Economic Community, and more. To conclude, let us briefly turn to the features of response processes which are illustrated by points in the narrative, which will partly explain why I chose to include certain 'facts' and exclude others.

The first and most basic question is, where in all of this is *the* response processs? My tentative answer is that it is embedded in the historical record of national water legislation, public actions and the actual effects evinced on a local level. A particular *kind* of response process is involved here, one that might best be called 'developmental' or even 'evolutionary'. It involves progressive escalation and reorganisation at higher levels of response and a relative absence of de-escalation. The process in question has been driven by a combination of circumstances contributing to increasing demand for water, as well as the *intensification* of industrial and urban strategies. At any given point in time the solution of water supply problems has promoted further *expansion* of the strategies in question. The long-term process has been incremental, involving small intensifying 'leaps' affecting the ways in which water resources are abstracted, distributed and otherwise controlled and the slow expansion of the new strategies and their consequences.

The application of response process principles involves a concern for particular increments in this unfolding process. It is probably best to take up the principles one at a time and to tentatively link them to particular points in the narrative. In terms of the response process features described above, the British drought illustrates the following:

(a) *Similar response to different problems.* A very obvious parallel exists between the way the British (and other industrialising nations) have coped with energy problems and water problems; developing new sources and exploiting progressively more marginal, expensive and *costly* sources, improving distributional systems and making them more extensive (electric grids v. the proposed national water grid which itself would be based on existing regional water grids).

(b) *Minimal response at onset.* This was characteristic of the British response to the 1975–6 drought at all levels, and was obviously one of the bases for charges of 'inaction'. Regional authorities were reasonably well prepared. Moreover, even at the height of the drought in 1976 there was a fairly clear recognition of the costs of 'maximum' responses such as the consequences of restricting industrial water allotments.

(c) *The causes of escalation may differ from phase to phase.* This is best exemplified in the history of national water legislation, different legislative Acts responsive to particular problems such as urbanisation, water quality, rising consumption, drought, but each Act contributing to the overall escalatory tendency.

(d) *Non-inevitability escalation.* Although various interests within and without government had proposed short- and long-run schemes and remedies that might help to cope with the present and future droughts, ultimately the national government did remarkably little and regional authorities much less than they might have done.

(e) *Reversibility.* Past water legislation has involved essentially irreversible responses at every level. Individuals became dependent on abundant good-quality water and indoor plumbing once the water system made it feasible. Dependency of this sort means irreversibility. At the same time, the graduated responses at the disposal of water authorities to regulate consumption to various degrees are designed to be appropriate to the problem at hand and *reversible*.

(f) *The restoration of equilibrium and the restoration of flexibility.* In this case, equilibrium involves the balance between demand for water and the capacity of the system serving the population unit in question. A given system loses flexibility as demand approaches a capacity that may not be readily augmented by expansion alone or a capacity which has been impacted by external disturbances such as a drought. In Britain this has happened when most aquifers are already heavily exploited, most suitable reservoir sites have been used and facilities for regional distribution are in use. Flexibility may be restored only by intensification, changing the boundary conditions, for example abstracting from rivers or transferring water between regions.

(g) *Changes in the units of response*. In the British case we can be concerned with the responses of individuals (and individuals of various kinds), fictive individuals such as business firms, communities, regions (including regional water authorities), and the nation and its government.

(h) *Loss of flexibility by lower-level units*. The impact of water restrictions imposed by water authorities on individual citizens in their homes is an obvious example.

(i) *The effectiveness of higher-level responses*. If we take as a case the creation of ten regional water authorities by the Water Act of 1973, the meaning of this should be quite clear. A single such new entity, the Yorkshire Water Authority, took over 11 localised water boards, the facilities of ten local water supply authorities, two joint sewerage boards, the facilities of 168 local sewerage authorities, and one river authority. This new unit is able to deploy the full resources of the region, integrating regional abstraction and distribution through a network of aqueducts, canals and pipelines, with planning and decision making over conflicting uses of water integrated too. There is likely to be water available somewhere which can be transferred to districts in need of it, and the availability of water for consumption can be enhanced through the management of conflicting uses.

(j) *Assessing the cost–benefit balance associated with escalation*. In a number of controversies cited, critics of government policy were more or less neatly divided between advocacy of escalation and advocacy of no action or minimal action. This evidently relates to a division between individuals and groups which will potentially benefit (at least in the short run) from escalation and individuals and groups who will bear the cost of lost flexibility.

(k) *The effectiveness of responses*. The question of effectiveness obviously needs to be answered for responses at different levels as well as from the standpoint of various tests. Starting with the responses of the water authorities themselves, a number of things can be said. Conservation measures were *successful enough* with water consumption being slashed by a third in many areas and by up to a half in hard hit areas subject to more stringent restrictions. A large amount of water was captured from sources not exploited in 'normal' times. Escalation to the most stringent short-term measures were avoided in all areas except South Wales and the south-west. Hence, the impact on industry and jobs, a great fear, was minimised.

Responses at the individual or domestic unit level appear to have been relatively ineffective, particularly in the absence of restrictions and rationing. Compliance with physical restrictions, on garden watering, car washing on up to the use of street hydrants appears to have been widespread. Economic incentives to conserve routinely are still lacking. Recent experience in California has shown that metering, in combination with high graduated water taxes, can have dramatic effects on consumption levels. The use of water meters is very rare in the UK. Hence, although water taxes have been going up and up over the past few years, there has literally been nothing for ordinary people to do about it. Restricting consumption provides them with no immediate and tangible benefits in the form of money saved.

Farmers, who felt the bite of the drought earlier than other people, seem to have responded effectively in several sectors by planting greater areas of certain crops (e.g. potatoes), by changing to 'drought' crops (maize, barley), or by not planting at all (peas). Cereal growers were hit hard in some areas but have a degree of flexibility because in any given year they get several chances to plant and harvest a successful crop. Farmers dependent on irrigation in many cases had to reduce their crop to fit their smaller water allotments. The livestock sector may have been hit the hardest in the short run because it had the least flexibility. Stockmen could elect to slaughter early and sell to freezer operators at low prices, but this was not widespread in the UK. High September and October rainfall may have helped stock and dairymen the most. The drought probably helped eliminate some marginal operations, but this would be consistent with government policy favouring the industrialisation of agriculture. Finally, although the prices of some food items have risen, it is probably impossible to say how much of this can be attributed to the drought and how much to inflation.

Postscript

This chapter represents an initial approach to the natural hazards field, conducted without being immersed in the existing technical literature as a specialist might be. It is not, however, without preconceptions. Rather, it was initially inspired by a desire to find case material that could be used to illustrate an approach to human–environmental interactions.

Drought was chosen as a promising kind of problem to work on. One outstanding point to emerge, however, was the obfuscation that surrounded the identification of drought as the core of the dangers involved. It is a type of mystification of the problem-field involving several factors:

(a) Only superficial attention is paid to the basic human problems that may be initiated by drought, such as loss of livelihood and life-support. These problems may be recognised, but they are not studied systematically, and certainly not with the same degree of precision (or research support) that is devoted to, for example, weather.

(b) Even less attention is devoted to the ways in which ordinary people, individually or as members of small communities, undertake – and must undertake – to cope with these and related problems.

(c) On the contrary, emphasis is most commonly placed on technological solutions, and on responses by big governmental organisations and, or 'outsiders'. Further, it seems that a very misleading picture of the costs, benefits and effectiveness of these kinds of response is then calculated.

(d)   There is an overemphasis on Earth and atmospheric systems, especially as the immediate initiators of difficulties, at the expense of examining the sociocultural (including political and economic) factors strongly influencing the outcomes. Moreover, coming fresh to this work one is struck by the way such recognition as there is of the influence of social factors assumes the form of 'blaming the victim'; for example, overgrazing, levels of consumption, overpopulation.

In summary, one began to suspect that perhaps the 'wrong' characteristics of the 'wrong' responses and effects are related to the 'wrong' environmental problems and their characteristics! In fact, the position most strongly reinforced by the studies of the Bushmen and the British is that a wide range of environmental hazards may be viewed most profitably as consequences of human activity – as 'unnatural' hazards! And this can arise in at least four senses: (a) that the hazard proceeds directly from human activity; (b) that the acuteness of the damaging effects are related to the intensity of human environmental exploitation, modification and density; (c) that development tends to encourage dependency and specialisation on the part of individuals and local communities, and hence reduces the ability of these units to respond, or narrows the range of *normal* environmental variability with which the units in question are able to cope *on their own*; and (d) that the involvement of outside, supra-local groups may render permanent the effects of an otherwise short-lived local problem.

All of this points to the necessity of paying closer attention to the actual situation of the people we study, focusing particularly on the consequence for them of their interactions with the natural and social environment. For us there is no objective environment – one that can be understood in its own terms and for its own sake. Rather, the environment with which we must be concerned is anthropocentric, determined by the capabilities of the people living in it and defined by the problems and opportunities which their activities either produce or expose. Here I have merely introduced some themes and principles in relation to some African and European case material. In Chapter 15 of this volume I will attempt to expand on them.

References

Baldwin, A. 1976. Give us this day . . . *Geog. Mag.* **XLIX** (8), 498–501.

Bateson, G. 1972a. The role of somatic change in evolution. In *Steps to an ecology of mind*, 346–63. New York: Ballantine.

Bateson, G. 1972b. Ecology and flexibility in urban civilization. In *Steps to an ecology of mind,*, 494–504. New York: Ballantine.

Burton, I. and K. Hewitt 1974. Ecological dimensions of environmental hazards. In *Human ecology*, F. Sargent (ed.), 253–83. Amsterdam: North-Holland.

Guenther, M. G. 1976. From hunters to squatters: social and cultural change among the farm *San* of Ghanzi, Botswana. In Lee and De Vore (1976, pp. 120–133).

Hall, N. 1975. The myth of the natural disaster. *The Ecologist* **5** (10), 368–71.

Hanna, L. W. 1973. *Environment and the future.* J. W. House (ed.), 164–218. London: Weidenfeld and Nicolson.

Hogg, W. H. 1969. Estimates of long-term irrigation needs. In *The Role of Water in Agriculture.* J. A. Taylor (ed.), 171–84. Oxford: Pergamon.

Howell, N. 1976. The population of the Dobe area !Kung. In Lee and De Vore (1976, pp. 138–51).

Lee, R. B. 1969. !Kung Bushman subsistence: an input–output analysis. In *Environment and cultural behavior.* A. P. Vayda (ed.), 47–9. Garden City: Natural History Press.

Lee, R. B. 1972a. The !Kung Bushmen and Botswana. In *Hunters and Gatherers today.* M. G. Bicchiere (ed.), 327–68. New York: Holt, Rinehart Winston.

Lee, R. B. 1972b. !Kung spatial organization in ecological and historical perspective. *Human Ecology* **1**(2), 125–48.

Lee, R. B. 1972c. Population growth and the beginnings of sedentary life among the !Kung Bushmen. In *Population growth: anthropological implications.* B. Spooner (ed.), 329–42. Cambridge, Mass.: MIT Press.

Lee, R. B. 1972d. The intensification of social life among the !Kung Bushmen. In *Population growth: anthropological implications.* B. Spooner (ed.), 343–50. Cambridge, Mass.: MIT Press.

Lee, R. B. 1972e. Work effort, group structure and land use in contemporary hunter–gatherers. In *Man, settlement and urbanism*, P. J. Ucko, R. Tringham and G. W. Dimbleby (eds), 177–85. Cambridge: Schenkman.

Lee, R. B. and I. De Vore 1968. Problems in the study of hunters and gatherers. In *Man the hunter*, R. B. Lee and I. De Vore (eds), 3–12. Chicago: Aldine.

Lee, R. B. and I. De Vore (eds) 1976. *Kalahari hunter gatherers studies of the !Kung San and their neighbors.* Cambridge, Mass.: Harvard University Press.

Mackinder, H. J. 1925. *Britain and the British seas.* Oxford: Clarendon Press.

Morren, G. E. B., Jr 1974. *Settlement strategies and hunting in a New Guinea society.* PhD dissertation in anthropology, Columbia University.

Morren, G. E. B., Jr 1977. From hunting to herding: pigs and the control of energy in Montane New Guinea. In *Subsistence and survival: rural ecology in the Pacific.* R. Feachem and T. Bayliss-Smith (eds), 273–315. London: Academic Press.

Prickett, C. N. 1969. The current trends in the use of water in agriculture. In *The role of water in agriculture.* J. Taylor (ed.), 101–119. Oxford: Pergamon.

Slobodkin 1968. Toward a predictive theory of evolution. In *Population biology and evolution.* R. C. Lewontin (ed.), 187–205. Syracuse: Syracuse University Press.

Vayda, A. P. 1971. Phases in the process of war and peace among the Marings of New Guinea. *Oceania* **42**, 1–24.

Vayda, A. P. 1974. Warfare in ecological perspective *An. Rev. Ecol. Systs.* **5**, 183–93.

Vayda, A. P. and B. J. McCay 1975. New directions in ecology and ecological anthropology. *An. Rev. Anthrop.* **4**.

Wisner, B., K. Westgate and P. O'Keefe 1976. Poverty and disaster. *New Society* **9** Sep, 546–8.

4 *Drought in the US Great Plains: shifting social consequences?**

RICHARD A. WARRICK

Lately, we have seen climatologists and meteorologists stepping into the limelight of urgent public debates. The mounting alarm over the perceived tightening relationship between food supply, climatic fluctuation, and social wellbeing has prompted many atmospheric scientists to take a hard look at climatic variability in the light of agricultural production in the United States. The approaches taken vary considerably, from the unravelling of climatic histories by tree-ring analysis to mathematical modelling of the general circulation. Emerging theories and conclusions reached can be characterised as conflicting and controversial (Are major droughts causally linked to cycles of sun-spot activity?). Yet, despite the ambiguities, there seems to be a surprising degree of unanimity with respect to one finding: climate in the US Mid-West is likely to be more variable in the future than in the immediate past (NAS 1976). It seems that this generation has been blessed with unusually favourable, stable conditions which, in all likelihood, will not be the norm of the future (cf. McKay below).

With thoughts of adverse climatic conditions rekindled in our collective mind, the notion of the dynamic interaction between climate and society demands greater attention. In broad terms, how do societies respond to climatic fluctuation, and how does the response influence vulnerability to such events over the long run? In the main, atmospheric scientists have been reluctant to tackle the question directly; similarly, most social scientists tend to hold climate constant in studying social change.

Related studies of human adjustment to geophysical hazards indicate that societies manage to adapt remarkably to a wide range of climatic diversity (Burton *et al.* 1978). However, the adjustment process is a complicated one which evolves within the context of continuous change in population patterns, technological innovation and social organisation. If one thing is clear, it is that the interaction between climate and society is dynamic and complex. Simple explanations of cause and effect are apt to fall short.

The Great Plains of the United States provides a rich source of data with which to explore in detail the relationships of climatic fluctuation and societal

* This chapter was originally prepared in 1977, and apart from minor revisions and updating of references it was not felt useful to our purpose here to make substantive changes. For further work on the research project see Warrick (1980), Warrick and Bowden (1981) and Bowden *et al.* (1981).

response. In this chapter, attention is focused sharply on the effects of drought over the last 100 years of agricultural settlement. What do we know about the social consequences of past droughts in the Great Plains? What mechanisms for coping with droughts have been adopted over time? What can we hypothesise as to the relationship between drought occurrence and social vulnerability? The remainder of this chapter addresses these questions.

The Great Plains and drought occurrence

The invasion of the Great Plains by agriculturalists intent on cultivating a region subject to a highly variable moisture supply took place relatively late in American history. Aided by government land policies, technological innova- tions, railroads and land promotional schemes, periods of generous precipita- tion in the late 19th century lured thousands of farmers westwards from more humid territory (Great Plains Committee 1937, Webb 1931). Few farmers recognised or understood the climatic adversities of their new home. It was a story all too common in modern agricultural settlement of supposed 'virgin lands' (cf. Chs 9, 11, 12). The fact that the deceptively subhumid condition of the Great Plains is inherently unstable and gives way periodically to chronic, widespread arid and semi-arid conditions has been painfully learned and relearned since those early years of settlement.

During the past 100 years, four periods of severe droughts have afflicted the Great Plains: in the 1890s, 1910s, 1930s and 1950s, or roughly every 20 years (Fig. 4.1). Less severe droughts occurred in the 1870s and in the 1970s. The striking regularity of major drought occurrence suggests that droughts are cyclic in nature. Among climatologists the subject is controversial. Some theories propose that drought occurrence is linked to regular cycles of sunspot activity (Willett 1975, Mitchell *et al.* 1979) and thus can be predicted, although the causal mechanisms are unknown. Other theories link drought to atmospheric pollution, either man-made (Bryson 1974) or natural, such as volcanic dust (Humphreys 1964). Drought also has been attributed to changes in surface conditions, for example, temperature or salinity changes of ocean currents (Namias 1956, 1963). In lieu of a detailed understanding of the causal mechanisms, droughts also may be described as a random series (Curry 1962) and thus forecast on a probabilistic basis.

If major droughts in the Great Plains occur every 20 years in a cyclic fashion, we would have expected a big one in the 1970s (Borchert 1971). Although scattered spatially and temporally, the Great Plains drought condi- tions in the 1970s, in conjunction with the severe drought in the western United States during 1976–7, may lend support to the notion of cycles. If droughts are random events, the relatively short historical record suggests that on the average we can expect droughts in the Great Plains about five times a century, without really knowing when. In either case, periods of

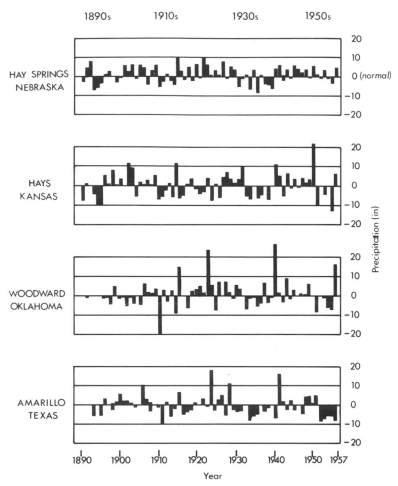

Figure 4.1 Major droughts in the Great Plains, showing inches of precipitation above or below normal for four localities. (Source: Warrick *et al.* 1975, adapted from Special Assistant to the President for Public Works Planning 1958.)

moisture deficiency are characteristic of the Plains and will occur again, bringing stress to agricultural and social systems.

Social consequences of drought Theoretically, the range of social consequences of agricultural drought is quite large, ranging from loss of income among individual agriculturalists to starvation and famine at the international level. These impacts are portrayed in Figure 4.2, which conveys in a simple way how they may be equated to particular levels of today's social systems.

With the unwelcome visitation of four major droughts during the past 100 years, what do we know of the ways in which social systems were affected by each occurrence? The entire picture is not yet clear, but preliminary comparative analyses of drought impacts suggest hypotheses for continuing research.

Figure 4.2 Range of social consequences of drought *via-à-vis* social system levels.

1930s v. 1950s: a comparison of drought effects A comparison of the drought of the 1930s with that of the 1950s is illuminating. In many respects, the physical characteristics of the two droughts were similar. Each lasted approximately the same length of time in the Great Plains, and each was accompanied by severe wind damage to desiccated soil, though not to the same degree. 1934 and 1936 were particularly bad years. During the 1930s, the worst-hit areas were concentrated in the northernmost and southernmost portions of the Great Plains. During the 1950s, the drought was most severe in the south-west and in southern portions of the Great Plains. Actually, the drought started during the 1940s in the south-west, and gradually spread northwards into the Plains. Though not spatially uniform, the two droughts were nearly comparable in meteorological and hydrological severity (Nace & Pluhowski 1965).

Each drought brought a marked decline in crop production (Fig. 4.3). Wheat, being sensitive to precipitation deficiencies and a principal product of the Great Plains, is a good indicator of the impact of drought on crop yields (cf. Chs 9–12). The Plains states experienced an average of 20–25% reductions in wheat yields in relation to preceding wet years during the 1930s; the drop in the 1950s was not as pronounced (Borchert 1971).* It should be stressed that we are referring here to an average yield, aggregated over the Great Plains states as a whole. This necessarily obscured the variation in yield from state to state, county to county, and farm to farm (which was often quite sharp), but nevertheless gives us some picture of the overall crop impact.

For the agriculturalist, the primary effect of drought was economic. As shown in Figure 4.4, gross farm income suffered during each drought. In the

---

* The sharp declines in yields prior to the 1950s, as depicted in Figure 4.3, can be attributed, in part, to a severe outbreak of wheat rust.

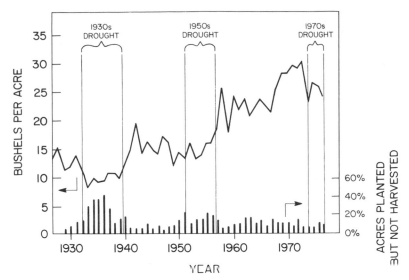

Figure 4.3 Wheat yields in the US Great Plains, 1927–77. (Source: US Department of Agriculture.)

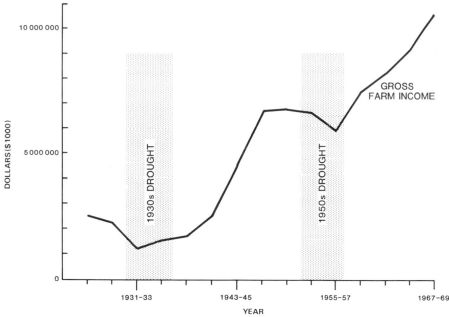

Figure 4.4 Gross farm income for the Great Plains region, 1925–69 (from Warrick *et al*. 1975). Based on 3-year averages: states included are North Dakota, South Dakota, Nebraska, Kansas, Oklahoma, Texas and Colorado. Gross farm income includes cash income from farm marketings, value of products consumed on farms, and government benefit payments. (Sources: data compiled from US Department of Agriculture 1927–37, *Yearbook of agriculture*; 1936–72, *Agricultural statistics*, yearly reports; 1971, *Farm income, state estimates, 1949–1970*; Washington, DC.)

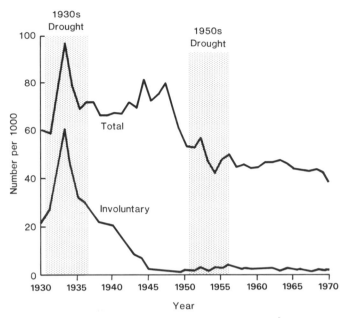

Figure 4.5   Farm transfer in the Great Plains, 1930–70.

1930s, this income loss compounded the problems of poor farm prices, maladjusted farm techniques and the general economic depression. The drop in farm income in the 1950s, although notably sharp, was proportionately less in comparison to total farm income.

Overcapitalisation in the 1920s had dramatically increased mortgage debts; the unexpected set of circumstances faced in the 1930s found many unable to meet expenses. Farm transfers, already high, accelerated (Fig. 4.5). Between 1930 and 1935 there was wholesale liquidation through foreclosures and voluntary deeding of farms to creditors (Great Plains Committee 1937, Kraenzel 1955). Drought in the 1950s did not have the same overall effect, although in some areas the number of farm sales ran high as farmers sold out to seek jobs elsewhere. Foreclosures were relatively rare in contrast to the 1930s, when there was no market for farms. Farms were often sold to neighbours in the 1950s, contributing to the increasing trend of larger and fewer farms (Ottoson *et al.* 1966).

One of the common images of the Dust Bowl period is the flight of thousands of Great Plains farm families from their ravaged land to the west coast, particularly California. Although there is a lack of consistent and comparable data on migration in the Plains states, the information available suggests that the total net migration during the era was no more than years preceding the big drought (Taeuber & Taylor 1937, Goodrich *et al.* 1936). Perhaps because a good portion of the migrants of the 1930s sought out specific west-coast locations as their destination, the impact of their decisions was more disruptive than otherwise. Migration also occurred during the

1950s drought; however, it was not the concentrated interstate movement of almost two decades earlier. The 1950s saw a good deal of movement within a region, as smaller farmers sold out to seek urban jobs.

One indicator of the severity of drought impact for the Great Plains' agriculturalists is the magnitude of the federal relief and rehabilitation effort generated by each drought. Both the 1930s and the 1950s droughts put in motion the flow of federal funds for disaster relief and aid for rehabilitation. In the 1930s, 21% of rural families in all areas were receiving federal aid by 1936 (Link 1937); the percentage ran as high as 89% in some hard-hit counties (Kifer & Stewart 1938). Total government benefits ran close to $1000 million.* The 1950s drought again elicited federal assistance, though total amounts were substantially lower. The relative importance of government payments (excluding crop insurance payments) as a proportion of total farm income in the grassland states is suggested in Figure 4.6. During the 1930s government payments comprised a large proportion of farm income, whereas in the 1950s it was negligible.

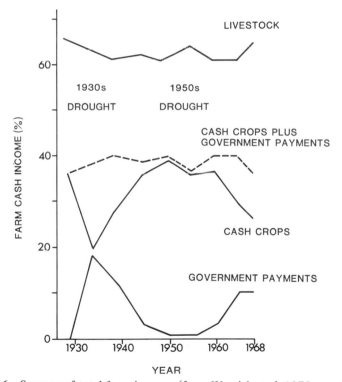

Figure 4.6 Sources of total farm income (from Warrick *et al.* 1975, as adapted from Borchert 1971, p. 14). (Note: percentage of total farm cash income derived from crops, livestock and government payments in grassland states since the inauguration of federal farm programmes. Based on data at 5-year intervals from *Statistical abstract of the United States*.)

* Compiled from Great Plains Committee (1937) and Link (1937).

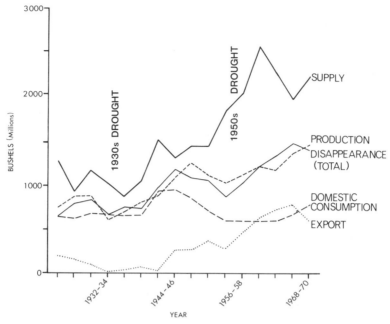

Figure 4.7 Supply and disappearance of wheat in the United States, 1923–70 (after Warrick *et al*. 1975). Supply is equal to all stocks, new crop production and imports. Disappearance is equal to domestic consumption (including feed and seed) plus exports. 'Wheat' includes flour and wheat products, and the figures are based on 3-year averages. (Source: data compiled from US Department of Agriculture 1936–72, *Agricultural statistics*, yearly reports; Washington, DC.)

Undoubtedly, one of the most serious social consequences of agricultural drought is the potential threat to the nation's food supply. To what extent was this an effect during the last two major droughts? Figure 4.7 depicts over time the relationship between wheat production, supply and disappearance, which includes both domestic consumption and exports. It is apparent that even with the dips in wheat production during the two droughts, food supply was never seriously threatened. In fact, it is ironic that as the Plains and the south-west were scorching under severe drought during the 1950s, and large amounts of federal aid were poured into the region, a ballooning problem for the United States was food surplus. Even with large areas experiencing market reductions in yield, farmers knew that their agricultural efforts were still contributing to the unwieldy surplus problem. It is of interest to note that exports of wheat also declined during these same periods, illustrating the buffer effect that the exportable margin of food had during bad production years.

Earlier droughts in the Great Plains   As crippling as the 1930s drought was to Great Plains farmers, Warrick and Bowden (1981) and Bowden (1976) suggest that earlier droughts of the 1890s and 1910s brought relatively far greater local hardships in proportion to the intensity and duration of drought, its areal extent and the number of people affected. For example, whereas malnutrition was a minor problem during the 1930s in some areas of the Plains, in the 1890s there were widespread reports of drought-related starvation and malnutrition in the drought-afflicted central and southern High Plains. Similar conditions accompanied the 1910s drought in the Dakotas and eastern Montana, though not as acute (Ottoson *et al*. 1966, Hewes 1975).

In comparison to later droughts, relief and rehabilitation in the form of government aid was not forthcoming during the earlier droughts. Plains states' governments were adamant about refusing to recognise drought disasters and personal misery. These effects ran contrary to the promotional images they were projecting (Baltensperger 1974). Federal and state governments had not yet come to grips with the concept of 'acceptable' aid in a period of laissez-faire capitalism (Ottoson *et al*. 1966, Bowden 1976). The drought-induced stress was borne almost entirely at the level of the agriculturalist, with modest support from within states or from neighbouring states (Dick 1975). This lack of relief intensified local problems and encouraged abandonment of farms and migration.

As previously discussed, outright abandonment of farms in the 1950s was rare; farms were sold off. In the 1930s abandonment of farms in the severely windblown areas did occur, and foreclosures and eviction of renters or sharecroppers were common. In the 1890s and 1910s, on the other hand, drought areas in the Plains witnessed massive abandonment of land by poorer farmers (relative to size of areas occupied and population). Unable to withstand the hardships, thousands simply walked off their farms (Bowden 1976).

A similar pattern is evident for population migration over time. The abandonment of farms during earlier Plains' droughts accounted largely for a vast exodus of farmers from large portions of the Great Plains. Some counties were stripped of over half of their populations, and others lost virtually all settlers in massive outmigration (Warrick 1980). By contrast, the 1950s drought resulted in little more than a shifting from rural to urban locations, which was barely perceptible from ongoing trends.

The overall pattern   In summary, a cursory examination of the social consequences of drought occurrence over the past 100 years suggests that drought impact at local levels has lessened dramatically since the first major droughts during early settlement. In the 1890s and 1910s the agriculturalist was extremely vulnerable to drought occurrence and, when drought struck, was forced to shoulder the burden of deprivation by himself. In the 1930s and the 1950s drought-induced stress on individual agriculturalists – farm owners, tenants and farm labourers – was reduced markedly.

In terms of social consequences specific to the national level, the impact of drought was relatively minor, even in the 1930s. Aside from the distribution of federal aid – a dribble when compared to the concurrent massive distribution of federal aid to a severely depressed 1930s economy – there were no food shortages, rising food costs, or shortage-related health effects. No drought crossed the national boundary to have significant impact at the international level.

Shifting drought vulnerability: a hypothesis

The above peek into past drought consequences does not necessarily lead to the conclusion that total impacts have lessened. The process appears much more complex. We know relatively little about the diffusion of effects throughout society. The apparent trends, however, allow us to formulate one central hypothesis about climate and society:

> It is hypothesised that with increasingly elaborate technology and social organisation, the local and regional impacts of recurrent droughts of similar magnitude *lessen* over time. However, in lessening, the impacts change in form and shift – spatially and socially – to higher system levels.

For example, it can be suggested that the harsh realities of starvation and spatial displacement facing the 1890s farmer were replaced locally during the 1950s by the hardships of paying insurance premiums, by slightly premature retirements and by a lingering uneasiness over receiving government support. The national obligation to bale out the Plains farmer shifts much of the stress to the US citizen. This stress takes the form of increased taxation and of rising prices for periodically scarce agricultural commodities.

If vulnerability to drought has indeed been altered, what mechanisms are responsible? In comparing the 1930s and 1950s, one apparent difference was the general condition of agriculture and the economy before and during the droughts: the occurrence of the 1930s drought found agriculture still suffering from the post-World War I collapse and the general economy in a severe depression; the drought of the 1950s occurred against a background of a healthy period of agricultural activity and a booming economy.

Moreover, it is certain that a number of drought-specific adjustments were adopted which, over various time periods, played a major role in effectively altering vulnerability to drought. Displayed in Figure 4.8 are ten modes of adjustment to drought which comprise fairly well the range of available mechanisms for dealing with drought hazard.

Between the Dust Bowl days and the 1950s, the adoption of a number of these types of adjustments increased rapidly. The 1930s saw for the first time the emergence of extensive federal institutions for relief and rehabilitation, the basic structure of which has continued with some elaboration up to the present. Conservation cultivation practices increased dramatically, and reached relatively high levels of adoption by the early 1950s, as did the use of financial and grain reserves. Agricultural managers increased the flexibility of their operations, as through increasing farm size. From the 1930s to the present the Great Plains experienced a six-fold increase in irrigation (Bor-

CONSERVATION OF AVAILABLE WATER
1. Conservation Cultivation Practices
2. Water Supply Protection

WATER AUGMENTATION
3. Weather Modification
4. Irrigation
5. Desalination

ALTER AGRICULTURAL CHARACTERISTICS
6. Operational Flexibility
7. Land Use Regulation
8. Prediction and Forecasting

SPREAD/SHARE LOSSES AND COSTS
9. Financial Protection
10. Relief and Rehabilitation

Figure 4.8 Alternative adjustments to drought hazards. Although most items listed are self-explanatory, a few need slight elaboration. *Conservation cultivation practices* include summer fallowing, stubble mulching, strip cropping, contouring, terracing and other agricultural techniques designed to reduce drought vulnerability. *Water supply protection* involves those specific actions taken to protect surface and ground waters, such as evaporation control, phreatophyte control and seepage reduction. *Operational flexibility* includes such practices as diversification, larger farm size, drought resistant crops, flexible cropping plans and others. Finally, *financial protection* refers specifically to financial reserves, reserves of feed and grain, and crop insurance.

chert 1971). The number of hectares covered under the Federal Crop Insurance Corporation rose rapidly from the initiation of the programme in 1938 and reached a peak in 1953 (USDA 1970). Much marginal land was tucked away under the Soil Bank programme.

The flurry of adjustment adoption was stimulated partly by a national resources co-ordinating committee, by the recommendations of the Great Plains Drought Area Committee,* and by a number of newly formed government agencies, such as the Soil Conservation Service and the Agricultural Stabilisation and Conservation Services. Also, the drought itself acted to accelerate trends already present in the agricultural sector.

The drought of the 1950s also generated a new interest in drought. As 20 years earlier, a committee was formed to examine the problem. Its conclusions, entitled *Drought: a report*, also outlined a number of recommendations (Special Assistant to the President for Public Works Planning 1958). A new emphasis was apparent. Water conservation and augmentation received considerable attention. Irrigation and river-basin development were promoted, as were weather modification, weather prediction or control, groundwater recharge, increasing runoff, evaporation control, desalination, phreatophyte† control and irrigation control lining. And as before, action was stimulated by

* See the committee's summary report (Great Plains Committee 1937).
† Phreatophytes are water-loving, riverine plants which consume large amounts of water through transpiration.

further governmental involvement – the Great Plains Conservation Programme was launched in 1956.

In short, with each drought considerable attention was focused on ways to
reduce the consequences. And seemingly, the evolution of drought-reduction
strategies reflects an increasing commitment to greater social organisation
and technological sophistication. In the 1930s the adoption, say, of financial
reserves or cultivation practices was largely a matter of individual choice. The
emphases that emerged from the 1950s, e.g. river basin development,
required effort and co-ordination far beyond the capabilities of the Great
Plains agriculturalist.

It is likely that in aggregate such adjustive mechanisms account for a large
part of the differences in impact between major Great Plains droughts. How
much of the difference will have to be determined by further research. Less is
known of earlier droughts. One immediate concern is: what kind of difference
are they making with respect to the likely impacts of future drought conditions on the Plains? A more fundamental question relates to the distribution
of drought effects at various system levels and to the potential for catastrophe.

Increasing catastrophe potential: a second hypothesis

The above information leads to a second major hypothesis:

> It is hypothesised that while local impacts from recurrent drought events of
> similar magnitude are lessened through an elaboration of technology and
> social organisation, the potential for *catastrophe* from events of rarer fre-
> quency is increased.

As noted above, the adoption of drought adjustments often required greater
hierarchical integration and specialisation in technology and social organisation. Since they are effective as buffers against relatively frequent events, they
may encourage the evolution of agricultural, economic and social systems
which are dependent upon them. The failure of these mechanisms under
severe stress might result in far-ranging, unexpectedly disruptive consequences. In an open system such as the Great Plains, this vulnerability may
be shared ever more widely, affecting previously unrelated areas or societies.

For example, at the international level, drought impact is considerable in
developing countries which are unable to compete with the industrialised
countries in purchasing surplus wheat on the world market. This problem is
exacerbated by the fact that many countries are becoming increasingly
dependent on the existence of wheat surpluses derived mainly from the
Plains. In the future, the consequence of major droughts in the Great Plains
may be the development of severe food 'shortages' outside the United States,
and possibly increased malnutrition and starvation and heightened interna-

tional tension as a result. At present, it is unclear whether or not such impacts would occur.

In short, taken together the two hypotheses suggest that, with each major Plains drought, the local and regional effects decrease, but the ripples of stress may be spreading out successively wider.

Examination of both hypotheses required a rigorous comparative analysis of the range of social consequences and mechanisms for each major Great Plains drought which goes well beyond the partial analysis presented here. The complex relationships between drought effects, adjustive mechanisms and climatic fluctuation need to be established and explored. In this regard, one crucial question to address is: given present patterns of drought adjustment, what would be the impacts if a severe drought, like that of the 1930s, were to strike the Great Plains in the near future? Ultimately, it is the answer to this question that underscores the critical importance of such research on climate–society relationships.

The importance of Great Plains drought research

In summary, this chapter has presented the results of limited analyses of the social consequences of, and social response to, major droughts in the Great Plains. The evidence suggests that the local impacts of drought have lessened progressively since early settlement in the latter part of the 19th century. The pattern of adjustive mechanisms shows an acceleration in adoption with each major drought event which, to an unknown degree, may be largely responsible for declining drought impact on agriculturalists. Over time, the sorts of drought adjustments adopted have required greater social organisation and technological sophistication. These findings have led to the formulation of two related hypotheses: first, that the impacts of recurring droughts of similar magnitude are being lessened and shifted – spatially, and socially – to higher system levels; and secondly, that while the mechanisms adopted have reduced vulnerability to higher-frequency events, they may be heightening the potential for catastrophe in the international context given the rare drought event.

The research problem areas – drought, social consequences, adjustive mechanisms – are ones for which contemporary society has deep concern. Greater understanding of the processes involved could provide practical insights in attempts to deal with the recurring problem of drought. For example, as the dust clears from the 1970s droughts in the west, the United States is once again faced with the question of how to respond effectively. One danger is that, under pressure, solutions will be adopted in haste without full understanding of the long-term consequences. From the west, cries for more reclamation projects already are loud and clear. It is possible that the United States may follow unintentionally a course which will increase significantly the potential for catastrophic loss from a future drought. Fuller knowledge of the likely long-term effects of drought mitigation measures could help guide decisions so as to correspond more nearly to desired goals in drought loss reduction.

Another danger is that the nature of the response may be based on an image of drought consequences which no longer applies. Are we fashioning our response around an image of destitute Great Plains farmers, giant dust storms and caravans of migrating families? If so, this image may be no longer appropriate to a 1970s or 1990s drought. If the above hypotheses are supported, they suggest that the consequences of climatic fluctuations, although lessening in some quarters, are being distributed in different ways throughout society. For the range of climatic hazards, we know relatively little about how impacts (losses, costs and benefits) are borne differently (Cochrane 1975). In the case of drought, the impacts may be hidden deep within the social fabric as, for example, in higher taxes, sky-rocketing meat prices, or spiralling fuel costs. In attempting to reduce the impacts at the level of the drought-afflicted Great Plains farmer, we may be exacerbating unduly the burden carried by others (e.g. the low income consumer in the north-east).

In general, the social response to drought has been based on our perception of the likely consequences, as gained through previously experienced impacts. It is much more difficult to conjure an image of the future under changing systemic conditions. Examination of hypotheses of shifting drought impacts provides a much needed historical perspective from which to understand the consequences of future droughts, and thereby to fashion drought policy to deal with them more effectively.

Acknowledgements

The research upon which this chapter is based has been supported by the National Science Foundation, grant numbers GI-32942 and ATM 77-15019. The author is grateful to Martyn Bowden, Robert Kates, William Riebsame and Daniel Weiner for many of the ideas presented herein. Major portions of this chapter are based on Warrick *et al.* (1975).

References

Baltensperger, B. 1974. *Plain folk and plains promoters: pre-migration and post-settlement images of the central Great Plains*. PhD dissertation. Clark Univ., Worcester, Massachusetts.

Borchert, J. R. 1971. The Dust Bowl in the 1970's. *Ann. Assoc. Am. Geogs* **61**, March, 1–22.

Bowden, M. J. 1976. *Desertification of the Great Plains: will it happen*. A position paper prepared for the UNEP component review of *Population, society and desertification*. Worcester, Massachusetts: Clark Univ., Prog. Int. Devel. Soc. Change.

Bowden, M. J., R. W. Kates, P. A. Kay, W. E. Riebsame, R. A. Warrick, D. L. Johnson, H. A. Gould and D. Weiner 1981. The effect of climate fluctuations on human populations: two hypotheses. In *Climate and history: studies in past climates and their impact on man*, T. M. L. Wigley, M. J. Ingram and G. Farmer (eds). Cambridge: Cambridge University Press.

Bryson, R. A. 1974. A perspective on climatic change. *Science* **CCLXXXIV**, no. 4138, 17 May, 753–60.

Burton, I., R. W. Kates and G. F. White 1978. *The environment as hazard*. New York: Oxford University Press.

Cochrane, H. C. 1975. *Natural hazards and their distributive effects*. Boulder, Colorado: Univ. Colorado, Institute of Behavioral Science.

Curry, L. 1962. Climatic change as a random series. *Ann. Assoc. Am. Geogs* **LII**, 21–31.

Dick, E. 1975. *Conquering the great American desert: Nebraska*. Nebraska: Nebraska State Historical Society.

Goodrich, C., *et al*. 1936. *Migration and economic opportunity*. Rep. Stud. Popn Redistrib. Wharton School of Finance and Commerce. Lancaster, Pennsylvania: University of Pennsylvania Press.

Great Plains Committee 1937. *The future of the Great Plains*. 75th Congr., 1st Session. Document # 114. Washington: Government Printing Office.

Hewes, L. 1975. The Great Plains, one hundred years after Major John Wesley Powell. In *Images of the Plains*, B. Blouet and M. Lawson (eds). 203–214. Lincoln: University of Nebraska Press.

Humphreys, W. J. 1964. *Physics of the air*. New York: Dover.

Kifer, R. S. and H. L. Stewart 1938. *Farming hazard in the drought area*. Works Prog. Admin, Div. Soc. Res. Monog. # 16. Washington, DC: US Government Printing Office.

Kraenzel, C. F. 1955. *The Great Plains in transition*. Norman: University of Oklahoma.

Link, I. 1937. *Relief and rehabilitation in the drought area*. Works Prog. Admin, Div. Soc. Res. Bull. 5, # 3. Washington, DC: US Government Printing Office.

Mitchell, J. M. Jr, C. W. Stockton and D. M. Meko 1979. Evidence of a 22-year rhythm of drought in the western United States related to the Hale solar cycle since the 17th century. In *Solar-terrestrial influences on weather and climate*, B. M. McCormac and T. A. Seliga (eds). Dordrecht, Holland: D. Reidel.

Nace, R. L. and E. J. Pluhowski 1965. *Drought of the 1950's with special reference to the midcontinent*. Geol. Surv. Watersupply Pap. # 1804. Washington, DC: US Government Printing Office.

Namias, J. 1956. Some meteorological aspects of drought, with special reference to the summers of 1942–1952 over the United States. *Monthly Weather Review* **LXXXIII**, 191–205.

Namias, J. 1963. Surface–atmosphere interactions as fundamental causes of drought and other climatic fluctuations. In *Changes of climate: Proceedings of the Rome Symposium*, 345–59. Geneva, Switzerland: UNESCO and the World Meteorological Organization.

NAS (National Academy of Sciences, US) 1976. *Climate and food: climatic fluctuation and US agricultural production*. Washington, DC: National Academy of Sciences–National Research Council.

Ottoson, H. W., E. M. Birch, P. A. Henderson and A. H. Anderson 1966. *Land and people in the northern plains transition area*. Lincoln: University of Nebraska Press.

Special Assistant to the President for Public Works Planning 1958. *Drought: a report*. Washington, DC: US Government Printing Office.

Taeuber, C. and C. C. Taylor 1937. *The people of the drought states*. Works Prog. Admin, Div. Soc. Res. Bull. Ser. 5, # 2. Washington, DC: US Government Printing Office.

USDA (US Department of Agriculture) 1970. *Economic considerations in crop insurance*. Washington, DC: US Government Printing Office.

Warrick, R. A. 1980. Drought in the Great Plains: a case study of research on climate and society in the USA. In *Climate constraints and human activities*, J. Ausubel and A. K. Biswas (eds). Oxford: Pergamon Press.

Warrick, R. A. (with P. B. Trainer, E. J. Baker and W. A. R. Brinkmann) 1975. *Drought hazard in the United States: a research assessment*. Boulder: Univ. Colorado, Institute of Behavioral Science.

Warrick, R. A. and M. Bowden 1981. The changing impacts of droughts in the Great Plains. In *Great Plains, perspectives and prospects*, M. Lawson and M. Baker (eds). Lincoln, Nebraska: Center for Great Plains Studies.

Webb, W. 1931. *The Great Plains*. New York: Ginn.

Willett, H. C. 1975. Do recent climatic trends portend an imminent ice age? In *Atmospheric quality and climatic change*, R. J. Kopec (ed.), 4–37. Paps 2nd Carolina Geog. Symp. Univ. North Carolina Studs Geog., no. 9.

5 *The Sahelian drought: social sciences and the political economy of underdevelopment*

JEAN COPANS

The Sahelian drought from 1971 to 1976 was a test both for African studies and for the politics of African governments and international agencies. Intellectual analysis and political responses have seemed both a naïve and a surprising answer to a conjectural phenomenon. Undoubtedly, new insights for empirical research, comparative historical analyses and theoretical adjustments have been offered, but most of the funds available in the period of the Sahelian drought research 'boom' have been channelled to the classical studies of social change, climate and climatic controls *per se*, and economic development. The 'end' of the drought was seen firmly to justify these associated traditional approaches and budget policies.

Yet most Africanists have not been able to understand or explain the economic and political causes of actual ecological imbalances. The limitations in scope of the various disciplines, the very fact of their separateness and the nature of the available social theories have rendered impossible a *natural and social history* of underdevelopment in contemporary Africa. That, however, is an essential prerequisite for understanding what happened in the drought.

As for the political economy, seen for example in the field of governmental decision and international aid, it has followed a familiar historical trend. A greater emphasis, at least verbally, has been placed upon needs and the impact of modernisation in the social and natural environment. But this concern has in fact enabled foreign investors and local dominant classes to foster social and economic consolidation of the market economy, in both the private and public sectors. Specifically, the great hydraulic and ranching projects are linking the African countries into an ever more complete interdependence with the economic structures and interests of the Western powers.

In effect the Sahel has been, and is, up for sale! The promises of the drought years now appear clearly as what they were intended to be, i.e. social and political tranquillisers. We must therefore review all aspects of the problem, for our critique of the common explanations and rationalisations will bear upon new theoretical – and political – proposals.

The most difficult task has not been the description of the common or so called 'scientific' bases of the drought, although it is not suggested that this was itself easy to do! The experience of the Comité information Sahel (1974) and the reviews of *Sécheresses et famines du Sahel* are, in my own case, examples that speak for themselves (Copans 1975).* It is in the process of theoretical reconstruction that the obstacles have become most prominent. Various problems arise in connection both with the 'conventional wisdom' and common reactions of social scientists to these sorts of crises. Thus the events of the past ten years have not significantly altered the economic situation of the Sahelian countries.† But they have compelled researchers as well as activists to look again for the real roots of such crises. I would emphasise my belief that to speak of theoretical reconstruction is not to fall into the pitfalls of speculation and metaphysics. Meanwhile the Sahel crisis has proved the uselessness of so-called 'urgent anthropology' which is only concerned with the plight of the 'true' primitive populations who may disappear by themselves or through ethnocide. The victims of modernisation, the marginalised populations of the underdeveloped world are excluded from noble ethnology, i.e. the recovery of leftovers. Our journalists, on the other hand, look for the sensational and the exceptional. Natural catastrophes and high mortality rates are enough for them.

Nevertheless we must understand the present, a task involving the explanation of the contradictory evolution of social relations, whether between men or between societies and their natural environments. This endeavour cannot view crises as simply a set of empirical events which blind us with their inevitability and tragedy. We still consider droughts as crises, and crises as accidents.

In the present chapter it is my purpose to contribute to this debate by presenting without equivocation the theoretical and practical implications of a radical socialist perspective on the Sahel drought and calamities in general. I am aware that both the ideas and language of such a position are widely disliked in the world of anglophone social science. Many indeed regard it as necessarily 'unscientific' as well as provocative. Be that as it may, we shall not proceed to understand even our disagreements unless positions are stated boldly.

The setting

The Sahel supposedly defines the southern belt of the Sahara, though it is a somewhat misleading term. The region stretches from latitude 14°N to 20°N and from the Atlantic to the Chadosudanian region (10–23°E). It covers roughly 2.5 million km², that is less than half of the area of the six countries that divide it politically: Mauritania, Senegal, Mali, Upper Volta, Niger,

---

* I am dealing in this chapter with my experience of the francophone areas. Secondly, I do not consider myself to be a specialist on the Sahel or on the study of drought and famine. But having done my fieldwork in the groundnut region of Senegal, I have been quite naturally involved in the recent debates and researches dealing with these problems.

† A consideration of Ethiopia would of course change the meaning of such an appreciation.

Table 5.1 Rainfall variability in the Sahel, 1972.

| | Rainfall (mm) | | Vegetation period | |
	Annual average	1972	Annual average	1972
Kaedi (Mauritania)	416	218	40	
Niamey (Niger)	534	343	75	15
Nigamena (Chad)	647	599	80	65
Kaolack (Senegal)	793	490	100	55

Source: following Y. Albony and B. Bonlenger, in Copans (1975, p. 47).

Chad. Of course, the northern regions of such countries as Ivory Coast and Nigeria are concerned as well. This geographical definition in fact encompasses two or three subregions meeting various criteria. For the FAO the real Sahel zone is the northern fringe where the annual rainfall varies from 100 mm to 300 mm and where the ecological potentialities allow only a pastoral economy. The southern region is dominated by agriculture – millet and sorghum as well as groundnuts are grown. The annual rainfall varies between 300 mm and 600 mm. In 1972 the variation in rainfall was quite brutal though hardly unpredictable. The consequent losses in production were very important in 1972–4. The overall estimates (from FAO) concerning cattle for instance, mention a drop of 25%, but this can vary according to the kind of cattle or of country – Mauritania for example lost up to 80% of its herds. Cereals and cash crops also showed large shortfalls in most areas (see Table 5.2).

Experts and the media estimated the number of drought-related human deaths for 1973 at close to 100 000 persons. Retrospectively this figure may be misleading in its apparent starkness, masking the really great damage in terms of more permanent social and economic disorganisation – migration to towns or other regions, an increased dependency on foreign aid and food relief. 'At the peak of the crisis, in April–June 1974, there were some 200 000 people entirely dependent on food distribution in Niger (5% total population). In Mauritania, 250 000 people (20% total population) moved temporarily and under dismal conditions into towns, completely destitute. In Mali, another 250 000 (5% total population) may have been forced into total dependency in towns' (Copans 1975). A blurred image of these phenomena can be gathered from following the evolution in farmer incomes and urban wage rates (ibid. p. 30).

Images

Our first question is a kind of tautology: when can we call a drought a drought? When is a famine a famine? Either we use a system that scales disasters like earthquakes so that we measure rainfall, the germination of plants and the quantity of available calories, or else we consider the phenomenon as a totality made up of historical and dialectical relationships.

Table 5.2 Production of selected crops for Sahelian countries, 1971–4 (1000 tonnes).

	Millet/sorghum			Groundnuts			Cotton		
	1971–2	1972–3	1973–4	1971–2	1972–3	1973–4	1971–2	1972–3	1973–4
Chad	639	490	430	75	75	76	109	104	115
Mali	715	474	530	152	134	120	74	72	58
Mauritania	80	50	25	—	—	—	—	—	—
Niger	1230	1130	780	171	140	50	8	5	1
Senegal	583	323	467	988	570	643	21	23	34
Upper Volta	772	769	1138	66	67	63	28	33	27

Source: E. Berg, in Copans (1975, p. 6).

Table 5.3 Changes in farm income and urban wages for the Sahelian nations, 1971–5 (1969/70 = 100).

		1971–2	1972–3	1973–4	1974–5
Niger	farmer income	86	69	25	82
	urban wages	98	90	80	111–27
Senegal	farmer income	125	77	86	192
	urban wages	97	95	94	111–63
Upper Volta	farmer income	98	126	115	134
	urban wages	95	99	98	118

Source: Copans (1975).

The first approach has been the main one influencing local powers and the relief agencies. Among other things it allows them to choose their own criteria. They can determine, following the nature of their interests, the moment and the gravity of the crisis. This procedure has the further virtue of being quantifiable and thus appearing to be scientific. It can enable us afterwards to define a solution in similar quantitative terms; that is, through the measure of relief aid.

Interpreting the crisis as a series of effects, and the solutions as a neutralisation of the effects, allows this conception to ignore the social logic of the human and natural complex of causes. A drought becomes a drought when someone wants it to be so. Historically, there have been 'droughts' nobody even mentioned. Now people do not stop talking about droughts. Any slight climatic change, any ecological imbalance calls immediately for a drought, the central feature being that this in itself is treated as if it were an explanation.

The absence of any historical study and the tacit refusal to view social reality in most of Africa as an economic and social structure of exploitation confirms the so-called commonsense explanation. Of course, I doubt if we are ready to understand where 'the development of underdevelopment' is leading us (cf. Ch. 14). We have not yet produced an adequate political theory of neo-colonialism, or understood the processes of domination and exploitation of the Sahelian populations. We still look for ups and downs – when will the drought become less severe? When will it stop? Will there be another one afterwards? Etc., etc. Nevertheless, at this point we should try to present the *conditions of production* of drought and famine and not give an abstract and quantitative definition.

One approach could be to examine the reactions of the local dominant classes. These reactions appear to fall into three categories. First, there are those who obviously have not understood what is going on. A persuasive explanation of this is that they are subjected to an ideological alienation which prevents them seeing reality as it is. Then I would single out those who did not *want* to understand what was going on, transforming what were manifestly social problems into philosophical debate. The remarks of President Senghor are an example (see Copans 1975, pp. 15–16, 24–5). Cynicism is the structural characteristic of the third attitude; whereby the crisis is used as a tool to further class domination. Drought becomes a means of bargaining through the world market in relief and aid. The readiness of the international agencies to play such a game shows clearly which interests and concerns ultimately benefit from Western humanism.

At the heart of the pragmatic approaches to the crisis we find a positivist view of reality which explains the very fact of these bargains. Are we before or after a drought? Is the drought more or less serious? The crisis becomes a barometer, and also an excuse for the errors of the past, which are then forgotten. History will begin anew as if nothing had happened before the drought and these responses to it. We are assured openly that this is the last time things will get out of control, that no drought will be able to produce such drastic effects in the future. Then we classify the facts. We fix the realm of drought and famine in time (before–after) in space (a more or less big region) in quantity (benign or disastrous). The phenomenon becomes a variable. And a variable can always be a marginal one.

All of these perceptions, attitudes and analyses stem from the ideology of the dominant classes which in turn shape the reports of journalist, government official and scholars. And for all the embellishments of language they are crude and rash reports needing no metaphors to get their message across. Three brief examples:

(a)   L. Tauxier, a French colonial administrator (in the Yatenga Cercle, of what is now Upper Volta) reacted very simply to the brutal mortality which struck 'his' population after a famine during World War I. His concern was the loss measured in terms of income tax, i.e. the drastic diminution of the number of taxpayers. We can still find similar concerns today.*

(b)   The FAO experts seem on the whole pleased at the disappearance of the cattle of the Sahelian nomads. They see these people as not producing meat for the market and drinking too much milk which is a waste of calories (see Copans 1975, vol. 1, pp. 15–16, 24–5).

(c)   On another level there are unmistakably 'racist' overtones to the attitudes of local political élites when condemning their fellow countrymen as 'inefficient' and unwilling to react positively to adversity. This comes out in all the local African newspapers.

Whatever the context, for more than a century we have had that well known policy of making the victim the culprit. The culprit is the person who does not pay his taxes, even if he *cannot* pay them, even if he is dead! The culprit is the person who does not know how to profit from market economy (why breed more cattle if these are not sold in the market place?). It can even be the person who obeys too well in assignments which prove to be quite stupid afterwards (in some situations the intensive use of fertilisers can be dangerous for future crops). The culprit is the bad producer. The culprit is an individual or a collection of individuals, but is never recognised as being caught up in a different socioeconomic system or history. After all how does one deal with the idea that the 'culprit' was in fact the prevailing (disastrous) production system; a system that produces producers unable to 'make it'; a system in which everything has been done so that they are essentially victims, albeit unwillingly, of past, present or future droughts?

Directions

To begin to deal with these problems our perspective must be fundamentally historical, but a history of concrete mechanisms and not of temporary prag-

---

* See excerpts of Tauxier's reports in Marchal (1907–73).

matic expedients which appear to dominate modernisation and even colonial-
isms as they impinge upon our problem. This history must be both social and
natural. Social relations are always relations of men with men, of men and
nature. The modes of exploitation of nature are the most difficult to explain.
Even Marxist theory, which has revolutionised social sciences and specifically
in relation to such issues, has not grasped adequately the nature of productive
forces at least in post-colonial and neo-colonial settings.

A concrete historical perspective   Africanists (and others of course) can use
anthropology and political economy to describe the evolution of African
societies. But the first has a microscopic view of reality, the second a macro-
scopic one. The duality (or supposed duality) of tradition and modernity, and
the separation of local level from world level, are built-in constraints of these
sciences. The unity – even on a theoretical basis – of these two disciplines is
illusory. The dialectics of participant observation and statistical tables of
economic output has to be invented, so to speak.

The nature of its tradition, its focus on the cultural level, on a closed
totality, has led anthropology to view changes as external variables, as
intrusions within the homogeneous social fabric. More decisive has been a
negative attitude towards the history of these societies, and only in the past
ten years have researchers begun to reconstruct some forms of the African
past. They have focused on recent history, that is, from 18th century onwards
where oral traditions or foreign documents, both European and Arabic are
considered more or less conclusive. This past is more political than economic.
When concentrating on the topic of droughts and famines it is a grave lacuna
because we can only explain the demopolitical reactions to such crisis. Therefore the conditions of production in past droughts and famines are still largely
ignored. We shall have to wait for new approaches in archaeology, historical
climatology, ethnobotany and zoology to be able to describe these situations
more accurately.

The silence of anthropology and the stammering of 'ancient' history are but
some of the intellectual obstacles we encounter. Underdeveloped capitalism
is a product of world imperialism. But usually domination and exploitation
are perceived as purely external factors which act *upon* the African societies.
That these forms are equally a product of the dominated societies is a point of
view dismissed by the ethnocentrism of most anti- or pro-imperialist positions. We leave the restricted horizons of the village communities for the mist
of invisible horizons.

We plead for a perspective based on an articulation of mediations. Regional
and national levels are made the relevant frames of analysis. We supposedly
must deal with the concrete content of theoretical analysis and not limit ourselves to the abstract logic of modes of production or social formations.*

* A theory of the state and of the arena of class struggle must take into account this level of
empirical research. See for example, Bolans *et al.* (1975). Definitions and uses of the Marxist
concepts of mode of production (forces and relations of production) and social formation can be
found in Seddon (1978), Hindess and Hirst (1975).

A natural and social history People are working on the history of African social formations. But they do not deal with the history of natural changes these societies produce. The history of material culture, of demography, the evolution of productive practices gives way for the moment to a history of cultures, states and economy as a sphere of exchanges.*

There is no linear – and parallel – evolution between the exploitation of nature and that within society. Yet such a relationship does exist. The basic concept of historical materialism that the mode of production is not a simple 'logical' organisation of the elements of an empirical description brings together productives forces and relations of production. It is indispensable to explain the natural history of groups – the demographic, physical, nutritional conditions of production, and so forth.

A self-sustaining economy, *sensu stricto*, has probably never existed. Recent studies in ethnic history demonstrate the relativity of frontiers between different social formations, especially at the level of economic exchanges. The fact of dependency, an articulation with the different forms and phases of capitalism, subsequently modifies the whole of local conditions of production. Focusing continuously upon the local phenomena of social relations, the anthropologist ignores the framework that ultimately determines events or their worth to society. Uneven local development that had been more or less autonomous changes into an uneven local development that is combined with other poles of development. The articulation with capitalism changes the nature of the law of uneven development of social formations. One-sided relations of domination and submission take precedence over relations of 'equality'; a market economy polarises and produces a hierarchy of the various social formations which can then be progressively dispossessed of all productive autonomy (see Pelletier & Goblot 1969, Lenin 1965).

This new history is both that of the spatial forms of relations of production and that of the changing technological, demographic and agronomic relations to the natural environment. It reveals that the absence of control over conditions of production imposed by colonial capitalism has actually been reinforced since the advent of neo-colonial independence. In these terms the means of control of the conditions of production are more and more complex while the actual exploitation of the natural (agricultural and pastoral) milieu takes no account of the conditions for:

(a)   the normal reproduction of the natural constraints of production (plant cover, moisture supply, soil fertility etc.);
(b)   the social reproduction of human labour force (demographic structure, nutritional status, social distribution of human and economic means etc.).

* See for example Cognery-Vidrovitch & Terray (1976) and Terray (1975). A good example of studies focused on productive forces can be found in the works of such historians of the French Middle Ages as C. Parrain and G. Duby. But we have not in the African studies all the richness and precision of the documents used in these analyses.

This exploitation turns out to be a 'super-exploitation'. It serves to impose more and more degraded conditions upon the direct producers who find difficulties even in maintaining their labour force at a minimum level. The conditions of reproduction are endangered by the state policies which are only directed at an increased production of surplus, *whatever the conditions*. Such a process must accelerate the rhythm of any crisis related to the climatic or other features of the natural environment. To the extent that the direct producers are more and more dispossessed from the control of the factors of production (and of the regulation of the natural and social reproduction process), they submit themselves to an exploitation against which they seem to be defenceless. This system quickens the process of separation between the producers and their natural conditions of production; it compels them to look for external help. The development of formal political and administrative structures, and the massive use of mystifying ideologies, are typical of this situation.

Such a history must examine those who suffer directly from these crises, but, of course, most studies only concentrate on this point. We must also consider the interests of those who *benefit* from such a situation. Social relations, because they are organised following patterns of unequal class and group relationship, always refract natural disasters in different ways. Immediate producers are affected *directly* by a drought. They are also affected as the natural effect makes its way through the social relations of exploitation. Within a social structure of unequal possession of means of production, of opposed classes, those who are dominated and exploited are those who are directly confronted with the 'hazards' of the social system. Dominant groups can always manipulate the relations of exploitation for their own benefit. They suppress the effects on the society as a whole, by having them bear primarily on the dominated classes. The food shortage, the access to help is unequally distributed from the start. This manipulation is a 'natural' characteristic of exploitative relationships and it does not stem from a cynical strategy of some individuals. Those who aggravate the crisis are those who can avoid feeling their effects.

The super-exploitation of those who work the natural milieu provokes repercussions at the ecological level. The investments to increase productivity are the producers' concern, whereas the fruits of any increase in productivity are monopolised by the state apparatus, the classes that control or operate it, the traders. The possibility of choosing new ways to exploit the milieu and the organisation of the means necessary to avoid any further degradation cannot be devised at the local level. Development technology in measuring progress in abstract figures denies any autonomy to the local producers. This technology goes hand in hand with a dispossession of decision, of knowledge, of the products of personal labour. Such a dispossession increases risks and uncertainties. In a materialist perception of social facts, natural causes can be considered as such in that they are categorised as 'natural' by the social structure of causes.

Empirical problems and theoretical concepts   Once this problematic is suggested, we must indicate the themes, construct the objects that enable us to approach these questions, questions of an empirical and theoretical nature – derived from social reality as perceived by the masses and as explained by theoreticians of various sorts. We shall show in our conclusion to what extent these questions – and the means chosen to find an answer – are *political*.

We shall single out for further comment the following five problems (cf. Copans 1975, vol. 1, pp. 28–36):

(1)   The conditions of production as related to an exploitation of natural environment. The control of the 'natural' factors of production – soils, pastures, cultures, etc.
(2)   The social organisation of the direct producers (peasants, herdsmen). The articulation between the use of the natural milieu and the social structure of exploitation.
(3)   The *national* system of exploitation – the contradiction between town and countryside, migration and internal market.
(4)   The role of the state apparatus and the national conditions for the reproduction of class exploitation.
(5)   Dependence and neo-colonialism. The development and humanitarian relief aid strategies in the context of an international class struggle.

The natural conditions of production have undergone an evolution through the successive agricultural policies. Numerous studies in geography, agronomy, rural economy and sociology have been devoted to the description of these production factors. Nevertheless two important lacuna can be considered:

(a)   The empirical approach to the natural milieu is separated into at least half a dozen natural sciences. A decisive barrier also separates these studies from those analysing social reality as an exploitation system.
(b)   In the background we always have productive forces. But the concept is not very well elaborated.[*] Anthropologists, for instance, are usually vague when considering the natural objects of the process. As long as pedological, botanical and zoological descriptions are juxtaposed to local ethnoscientific logic and theories of relations of production, we will not be able to understand how the social relations of exploitation modify the very form of natural relationships. On the other hand we might deem it necessary to over-ride the idealistic ethnoscience of mythologies and kinship classifications so as to construct an ethnoscience of the material conditions of production – a benefit both for the informant and the researcher. The fundamental objective of our approach lies in explaining the relations involved in developing the natural milieu as

---

[*] Even F. Pouillon in his paragraph on 'The thesis of the priority of productive forces' concentrates primarily on the means of production and technology (cf. Pouillon 1976).

relations of exploitation between men. We must discover the strategies
of exploitation which are also conditions and means for the 'exploitation' of the natural milieu. These relations can in turn show where social
relations of exploitation fit in. We must grasp the totality of the social
constraints (economic and non-economic) of the production. Economic
anthropology has emphasised the labour process, the technological cus-
toms and the exchange of products. Sometimes it forgets the importance
of superstructural factors (kinship, ideology). Of course everybody men-
tions the role of kinship within the relations of production but we are
often confusing the kinship system (which as such is not a strongly built
mechanism) with kinship relations, in which some function as relations
of production and others do not.* Meanwhile ideology is not just a
reflection of conditions. It is also an organisational scheme of social
practice and as such is part of their practical effect. We are thus calling
into question all of our classical anthropological assumptions.

We content ourselves too often with the local and communal dimensions of
our study area. But the constraints of the exploitation system have long been
determined from outside the communities. It is impossible today to understand the local systems in various parts of the Sahel as being purely agricultural. The relationships between town and countryside, and the migratory
process which links these two realities, create new conditions for the reproduction of labour force and therefore of all social relations (Amin 1974,
Amselle 1976). The process of peasantisation and proletarisation are basically produced by the same causes (though they are differentiated effects).
The urbanised masses (producers and non-producers) are a component of the
social uses of the natural milieu. The pseudo-unemployed, the marginalised
population (see Gutkind & Wallerstein 1976, Gutkind & Waterman 1977)
are the other side (and also an indirect cause) of the super-exploitation of
agricultural producers. These phenomena are amplified and quickened by
drought.

Once we have marked the various mechanisms of exploitation, we must
construct the national class system of exploitation and the arena of class
struggle. We must study carefully the state apparatus because it is the nexus of
all social relations. After 15–20 years of neo-colonialism the national basis of
the state and the conflicts it controls (or fails to control) has a definite
sociological and political meaning (e.g. Dunn 1978). We can no longer view
the state as an illusion, as a veil that camouflages a brutal external intervention – though this can also still be true in many cases. Some social groups have
evolved and occupy the decisive sectors of the state; they tend to organise the
reproduction of the system for their own benefit and not only for their foreign
partners. Institutions and policies intended to establish the national conditions of class domination and its reproduction are today a fact we have to take

* It would be instructive to show the formalist logic of both functional and structural anthropologists in the approach to this domain.

into account. We shall understand the true effects of drought when we can show to what extent local bureaucracies and bourgeoisies have utilised them in order to consolidate their power. *We can no longer separate the natural phenomenon and the necessary political translation of its effects.*

Finally, we consider the international level of dependence and underdevelopment. Indeed, the natural and social transformations under study are the result of the historical process of imperialist expansion. We must single out the new changes in this respect.

(a)   To what extent has the world division of labour been reorganised in the past ten years? (cf. Feder 1976)
(b)   Are not the new forms of dependence involving a more and more precarious position for the Sahelian countries?
(c)   What is the meaning of the production of foodstuff (vegetables and meat) for the world market?
(d)   To what extent is this phenomenon expressed by an increase of class exploitation and a rapid development of class differentiation?
(e)   Is not this process the beginning of an autonomous economic strategy on the part of the national bourgeoisies?

All these questions – and others – show how weak are our theoretical definitions of the socioeconomic background of drought and its neo-colonial overtones. Drought and famine demonstrate also other dimensions of the dependence process. What is called humanitarian aid is in fact an astute (and cheap) means of preserving domination and a beggar's mentality among the dominated. World food relief can also serve American imperialist strategy (see Meunier 1975, Berlan *et al.* 1975). If this policy helps solve some social and nutritional problems, that is also the perspective of the dominant classes' interest, be they African or Western. Therefore we are not exaggerating when we conclude that the Sahel crisis of the past ten years is a component of the international class struggle. For the time being, bureaucracies and bourgeoisies keep the initiative. But things could change in this respect.

Conclusion

The study of droughts and famines is undoubtedly fashionable, although many studies deal with it merely by changing titles. Hence we write about 'Social change consequences of drought' or 'Human and natural environment and the effects of drought'. Words are changed but not the content.*

Most of the researchers who have been concerned with drought and famine have viewed them through a single relationship of cause and effect. Then,

---

* In fact most research in France since 1974 has been conducted in geography and economics. Very few anthropologists (with the exception of C. Raynault) are studying this topic. Apparently things are quite different in British and American social sciences.

when solutions have been proposed, the relationship became that of remedying the effects. But we must contest this positivist and mechanistic point of view and propose a more historical and dialectical stand. What we can call causes, effects and solutions are all elements of the same structure. They are different moments of the same process. Hence solutions often contribute more to the existence of the same causes and effects than to their disappearance. Causes, effects and solutions are not autonomous objectives, objective facts which can be analysed as such. The social and historical totality, and the local mechanisms of the various modes of exploitation, disintegrate the so-called objects, droughts and famines.

One may ask if droughts and famines are just a collection of accidents whose statistical probabilities are more or less definite. Equally one can ask if they do not reveal an extreme evolution in the conditions of an enlarged reproduction of imperialism, i.e. an extreme evolution for the dominated societies and their own use of natural resources. Let us make a comparison and one of paradox. Who is really responsible for labour accidents in factories? The very expression 'labour accident' suggests an involuntary and abnormal phenomenon. But it is not so. The cost of work security and the refusal to let the worker control the material conditions of his work place are a logical product of relations of exploitation. A labour accident is a normal moment of the labour process within such a system. Like unemployment it is a structural feature and it contributes to fix the price of the labour force. Bosses always view the workers as being responsible for their own fate, because they are careless, but that is the exploiter's point of view!

Drought is a potential effect of social super-exploitation provoking degradation of the regulating mechanisms of the natural environment. Famine on the other hand is like an indefinite *période de sondure* – the time between the end of supplies from the previous harvest and those from the next one. A prior golden age is purely hypothetical. It is the gradual or brutal dispossession (a non-reversing tendency) of the control of all factors of production which is incriminating. Famine is a definite proof that the so-called technological process is only possible in return for an alienation of the direct producers. Droughts and famines are becoming *regulating devices* of Sahelian underdevelopment, much as inflation and underemployment are regulating devices of the current crisis of imperialism.

All of these remarks lead to the conclusion that (human) ecology can only be a political science. The science of the utilisation of the natural milieu must be first of all the science of the social exploitation of those who make use of this milieu. The Sahelian crisis and all natural disasters of the same kind demonstrate a direct repercussion of nature upon the social relationships of production. Social exploitation works out partially through the mechanisms of natural evolution; our object is located at the very place where the relations between man and nature mask the more subtle forms of exploitation of man by man.

Once we have defined the object and the theory of this science we must try to determine the nature of its practice. For science has been put into question during the Sahelian events. It has been proved to be a hyperspecialised practice, a body of knowledge integrated as such in the exploitation system whether in looking for the causes or the solutions. There is a total opposition between the pseudo-neutral objectivity of the observer and the initiatives of those subjected to disorganisation and marginalisation. There can be no common experience between the specialist in 'better' development and those who are dispossessed. To explain the roots of exploitation without acting publicly and actively to suppress them is a mutilation of Marxist theory. Of course there are various ways of intervening. An instructive experience is that of the Comité information Sahel, its publications and public initiatives (Copans 1975).*

To evoke a science for the victims of exploitation, in this case of drought, simplifies the transformation of research objectives and of explanatory theories. A liberation from the constraints of the natural milieu can be effective only if there is a change in the control of these conditions. These transformations are geared to the abolition of the actual system of exploitation evolved by imperialism and reproduced by the neo-colonial states. The science of these transformations is therefore a science of revolution.

Those who perceive the political background to so-called natural disasters can rely on the victims' intuitions. For they know that the tragedy they live can be traced back to human causes.† Fatalism in the case of natural hazards does not exclude a more or less clear consciousness of the effects of exploitation relationships in the triggering or aggravation of the natural process (see Copans 1975, vol. 2, pp. 102–19). The well known 'Science for the people' has to become a science *from* the people *by* the people. For the struggle against the drought and the famine begins with the struggle against those who profit from it.

Natural hazards specialists must be aware that they benefit *also* in a certain way from this situation. Surely nobody takes seriously anymore the argument that the betterment of human knowledge and the development of objective science is our purpose? The struggle against drought and famine starts at any time and in any place. 'Experts' should not exist, not even 'red' ones!

References

Amin, S. (ed.) 1974. *Modern migration in Western Africa*. Oxford: Oxford University Press.
Amselle, J. L. (ed.) 1976. *Réseaux et processus migratoires: les migrations africaines*. Paris: Maspero.
Alige, M. 1975. *Théories des pouvoirs et idéologie*. Paris: Hermann.

* The Comité has stopped its activities at the end of 1976.
† Susman, O'Keefe and Wisner (Ch. 4) describe the reactions of the inhabitants of Guatemala City slums after the earthquake of February 1976. They come to call it a 'classquake'!

Berg, E. 1975. *The economic impact of drought and inflation in the Sahel*. Ann Arbor, Michigan: Univ. Michigan, Center for Research on Economic Development, 22.

Berlan, J. P., J. P. Bertrand, J. P. Chabert, M. Marloie and P. Spitz 1975. Blè et soja, penuries sur commande. *La Recherche* no. 56, mai 1975, 408–17.

Bolans, J. L., C. Coulon and J. M. Gastellu 1975. *Autonomie locale et intégration Nationale au Sénégal*. Paris: Pedone.

Comité Information Sahel 1974. *Qui se nourrit de la famine en Afrique?* Paris: Maspero.

Copans, J. (ed.) 1975. *Sécheresses et famines du Sahel*. Paris: Maspero.

Copans, J. 1977. Politique et religion, d'une relation idéologique interindividuelle à la domination impérialiste: les Mourides du Sénégal. *Dialectiques* no. 21, automne, 23–40.

Cognery-Vidrovitch, C. 1976. The political economy of the African peasantry and modes of production. In Gutkind and Wallerstein (1976).

Dunn, J. (ed.) 1978. *West African States: failure and promise*. Cambridge: Cambridge University Press

Feder, E. 1976. The new world bank programs for the self liquidation of the Third World peasantry. *J. Peasant Studs* **3**, no. 3, 343–54.

Gutkind, P. C. W. and I. Wallerstein (eds) 1976. *The political economy of contemporary Africa*. California: Sage.

Gutkind, P. C. W. and P. Waterman 1977. *African social studies: a radical reader*. New York: Monthly Review Press.

Hindess, B. and P. Q. Hirst 1975. *Pre-capitalist modes of production*. London: Routledge & Kegan Paul.

Lenin, V. I. 1965. *The development of capitalism in Russia, Collected works*, vol. 3. Moscow.

Marchal, J. Y. 1907–73. Récoltes et disettes en zone nord-soudanienne. In *Chronique des saisons agricoles au Yatenga* (Haute Volta), Paris: ORSTOM (multicopied).

Meunier, R. 1975. L'aide d'urgence et les nouveaux projets de développement. In Copans (1975, vol. 1, pp. 109–29).

Pelletier, A. and J. J. Goblot 1969. *Matérialisme historique et histoire des civilisations*. Paris: Editions Sociales.

Pouillon, F. 1976. La détermination d'un mode de production: les forces productives et leur appropriation. In *L'Anthropologie économique*, F. Povillon (ed.), 57–85. Paris: Maspero.

Seddon, D. (ed.) 1978. *Relations of production, Marxist approaches to economic anthropology*. London: Cass.

Terray, E. 1975. Classes and class consciousness in the Abron Kingdom of Gyaman. In *Marxist analyses and social anthropology*, M. Bloch (ed.) New York: Halstead Press.

6 Underdevelopment and hazards in historical perspective: an Irish case study

COLM REGAN

> There was no want of food of another description for the support of human life. On the contrary, the crops of grain had been far from deficient, and the prices of corn and of oatmeal were very moderate ... those districts in the south or west presented the remarkable example of possessing a surplus of food whilst the inhabitants were suffering from actual want ... The calamity of 1822 may therefore be said to have proceeded less from the want of food itself, than from the want of adequate means of purchasing it; or in other words from the want of profitable employment.
>
> Report of the Select Committee on the
> employment of the poor in Ireland (1823)

Introduction

The struggle for land has constituted a major theme in Irish history for at least the past 350 years. In the economic and political circumstances of the period from the 17th to the 20th century, access to land ensured some measure of security and stability. For those without access to land, or to sufficient quantities of it to sustain themselves, the reality was most often one of economic and social marginalisation, emigration and, periodically, starvation. The situation became particularly acute in the first half of the 19th century when starvation and death became a frequent phenomenon reaching a peak in the infamous 'Great Starvation' from 1845 to 1848.

The details of the famine have been described so often as not to require elaboration here; indeed, the event has by now entered the lore of research on hazards and disasters. Despite various debates and difficulties over the accuracy of statistics, there is general agreement that in the period 1845–8, approximately 1.00–1.25 million people died from starvation and from associated diseases such as pestilence, dysentery, relapsing fever and cholera. Between 1846 and 1851 nearly a million persons emigrated; whole families and neighbourhoods were broken up, scattered or wiped out. These emigrants often suffered loss of life in transit or on arrival at their destination

Figure 6.1 Ireland.

(O'Brien 1921, Edwards & Williams 1957, Woodham Smith 1962). The particular events of those years were unique only in scale as starvation had occurred before, a total of 23 times between 1739 and 1844 (O'Brien 1921, p. 222). The previous highest figure for loss of life was in 1739–40 when approximately 300 000 died. In the 18th and 19th centuries then, it is clearly possible to argue that starvation, disease and death had become 'normal' features of Irish society, albeit by no means 'natural'. In a word, the majority of the population of Ireland during these centuries had become vulnerable; their survival depended on the delicate balance between population growth and the ability of the subsistence sector (which had been greatly disrupted by the spread of a monetary economy) to absorb that growth. The recurring starvations and, in particular, that of 1845–8 were the specific and, in many ways, inevitable result of that vulnerability and the crises which it periodically produced.

The period prior to and incorporating the famine was, in many ways, a watershed in the social and economic history of Ireland, although many historians now argue that its immediate impact should not be overestimated (e.g. Cullen 1972). The period witnessed the final collapse of pre-capitalist Ireland and its incorporation into an industrial capitalist economy based upon England. The famine also completed the work of processes begun far earlier, e.g. the penetration and expansion of a market economy, the creation of an industrial reserve army of labour and the entrenchment of Ireland's role as a major agricultural producer for industrial Britain. The nature of economic development and its effects on both rural and urban populations in this period must be firmly situated in the logic of this expanding capitalist system and its connections with its subordinate economies. The consecutive influences of absolutism, mercantilism and, finally, industrial capitalism, conditioned and influenced development in Ireland and subjugated the majority of the Irish peasant population to socioeconomic forces which made the horrors of 1845–8 almost inevitable.

Issues of interpretation

One of the most consistent criticisms of orthodox 'natural hazards' research and theory over the past few years has been its lack of historical perspective. Third-World studies aside, the 'Great Starvation' in Ireland provides one of the most interesting and informative historical case studies. This is true not only because of its well documented historical background but also because it has been the subject of many conflicting interpretations and analyses. There is as much to be learned about ideology in historical research as there is about Ireland specifically. This is as true of both latter-day academic research as it is of contemporary political and economic commentary.

Two popular contemporary interpretations of the disaster attributed it to divine retribution for, on the one hand, the government's recent support for the establishment of a popish seminary in Maynooth and, on the other, for intemperance and licentiousness. Charles Trevelyan, Under-Secretary at the British Exchequer (who had responsibility for Irish relief measures), saw the famine as a 'direct and wise intervention of providence' (Verriere 1979, p. 62). There were many nationalists, particularly in the aftermath of the starvation, who viewed it as an excellent example of English maleficence towards

Ireland; this view is best expressed in the saying that 'Providence sent the potato blight, but England made the Famine'. This view was incorporated into the nationalist interpretation of Irish history, which survives today in various forms. In Britain, many including J. S. Mill attributed the disaster to the rackrenting aristocracy, others to the lack of a modern agricultural sector, while the most celebrated interpretation was offered by Thomas Malthus who argued that 'overpopulation' was the problem (Edwards & Williams 1957, Black 1960).

In more recent years two conflicting schools of thought have emerged. One, which is part of a general revisionist trend in Irish history and which seeks, for the most part, to disassociate Irish underdevelopment from British colonialism, emphasises demographic and adaptive factors while arguing that one reason why the situation became so serious, particularly in the west, was that area's lack of integration into the national (and by implication, international) economy (e.g. see Cullen 1972, Mitchell 1976). While many Irish geographers and historians would argue a neo-Malthusian version of the starvation, few would go as far as British historian A. J. P. Taylor who recently characterised the Lancashire cotton famine of 1861 as a 'man-made' disaster whereas the Irish famine was a 'natural catastrophe' (1978).

In contrast to this type of analysis, there are those who stress the structural roots of starvation in the marginalised economic and social conditions of the majority of the Irish peasantry in the period. Perhaps the clearest and most forthright statement of this view is offered by James Connolly who argued in 1910 that 'It is a common saying amongst Irish nationalists that "providence sent the potato blight; but England made the Famine"'. The statement is true, and only needs amending by adding that England made the famine by a rigid application of the economic principles that lie at the base of capitalist society'. This analysis has been echoed by Strauss (1951), Gibbon (1975) and Verriere (1979). The emphasis here has been on the impact of Irish integration into the British colonial system and its effects on development. Again, as in the case of the revisionists, the analysis stretches far beyond the period 1845–8 and involves issues of general debate on the interpretation of Irish economic history.

The historical context

In the case of Ireland the initial feudal expansion from England, from the 12th to the 16th century established a weak and regionally isolated regime which eventually retreated (or became assimilated) in the face of strong opposition from Gaelic society and weak support from England (Beckett 1966, Bottigheimer 1971, Nicholls 1972). Apart from those areas of the east coast where settlement was densest, Gaelic society was altered very little, most regions remaining relatively autonomous especially in the west and north. By the beginning of the 16th century the actual authority of the Crown depended, in large measure, on various local lords; Gaelic society had experienced a resurgence and many Gaelic lords presented both a military and political threat to the English Crown. However, by the end of the 17th century this situation was completely reversed, the authority of the Crown and parliament had been established, many Gaelic and Anglo-Irish lords had been defeated and, most importantly, vast tracts of land had changed ownership. From this period onwards Ireland became increasingly locked into the rhythm and logic of British development, albeit in an uneven fashion. James summarises the situation thus: 'For England's medieval rulers the conquest of Ireland represented more an adventure than a set policy. In Stuart and Hanoverian times when England aspired to be a commercial and colonial power, control of Ireland became a necessity' (1972, p. 2).

This transformation in effective administration and control in Ireland was, in large measure, the result of the emergence in England of the absolutist state. For the first time it now became possible to overcome the local parcellised nature of feudal society and to establish a centralised state. That state introduced a standing army, a permanent bureaucracy, national taxation, a codified law system and, most importantly, the beginnings of a unified market system (Dobb 1947, Hill 1967, Anderson 1974, Hilton 1976, Tigar & Levy 1977). It now became increasingly possible (and necessary) to subdue and control Ireland. Policies adopted in this period included increased involvement in areas outside the east coast, a policy of land surrender and regrant (thus finally, *de jure*, abolishing the clan system of ownership) and initial, though largely unsuccessful, attempts at land colonisation (Froude 1872–4, Butler 1917, Beckett 1966, Moody *et al*. 1976). This initial phase of absolutist expansion created the basis upon which the second and far more extensive expansion of control in the 17th century could be effected.

Following the defeat of the monarchy in England and the establishment of a parliament increasingly dominated by, and reflective of, the needs and requirements of merchant capital, relations between England and Ireland became increasingly conditioned by the philosophy and practice of mercantilism (Strauss 1951, Hill 1961). The latter was bellicose in nature: it emphasised the necessity (and profitability) of warfare and consequently the prosecution of a conquering foreign policy. The principal aims of mercantilism were to assist the process of capital accumulation in its infancy. Colonial areas, such as Ireland, were to be kept as sources of raw materials and as agricultural areas producing for the benefit of the colonial power. Another feature of mercantilist practice, and one which had an immediate and long-term effect in Ireland, was a vigorous policy of attempting to prevent the emergence of potentially competitive industries in the colonies. In short, mercantilism was a vital element in the promotion of capitalism in its period of primitive accumulation (Dobb 1947, Anderson 1974, Magdoff 1978). The results of Ireland's increased integration into this system are succinctly commented upon by Strauss: 'The peculiar and tragic combination of a primitive feudal land system [*sic*], riveted to a modern country in the mercantilist stage of capitalist development, enveloped Ireland in a mesh of sufferings and contradictions which determined her destinies for a very long time' (1951, p. 12).

Part and parcel of this vigorous foreign policy involved a series of land confiscations and plantations, beginning approximately in 1585 and ending in 1690. For economic, political and strategic reasons, these plantations involved substantial aristocratic landholders, small-scale tenant farmers, soldiers and, of particular importance initially, merchant adventurer companies (Butler 1917, Simms 1956, Clarke 1976). These companies had no great desire to develop the land and they merely used it as a lucrative means of speculation (Rabb 1967, Bottigheimer 1971).* Between 1640 and 1688 the amount of land held by English and Scottish settlers almost doubled to 78% of the total, an increment, in that period of some 2.8 million ha (Butler 1917). Having fled the country or been beaten in battle, many Gaelic and old English lords were dispossessed and driven westwards into Connacht while the majority of the population were transformed into a substantial tenantry paying money rent, and into large numbers of landless and subsistence farmers.

In the new order of things land ceased to be the basis of social existence and became a marketable commodity. This is best exemplified in the adventurers' investment not in land *per se* but in what Rabb (1967) calls 'futures', i.e. land as a commodity which could be sold profitably to others in the future. This transformation also facilitated the emergence of a more individualist use of land 'determined solely by the principle of maximising the incomes of those who had acquired ownership of it through the violence of the seventeenth century' (Crotty 1966, p. 32). Thus we can identify the emergence of increasingly capitalist agricultural estates, specialising in commercial livestock rearing, alongside a 'native' subsistence economy increasingly geared towards the provision of subsistence crops such as turnips and potatoes. The majority of the population became ever more dependent on the latter crops while grain and other cash crops went to pay rising rents. This situation was made all the more precarious by the impact of mercantilism on trade and industry.

The nature of mercantilist trade policy became abundantly clear in the Irish case. Until 1663 there existed no restrictions upon trade and manufacturing in Ireland nor duties on Irish goods imported into England (Murray 1907, p. 6). Such a situation was of benefit to a Crown dependent on extracting finance from Ireland but not so to a Parliament increasingly representative of merchant and manufacturing interests. The policy adopted from 1660 onwards indicated that Ireland was henceforth to be treated as a dependency of England and would thus be prevented, as far as possible, from adopting policies injurious to dominant class interests there.† Prior to 1660 Ireland had developed a cattle exporting trade worth approximately £4 million annually.

* These merchant adventurer companies form a particularly interesting study of primitive accumulation.

† The fact that various class interests in Ireland opposed these measures and were, to some extent, successful in modifying them, does not alter the intent or policies of mercantilism. However, this remains a matter for debate in Irish economic history (e.g. Cullen 1968, 1972).

The Cattle Acts of 1663 and 1665 prohibited (at the behest of cattle-breeding interests in the west of England) the import of Irish cattle, sheep or swine. These restrictions were countered by the growth of a provisioning trade which dealt directly with continental Europe and the plantations (O'Brien 1919, Cullen 1972). The Navigation Acts of 1670 and 1671 prohibited the import of goods directly into Ireland except through England, hence effectively damaging the Irish shipping trade which could no longer carry goods directly home, thus placing it at a disadvantage. Further Acts regulated the terms and duties to be imposed on trade in various commodities thus helping to limit the growth potential of industry (O'Brien 1919, Cullen 1972).

Hand in hand with restricting trade went a series of Acts hindering and delimiting the emergence of manufacturing industry in Ireland. Industry was only to be fostered where it did not conflict with the rapidly expanding English system (Hobsbawm 1961). High import duties on Irish goods entering England, the banning of wool exports, Acts prohibiting the export of glass, (and the import of foreign, non-English made glass), silk or gloves, the import of non-English hops for brewing and prohibitive taxes on beer exports all hampered and stunted Irish economic development. Through pursuing such policies British merchants and manufacturers sought to secure a plentiful supply of raw materials to encourage their own home industries and to prevent potential competition. Many of these restrictions were relaxed after 1750, but by this time English trade and manufacturing had already been given an important advantage and it proved particularly difficult for Irish manufacturing to compete, especially in the period of 19th-century laissez-faire (Murray 1907; O'Brien 1918, 1921). Further to this, the precarious base and small scale of Irish industry, its regional concentration (on the east and south coasts predominantly), and the small size of the home market, militated against its capacity to absorb surplus agricultural population.

Throughout the 18th century the relative success of the provisions trade, along with other factors, such as the Penal Laws (which prevented Catholics from obtaining long leases, thus directing them into cattle rearing which yielded high, short-term and easily realisable profits); the fact that Irish grain was allowed into the English market only when the price was over 48 shillings a quarter, plus the fact that arable land was exempted from tithes (payable to the established Church), all ensured the growth of pasture land over arable, at least up to 1780. The restrictive legislation plus absenteeism among many landholders significantly reduced the application of capital to the land thus preventing many improvements adopted, in this period, in English agriculture. Throughout the 18th century there was little improvement in land. Leases on land in many countries had restrictions on ploughing and, despite some efforts to increase tillage, production continued to decline until 1750.

Starvation and death occurred in 1727–8 and in 1741–2, thereby precipitating legislation designed to increase grain production, yet this only succeeded when demand for grain increased in England and when the Penal Laws were finally repealed. Between 1770 and 1846 the Irish grain trade thrived, as did other basic agricultural foodstuffs. However, the remainder of Irish agriculture, and particularly the subsistence sector (concentrated heavily in the western half of the island) continued to be depressed and backward. Many travellers and observers of the period were unanimous in characterising agriculture as particularly backward with respect to methods and crop returns (see Maxwell 1954).

Landlords, farmers, cottiers and labourers

Many of the new landlords who had acquired land during the 17th century resided in England or had returned there during the restrictive period of mercantilism, or lived in urban centres such as Dublin, to which centres remittances of rent were sent (O'Brien 1921). Estimates vary as to the amounts remitted although a reasonable figure would appear to be approximately £1.2 million per annum towards the end of the 18th century (Cullen 1972, p. 20). Although absenteeism declined after 1750–60, there is considerable debate and disagreement over its impact. Nonetheless it is fairly certain that it led to the neglect of land, the emergence of a 'middleman' system from which rent abuse frequently arose, and to a general neglect of agricultural methods. The desire to maximise rents also aided the process of subdivision. More rigid management of estates did not occur until after 1800, although many of the earlier practices continued until after 1850.

Particular faith was placed by many political economists in the 18th century on those farmers whose fortunes arose from the cattle and provisions trade. The wealthiest of these farmers tended to live in the south and east of the island and their occupation consisted primarily of buying and selling. Rather than being a farmer on the English style, the Irish grazier was a speculator in cattle; an important distinction as most commentators believed that this lack of a dynamic capitalist farmer class was one of the chief reasons for the backward state of agriculture. Thus much of agriculture was not labour intensive and those farmers who did invest in land generally continued to rackrent it and often lived far above their means. Most of the smaller farmers were unable to employ wage labour due to their own precarious position and their reliance on cheap family labour. In cases where labour was employed, wages were paid in land, or partly in cash. The typical small farmer usually held land from either the landlord or the middleman, rent was paid in cash, he possessed little capital and was increasingly vulnerable to disaster as the 18th century progressed (Green 1957, Crotty 1966, O'Tuathaigh 1972). In the circumstances of pre-1845 Ireland, the emergence of such a class was severely limited and this class remained weak – numerically, economically and politically.

The majority of the population consisted of either cottier tenants who rented small tracts of land or landless labourers whose plight was the most severe. These tenants and labourers plus their families lived in abject poverty,

often amid squalid conditions, and suffered from a permanent state of under-
or unemployment. Land was usually held from an agent, middleman or head
tenant; rent was paid by the sale of cash crops or pigs (periods of stress were
often marked by an upsurge in the sale of pigs) and the family's living was
provided by the subsistence crop which was, for the most part, potatoes
(O'Neill 1955, Green 1957, Crotty 1966, Beckett 1966). Cottier tenants who
had potato ground were far better off than those landless labourers who had
to rent land in conacre. The latter was a system whereby labourers rented
fertilised land, sowed the seed, tended and harvested the crop and paid the
rent in either cash or, more likely, labour service (Beames 1975). Conacre
amounted to speculation in food and if the gamble failed disaster often followed. The digest of evidence before the Devon Commission of 1845, set up
to enquire into the state of landholding, concluded that those who rented
conacre: 'if the season is good . . . derive a considerable profit; if the crop fails
he is ruined. He is in the position of a gambler who plays for a stake that he
cannot pay if he loses; and he frequently does lose, from the uncertainty of
the potato crop' (Kennedy 1847, p. 522).

The annual income of labourers was small and they depended almost
entirely upon the subsistence sector for survival. Wages were low and competition great; the Poor Enquiry Commission of 1837 concluded that there were
in Ireland about five agricultural labourers for every two on similar-sized
farms in England. The precarious and vulnerable nature of their existence was
clearly demonstrated by their yearly distress while the new potato crop was
ripening. August to September were generally referred to as the 'hungry
months'; during these months many labourers emigrated eastwards or over to
Britain while the remainder of the family often went begging. As reclamation
of marginal land or recourse to mountain sides became one way of trying to
increase the subsistence crop, more and more people began to move onto
more and more marginal land (Freeman 1957). As the 19th century progressed, the distinction between the labourers and the small farmers became more
blurred. By 1845 the Devon Commission could report that: 'the testimony
given is unfortunately too uniform in presenting the unimproved state of
extensive districts, the want of employment and the consequent hardship and
poverty under which a large proportion of the agricultural population continually labour'.

Subdivision and 'overpopulation'

Two related processes which, in the opinion of observers, prevented the
spread of capitalist farming (especially in the west and south) were those of
subdivision and 'overpopulation'. Both were cited as reasons for sustained
poverty, unemployment and unimproved methods in agriculture. Subdivision
was the only method by which newly married couples could gain access to
land and thus to survival. Prior to 1800 this process was often fostered by

absentee landlords as one of the most effective methods of increasing rent rolls.

Due to the lack of industrial employment, high prices for agricultural produce up to 1815 and the desire for readily available cash, subdivision could continue as long as the subsistence sector was undisturbed. Legislation enacted in 1793 further promoted subdivision by enfranchising all those with a freehold of 40 shillings or more; thus a landlord's political power was often based on subdivision. The evidence presented to the Devon Commission provides some interesting examples of this process; evidence was presented from one townland in Mayo which contained 239 ha, of which 168 were bogland. The approximate total of profitable land was 68 ha which was supporting 110 landholders and their families (Kennedy 1847, p. 446).

Another process which went hand in hand with subdivision was that of making the tenant responsible for improvements, either in buildings or land, and increasing rent accordingly. Such a tendency (least widespread in Ulster) prevented improvements in agriculture and promoted the generally backward state of production. In summary then, the period from 1750 to 1815 was characterised by subdivision because 'high prices for agricultural products which tended to replace pasture by tillage tended to increase the number of middlemen which lived from rents derived from land and also decreased the size of the average farm as owing to the general want of capital, it was impossible to find tenants for larger tillage farms' (O'Brien 1921, p. 44).

In these circumstances the subdivision of more and more marginal land was the only possible solution for the majority of the peasantry, a solution made possible only by reliance upon the potato. In the circumstances where the latter should be diseased or lost, disaster would be the inevitable consequence as indeed it was in 1845–8. E. R. R. Green has commented that 'The English bias in favour of large-scale capitalist farming and the belief that the natural economy of Ireland was grazing led easily to the assumption that overpopulation was the whole problem' (1957, p. 117). The overpopulation argument was used extensively within government debates and discussions on Irish policy. Those classical economists who advised the British government argued that the preconditions for economic development could only be created by the clearance of large numbers of peasants from the land and the creation of an urban proletariat. Thus Malthus argued that 'the land in Ireland is infinitely more peopled than in England and, to give full effect to the natural resources of the country, a great part of this population should be swept from the soil into large manufacturing and commercial cities' (quoted in Black 1960, p. 86).

The population of Ireland rose by 33% between 1735 and 1785 and had reached a total of 8.2 million by 1841, an increase of 105% in a century. In such circumstances the overpopulation theory seemed reasonable and formed the basis of what little government action did occur. In the public eye the Irish population was seen to be lazy and indolent, overfertile and feckless as a result of the ease of subdivision, a view which influenced many government commissions and which strengthened the tendency towards eviction and emigration after 1815. Government commissions in 1823, 1827, 1830 and 1838 all agreed that reduction of population was a precondition for economic progress. Hence the various efforts at promoting eviction and emigration which resulted in an outward movement of some 140 000 to the United States and 600 000 to Britain in 1780 to 1845 (O'Brien 1921). Given the lack of industrial employment, overpopulation theorists argued that emigration was the only viable solution.

The opinions of the overpopulation theorists did not go unopposed, by nationalist politicians, priests and some government administrators, all of whom attributed much of the distress to the lack of lucrative employment and the unequal distribution of land. They indicated that population density had only a marginal effect on poverty as Ulster, the area with the highest population density, was considered to be the most prosperous and the ideal type for British-style agriculture. Ulster's population density was 157 persons per square kilometre; one of its counties had the highest density in Ireland at 197 per square kilometre and, of the top six counties in population concentration, five were in Ulster (Freeman 1957).

While these areas of Ulster were the most densely settled they were also the areas least affected by the starvation. To those who opposed the overpopulation theorists, the solution to the problem lay in bettering the condition of the mass of people through providing continuous employment. Others pointed to the fact that in the distressed circumstances of the period after 1815 reliance on family labour became vital and that therefore population growth was highest amongst the poorest classes. The evidence presented before the

Table 6.1 Estimates of the Irish population in the 18th and 19 centuries.

Year	Population	Source
1767	2 544 276	hearth money collectors
1778	3 000 000	Young's *Tour in Ireland*, vol. II
1785	2 845 932	hearth money collectors
1790	3 750 344	Beaufort 1792
1804	5 400 000	census commissioners 1821
1813	5 937 856	incomplete census
1831	7 767 401	census
1841	8 175 124	census

Source: Freeman, (1957, p. 15).

Table 6.2 Rural population densities in Ireland, 1841.

Province	Population/km^2
Leinster	95
Munster	128
Connacht	149
Ulster	157

Source: Freeman (1957, p. 34).

Devon Commission supported much of this view. A landlord argued that while 'in the south and west of Ireland immense poverty and suffering occur in connection with dense population and minute subdivision of land, but do not occur in the parts of Ulster I have referred to, connected with a very high degree of peasant prosperity and the absence of pauperism' (quoted in O'Brien 1921, p. 69).

Much of the evidence presented at the commission was supported by the economists J. S. Mill and R. Kane. Even the British Prime Minister stated in the House of Commons in January 1847 that 'if a good agricultural system was introduced into Ireland; if there was good security for the investment of money in land; if the proprietors themselves would undertake the task of improving the country, and if other classes would co-operate with them – I say I do not think the present population of Ireland is excessive' (quoted in Black 1960, p. 125). Yet despite such influential opinions, few economists and politicians recognised the fact that structural change in Irish agriculture was necessary but instead continued to argue that the problem would be solved by eviction and emigration.

By the beginning of the 19th century the regional pattern of development had become firmly established and the area which would feature most prominently in the starvation was clearly distinguishable. In Ulster small farms predominated with supplementary income often provided by spinning and weaving. In the midlands, east Munster and parts of east Connacht there were many large holdings, commercially farmed and containing a high proportion of cottiers and landless labourers. While the eastern areas contained many pockets of small holdings, they were nonetheless the most commercially integrated area and they contained a high percentage of the largest farms. However, the condition of large parts of the western seaboard had become a matter of serious concern; subdivision, on a very minute scale, was normal (often on the most marginal of land) as also was widespread (un)underemployment and poverty. It was this area which was hardest hit by the events of the period from 1800 to 1850.

Ireland 1815–45

The capitalist sector of Irish agriculture experienced a boom period up to 1815; fuelled to a large extent by the industrial revolution in Britain, the Napoleonic wars in Europe and bounties on grain in Ireland. Alongside political factors (such as the 1793 enfranchisement of 40 shilling freeholders), these forces tended to increase the value of land, contributed to subdivision and to increased reliance on the potato. During this period livestock and agricultural exports increased, the provision trade expanded, and increased investment in land occurred. Such investment tended to push up rents, forced more people on to more marginal land and helped to increase eviction and emigration (O'Brien 1921, Cullen 1972, Donnelly 1975). Duffy has indicated that in many cases it was the poorer land that experienced most subdivision and mismanagement as absenteeism tended to be highest there (1977, pp. 14–15).

The delicate balance between the export cash-crop sector and the subsistence sector was disastrously affected by the ending of the Napoleonic wars in 1815, the triumph of free trade in England in 1846 and the depression that followed. Between 1815 and 1820 the volume of exports rose by 10%, yet the total value fell; grain prices fell by 50% between 1818 and 1820 (Cullen 1972, p. 101). By 1800 much of the plantation trade was in the hands of North American traders, while Irish traders also lost the West Indian trade. Irish producers were now almost totally dependent on the English market which accounted for almost 80–85% of Irish exports by 1800 (Cullen 1968, p. 48). In such circumstances any crisis or depression in England (such as occurred between 1820 and 1840) would have widespread repercussions in Ireland.

The English market for Irish agricultural goods was no longer assured as grain was increasingly imported from Europe. The value of Irish exports continued to fall in the 1830s; more and more land was converted to tillage, and landlords desperately attempted to expand capitalist style agriculture through better management of estates and the clearance of peasants from the land. Enclosure, eviction and emigration became the chief solutions. The ranks of the unemployed rural proletariat were further swelled by the return of ex-soldiers after 1815. Yet more marginal land was occupied, begging increased rapidly and many urban areas became ghettoised.

Table 6.3   Value of Irish exports and imports, 1700–1816.

Year	Exports	Imports
1700	814 746	792 473
1720	1 038 382	891 678
1740	1 259 853	849 678
1760	2 139 388	1 647 592
1780	3 012 179	2 127 579
1801	3 714 779	5 584 599
1811	6 099 337	6 564 578
1816	7 076 123	6 106 878

Source: Cullen (1972, p. 54).

Table 6.4   Wheat and flour exported to Great Britain, 1800–42.

Year	hl	Year	hl
1800	2 178	1825	1 151 547
1805	244 509	1830	1 540 319
1810	367 513	1835	1 924 323
1815	551 159	1840	507 236
1820	1 173 033		

Source: O'Brien (1921, p. 99).

Table 6.5   Oats and oatmeal exported to Great Britain, 1800–42.

Year	hl	Year	hl
1800	7011	1825	4 739 321
1805	591 168	1830	4 278 130
1810	1 432 800	1835	5 300 271
1815	1 737 528	1840	5 925 655
1820	2 664 289		

Source: O'Brien (1921, p. 101).

Throughout this period the British government and the Irish administration considered various methods by which the 'excess' population could be decreased. Public works, reclamation, assisted emigration and the introduction of a Poor Law (1838) were all expedients adopted to help the spread of capitalist farming. At no stage did the government or its economic advisers (e.g. Nassau Senior) believe that structural change in property relations was necessary; all agreed (with the notable exception of J. S. Mill) that the rights of private property were inviolate and this view was to persist throughout the starvation. In short the tenantry had now become a liability to the landlords, a situation exacerbated by Catholic emancipation, achieved in 1829 at the expense of the 40 shilling freeholders. Shorter leases became the norm as more and more tenants competed with each other to pay higher and higher rents. Those who suffered most were the cottier tenants and the landless labourers who had previously paid little cash rent and who now relied solely on the potato. By 1830 a select committee report declared over one-third of the population to be unemployed, the 'poor houses' were full and the future appeared to be extremely bleak.

The depressed and precarious state of agriculture immediately prior to 1845 was paralleled, to a significant degree, in industry. The Act of Union of 1800 opened Ireland to the impact of full competition with the more advanced factory-based system of industrial Britain. Given the increased rate of concentration and centralisation within British industry, and given the history of mercantilism in Ireland, it was inevitable that Irish industry would find it difficult to compete.

With the important exception of northeastern Ireland, most domestic or small-scale industries experienced a decline. Cotton went into depression in 1825, linen did not revive until after 1830 and was increasingly regionally concentrated in the north-east and adjacent areas while wool manufacturing declined considerably also. Textile production in the south declined to one-eighth of its previous volume; many mills went bankrupt and only in the north-east was the transition back to linen successful. The industrial crisis of Ireland prior to 1845 was, as Cullen notes, 'due more to the impact on the Irish economy at large of sharp recession in England than to any other factor' (1972, p. 107). The subsequent dislocation and distress ensured that Irish industry would be wholly incapable of absorbing surplus agricultural population which, in turn, left those who could not emigrate totally dependent on the subsistence sector. The regional impact of such distress is noted by Cullen, 'In the poor districts of the north west and west and in the peninsular regions of the south west, . . . whole districts barely subsisted or were reduced to that condition by the decay of the textile industry' (1972, p. 117). While more and more people became dependent upon the potato, the crop itself became less reliable. Due to pressure of cultivation on more marginal land and to the decreasing size of subsistence plots, the varieties of potato used declined in quality. The better 'minnion' and 'cup' varieties were replaced by the more prolific coarse 'lumper'. The last type did not keep well and usually went bad in August. The combination of all the processes operating in the period from the beginning of the 19th century are neatly summarised by E. R. R. Green: 'The proportion of the population of Ireland dependent on the potato had increased steadily, not only under the pressure of an overgrowing population but by high rents, fluctuating prices, collapse of the domestic system of industry, the gradual decline of tillage among big farmers and the adoption of improved implements, all of which reduced employment' (1957, p. 122).

The Great Starvation 1845–8

The potato blight caused by the fungus *Phytophthora infestans* first appeared in September 1845 in Ireland. Prior to that date it had been recorded in continental Europe and in England, including the Isle of Wight. Immediately those who understood that the blight would hit Ireland were aware of the disastrous consequences that would follow in its wake. In announcing the blight in a delayed edition, the *Gardener's Chronicle* stated on 13 September 1845 'We stop the press with very great regret to announce that the potato murrain has unequivocally declared itself in Ireland. The crops about Dublin are suddenly perishing . . . Where will Ireland be in the event of a universal rot'.

The initial and subsequent reports on the disease were played down by the British government, who maintained that reports from Ireland were usually exaggerated, and local landlords, lest they be forced to pay the cost of relief. The full extent of the disaster was revealed when the potatoes were dug from the ground and rotted within a few days. Anticipating the calamity that would result, the Home Secretary, Sir James Graham, advised the British government to act quickly to set up relief committees, to organise public works and to import food for distribution (O'Brien 1921, Edwards & Williams 1957, Woodham Smith 1962). The reaction of the British government was severely hindered by a rigid adherence to the economic doctrine of free trade and to the rights of private property. Throughout the entire period of the starvation numerous observers pleaded with the government to ban the export of food (an expedient adopted in continental Europe during these years), to open the ports, to create and stock food depots, and to provide free food for the starving and always the answer was hedged by comments on the need to avoid interrupting normal trading patterns and profit making. Medical officers, relief officers, relief committees and, eventually, all those directly concerned were prevented from dealing effectively with the situation due to the over-whelming dominance of this philosophy. As *The Times* (London) commented on 26 June 1845, 'They are suffering a real though artificial famine. Nature does her duty; the land is fruitful enough, nor can it be fairly said that man is wanting. The Irishman is disposed to work, in fact man and nature together do produce abundantly. The island is full and overflowing with human food. But something ever intervenes between the hungry mouth and the ample banquet'.

Tables 6.6 and 6.7 attest to the fact that during the starvation food con-tinued to be exported from Ireland. Various people, from ships captains and government officers to nationalist politicians and religious groups, all unre-servedly condemned this situation. Debate has occurred as to whether suffi-cient food was available to feed all those in distress. O'Neill (1952) concludes that sufficient would have been available for 1845, but that after that date planting was affected and thus agriculture became more deficient. However, the export/import system was totally illogical with wheat, barley, oats, wheatmeal flour, barley meal and oatmeal all being both imported and exported throughout the period 1845–8 (O'Neill 1952, p. 106).

The major point of interest here is that despite this situation the govern-ment refused to act, the later Prime Minister, Russell, informed electors in London in 1845 that 'We ought to abstain from all interference with the supply of food. Neither a government nor a legislature can ever regulate the corn market with the beneficial effects which the entire freedom of sale and purchase are sure of themselves to produce' (O'Neill 1952, p. 103).

Table 6.6   Exports of provisions from Ireland to England, 1842–5.

Year	Wheat (hl)	Barley (hl)	Oats (hl)	Wheatmeal (hl)	Oatmeal (hl)
1842	326 242	146 225	3 705 506	913 959	4 510 523
1843	559 688	321 165	4 542 000	2 074 619	4 962 560
1844	582 366	263 611	4 390 424	2 441 306	3 346 826
1845	1 083 798	270 706	4 885 009	4 136 016	3 079 915

Source: evidence presented by Daniel O'Connell in British House of Commons, from Foster (1846, p. 615).

Table 6.7   Exports of livestock from Ireland, 1847–50.

Year ending 5 January	Oxen, bulls and cows	Calves	Swine	Sheep
1847	186 438	6363	480 827	259 257
1848	189 960	9992	106 407	324 179
1849	196 042	7086	170 787	255 628
1850	201 811	9831	68 053	241 061

Source: O'Brien (1921, p. 373).

The Great Starvation and the period immediately following it represented in condensed form the results of processes that would otherwise have taken decades to reach final conclusion. Ireland has yet to recover fully from the loss of one-half of its population between 1821 and 1881, the majority of that loss occurring in the period 1841–51. Deaths from starvation, pestilence, cholera, dysentery and losses from emigration reached huge figures. An estimated 250 000 died from pestilence, 99 000 from dysentery, 30 156 from cholera and 87 800 emigrated between 1845 and 1848. A further 6100 died en route to Canada and the United States, 4100 on arrival and an estimated 1900 shortly afterwards (O'Brien 1921, pp. 240–6). Given such figures it is inevitable that the starvation should haunt Irish economic, social and political life for the next five decades. The horrors of the period were ingrained upon the minds of the peasantry and much of the consequent hostility towards England originated in the apparent callous disregard exhibited by the administration. For sheer scale and horror the Great Starvation ranks alongside other infamous episodes of empire, i.e. the treatment of the indigenous peoples in North and South America, Africa and India. It also shares many parallels with similar 'famines' in the underdeveloped countries and continents today.

When extensive starvation began to manifest itself in 1846, it was estimated that one-half of the population was directly dependent on the potato. Under the Peel administration (up to 1846), the majority of relief was to be limited to local committees, 'poor houses', public works and an extremely limited importation of Indian corn meal. The measures had some success but made no lasting impression on the overall situation. The Poor Law system had been introduced in 1838 and was in operation over the entire country by 1843, but it was hopelessly inadequate, being able to cater for a maximum of only 100 000 persons. The reliance on local organisation of relief was inadequate in the light of landlord desires to avoid cost and also to clear land wherever possible. The administration of public works was inefficient (such was the case throughout the period) corruption was rife and the payment of money wages to those unaccustomed to it caused much confusion (O'Brien 1921, Edwards & Williams 1957, Donnelly 1975). Ignorance of Irish conditions caused British and Irish administrations to assume that, once wages were paid, food could be easily purchased; however, such was not the case as the trading and distribution system was underdeveloped due, to a large extent, to its external orientation in previous decades. The final measure adopted by the Peel administration was the importation of £100 000 worth of Indian corn meal. This requisition was kept secret for a long time; its distribution was limited to the western half of the country and its use was governed by the fact that no trading network existed which could be disrupted.

With the fall of Peel's administration, in the wake of the repeal of the Corn Laws, the administration of Russell was even more committed to a rigid adherence to the rules of orthodox economies. The government and the administration were adamant that no relief measures were to become a burden on the exchequer, that no actions taken were to interfere with normal trade and profit, and that no one was to receive aid unless destitute. The last stipulation was achieved with a vengeance in June of 1847 when the notorious Gregory clause was added which admitted to relief no-one with more than 0.1 ha. On the importation of foodstuffs Russell was adamant, 'We do not propose to interfere with the regular mode by which Indian corn and other kinds of grain may be brought into the country' (Edwards & Williams 1957, p. 223). The reason for this was clear, 'trade would be disturbed . . . supplies which are brought to us by the natural operations of commerce would be suspended . . . the intermediate traders . . . would have their business entirely deranged' (ibid.). Trevelyn, the Under-Secretary at the Exchequer, exercised a huge influence on Irish affairs and insisted that all actions should never conflict with private profit: 'The supply of the home market may safely be left to the foresight of private merchants' (ibid.). Throughout the period of distress Trevelyn instructed field officers who administered various relief measures, and who often reminded the administration that the measures adopted were hopelessly inadequate, not to interfere with the continuing exports of food, and that all sales of imported corn meal were to realise 15% profit, considered to be the national average. What this meant in reality was that corn meal which was normally bought at £13 a tonne was sold for £19 (ibid., p. 225). The government agreed that relief depots would only be opened where merchants did not operate effectively; sales of meal would only be sanctioned when all local supplies ran out. Again, public works were limited in scope, corruption was rampant and many clerks of works took the opportunity to advance loans at exorbitant interest rates, as also did many merchants. In October of 1846 the total number of people employed on public works reached 250 000, yet by spring 1847 the figure was 720 000. Many private charities did significant work through soup kitchens (later adopted by the government), medical assistance and food distribution. By August of 1847 over 3 million people were receiving rations at government soup kitchens and yet exports from the island still continued.

The export of food from the country at this time, and the regulations governing relief, provided stark evidence of the British government's adherence to an economic doctrine of free trade despite the cost to such areas as Ireland. At the conclusion of an inquest in Lismore (Co. Waterford), the jury, in returning a verdict that 'death was caused through the negligence of the government in not sending food into the country in due time', was echoing the sentiments of many Irish people at the time. It was inevitable, given the political climate of Ireland and the control wielded by the national bourgeoisie over the peasantry, that much of the blame for the starvation would be laid on English political control of Ireland. Hence, much of the politics of 'post-famine' Ireland centred around the quest for national independence and, as a result, much of the economic aspect of the starvation was lost.

The years immediately following the period 1845–8 provided an accurate insight into the importance of the Starvation in Irish economic and social history. As we have already noted, the task of sweeping the peasantry off the land was hastened and the consolidation of farms proceeded apace. Subdivision, so very characteristic of the pre-1845 period, gave way to consolidation, and the small proprietor almost disappeared (see Table 6.9). 'The labouring class almost totally disappeared and the consolidation of land holdings which followed in the wake of the Famine signalised the passing of the small holder' (Edwards & Williams 1957, p. XIII). Much of this consolidation of land was achieved through increased evictions. O'Neill provides evidence of clearances in Tipperary, Clare and Roscommon, and estimates that between 1849–51 a total of 50 000 families were evicted. He also notes that there were 275 000 fewer families in rural Ireland in 1851 than in 1841 (1955, p. 163). Furthermore, Strauss notes that, after the starvation, 'Of 32,610 landed proprietors, just over $\frac{1}{2}$ (18,100) held a mere 474,000 acres [191 827 ha] or 2.3%, a further $\frac{1}{4}$ (8,010) held 1,956,000 acres [791 593 ha] (9.7%) and the remaining 6,500 landowners held 17,720,000 acres [7 171 284 ha] (88%) with estates averaging 2,726 acres [1103 ha]' (1951, p. 137). This consolidation of land also meant that the decline experienced in tillage prior to 1845 continued unabated into the 1870s. Cullen estimates that the volume of arable land fell from 1.7 million ha in 1855 to 1.5 million in 1864 and further still to 1.3 million in 1870 (1972, p. 137).

The Starvation had momentous effects on the structure of Irish society as the trend towards early marriage was reversed. Emigration tended to remove the most able members of the community and there were a disproportionate number of old and young people in the population structure. Emigration now took on a systematic aspect, for the first time in areas of the south and

Table 6.8 Irish emigration figures for period 1845–1900.

Year	Emigrants	Year	Emigrants
1845	61 242	1851–60	1 163 418
1846	105 955	1861–70	849 836
1847	210 000	1871–80	623 933
1848	178 159	1881–90	770 706
1850	209 054	1891–00	433 526
1851	249 721		

Source: Cullen (1972, pp. 134–5) and O'Brien (1921, p. 240).

Table 6.9 Number of agricultural holdings in Ireland in the period 1841–71.

Year	Land under	Hectares			
		0.4–2.0	2.0–6.0	6.0–12.1	over 12.1
1841	135 314	310 436	252 799	79 342	48 625
1851	37 728	88 082	191 854	141 311	149 090
1861	40 080	85 469	183 931	141 251	157 833
1871	112 787	74 809	171 383	138 467	159 303

Source: Pomfret (1930, p. 42).

Table 6.10 Rate of population decline in Ireland 1841–81.

Year	Leinster	Munster	Ulster	Connacht	Ireland
1841–51	15.3	22.5	15.7	28.8	19.9
1851–61	12.9	18.5	4.8	9.6	11.5
1861–71	8.1	7.9	4.2	7.3	6.7
1871–81	4.5	4.5	4.9	2.9	4.4

Source: Lee (1973, p. 2).

west; the annual outflow reached a figure of 200 000 and represented 'something which was more a headlong scramble from a stricken area, more a flight of refugees than an emigration' (Edwards & Williams 1957, p. 321). Another major impact of the starvation was felt in the numbers of Irish language speakers in the country. Prior to 1845 the number had been increasing due to population growth, and since their representation was highest amongst the poorer classes, their numbers declined rapidly. Those who emigrated had to adopt English in order to survive, while at home the percentage of Irish speakers had declined to 25% by 1851 (O'Tuathaigh 1972, p. 158).

The pressure for national independence received further impetus from the events of 1845–8. Thus, in the Young Irelanders movement, a struggle occurred between the reformist elements and those advocating armed insurrection; the latter group carried the issue and an abortive rebellion was attempted in 1848. Throughout the remainder of the 19th century the focus of political action remained upon the national question and thus many of the economic and social aspects of underdevelopment remained neglected. However, local reaction to economic ills were expressed through increased agrarian crime, attacks upon landlords or their livestock and farms. Still, throughout the century much energy was diverted into the struggle for survival as starvation still threatened again in the 1860s and 70s (O'Neill 1955). It was not until well into the 20th century that many of the social and economic legacies of the starvation period were overcome.

Conclusion

This chapter has attempted to analyse the economic, social and political roots of the Great Starvation in Ireland. I have argued that throughout the 18th and early 19th centuries, the peasantry experienced intensive marginalisation, both economically and politically; Irish industry was stunted and warped in its development by consecutive policies of mercantilism and free trade; agriculture was export-cash-crop oriented and was both inefficient and unreflective of local or national needs. The development of capitalism in the Irish countryside was dependent on the conservation of the subsistence sector to support the majority of the population. This specific articulation within the Irish economy was the result of the uneven manner in which pre-capitalist Ireland was integrated into British industrial society. As has already been noted, this conclusion is clearly consistent with the results of research into similar catastrophies in many Third World countries today. Apart from its immediate and horrific impact, the central importance of the Great Starvation in Irish history was that it threw into stark relief the reality of the political economy of underdevelopment in a peripheral colonial society.

Acknowledgements

The author gratefully acknowledges the help of Hilda Maguire in commenting on an earlier draft of this paper.

References

Anderson, P. 1974. *Lineages of the absolutist state*. London: New Left Books.
Beames, M. 1975. Cottiers and conacre in pre-famine Ireland. *J. Peasant Studs* **82**, no. 3, 352–4.
Beckett, J. C. 1966. *The making of modern Ireland 1603–1923*. London: Faber & Faber.
Black, R. D. C. 1960. *Economic thought and the Irish question 1817–'70*. Cambridge: Cambridge University Press.
Bottigheimer, K. 1971. *English money and Irish land*. Oxford: Oxford University Press.
Butler, W. F. 1917. *Confiscation in Irish history*. Dublin: Talbot Press.
Clarke, A. 1976. *Pacification, plantation and the catholic question 1603–'23* (with R. Dudley Edwards). In Moody *et al.* (1976, pp. 187–231).
Connolly, J. 1910. *Labour in Irish history*. Dublin.
Crotty, R. 1966. *Irish agriculture production; its volume and structure*. Cork: Cork University Press.
Cullen, L. M. 1968. *Anglo-Irish trade, 1660–1800*. Manchester: Manchester University Press.
Cullen, L. M. (ed.) 1969. *The formation of the Irish economy*. Cork: Mercier Press.
Cullen, L. M. 1972. *An economic history of Ireland since 1660*. London: Batsford.
Dobb, M. 1947. *Studies in the development of capitalism*. New York: International.
Donnelly, J. S. Jr, 1975. *The land and people of nineteenth-century Cork*. London: Routledge & Kegan Paul.
Duffy, P. 1977. Irish landholding structures and population in the mid-nineteenth century. *Maynooth Review* **3**, (2), 3–27.
Edwards, R. D. and T. D. Williams 1957. *The Great Famine, studies in Irish history 1845–52*. New York: University Press.
Foster, T. C. 1846. *Letters on the condition of the People of Ireland as published in London Times*. London: Chapman and Hall.
Freeman, T. W. 1957. *Pre-famine Ireland*. Manchester: Manchester University Press.
Froude, J. A. 1872–4. *The English in Ireland in the eighteenth century*. vols. I & II. London: Green.
Gibbon, P. 1975. Colonialism and the Great Starvation in Ireland, 1845–9. Race and Class part 2, 131–9.
Gill, C. 1925. *The rise of the Irish linen industry*. Oxford: Oxford University Press.
Green, E. R. R. 1949. *The Lagan Valley 1800–1850*. London.
Green, E. R. R. 1957. Agriculture. In Edwards and Williams (1957).

Green, E. R. R. 1969. Industrial decline in the nineteenth century. In Cullen (1969, pp. 89–100).

Hill, C. 1961. *The century of revolution 1603–1714*. London: Nelson.

Hill, C. 1967. *Reformation to industrial revolution*. London: Weidenfeld & Nicolson.

Hilton, R. (ed.) 1976. *The transition from feudalism to capitalism*. London: New Left Books.

Hobsbawm, E. 1961. *The age of revolution*. London: Weidenfeld & Nicolson.

James, R. G. 1972. *Ireland in the empire 1688–1770*. Cambridge, Mass.: Harvard University Press.

Kay, G. 1975. *Development and underdevelopment: a Marxist analysis*. London: Macmillan.

Kearney, H. R. 1958. Mercantilism and Ireland 1620–40. In Williams (1958).

Kennedy, J. (ed.) 1847. *Digest of evidence taken before her Majesty's Commissioners of enquiry into the state of the Law and practice in respect to the occupation of land in Ireland*. Dublin: Hodges & Smith.

Lee, J. 1969. *Capital in the Irish economy*. In Cullen (1969, pp. 53–64).

Lee, J. 1973. *The Modernisation of Irish society, 1848–1918*. Dublin: Gill & MacMillan.

MacCurtain, M. 1972. *Tudor and Stuart Ireland*. Dublin: Gill & MacMillan.

Magdoff, H. 1978. *Imperialism: from the colonial age to the present*. New York: Monthly Review Press.

Malcomson, A. P. W. 1974. Absenteeism in eighteenth century Ireland. *Irish economic and social history* no. 1.

Marx, K. (ed.) 1970. *Capital*, vol. 1. Moscow: Progress.

Maxwell, C. 1954. *The stranger in Ireland*. London: Jonathan Cape.

Mitchell, F. 1976. *The Irish landscape*. London: Collins.

Moody, T. W., F. X. Martin and F. J. Byrne (eds) 1976. *A new history of Ireland*, vol. III. Oxford: Clarendon Press.

Murray, A. E. 1907. *Commercial relations between England and Ireland*. London: King.

Nicholls, K. 1972. *Gaelic and Gaelicised Ireland in the Middle Ages*. Dublin: Gill & MacMillan.

O'Brien, G. 1918. *Economic history of Ireland in the eighteenth century*. Dublin: Maunsel.

O'Brien, G. 1919. *Economic history of Ireland in the seventeenth century*. Dublin: Maunsel.

O'Brien, G. 1921. *Economic history of Ireland from the Union to the Famine*. London: Longmans.

O'Neill, T. P. 1952. Food problems during the Great Famine years. *J. R. Soc. Antiquaries of Ireland* **LXXII**, part II, 99–108.

O'Neill, T. P. 1955. The Irish land question, 1830–50. *Studies* **XLIV**, Autumn, 325–36.

O'Tuathaigh, G. 1972. *Ireland before the Famine, 1798–1848*. Dublin: Gill & MacMillan.

Pomfret, J. 1930. *The struggle for land in Ireland*. Princeton, NJ: Princeton University Press.

Rabb, T. K. 1967. *Enterprise and empire: merchant and gentry investment in the expansion of England 1575–1630*. Cambridge, Mass.: Harvard University Press.

Simms, L. G. 1956. *The Williamite confiscation in Ireland 1690–1703*. London: Faber & Faber.

Smyth, J. 1974. The changing nature of imperialism in Ireland. *Bull. Conf. Social. Econs*, Spring, II, 61–84.

Strauss, E. 1951. *Irish nationalism and British democracy*. London: Methuen.

Taylor, A. J. P. 1978. When the bobbins stopped. *Observer Review*, Sunday 9 April.

Tigar, M. and M. Levy 1977. *Law and the rise of capitalism*. New York: Monthly Review Press.
Vérrière, J. 1979. *La Population de l'Irlande*. Paris: Mouton.
Williams, T. D. 1958. *Historical studies*. London: Bowes & Bowes.
Woodham Smith, C. 1962. *The great hunger*. London: Hamish Hamilton.

Part II

HAZARDS IN CONTEXT:
problems of agricultural development and food security

7 Interpreting the role of hazards in agriculture

KENNETH HEWITT

The previous chapters have been concerned with the interpretation of individual disasters or sets of disasters. What they show is that, even in sudden calamities, prior human circumstances rather than a chance natural extreme carry the larger burden of responsibility for disaster. They show governments and scholars responding to these disasters vigorously. But if our authors have identified the problem properly, if the main purpose is to bring aid to the needy, then those responses are often inadequate and they even make matters worse. Moreover, the failings seem to flow from politicoeconomic, agency-centred or ethnocentric preoccupations tangential to the disaster and its victims' needs. Whether or not that is a deliberate moral or technical choice, or merely a 'side-effect' of the institutional arrangements and predicaments of the actors involved, is a large question. Its implications for research, however, seem rooted in what I described above as 'the dominant consensus' concerning disaster (see Ch. 1).

Yet, if the study of disaster is the acid test of the adequacy of the dominant view, the identifying of natural hazards by the natural processes that initiate damages has itself proven a coercive approach. It can lead even those with social-science concerns back into a geophysically centred style of discussion.

If sociocultural conditions are so important; *if* there are decisive continuities between ongoing and crisis situations; *if* institutional response to disaster must always be consciously measured against institutional priorities, preoccupations and ideology; *then* a focus upon the occurrences and dimensions of an objective damaging 'agent' may well make us miss the point. If 'risk' itself is the issue, presumably the *range of risks* for community or institution should be the context for evaluating any one risk. However, that brings one up against the evidence that people and institutions differ widely in what are for them (or what they recognise as) risks. In other words, risks are highly differentiated socially, and from place to place and time to time. Nearly all circumstances that appear as risks also have a beneficial component for some people all of the time and for most of us some of the time. This is obvious in the case of streamflow, rainfall or snow-on-the-ground. They involve 'benefits' and 'risks' (see Whyte & Burton 1980). However, society itself differentiates these risks and benefits by its behaviour, organisation and expectations. In particular, civil societies have long practised the deliberate arts of redistributing risk from one area, group or project to another. Businesses pass on commercial risks to consumers; from one group of consumers to another; from individuals to groups or governments and so on. The dominant view evidently proceeds from the assumption that society has *not* done that with natural hazards. They are treated as random misfortunes that may strike anywhere, albeit dependent in a probabilistic way upon the frequency of natural events, relative numbers and level of advancement of human 'targets' and their location relative to 'high hazard' geophysical features (Burton *et al.* 1978). But is this entirely so. If it is not, then that would indeed be a sense in which these are 'unnatural hazards' (see Chs 13 & 14).

One simple strategy for changing our perspective is to consider natural hazards in the context of particular sectors of economic life. An area in which that is far from being 'academic' is agricultural development and food security. Scarcity and famine here, crop loss and glut, have long been identified with the vagaries of weather and climate in particular. Drought is the most widely found accompaniment of famine. Debates about climatic change and food supply are a current vogue of 'doomsday' climatology and its critics (Schneider 1976, Bryson & Murray 1977).

The chapters in Part II present a spectrum of studies of hazards in the context of agriculture and food supply. They are, in many ways, 'low key' studies of a more traditional sort that geographers carry out. They discuss crop hazards at various levels of severity, rather than individual major disasters. They look at particular geographical areas of various sizes, drawing upon a range of data from personal field work to government statistics. And yet they are an essential complement to the message of the more frankly discursive or conceptual chapters.

Most chapters involve the role of the atmospheric environment. Nevertheless, the concerns developed in the bulk of the literature on agro-climate or climate and food supply, are not so central here. There is little about climatic 'cycles' or the threat of climatic changes *per se*. In fact, we have little to say about the meteorological features of storms, droughts and so forth. We do not add to models and speculations concerning supposed warming or cooling trends or, for example, the possible consequence of CO_2 build-up in the atmosphere. Nor is there discussion of the 'population–food equation' in global terms. Again I believe these to represent a limited and partial if 'dominant' perspective on our problem. In monopolising commentary and public awareness that again has produced a distorted view, reflecting the placement of the problem in a technocratically convenient light.

The material used in these chapters is not in itself unusual. Much of it is derived from sources tailored to the dominant consensus. Yet the message that emerges is different. It shows the form and degree of risks to depend integrally upon the sociocultural contexts involved, the ongoing systems of occupancy of the habitat and especially the wider economic and political forces to which their agricultural efforts are subject. From a tiny settlement of Mennonite farmers in Paraguay, to the Soviet Union and multinational contexts of the grain trade, human initiatives are shown to govern exactly those aspects of agriculture that prefigure climatic risks. But we also see another widespread feature. Whether in Belize or India or Canada the conditions, goals, ideas behind these globally felt initiatives develop outside, and often with small regard for, the predicament of the farming community itself, or those whose food needs are the greatest.

Actually, it is the need for sustained discussion of climatic hazards *in relation* to agricultural development and food security that must be emphasised. Of themselves, the agricultural issues we raise are well known in studies of agricultural development (or 'underdevelopment'). But there, we find little concern over the problem of natural hazards. With rare exceptions there is a comfortable assumption that crop losses lie in a different arena from the development of a rational agriculture. Here, as elsewhere, economic development has tended to ignore the adage about 'planning for the worst and hoping for the best'. It is literally sold as planning for 'the best' while ignoring 'the worst'. Yet most of the chapters in this book demonstrate the essential interdependence of the state or style of agriculture and the risks from natural events.

By way of introduction again, I shall stand back from the details of particular cases and ask about the problems of climatic hazards in agriculture generally, sketching some of the background to a socio-cultural and geographical perspective on them.

Agricultural losses

Some sense of the scope of the problem as it is commonly described can be derived from annual reports of the UN Food and Agriculture Organisation (Table 7.1). Every year, serious losses or exceptional harvests are attributed to weather variations. A broad range of weather phenomena is involved as damages are reported from virtually all climates where agriculture is practised (Table 7.2). Nor do the failures seem peculiar to one or two types of agriculture. Severe problems occur in socialist as well as capitalist agriculture; in industrialised, affluent areas and impoverished ones; and, for that matter, in theocratic as well as secular states.

In the perspectives of human geography or anthropology it would be quite mistaken to assume automatically that these many separate events belong in every sense to a single coherent set. They represent the classifying of events by cause and consequence in the context of the official compilation of agricultural statistics. Even were officials of the respective countries equally in touch or reliable about events on the ground, the exact nature of 'wind damage' or 'drought loss' is ambiguous even on purely biophysical grounds. More importantly, the meanings or implications of these damaging events differ greatly as a function of the state of a given agriculture: its social, economic, technological and environmental contexts. It is with these issues, as they bear upon the interpretation of risk and responsibility for damages – but also in relation to who eats and who does not – that we are concerned here. And that requires us

Table 7.1 Natural short-term events affecting food and other agricultural products, 1962–75.

Year	Agent	Location	Effect
1962–3	drought, excessive rain	western Europe	15% decline in wheat production
	cold spell, frosts	eastern Europe	wheat and barley crop destroyed in Ukraine
1963	frost	Brazil	5% decline in coffee production
	drought	South Africa	maize production down 20%
	flood	China	prevents expansion of cotton hectareage
	9-month drought	China	rice crop down from 80.6 million tonnes to 78.4 million
	floods	China	cotton crop affected
	bad weather and flooding	Afghanistan, Iraq, Jordan and Syria	grain production reduced
1963–4	severe winter and spring frosts	USSR	hampered sowing of wheat and barley
	drought	USSR Siberia and Kazakhstan	wheat production deliveries down 21%
	unfavourable weather	USSR	forage crop poor and resulted in decreased milk production
	adverse weather	eastern Europe	agricultural production down
	severe frost	North America, Florida	citrus fruit crop declined
	wet, cold spring weather	Japan	sharp fall in barley harvest
	drought	South Africa	maize production 20% less than the year before
1965	bad weather	western Europe	projected increases in agricultural production not realised
	excessive rain	Europe	reduced winter wheat plantings
	drought	Far East	wheat crops in India and Pakistan decline by 5%
	excessive rain	United States	decline in wheat production by 7%
	drought	north-west Africa, Near East	decline in wheat production
	drought	Argentina	wheat production fell more than 30%
	drought	China	wheat production down 7%, coarse grains 3%
	drought	eastern Europe	6% decline in agric. production
	drought	China	wheat estimated to have fallen by 7%, coarse grains by 3%
1965–6	drought	central, southern and eastern Africa	2% decline in total agric. production

Table 7.1–*continued*

Year	Agent	Location	Effect
	drought	Morocco	wheat crop estimated to be only two-thirds of previous year
	bad weather	eastern Europe	agric. production failed to increase over level of 1964–5
	adverse weather	western Europe	quality of wheat harvest adversely affected with parallel reduction of fruits and vegetables
	adverse weather	USSR and eastern Europe	crop production down with 20% reduction in USSR wheat crop
	serious drought	Australia	decline of 6% in agric. production with a 30% drop in wheat crop
	drought	Argentina	30% decrease in wheat
	failure of rains	India	total output of food grains falls from 88.4 million tonnes in 1964–5 to 75 million in 1965–6
1967	unfavourable weather	United States	cotton production fell by 20%
	bad weather	Ireland	fish catches 30% lower than previous year
	storms	western Europe	30 million m^3 of forest destroyed
	drought	southern Europe	grain crops seriously affected
	drought	south-east Australia	agric. production in Oceania fell by 11%
	drought	Cuba	sugar production declined sharply
1968	drought	Italy	1968 agric. production fell slightly short of 1967 level
	drought	eastern Europe	vegetable production fell by 10%
	cold spell, excessive rain	Central and North America	maturity and harvest of wheat affected
	drought	Latin America	national emergency in Chile, 30% increase in Peru's wheat imports
	drought, cold spell	Brazil	coffee production lowest in 12 years
	bad weather	eastern Europe	agric. output stagnated after 5 successive years of growth
	bad weather	Latin America	reduces agricultural production by 2%
1969	bad weather	North America	cotton production fell 9%
	heatwave	Poland	poor potato and sugar harvests
	bad weather	Lebanon	7% fall in total output
	excessive rain	Libya	wheat sowing operations delayed

Table 7.1–*continued*

Year	Agent	Location	Effect
	cold, dry spell	Turkey	wheat production kept below expected level
	excessive rain	West Africa	a factor in the 35% decline in agric., fishery and forestry exports
1970	drought, blight	United States	wheat output falls by 14 million tonnes
	floods	Hungary, Romania	loss of 560 000 and 300 000 ha respectively
	drought	New Zealand	agric. production unchanged, losses in dairy market products
	bad weather	western Europe	wheat production down by 5%
	bad weather	eastern Europe	combined production index fell slightly
	drought	Argentina	reduced size of wheat crop by 40%
	excessive rain	Brazil	intensified forest operations
	bad weather	West Malaysia	rubber output fails to grow despite increases in other crops
1970	Cyclone, tidal wave	East Pakistan	rice crop hit, total output fell by 10%
	drought	West Pakistan	reduced wheat production by 10%
	drought	Near East	reduction in output in Afghanistan, Iran, and Iraq; widespread crop failure and extensive livestable losses
	drought	southern Africa	livestock losses and crop failures
	drought	Australia, South Africa	world wool production remained unchanged
	Frost, drought, blight	Brazil	8% decline in world coffee production
1971	Excessive rain, hail, drought	Brazil	adversely affected potato planting
	drought, floods	Far East	adversely affected prospects for cereals and other crops
	typhoon, blight	Philippines	rice crop declines by 2%
	storms, excessive rain	East Germany	wheat and barley crops expected to be 15% lower
	adverse weather	South America	regional production of potatoes fell 16%
	blight, drought	United States	wheat and feed grain production sharply curtailed
	bad weather	Far East	output of rice in several countries declined
	drought	Afghanistan	agric. production drops

Table 7.1–*continued*

Year	Agent	Location	Effect
	bad weather	Near East	adverse effects in agric. production of several countries
	drought	Iran	heavy losses of livestock
1972	bad weather	USSR	spring wheat crop 20% below 1971 level
	cold spell, drought	USSR	a third of winter wheat crop lost
	floods	United States	cotton harvest 6% below 1971 level
	cold spell	western Europe	growth hindered, harvesting and grain quality down in varying degrees
	floods	Far East	damage in Pakistan, India, and Bangladesh where considerable areas under rice and cotton affected
	drought	Bangladesh	requires an increased allocation of scarce foreign exchange to import more food grains
	typhoon, floods	Philippines	targeted 6% growth of foodgrains not realised
	dry spell	India	foodgrains output declines by 5 million tonnes
	earthquake, drought	Nicaragua	capital destroyed, necessary to obtain food relief
	dry spell	Ecuador	coffee production drops 18%
	drought	Africa	agric. production increased only by 1%, food relief for Sahel initiated by FAO
	bad weather	United States	feed grain production falls short of previous year's level
	bad weather	Italy	soft wheat crop reduced by 15% and hard wheat 20%
	bad weather	USSR	'growing conditions worst in 100 years'
1973	drought	Africa, Sahelian zone, west Africa, eastern and southern Africa	7% below that of 1961–5
1973–4	adverse weather	Oceania	lower production of sheep
	drought	India	groundnut oil production drastically cut
	frost	Africa	coffee crop affected
	frost	Brazil	coffee crop decreased

Table 7.1–*continued*

Year	Agent	Location	Effect
	drought	Africa	cocoa bean production in the main west African producing countries was badly affected by drought
	flooding	United States	cotton crop drastically reduced by flooding in the Delta region
	floods	Bangladesh	jute crop was about 9% smaller
1974–5	drought	United States	drastic reduction in maize production
	erratic monsoon season	Bangladesh	rice crop affected
	drought	Pakistan	reduced rice yields
	adverse weather	northern and eastern Europe	decrease in sugar production
1974	Hurricane Fifi	Honduras	80% of banana crop lost
1974–5	adverse weather	Nigeria	cocoa bean crop reduced
	drought, excessive rainfall	US Texas and Cotton Belt	cotton crop down 10%

Source: FAO Annual Report, *The state of food and agriculture.*
Note: the FAO data is accepted as given although it does not always agree with some other sources. Thanks are due to Mr William S. Petti, Rutgers University, and Mr John Bowen of WLU for assistance in preparing this Table.

Table 7.2   Number of major events affecting food and other agricultural products, 1962–75.

	Oceania	Far East	Near East	Africa	Latin America	Western Europe	Eastern Europe	North America	Total
drought	5	11	5	11	11	5	3	5	56
excessive rain	0	0	1	2	2	1	2	1	12
cold spells	0	0	1	0	1	1	3	0	6
volcano	0	0	0	0	0	1	0	0	1
typhoon	0	2	0	0	0	0	0	0	2
cyclone	0	1	0	0	0	0	0	0	1
earthquake	0	0	0	0	1	0	0	0	1
frosts	0	0	0	1	4	0	1	1	7
floods	0	6	1	0	0	0	1	2	10
storms	0	0	0	0	1	1	1	0	3
heatwave	0	0	0	0	0	0	1	0	1
blight	0	1	1	0	1	0	0	2	5
tidal waves	0	1	0	0	0	0	0	0	1
hail	0	0	0	0	1	0	0	0	1
bad weather	1	3	4	1	2	5	8	3	26
total	6	26	13	15	24	15	20	16	134

Source: after FAO Annual Reports.

again to recognise the extent to which climatic risks are *not* explained by climate, or disaster by the peculiarities of calamitous events. Sorokin (1942), for example, discussing even the major calamity of famine described 'the unfavorable play of natural forces such as drought, flood, fire' as being among the 'supplementary conditions'. These may 'make real' the society's margins of safety in food or lack of them. But after extensive studies he was prepared to go no further in defining causality than to say 'mass famine' is 'chiefly the result of sociocultural circumstances, that make society unable to cope with the food problem under current conditions' (1942, p. 293). He had examined far too many cases where starvation, even during droughts or blights, was largely a socioeconomic phenomenon, whether seen in absolute food insufficiency or failure to deliver available food to the needy (cf. Regan above, Ch. 6).

In the context of more common, less catastrophic risks to agriculture, the role of the socioeconomic circumstances in which losses operate must be even more obvious. Such at least is a viewpoint to be found in much of the agricultural development literature. One of the early studies of agricultural occupancy of flood-prone areas by a geographer contains an elaborate statement of essentially this argument:

'occupance responds to a variety of conditions among which the flood hazard is not often of primary significance. In addition to external factors the total resource complex within each management unit is important . . . That the flood hazard does not dominate agricultural occupance is not the result of any lack of awareness on the part of the farmer. Rather, it is that the significance of flood hazard is conditioned in its effect by other factors . . . In consequence it is not good sense to talk of floodplain land use without reference [to these]' (Burton 1962, p. 144).

Perhaps the reason that this kind of awareness often fails to penetrate substantive research is the elementary result of the partitioning of hazards into a separate arena of isolated events, as was discussed in Chapter 1. That tends to lead to a narrow geographic analysis in two senses. First, it directs attention to the immediate processes of damage in the interaction of a damaging agent and vulnerable crop or the potential for such interaction. But secondly, even in the context of a broader risk management interest, it tends to define the problem in what one could call a 'vertical' view of man–environment or crop–climate relations. Here, interpretation turns upon the local associations of particular weather events or regional climate statistics, and a particular agricultural setting. That might be a wheat farm, a reclaimed delta, or area of marginal numbers of frost-free days. In other words the 'vertical' view confines attention to analysis, explanation, and manipulation of local biophysical and crop practice conditions.

Today, there is a good deal of fiction in discussing even the agriculture of whole nations in terms of their internal context of farming and agro-climate.

The essential context of agricultural development and the risks attending it have long been tied to more or less extensive or 'horizontal' systems of interdependency. These may be partly among complimentary and competing agricultural areas or systems, but also and increasingly between agriculture and the larger space economy. To quote Burton again: 'The day of the "isolated state" in agricultural production of any kind is over. All the world's farmers, peasants, shifting cultivators, nomads and agribusinesses have been swept and continue to be swept yet more inexorably into complex global systems of production and distribution . . .' (personal communication 1981). Not only do these arrangements link together the predicaments of people in very different hazard settings: they create networks, centres and orders of power able, say, through the extensive geographies of food economy, to shape local food risks from a distance, sometimes beneficially, often detrimentally, but never unimportantly. It is here too, however, that one must echo Susan George's complaint that all too often these developments are seen to be 'the result of nameless forces, and, so to speak, in the passive voice. Such and such happens, this or that occurs, but there are no living, visible actors on the stage' (1976, pp. 11–120). Yet there are 'actors' involved. It is rarely possible nowadays to see them as individuals. Rather they appear as the 'positions' and styles of operation of more or less large institutions and the interests they serve. Within nations, among the different institutions putting pressure upon farmers, and between states and social groups in the international system, there are considerable differences involved in power and authority over food producing and the allocation of food produced among competing demands. This is not a new development (Wallerstein 1974).

Even the geographer not willing to enter the 'politics of food' debate can find, in some of the main concerns of cultural geography, the background that reveals how inadequate is that 'vertical' or localised view of hazards. I refer to the considerable body of work discussing 'man's role in changing the face of the earth' (Thomas 1956), and in particular the whole question of the origins and dispersal of agricultural domesticates and practices (Sauer 1952). These questions are integral to the forms and development of agricultural risks, essential cultural–historical background to the more recent developments of political economy.

Background to a vulnerable agriculture

Although agricultural regions show a broad relation to climate, climate itself contains few clues as to how and why the history, the geographical spread and system features of agriculture have arisen. Today's major crops originated and were first domesticated in tiny, not to say unusual, ecological zones (Harlan 1975, Ucko & Dimbleby 1969). Nowadays, as through most of history, they yield nearly all of their product over huge, relatively diverse areas, far removed in location and climate from the hearth zones. Breeding and selection for climatic tolerance have been an essential part of this development. Even more important have been drastic modifications of newly colonised areas. Much of that effort may appear to make the immediate crop environment more closely resemble the habitats of the source regions.

Even so, most crop plants are grown well beyond their optimal habitats. They flourish only because of human assistance. Without it many would die out altogether. The survivors would be found in greatly contracted geographical areas. Here then, in the most general features of agricultural geography, one finds human history setting out the broad patterns of crop lands and their vulnerability.

The extraordinary dominance of wheat, rice, maize and potatoes in agricultural production (Harlan 1976) and the areas they involve, has far more to do with human history and institutions than superior climatic hardiness or, indeed, nutritional quality. Much the same can be said of the pre-eminence of pork, beef and poultry in meat production, or the common cow in milk products.

The remarkable spread and adoption of manioc, maize and potatoes from American sources, following the European voyages of discovery and conquest, became in due course largely a matter of feeding colonial and other dependent impoverished populations with cheap uniform bulk diets – while the superior cash crops were shipped to industrial heartlands. Sometimes this was a matter of deliberate introduction. Sometimes such crops were adopted, perforce, to become the staples of peasants or slaves having to support themselves on poor or tiny areas of land. Equally important, as factors behind the adoption of such crops, was the sudden surge in numbers felt by colonial peoples under the impact of the 'imperial peace'. For along with the new demands of its rulers for land reform, commerce and taxation came the impact of modern medicine and increased, albeit still limited, ability to reallocate food in emergencies, reducing death from famine.

Wet rice cultivation in Asia has been shown to have waxed and waned with the degree of spatial extent of central control by states and empires – with a concomitant specialisation ('peasantising') or diversification ('tribalising'?) of rural economies. These sorts of historical variations have occurred in spite of, rather than because of, climatic variations. This can be seen in an interesting fashion from the exceptional data on cultivation in Japan, for example (Takahashi & Yoshino 1976, Part III).

Similar considerations apply to the development of the economies of wheat, maize, cattle and sheep in western North America, Argentina, Australasia and other areas treated as 'open lands' in the 19th century. How little this really owed to rugged individualist frontier farmers pushing back the wilderness! How much it reflected, within a general framework of colonial and mercantile expansionism, evolving strategies to feed the growing masses of urban industrialised wage-earning workers in Europe, and later, in other rapidly urbanising areas. Nor can one attribute this in any great measure to chance, or the opportunities produced by, say, 'the American environment'.

Armytage (1965), in a fascinating study, has shown how the prototypes of modern technocratic exploitation of science and discovery played a large role here. There have been many fumblings and blunders like the ill fated East African 'groundnut scheme'. In terms of the provision of new surpluses for commerce there were inordinate 'successes' too. The overall transformation of agriculture was inescapably wedded to and dependent upon the initiatives of state, imperial and private organisations investing in centrally controlled food and related trading arrangements (cf. Ch. 12). Nor was that something appearing suddenly in the 19th century, though its scale was vastly expanded. The grain trade, sugar plantations and spices had been important factors in the commercial strength and development of European states even before the era of mercantilism, or its ostensible replacement by laissez-faire capitalism and industry (Sombart 1913, Jones 1959, Craton 1974, Wallerstein 1974).

Such developments created agricultural communities – not to mention the huge numbers of people dependent upon them – that in due course also proved vulnerable to large-scale dislocation by drought, pests, crop disease and other natural hazards (Walford 1879, Woodham Smith 1962; Ch. 6). That is as much a part of the record as their clear ability, overall, to sustain large populations and agriculture-based industries.

In the case of North America the problem came to a head in the early decades of the 20th century and notably the 'Dust Bowl' years. Slowly, since then, affluent states began to accept a more general responsibility for the problem. This has taken such forms as state-supported weather insurance and price supports; huge subsidised storage facilities and such agencies as the Canadian Wheat Board, and state-financed flood and irrigation schemes. As a result, vulnerability to losses, though hardly reduced in magnitude, has been greatly reduced in severity for these nations and their farming communities, as shown in the chapter by Warrick above. But even that has only occurred in concert with, and largely because of, two other developments.

First, there is the ever more complete integration of farming with the commercial, political and life-style features of the urban–industrial majority (Johnson & Kilby 1975). Secondly, agriculture has become integrated with the corporate economy in a vertical as well as horizontal sense (Walsh 1975, Troughton 1981). That is to say, agricultural products are often part of more or less long lines and complicated networks of re-processing, allocation of by-products to food or non-food manufacturers; of techniques for preparation, preservation, packaging. These go along with an extensive redistribution in space. As one example, the industrial and commercial ramifications of maize create a system to be compared with the major metallurgical industries.

Among the results, total raw food production or capacity may be a secondary consideration, or at least one highly dependent upon others, in the measure of performance within agriculture and agribusiness. 'Planned scarcity' is but one obvious corollary of the dependence of food production upon non-farm considerations. In the past several decades North American governments have used large amounts of tax dollars to manage production, paying farmers not to grow, and ensuring land is left fallow. The quantities of food consequently not grown outstrip losses in almost all weather disasters. They are close to the requirements to wipe out global malnutrition at its current levels. At the same time, exports of foodstuffs to paying customers and the management of these exports to improve prices for home business outstrips gifts or long-term low-interest loans to help impoverished nations overcome food problems or crop failure. These matters are documented at length in George (1976, Ch. 6) and Morgan (1978, Ch. 14), who supply useful bibliographies of other sources.

Today's weather problems occur in a global food context which is only partly distinguished by the numbers of people involved and unprecedented quantities of Earth resources tied up in human economies. Also, the sorts of organisation and large-scale input of inanimate energy we associate with industrialisation have spread increasingly into crop production (Steinhart & Steinhart 1974, Ch. 6; Leach 1975, Pimentel *et al.* 1973). Except for climate, these support drastic modifications of the crop environment. The ability to achieve very large yields in good years, along with massive transportation and storage facilities, allow a substantial smoothing out of supply fluctuations in space and time. Worldwide networks of finance and trade enable particular regions to be cushioned against the problems of dearth or glut. Along with means of rapid delivery of emergency aid, such developments apparently weaken the so-called 'malthusian checks'.

On the other hand, the absolute scale and complexity of risks, and the potential scope of disaster, have expanded enormously. It seems too that in many areas survival of disaster through emergency action is traded off against ongoing chronic hunger and malnutrition. Then there is the vexed question of the risks of shifting to greater dependence upon complex human institutions that are themselves economically and politically vulnerable. Does that create new dimensions of risk from nature, given that institutions continually change policies according to their more immediate economic and political 'climate', and may fail?

Meanwhile there is a fundamental difference between the political economy of food and agribusiness in high-technology commercial contexts, and the desire to create production agriculture in the same mode, in order to feed the hungry or supply the food-poor nations directly. However, the 'green revolution' is already, in its commercial impact and its failures as well as its ability to vastly increase production, exhibiting many of the features and making the kinds of demands for economic restructuring comparable to the surplus-oriented grain monocultures already in place (Johnson 1975, Scrimshaw & Taylor 1980). The issue here is not only whether it is 'good' or 'bad', though we should think hard about that. Rather one must recognise the profound influence it has upon the development of food systems and the relative importance of various pressures or risks upon farming. It makes a mockery of any study of natural hazards that treats food production as a sort of autonomous mechanical accommodation between crop or farmer and climate.

The susceptibility of the international space economy of food to economic and political manipulation by dominant states and institutions is not the smallest factor in the geography of food scarcity and security. Weather and other losses at the production end may seem the clearest source of food shortage and indicator of the role of natural hazards. But there is a more or less large distance, organisationally as well as geographically, between production or its failures and the final consumption of food. At least half of today's world population is normally dependent upon extensive systems of food distribution. Virtually everyone is dependent upon them in food crises. As some of the later chapters show, these arrangements for the storage, processing and allocation of food are far from straightforward in their relation to need, and are not necessarily benign. What one must emphasise here, however, is that they reflect back powerfully upon agriculture. Their importance is not limited to patterns of consumption and who may go hungry. The non-farm elements of food systems have had, and increasingly are having, a profound effect upon what is grown, can be grown, where and with what risks (Schuphan 1965, Hewitt 1976). As they become more extensive and complicated these elements introduce more opportunities for the food system to be shaped by considerations other than agricultural productivity and food need. The pressures to produce cash crops for export in food-poor countries that are also poor in foreign exchange and commercial opportunities is but one example (Myers 1981).

An outstanding feature of the world scene is the vast area engaged in, or otherwise feeling the impact of, 'modernisation' programmes (Hutchinson 1972, Ch. 10; Hopper 1976, Morgan 1978, Scrimshaw & Taylor 1980). Although agriculture can nowhere be called set and unchanging, nations of the tropics and subtropics are especially engaged in transformations of their agricultural base (see Chs 5, 8, 10 & 14).

A generally valid point about hazards is that during periods of socioeconomic change and technical innovation, benefits are heavily compromised by the dislocations in well tried arrangements and the risk-prone experiments with techniques developed in other contexts. Such social and economic transformations involve a large measure of trial and error (cf. Chs 9 & 11). Even when agriculture is successfully reformed, it has commonly been to the disadvantage of some, and often greater vulnerability among people and factors not directly involved in the development (George 1976). We repeatedly encounter food shortages and misery among peoples displaced by change, among those unable to compete in the new circumstances, or otherwise off-balance in the new social and political arrangements. This is the message of our chapters on the Sahel, the New Guinea Highlands, the Bushmen and Belize (Chs 2, 3, 5, 8 & 13). It can be compounded by the ever-greater role of central governments and other institutions more or less far removed from rural peoples.

After all, much that is accepted as essential to the achievements of high-production agriculture today depends upon the ability of institutions and resources outside the producing and consuming of food to influence farming. Investment practices, the futures markets, research and education, government policies – are variously championed as the strengths of the food systems of the affluent industrial world, and the necessary instruments to improve diets elsewhere. But these items are themselves subject to fluctuating events and varying relative impacts upon agriculture. If they have any influence at all, their changes are also likely to be reflected in the conditions of risk for crop and grazing lands.

In such extensive geographies of economic, technical and political influence, even disaster can acquire an ambivalent relation to wellbeing. One man's calamity is another's 'windfall'. There is a long history of farmers bearing more of the risk of crop failure and benefiting less from good performance than other sectors. But it is also not uncommon for them to lose part of a crop to weather damage and be more than compensated by prices driven up by scarcity (Morgan 1978). In recent years North American grain producers have benefited greatly from harvest failures elsewhere, as shown by McKay (Ch. 12) and Hewitt (Ch. 10). The matter looks very different to United Nations statisticians calculating total food need. It will seem unfortunate to anyone concerned about poverty, which equates with hunger much of the time, and starvation, when food is scarce and prices rise. But then, it is far from clear that expanding agricultural production or occasions of bumper harvest do very much for these folk anyway (George 1976, Ch. 5; Eckholm 1979).

Disastrous food losses to weather are in any case not simple in relation to social conditions. Agricultural development may be harmed by damaging natural events, especially as weather is perceived as a major risk for investment. Cheap foreign grain sent to relieve hunger may actually harm development if it penalises enterprising local farmers who could have benefited from higher prices. Nor is there any lack of evidence for those who look beyond the rhetoric, indicating that food assistance, even in famine, is generally sent if and only if a political or economic advantage can be seen to flow from it (Wallenstein 1976, Rothschild 1976). But the aftermath of disaster may also provide the setting where government or the private sector can penetrate an area and bring about agricultural reforms and intensification fitting its interests, but previously resisted. This is indicated in Copans' work on the Sahel (see Ch. 5 & notes). But, as Morgan (1979) puts it 'to blame the merchants (e.g. of grain) for conditions that have promoted enormous food imports and continuing malnutrition is to miss the economic and political point, which is that commercial markets, not famines, interest merchants' (p. 446).

Of course, *not* to blame them and government agencies for promoting a very different image of the conditions of agricultural investment and food assistance would also be to 'miss the point'. However, the issue here is that since it is almost invariably only the poor and already malnourished who suffer starvation and death in drought, flood, or unseasonable frosts (Bhatia 1967, George 1976, Ch. 1); *and* since most countries with chronic malnutrition problems have not failed to raise agricultural production faster than population in recent years (United Nations 1974); we must surely look closely at the interdependence between the conditions of agricultural development and the meaning of natural hazards in food security. That is the main subject of the chapters that follow.

References

Armytage, W. H. G. 1965. *The rise of the technocrats: a social history*. London: Routledge & Kegan Paul.

Bhatia, B. M. 1967. *Famines in India, 1860–1965*, 2nd ed. New Delhi.

Bryson, R. A. and J. T. Murray 1977. *Climates of hunger: mankind and the world's changing weather*. Univ. Wisconsin, Madison.

Burton, I. 1962. *Types of agricultural occupance of flood plains in the United States*. Univ. Chicago, Dept. of Geography Res. Pap. no. 75.

Burton, J., R. Kates and G. F. White 1978. *The environment as hazard*. New York: Oxford University Press.

Craton, M. 1974. *Sinews of empire: a short history of British slavery*. New York: Anchor Books, Doubleday.

Eckholm, E. P. 1979. *The dispossessed of the Earth: land reform and sustainable development*. Worldwatch Inst. Pap. no. 30, Washington, DC.

George, S. 1976. *How the other half dies: the real reasons for world hunger*. Harmondsworth: Penguin.

Harlan, J. R. 1975. *Crops and man*. American Society of Agronomy, Madison.

Harlan, J. R. 1976. The plants and animals that nourish man. *Scient. Am.* **235**(3), 88–97.

Hewitt, K. 1976. *Lifeboat: guide to a habitable earth*. Toronto: Wiley.

Hopper, W. D. 1976. The development of agriculture in developing countries. *Scient. Am.* **235**(3), 196–205.

Hutchinson, J. B. 1972. *Farming and food supply: the interdependence of countryside and town*. New York: Cambridge University Press.

Johnson, B. F. and P. Kilby 1975. *Agriculture and structural transformations: economic strategies in late-developing countries*. New York: Oxford University Press.

Johnson, D. G. 1975. *World food problems and prospects*. Am. Enterprise Inst. for Public Policy, Foreign Affairs Study no. 20.

Johnson, K. and P. O'Keefe (eds) 1979. *Environment and development: community perspectives*. Int. Devel. Prog. monog. Clark Univ., Worcester, Mass.

Jones, W. O. 1959. *Manioc in Africa*. Stamford, California: Stamford University Press.

Leach, G. L. 1975. The energy costs of food production. In Steele and Bourne (1975, pp. 139–63).

Morgan, D. 1979. *Merchants of grain*. Harmondsworth: Penguin Books.

Myers, N. 1981. The hamburger connection: how Central America's forest became North America's hamburgers. *Ambio* **10**(1), 3–8.

Pimentel, D., L. E. Hurd, A. C. Belotti, M. J. Forster, N. A. Oka, O. D. Sholes and R. J. Whitman 1973. Food production and the energy crisis. *Science* **182**, 443–7.

Rothschild, E. 1976. Food politics. *Foreign Affairs Quarterly* **54**(2), January, 285–307.

Sauer, C. 1952. *Agricultural origins and dispersals*. American Geographical Society, New York.

Schneider, S. H. 1976. *The genesis strategy: climate and global survival*. New York: Plenum Press.

Schuphan, W. 1965. *Nutritional values in crops and plants*. London: Faber & Faber.

Scrimshaw, N. S. and L. Taylor 1980. Food. *Scient. Am.* **243**, no. 3, 78–99.

Sombart, W. 1913. *Luxury and capitalism*. (transl. W. R. Dittmar, 1938). New York: Columbia University Press.

Sorokin, P. A. 1942. *Man and society in calamity*. New York: E. P. Dutton.

Steele, F. and A. Bourne (eds) 1975. *The man-food equation*. New York: Academic Press.

Steinhart, J. S. and C. E. Steinhart 1974. *Energy: sources, use and role in human affairs*. North Scituate, Mass.: Duxbury Press.

Takahashi, K. and M. Yoshino (eds) 1976. *Int. Symp. on Recent Climatic Change and Food Production*. Univ. Tokyo.

Thomas, W. L. (ed.) 1956. *Man's role in changing the face of the Earth*. Chicago: University of Chicago Press.

Troughton, M. 1981. Industrialization of agriculture. *Proc. Geog. Inter-Univ. Resource Mgmt Sem.* (GIRMS) **11**, 74–99. Dept. of Geography, Wilfred Laurier University.

Ucko, P. J. and G. W. Dimbleby (eds) 1969. *The domestication and exploitation of plants and animals*. London: Duckworth.

United Nations 1974. *Assessment of the world food situation*. World Food Conf. E/Conf. 65/3. New York: United Nations.

Walford, C. 1879. *The famines of the world, past and present*. New York: Burt Franklin.

Wallenstein, P. 1976. Scarce goods as political weapons: the case of food. *J. Peace Res.* **13**(4).

Wallerstein, E. 1974. *The modern world system*. New York: Academic Press.

Walsh, J. 1975. US agribusiness and agricultural trends. *Science* **188**, 531–4.

Whyte, A. V. and I. Burton (eds) 1980. *Environmental risk assessment*. SCOPE Report no. 15. Chichester: Wiley.

Woodham Smith, C. B. 1962. *The great hunger: Ireland 1845–1849*. New York: Harper & Row.

8 *The place of climatic hazards in food scarcity: a case study of Belize*

JERRY A. HALL

Introduction

The society involved in the following study seems typical of areas severely constrained by unfavourable natural resources and serious environmental hazards, (hurricanes, floods, droughts, irregular onset of the rainy season etc.). Yet an analysis of the overall extent of resource development in relation to natural hazards suggests that human activity, notably the history of the colony and biased attitudes of the national government, are also to blame for the form and degree of risk. Hazards can be viewed as a function of both natural events and 'human-use systems' such that variations in either, have a potential impact on damages (Burton *et al*. 1978, p. 41). It is necessary to begin, therefore, with some cautions about the studies that have been applied to the Tropics generally and Central America in particular.

Thus, in terms of the development of agricultural resources, the world is shocked each year, or used to be shocked, by United Nations' figures on world hunger, malnutrition and starvation. Two-thirds of the world's people live in countries with national average diets that are judged as nutritionally inadequate (FAO 1977). A closer look at the distribution of hunger emphasises the fact that the diet-deficient areas are concentrated in Asia, Africa, South America, Central America and the Caribbean (Brown 1978). In other words the problem is found largely in the Tropics and Subtropics. Yet, the problem generally is not so much what tropical agriculture fails to produce, but rather *what is produced*.

The recent history of the more productive tropical agriculture has a progressively greater concentration on cash and plantation crops, neglecting the production of local staples (Thurston 1971). Agricultural research in tropical areas has been and still is predominantly directed to cash and plantation crops. Cash crops may be a source of foreign currency for the developing countries, but the production of cash crops demands a strong dependency on stable weather conditions and stable world markets. An interruption of either weather conditions or world markets reduces the acquisition of foreign capital. Also, since so few staples are produced locally, a small shift in weather conditions can initiate a large-scale disaster in the nation. Scarce foreign capital is then consumed in the emergency purchase of staples and the whole country is left poorer.

Figure 8.1   Belize study area.

Belize, a small internally self-governing colony of Britain located on the east coast of Central America, is no exception (Fig. 8.1). This micro-state of approximately 22 015 km^2 and a population estimated at 135 000 in 1980 is unique, however, in its vigorous planning for independence from Britain. Many questions arise concerning the ability to achieve independence, primarily because Belize traditionally has not been able to feed herself. Other major problems relate to a heavy dependence on a foreign-dominated cash-crop economy, a limited industrial base, and an increasing negative balance of trade.

Belize is not able to feed herself even though she has some 1 million ha of arable land lying idle. The limited development of rural land is a function of government priorities, Belize's colonial legacy and hazards in agro-climate.

Historically, the long-term developmental plans for Belize have called for greater exploitation of the forests and the increased production of foreign-dominated commercial agriculture (Thomson 1976). Recently the emphasis on timber exploitation has been reduced, and after 300 years of dependence

Table 8.1 Composition of Belizean exports, 1971–5.

	1971 $(Belize)m	%	1972 $(Belize)m	%	1973 $(Belize)m	%	1974 $(Belize)m	%	1975 $(Belize)m	%
fish	2.5	10	2.7	9	2.7	6	3.3	4	3.8	4
citrus products	3.7	15	4.0	13	4.4	10	5.4	6	5.2	5
sugar and molasses	13.2	53	17.8	57	23.0	55	58.8	71	81.7	79
wood and forest products	1.5	6	1.9	6	3.7	9	5.2	6	2.1	2
clothing	2.0	8	3.9	13	6.3	15	8.3	10	7.4	7
other	1.8	7	0.8	3	2.1	5	2.4	3	2.7	3
total	24.7	100	31.1	100	42.2	100	83.4	100	102.9	100

Source: Belize Abstract of Statistics 1975, Belmopan, Belize.

on forest exports, agricultural exports of tropical cash crops such as sugar, citrus and bananas now dominate (Table 8.1). Sugar and molasses, for example, account for over 80% of the total exports compared to 2.1% for wood products (Table 8.1).

Further evidence of the bias towards commercial crops is evident in the allocation of government grants and loans. Private and foreign investors are granted or loaned millions of dollars while it is still almost impossible for peasant farmers to gain sufficient loans to acquire their own farms and equipment. That is not to indicate that no aid is going to peasant farmers. For example, more and better trained agricultural extension officers are appearing, but the scale of aid is strongly tilted in favour of commercial cash crops.

A critical factor in increasing food production involves landownership. 3% of the population owns over 95% of the land. The majority of peasant farmers own no land at all (Krohn 1978). The bulk of the privately owned land is held by foreign owners and lies idle or is in forests. A recent land tax developed by the government to be placed on all foreign-owned land has not been applied to several of the large landowners. Peasant farmers traditionally rent a few hectares of river land or jungle and establish swidden or slash and burn economies. It is these peasant farmers who contribute the bulk of the staples for the nation.

Local production of staples

In 1975, 40% of Belize's total imports were food (Table 8.2). The dollar value of food imports has increased each year. Given Belize's deficit balance of trade, which stood at $(Belize) 62 million in 1976, the importation of food that could be produced locally absorbs precious foreign reserves that might otherwise be put to better use. Meanwhile, if the capital for staple food importation was redirected to developing peasant agriculture, there is every reason to believe Belize could become self-sufficient in food.

The reasons that self-sufficiency probably will not occur in the near future include: the government's bias towards commercial agriculture, the colonial legacy which has resulted in the lack of a viable rural agricultural society (two-thirds of the Belizian population resides in urban centres), and the extreme effects of weather variability on peasant production. Belize has no traditional agricultural society. Farming is not considered a viable occupation by the populace, and rural population density is less than one per 2.6 km^2 (Floyd 1972). The resistance to enter the farming profession in part relates to Belize's colonial legacy and in part to uncertainties associated with an unreliable agro-climate. As a result, the number of farmers producing staples is small. And each year some sector of peasant agriculture suffers crop losses and, or reduced yields because of weather hazards.

In summary then, it appears that Belize experiences the typical Third World type of food scarcity. Belize is unusual, however, in that peasant

Table 8.2 Composition of Belizean imports, 1971–5.

	1971 $(Belize)m	%	1972 $(Belize)m	%	1973 $(Belize)m	%	1974 $(Belize)m	%	1975 $(Belize)m	%
Section C – food	15.2	26	17.2	25	18.8	26	29.6	26	40.0	25
01 meat	1.9	3	2.0	3	2.2	3	2.5	2	4.4	3
02 dairy products and eggs	4.2	7	4.6	7	4.9	7	8.8	8	10.6	7
04 cereals	2.4	4	3.1	4	3.2	4	6.2	6	8.7	6
05 fruits and vegetables	1.4	2	1.3	2	1.6	2	2.0	2	4.0	3
08 animal feed	0.6	1	0.8	1	1.2	2	1.7	2	2.0	1
09 margarine and lard	1.3	2	1.8	3	1.8	2	2.8	2	3.5	2
Section I – beverages and tobacco	2.9	5	2.3	3	3.0	4	4.4	4	2.9	2
Section II – crude materials	0.3	1	0.4	1	0.6	1	1.2	1	1.0	1
Section III – mineral fuels	3.4	6	3.5	5	4.9	7	11.5	10	13.5	9
Section IV – animal and vegetable oils	0.2	—	0.1	—	0.1	—	0.2	—	0.3	—
Section V – chemicals	5.0	9	6.9	10	6.6	9	11.4	10	18.8	12
54 medical and pharmaceutical	1.1	2	1.9	3	1.5	2	2.0	2	4.1	3
55 perfumes and soaps	1.5	3	2.0	3	2.2	3	4.4	4	6.5	4
56 fertiliser	0.7	1	0.4	1	0.5	1	1.4	1	1.6	1
Section VI – manufactures	11.2	19	13.5	19	14.1	20	19.4	17	28.6	18
65 fabrics	1.4	2	1.9	3	2.5	4	5.2	5	7.5	5
Section VII – machinery and transport equipment	13.6	23	15.8	23	15.2	21	20.7	18	37.7	24
73 transport equipment	6.3	11	6.8	10	6.2	9	10.0	9	15.7	10
Section VIII – miscellaneous manufactures	6.4	11	8.9	13	8.4	12	13.7	12	14.9	9
84 clothing	1.7	3	1.3	2	1.5	2	3.9	3	1.5	1
85 footwear	0.7	1	0.9	1	0.7	1	1.1	1	1.3	1
Section IX – miscellaneous	0.5	1	0.6	1	0.5	1	0.6	1	0.4	—
total	58.6	100	69.3	100	72.3	100	112.7	100	158.0	100

Source: Belize Abstract of Statistics 1975, Belmopan, Belize.

agricultural development has been retarded while millions of arable hectares lie idle. This, and the type of agriculture that does exist, are integral to an understanding of the impact of climatic hazards.

The colonial legacy

To understand the Belizian economy, its reliance on Britain and the limited subsistence agricultural development, one must consider the country's colonial heritage. The cultural remnants of this exploitative system still linger. They serve to hinder growth and development today (Bolland 1977).

The mercantile system was colonialism's economic corollary and it functioned well from the Belize settlement's earliest days. Logwood was cut by the settlers and shipped to England in exchange for virtually all of their food and manufactured goods. Later when specialty woods like mahogany and rosewood replaced logwood as the principal export, the system remained unchanged. There was arable land, but the development of peasant agriculture was restricted. Large landowners discouraged it for fear of losing their valuable forestry labour force. The settlers, many of whom were slaves, seemed to prefer the seasonal nature of logging and there were no incentives from England to support local agrarian development (Krohn 1978).

Logwood was the only basis of British Honduras' (now Belize) settlement in the 17th and early 18th centuries. Small temporary camps first occupied the north coastal areas. Later in the 18th century small isolated camps were developed in the interior. Food stuffs and trade materials from England were traded for wood. At no time were there extensive rural settlements attendant to the log camps. Very few timber trails were blazed because the rivers acted as adequate transportation routes for logs and supplies.

The use of natural waterways actually discouraged the development of seasonal tracks and other roads. It was not until the early 1930s that major roads were constructed and even today only three main roads exist so that large parts of the country remain remote. Rivers crossed by secondary roads are forded on hand-operated ferries that cannot run during the high flood periods. Transportation is further reduced during the rainy season and after the all-too-common hurricanes, because of floods and washouts.

Development of subsistence farmers

Some peasant agriculture did indeed develop. The timber merchants had to face the problem of feeding their slaves. Labour was always in short supply, so full-time farming could not be encouraged. The nomadic conditions of the industry and the absence of roads made permanent farms unacceptable. Imported food products were easily transported and stored, but imported goods were expensive. As the role of timber in the economy began to fall, the need for a local food source developed.

There is evidence to suggest that part of the staple demand was met by allocating provision grounds, called plantations, to the slaves for their own use (Ashcroft 1973). The provision grounds were devoted primarily to subsistence production, but a substantial amount of the harvest was exchanged in the nearby camps for cash. Slowly a subsistence farming system evolved, based on free time and borrowed land. Generally the land farmed was near a logging camp and a river. The logging camp supplied the workers' primary source of income and acted as a market for surplus harvest while the river supplied fertile alluvium.

Forestry demanded an agricultural cycle that could be adapted to its needs. The time allocated to farming was small and therefore elaborate sedentary agricultural systems were not evident (Ashcroft 1973). Only simple tools were available in the bush camps (machete, axe and fire). A simple slash and burn, shifting cultivation was adopted. Crops included staples such as swamp rice on the flood plains and maize, cubits, beans and root crops in upland locations. The agrarian cycle was also related to logging and river schedules.

By the 1920s rural land use had developed very little. The timber industry began to mechanise and the work period was reduced to six months. Several isolated timber camps were closed. Timbermen's incomes fell and many left the camps and wandered to the coastal towns. The part-time farmers could not sustain their families by farming alone and several camp provision grounds were abandoned. Other part-time farmers retained their farms and searched for occasional work in distant camps for part of the year.

By 1980 subsistence farmers had spread along the rivers and along the more recently completed roads. Rural population density is still very low, with less than 10% of the country's population involved (Fig. 8.2).

The agricultural or *milpa* system of slash and burn has not changed substantially and temporary lands are rented each year. Subsistence crops are essentially the same as in the past. Some farmers along the major rivers have now occupied permanent fields and produce some root and fruit crops for sale, but the operations are still part-time.

The average peasant farmer spends about 150 days on his fields. Because he does not produce sufficient income for his family's survival, he uses his free time to hunt, fish, or work off the farm. Harvest surpluses, where evident, are sold at nearby villages or are carried to a city market. The cropping schedule has not changed significantly, so that the harvest brings a glut of products to market and off-season periods require the importation of staples. Sufficient progress in agricultural extension services is not evident. Government policy still appears to favour increasing the role of foreign-operated cash-crop systems.

Thus the present state of affairs involves crude milpa farming methods, an inadequate and cumbersome transportation system, poorly developed marketing arrangements and limited agricultural extension system, which com-

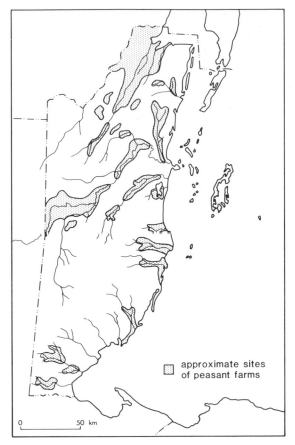

Figure 8.2 Rural population distribution.

bine to discourage expansion of domestic staple production. Behind these factors stand the exporting–importing interests which work to maintain arrangements as they are. Therefore, most rural people have little choice but to respond to the fluctuating fortunes of forestry and the rising influence of foreign-based cash cropping by attempting to maintain the old part-time pattern. The result has led to a broader and more entrenched state of poverty for the entire country.

Problems in agro-climate

The colonial legacy and present day social and economic conditions have retarded the progress and development of Belizian peasant agriculture. Crop failures and reduced yields associated with climatic hazards further reduce the interest in peasant agriculture.

On the surface, the general description of weather and climate for Belize

shows little indication of climatic hazards. Recently, several authors have
considered the climate of Central America (including Belize) and the role of
climate in tropical agriculture (see Walker 1976, Hall 1973, Schwendtfeger
1968, Portig 1965, Bushong 1961, Romney 1959). According to the Belize
studies the range of temperature is moderate, with no records below 7°C, so
that frost and cold setback are not problems. Even the average annual precipitation (Fig. 8.3) illustrates a range from 5000 mm in the south to
1525 mm in the north. It is, rather, the extreme variability of precipitation in
terms of onset and amount that constitutes the most serious climatic hazard
for agriculture.

Belize is in a transition zone between large-scale atmospheric systems (Fig.
8.4). As each system gains its seasonal control there are spectacular shifts in
precipitation and wind conditions (Fig. 8.5). This variability is the source of
hazards for Belize's rural development and agriculture, especially in the transition between atmospheric systems.

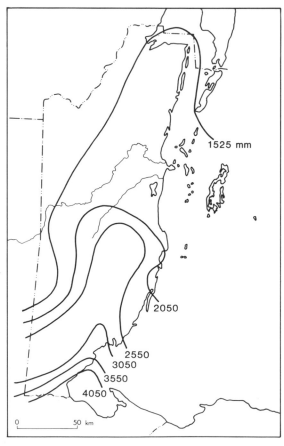

Figure 8.3 Belize average annual rainfall.

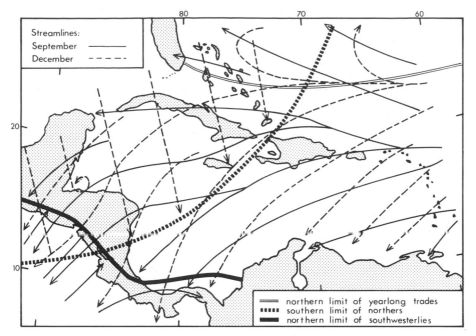

Figure 8.4 Large-scale atmospheric controls.

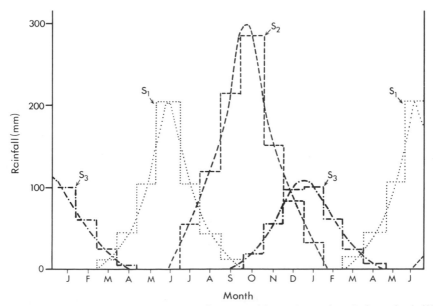

Figure 8.5 Rainfall distribution and regime transitions. Annual variation of rainfall in Belize: S_1, first zenithal rains; S_2, second zenithal rains; S_3, rain due to northers. The transitions between regimes are the periods of great agro-climatic hazards.

Agro-climatic hazards and the human response   The most violent short-term hazards to plague Belize are the hurricane and tropical depression, for the country is located in one of the most active hurricane areas of the Caribbean. Hurricanes and violent depressions have struck Belize at least one year in five. Historically, the loss of life, property damage and crop destruction, have been very high. Belize City still bears the imprint of the 1931 and 1961 (Hattie) hurricane damages. In both cases the entire city was under almost 4 m of water during the storms. Punta Gorda was partially destroyed along with thousands of hectares of forest by a hurricane in October 1945. Hurricane Janet (September 1955) levelled the northernmost city of Corozal and destroyed the developing coconut industry. In July 1960 Hurricane Abby hit the Stan Creek area causing considerable urban damage as well as destroying 85% of the banana crop. Hurricanes Carmen and Fifi both moved over Belize in September 1974, resulting in severe damage to corn, fruit trees and sugar cane in the north as well as destroying 90% of the banana crop in the south.

Peasant farmers' response to hurricanes involves short-term adjustment such as rebuilding shacks and replanting. Food shortages are offset by hunting and gathering. Urban poor, dependent on the meagre flow of peasant staples, search for handouts, steal or go hungry. The notable responses of the Belizean government have been to move the capital to Belmopan, 100 km inland, and to install a long-range radar unit at the international airport. As yet the value of the radar as a warning device is minimal to the peasant farmer.

Beyond the physical destruction of hurricane winds and the flooding by torrential rains, there are several less violent climatic influences that work to reduce agricultural development and potential. The extreme variation of monthly (Fig. 8.6) and annual precipitation, the irregular onset of the rainy season, the irregular duration of seasonal droughts and abnormal extensions of the wet season are all common hindrances to agricultural production and planning. However, the impact of these less violent influences on peasant agriculture depends on their occurrence relative to the farmers' cropping schedule.

Agro-climate and crop scheduling   The crop schedule originally established by peasant farmers related to the earlier timber-falling schedule, and in some degree to folklore, rather than to climatic variation. Broadly, however, the schedule ties in quite well with the weather regime, except that critical events such as planting and harvesting tend to occur during precipitation transition periods (Fig. 8.7). In these periods, precipitation is extremely variable and almost impossible to predict.

The following case study, derived from questionnaire responses or peasant and commercial farmers in the Central Farm area of Central Belize, is presented to illustrate the relationship between typical cropping schedule and climate variation. Meteorological data are based on reports from the Central Farm Agricultural Experimental Station (Hall 1978).

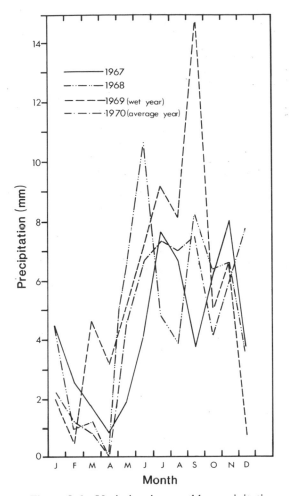

Figure 8.6 Variation in monthly precipitation.

January is the transition month in which the wet season ends and the dry season begins (Fig. 8.7). Belize comes under the influence of the subtropical high inversion. Winds are from the north and north-east with occasional bursts of cold northwesterly air from North America. Precipitation generally occurs as low-intensity rain, in periods from one to two days, and there are about 17 rainy days. It is now that milpa and commercial red kidney beans are harvested. Generally, the soil moisture is still at field capacity and moisture hazards involve excess precipitation that can delay harvesting and induce sprouting of the unharvested beans.

In *February* precipitation decreases to about 75 mm. During this month the subtropical high-pressure system gains control. Evaporation exceeds precipitation generally by mid-February and the dry season begins. Farm

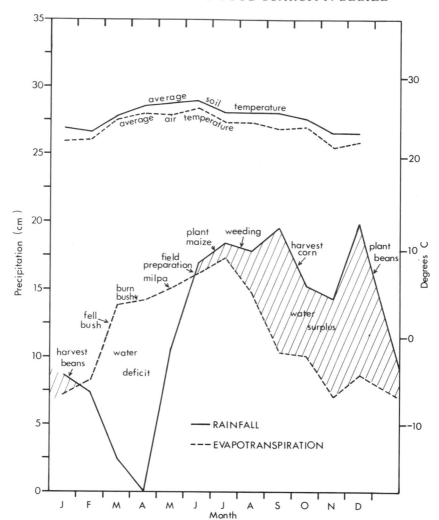

Figure 8.7   The agricultural schedule and agro-climate.

activities are limited to the selection of new milpa plots and therefore climatic hazards are minimal.

March to *early June* is very dry as the influence of the stable subtropical high-pressure system is felt. Generally, there are less than ten rainy or cloudy days per month during this period. As the Sun passes the equinox and approaches its summer solstice, land temperatures begin to rise. Soil moisture falls below field capacity and grasses and forest vegetation brown off. Primary farm activities involve the slashing and burning of milpa plots.

April is often the driest month, with no precipitation falling at several stations. Milpas are burned during this period with some danger of runaway fires.

During *May* the Sun is directly overhead. Temperatures rise and local land heating contributes to convectional showers, which are intense and of short duration. Precipitation levels for the month may rise about 10 mm, but showers are scattered and precipitation is not reliable. Locally the short-term high-intensity precipitation causes erosion of burned fields. It is during May that peasant farmers begin planting their milpas. Soil moisture is still deficient but the peasant farmer hopes to gain an early sprout from the shower moisture so that plants will be established before the onset of the actual rainy season. But precipitation is so unreliable that germination failure is quite common. Peasants respond by replanting until they either gain a sound germination or run out of seed.

The rainy season generally begins in *June* and continues erratically until *early August*. Land temperatures are the highest of the year and convective precipitation dominates the weather. Monthly precipitation may rise above 150 mm and is accompanied by high runoff and local floods. It is necessary that crops be well established by this time as poorly developed plants are easily washed out of the soil. The saturated surface soil conditions and high erosion potential reduces the success of replanting.

July is similar to June except that soil moisture is at or near field capacity and precipitation becomes more variable. In some years, for example, only 100 mm of rain may fall, while in other years such as 1961 hurricanes may bring as much as 250 mm additional rain. Easterly waves become more evident in July. Each storm may last for several days, producing continuous torrential downpours and flooding of low-lying areas. Little labour is put into the farm during the rainy season and farmers tend to use time to hunt or to work in a nearby village.

August is a transition month. The sun migrates south of the colony toward the Equator and the land begins to cool. Precipitation declines and the drier conditions benefit the maturing of the grain crop planted in May. August is also a rest or off-farm period for the peasant. Climate hazards are associated with the onset of deep tropical depressions and hurricanes.

September and *October* are cloudy months, and average air temperatures begin to fall. The large-scale circulation shifts, as the subtropical high begins to move southwards. The first northern air from the continent begins to interact with warm sea breezes causing local storms. Winds shift from the north-east to the north and north-west as masses of continental air begin to dominate the area. Northwesterly air flow is generally accompanied by low-intensity rain over longer periods. September and October exhibit a variable rain pattern because of the transition of the large-scale systems. It is now that the milpa harvest begins. Milpa corn cobs are broken to induce drying and they are hand-picked in the drier period of late October. If precipitation amounts are higher than normal, the cobs decay and the saturated soils make harvesting difficult.

During the months of *November* and *December* Belize comes under the influence of cool northern air and irregular periods of southeastern air off the subtropical high-pressure system. Continental air gives rise to frontal-like storms and precipitation. Agricultural activities are restricted as soils become too wet for ploughing. Precipitation declines in late December and preparation for kidney bean planting begins. Accumulated soil moisture, humidity and days with rain become critical factors for bean production. An excess of these factors reduces the ability of the bean plant to survive. Since precipitation is not reliable, bean production involves more hazards in many ways than milpa corn production.

To summarise: The weather problems in agricultural production are largely associated with the variability of the precipitation pattern. It is quite apparent that variability in the timing, amount and intensity of precipitation are primarily due to the interaction of large weather systems which migrate through the year. Belize is in a transitional weather zone, rather than in a stable zone dominated by either the tropical or mid-latitude systems. The agricultural year is beset with a series of weather-related hazards. Peasant farmers are subsistence farmers who rely on the harvest to feed their families. Adjustments to climatic hazards simply include replanting until a crop succeeds. Feast and famine sequences are common. On occasion, however, extreme droughts or floods extend beyond the normal range of adjustment of the farmer. Entire crops are lost throughout the nation and severe hardships are experienced by rural and urban dwellers alike. An example of such a disaster occurred in 1975 when there was no rainy season.

The drought of 1975

In 1975 the rains did not come in May to end the dry season – nor did they come in June, July, or August. Millions of dollars in staple and cash crops were lost as seeds and young replants shrivelled in the hot sun. Thousands of local and imported livestock starved as pasture grasses died. This was a rare event, a drought of unprecedented length (Fig. 8.8).

In 1975 the dry season began early in February and, for some areas of the country, lasted until September. Rainfall during this period was only about one-third of normal. The usual heavy July thunder showers of the rainy period did not materialise, except in the far southern Toledo district where scattered showers occurred mainly along the coast. Rainfall in the northern districts was insufficient to sustain crop and pasture growth. There was hardly a crop or livestock enterprise that was not directly or indirectly affected, and the effects continued to be felt for several years.

Virtually all facets of peasant and commercial agricultural production were affected by the drought. Grain production is estimated to have reduced by 50%; that is, from a forecast production of 2.5 million kg to a production of around 1.25 million kg. Many farmers had to replant their fields two or three times. This resulted in a scarcity of seeds towards the end of the planting

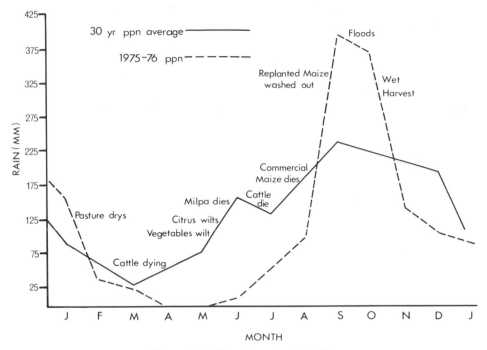

Figure 8.8 The drought of 1975.

season. In some areas there was poor germination of maize plants while in others the young maize plants were stunted due to a lack of adequate soil moisture. Rice production was reduced directly by the drought but was also affected indirectly by a build-up of armyworm populations which damaged the rice crop. Paddy rice production was as low as 1.25 million kg compared with 3.0 million kg in 1974. There was a shortfall of around 2.5 to 2.7 million kg of finished rice. This had to be replaced by imports from commercial suppliers.

Commercial crops were also affected. Sugar cane losses equalled half of the normal production and the more recently planted sugar cane fields were stunted because of water stress. Several cane fields planted in May did not germinate. The 1976 crop production was also down because of the water stress problem of 1975. In the citrus industry the orange crop, which experienced a 25% decrease, bore the brunt of the effects of the drought. Most of the grapefruit crop was harvested before the dry season could take its toll, but the effects of the drought on grapefruit were felt in 1976 because of poor flowering and fruit development. Tropical produce experienced problems with about a 10% decline in production, and an equal amount of fruit was rejected because of poor quality. The banana industry was also severely affected by the drought. Shipments of fruit had to be suspended in April because there was insufficient quantity of high-quality fruit to warrant a ship stopping over in Belize. Exports did not commence again until after

December 1975. The shortage of coconuts caused by the two hurricanes of 1974 was exacerbated by the drought. Due to water stress, bearing plants shed their young nuts, resulting in a reduction of the amount of mature nuts available for consumption. The drought also resulted in a shortage of plantains and other starchy food crops, including root crops. Bearing plantain trees toppled over, young suckers died, and stunted growth of others occurred. Planting of root crops had to be delayed until the onset of the rainy season. Since these plants do not come into production until some six to nine months after planting a continuing shortage of starchy food crops was evident into 1976.

The drought caused millions of dollars (Belize) in livestock losses during the dry period. Of the commercial livestock, cattle were hardest hit by the drought. Improved pasture stood up to the drought until the end of April, but cattle on unimproved pastures began to lose weight as early as April. By the end of July, an estimated 200 head of cattle had died due to a lack of adequate feed and water supplies. By September, an estimated total of 525 head of cattle were lost, mainly in the western (Cayo) district. Losses in the northern districts were minimised to some extent through the supplementary feeding of sugar cane tops and chopped, whole cane to the cattle. The greatest loss in cattle was that of body weight gain. Based on a cattle population of 45 000 head and an average weight loss of 22.5 kg per animal, the loss of beef production was approximately 1.01 million kg, or a loss of around $3 million to the industry. Pig and poultry production were mainly affected by the shortage of corn and other grains.

The immediate effects of the drought were hunger and the importation of staples. The long-range effects, however, include a mounting pressure to induce the Department of Agriculture to shift some of its priorities from commercial to peasant agriculture and to establish a long-term agricultural programme in concert with the agro-climate. An integral part of such a programme must be good agro-climatic information, and the assessment of risks from weather extremes. But very little work on climatic hazards has been completed for Central America although models for statistical forecasts are available and have been used to good advantage elsewhere. Agro-climate calendars have, for example, become common in the mid-latitudes and have gained some success in the savanna areas of the world (see Benoit 1979, Glover & Robinson 1953, Gramzow & Henry 1972, Hall 1978, Manning 1956, Shaw 1975, Walker & Rijks 1968).

The preceding section emphasises the roles of extreme weather hazards and weather variability in reducing crop production. The peasant farmer's response to weather hazards is to continue replanting until a crop succeeds or he runs out of seed. There are limits to the success of this adjustment. Late-planted crops are pushed into overly wet or drought conditions which normally reduce the yield.

It is obvious that any advance or progress in agricultural development must be accompanied by and adjusted to some type of agro-climate calendar; that is, a device that estimates to some extent the onset and duration of the rainy season and the distribution of rainfall within that season. The statistical manipulation of meteorological data requires reliable long-term records for several weather stations in the country. Belize has recently reorganised its meteorological office, and daily weather records for the country's meteorological stations are now stored at the international airport. Also, a trained meteorological officer oversees the operation of data reporting and storing. A long-range radar system is in service to locate and track severe tropical storms.

The first step has been taken to establish an agro-climate calendar by Walker (1976) while working with the British Ministry of Overseas Development in the Belize river valley. Walker established estimates for the first week of the rainy season for the Belize river valley.

I am presently involved in establishing a national agro-climate calendar in co-operation with the Belize Department of Communications and Department of Agriculture. Initial interest has been concentrated on the onset of the rainy season across the country.

In an earlier section it was noted that the dry season begins in mid-February and generally extends to mid-May. The actual onset date varies spatially as well as temporally across the country. Since soil moisture is too low to support germination in the dry period the farmer needs to know the best date for successful planting. The average date of the onset is of little value because of the extreme variation in the event. The onset has arrived as much as a month and a half early, and in 1975 (the year of the drought) the rainy period did not occur at all.

A central issue in any improvement of our knowledge is, however, its relevance to and integration with the actual system of farming, notably the scheduling pattern of peasant agriculture and the onset of specific precipitation regimes. A method which strives to do this involves estimating the probable start of the rainy seasons and droughts for specific periods of the year and directing agricultural events (e.g. land preparation, seeding, harvesting, etc.) to the periods with the *best* estimates for acceptable climatic conditions.

A clearer picture of precipitation distribution during the dry period and an indication of the probable start of the rains may be noted in a pentad analysis of the long-term precipitation record for May and June. (A pentad is a unit of five consecutive days.) Field analysis of germination conditions at the Central Farm Agricultural Experimental Station indicate that a pentad with 25 mm of precipitation is sufficient to support germination. If this first wet pentad is followed by continuous wet pentads, the rainy season is said to have begun. To ascertain the probable date of the first wet pentad for a specific station, each year of the data record is divided into units of five days. The precipitation distribution for the units is tabulated for the long-term record. The statistical probability of a wet pentad occurring at a specific date is noted. Thus a calendar of dates for the onset of the rainy period and the probability statements associated with them may be isolated for all the stations in the country which have sufficiently long records. Figure 8.9 indicates the average date of the first 50% chance of the total of 25 mm rainfall in five days for various stations in Belize. Generally the maps show that the onset of the rainy period is much later in the north than in the south and therefore planting of spring crops should be at least a month later.

Figures 8.7 and 8.8 show that the planting of milpa corn (for example) is much too early in the season relative to the best probable data for reliable precipitation. Similar disparities appear for harvesting corn and planting beans.

Much more work is necessary, of course, to relate the rate of soil moisture build-up to the occurrence of wet pentads in order to isolate more optimum planting times for each area covered by meteorological data. Also, data on droughts, unusually wet periods and violent storms need to be tabulated and related to the agro-climate calendar. More information on the probable onset of the rainy season, droughts and violent storms in Belize could also be gained by a closer examination of the large-scale weather conditions of countries

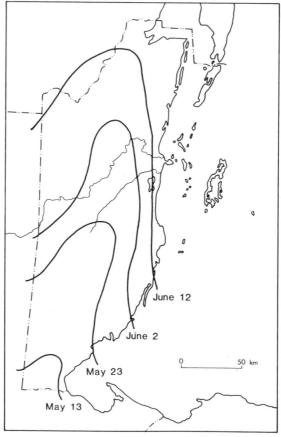

Figure 8.9   Average date of onset of the rainy season.

around Belize. Closer co-operation between these countries concerning the onset of the rainy seasons could lead to more accurate extrapolation or precipitation data. The chance of this co-operation is good, as Belize now has a qualified full-time meteorologist on staff. An effective programme to integrate weather forecasts and to incorporate weather data presently being analysed into a peasant crop schedule has not, however, been developed yet. An obstacle which must be overcome is the lack of an effective agricultural extension programme which is committed to the education of the peasant farmers, not only in terms of agronomic techniques but also in terms of translating climatic data into specific periods for planting, harvesting, etc. Unless peasant farmers are made aware of the weaknesses of their present agricultural schedules and the risks associated with its maintenance, few advances can be anticipated in the production of staples.

Conclusions

The case study of Belize emphasises specific problems that relate to that country's agricultural development. Perhaps the central issue is that the peasant agrarian system has been, and still is, biased by a colonial legacy and influenced by a forestry-garden complex that no longer exists such that, now, there is little relationship between the scheduling of crops and the agro-climate. But many Belizian problems are coincident with those of other so-called Third World countries. First, the bulk of peasant farmers only farm part-time. Many engage in slash and burn on rented or squatted land. Secondly, farm fields are small, fragmented and isolated from urban centres. Thirdly, trails leading to all-weather roads are of poor quality and are often flooded. Fourthly, the sale of surplus crops is not regulated by marketing boards and it suffers from glut or famine effects. Fifthly, land availability and farm credit are restricted by government bias. Sixthly crop production is influenced and restricted by folklore interpretations of agro-climate factors. But the folklore that directs planting and harvesting schedules is out of phase with precipitation regimes, while random hurricanes and droughts further decrease the stability of agricultural production.

In order to solve its food scarcity problem, the Belizian government must first recognise the importance and complexity of the problem and then implement realistic long-term developmental plans. There is some evidence that the officials of the Ministry of Agriculture are attempting to aid the peasant farmer. For example, tax land is being made available to peasants at a low annual cost. There has been a small increase in the number and activity of the agricultural extension officers. More farm visits by extension officers and seminars are being held. A marketing board, which has been established for large volume commercial sales, is now accepting some peasant crops. Also a few peasants are coming forward requesting agricultural extension aid. The overall impact of the government's activities and the acceptance of help by the peasants, however, has been small.

Solutions to the food scarcity and agro-climate problem referred to in the case study could be significantly improved with detailed agro-climate calendars, for example. These could well be developed for most of the Third World in the near future. However, that requires adequate data collection and manipulation. The implementation of improved subsistence agricultural programmes based on these calendars will depend on the political climate of the country. Meanwhile, it is also possible for the agro-climate calendar described above to be used simply to allow commercial large-scale agriculture to be more cost-effective and further exasperate the problem of self-sufficiency in food production. During my tenure in Belize there were verbal commitments to gaining solutions to Belize's staple-scarcity problems.

Recently, Belize gained her independence from England and these verbal commitments are now critical to her survival as a nation.

References

Ashcroft, N. 1973. *Colonialism and underdevelopment: processes of political economic change in British Honduras*. Columbia: Teacher's College Press, Columbia Univ.

Benoit, P. 1979. *A review of agroclimatological studies and drought in the West African Savanna*. 9th An. Conf. Afr. Studs, Winnipeg Univ.

Bolland, O. N. 1977. *The formation of a colonial society*. Baltimore: Johns Hopkins University Press.

British Honduras (Belize) 1967. *Development Plan 1964–1970*. Office of Premier Government Printing Office.

Brown, L. R. 1978. *The twenty-ninth day: accommodating human needs and numbers to the Earth's resources*. New York: Norton.

Burton, I., R. W. Kates and G. F. White 1978. *The environment as hazard*. New York: Oxford University Press.

Bushong, A. D. 1961. Agricultural settlement in British Honduras. Unpublished PhD dissertation, Florida Univ.

Department of Agriculture 1969–78. *Monthly review of agriculture*. Belize.

Department of Statistics 1970. *Census of British Honduras, 1970*. West Indies Population Census, Kingston, Jamaica.

Floyd, B. 1972. *Belize: traditional and modern ways of using land resources*. Focus, Amer. Geogr. Soc., New York, vol. XXIII, no. 3.

FAO (Food and Agriculture Organization) 1977. *The fourth world food survey*. Rome: UN, FAO.

Glover, J. and F. Robinson 1953. A simple method of assessing the reliability of rainfall. *J. Agric. Sci*. no. 43.

Gramzow, R. H. and W. K. Henry 1972. The rainy pentads of Central America. *J. Appl. Meteorol*. **II**, June.

Hall, J. 1973. *Mennonite agriculture in a tropical environment*. Unpublished PhD dissertation, Clark Univ.

Hall, J. 1978. *Precipitation regimes transitions as climatic hazards*. Conf. Latin Am. Geogs, Sonoma State College.

Krohn, S. (ed.) 1978. *The economy of Belize 1978*. Belize City, Belize: Brukdown Publications.

Labour Department 1964. *Manpower assessment report 1964*. Government Printing Office.

Manning H. L. 1956. *The statistical assessment of rainfall probability and its application to Uganda agriculture*. Proc. R. Soc. no. 47.

Ministry of Agriculture and Lands 1969–78. *Annual report*. Government Printing Office.

Portig, W. H. 1965. Central American rainfall. *Geog. Rev.*, January.

Romney, D. H. (ed.) 1959. *Land in British Honduras*. Colonial Publication no. 24. London: HMSO.

Sampson, H. C. 1929. *Report on development of agriculture in British Honduras*. London: HMSO.

Schwendtfeger, W. (ed.) 1968. *Climates of Central and South America*. Volume 12 of World Survey of Climatology. Amsterdam: Elsevier.

Shaw, A. B. 1975. *Rainfall variability and its effects on rice cultivation in Guyana*. Unpubl. MA thesis, Wilfrid Laurier Univ.

Thomson, B. P. 1976. *Current economic situation and prospects – Belize*. Belize Government, Belmopan.

Thurston, D. H. 1971. Tropical agriculture: a key to the world food crises. In *Population and food* R. S. Leisner and E. J. Koromandy (eds). Dubuque, Iowa: Wm. C. Brown.

Walker, J. T. and D. A. Rijks 1968. Computer programme for the calculation of confidence limits of expected rainfall. *J. Agron. Sci.* **58**.

Walker, S. A. 1963. *Summary of climatic records for Belize*. Supplies Report Land Resources Div. Ministry Overseas Dev. no. 3.

Walker, S. H. 1976. *The agricultural development potential of the Belize Valley*. Belize, Land Resources Study 24, Ministry of Overseas Development, Surrey, England.

9 *Food production under conditions of increased uncertainty: the settlement of the Paraguayan Chaco by Mennonite farmers*

A. HECHT AND J. W. FRETZ

With an ever-increasing world population the food requirement grows too. This is especially true of areas of the world such as South America, Africa and Asia. One result has been agricultural expansions into ever more hostile and/or agriculturally marginal areas (Bergstrom 1973, p. 31). During periods of unfavourable environmental conditions, as experienced recently in the Sahel (see Ch. 5), this appears as a hazardous situation bringing untold misery. Yet, in the next fifty years such lands may have to be exploited even more, to produce enough food for the world – at least for some of its more vulnerable peoples. The question of how agriculturists can cope with the hazards or uncertainties of such marginal habitats is therefore of great concern. It is particularly relevant to examine cases where settlers have attempted to develop modern productive agriculture and have done so with some success.

Within the interior of South America lies the Gran Chaco plain (Fig. 9.1). It is a region of marginal agricultural potential. Nevertheless, it is being probed more and more for potential settlement. The Chaco Austral in Argentina, an extension of the Pampas, already has a number of settlements on the southern, eastern and western margins. The Chaco Central, just north of the Chaco Austral, now has a railroad line running between its eastern and western margins, the latter in the foothills of the Andes. Settlements have begun to dot this railroad although the area is by no means fully inhabited (Buenstorf 1971). But the really virgin region is the Chaco Boreal of Paraguay and Bolivia. The population density here is less than one person per 2.6 km². Except for a few military outposts, scattered groups of native Indians and a few settlers, the region is empty.

It was here, however, that a conservative group of Canadian Mennonites, German–Dutch in origin, settled in the late 1920s (Fig. 9.2). Although their reason for going to the Chaco was to get away from the encroaching 'world' in Canada, they nevertheless were the first to attempt to establish an agricultural settlement in the Chaco Boreal. The isolation provided by Chaco was wel-

Figure 9.1   South America.

comed on religious grounds. But it has taken 50 years to establish a viable economy. The main problem is a natural environment marginal for agriculture and also unpredictable and highly variable. Subsistence food production and later commercial crops turned out to be a precarious occupation, especially when combined with price fluctuation in the nascent market system of Paraguay. Nevertheless, the settlement survives and a closer look at its experience, albeit involving a unique type of society, offers useful pointers to the broader problems of these hazardous locations.

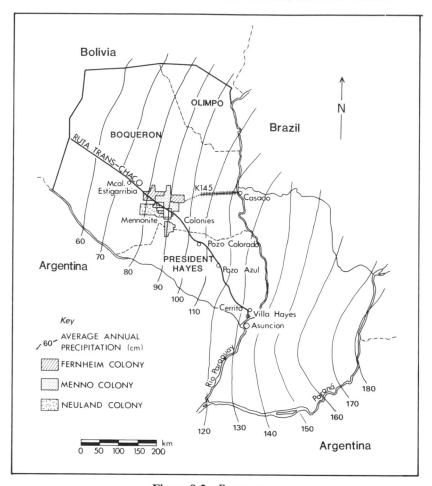

Figure 9.2   Paraguay.

Environmental milieu

The Gran Chaco Region occupies some 1 million km². It extends some 1200 km from the headwaters of the Mamore river system in Bolivia to the northern regions of the Argentinian Pampas (Fig. 9.1). It stretches from the foothills of the Andes to the Paraguay–Parana Rivers, some 650 km to the east (Shannahan 1927). The whole region is of relatively low elevation, being some 170 m above sea level at the Mennonite settlements in the Chaco Boreal (Krause 1952). The Chaco plain was formed by alluvium deposited by rivers flowing out from the eastern slopes of the Andes. In the level terrain, with sandy soils and high evaporation, a number of these streams do not have incised beds and they change course relatively frequently. No permanent surface streams originate in the Chaco itself. During the rainy season water collects in shallow low-lying areas, is absorbed into the ground, or evaporates.

The soils of the Chaco Boreal region are mainly fine sandy loams and silty clays. They are covered with shrub forest or coarse grasses. The bushlands in most instances have been formed on the finer sediments where there is a high moisture-holding capacity but low permeability; here there are large swamps during the rainy season. On the other hand the coarse grasses grow on the fine sands where permeability is extremely high. The soils have formed relatively recently and are quite rich in nutrients, at least in comparison to eastern Paraguay where subtropical conditions have caused greater leaching. The Chaco soils therefore have a fair to good potential for food production.

As indicated before, the real problem of the environmental milieu is climate. And among the climatic problems, precipitation variability is the main one. The local inhabitants recognise it and incorporate it in their way of thinking. For example in the local bimonthly paper *Mennoblatt* (1977, vol. 48, no. 2, p. 5), printed in Filadelfia, Chaco, a story is told (in the German vernacular) to indicate that the moisture variation in the Chaco is sometimes rather large. Last winter, we are told, the pasture grass was so short (little rain) that even the grasshoppers had to bend down when they wanted to feed! This summer, in Neuwiese (a village), the grass is growing so fast (much rain) that the caterpillar was unable to feed since he had to climb continuously in trying to get to the top of the plant!

Precipitation variation can be examined in terms of: (a) yearly variation or variation in total rainfall per growing season, (b) variability within the growing season, (c) spatial variability in rainfall and (d) the effectiveness of the precipitation. In the Chaco all four are of substantial importance. Table 9.1 shows yearly average precipitation at two stations in the Mennonite colonies of the central Chaco Boreal (Fig. 9.2). At each station the minimum is less than half the maximum. Such variation seems the norm for savanna-type climatic regions. When combined with the soil types found in the Chaco however, severe flooding, especially on the fine clayey soils, alternates with drought on the sandy campo soils.

A glance at a map of South America indicates that the Chaco lies in the eastern shadow of the Andes. This to some extent affects its precipitation. It is

Table 9.1 Average annual rainfall for growing season at two Mennonite colonies (mm).

	1955	1956	1957	1958	Year 1959	1960	1961	1962	1963
Filadelfia	611	596	1109	822	1016	1123	897	621	840
Halbstadt	—	821	1002	858	1342	1218	831	611	1077

	1964	1965	1966	1967	Year 1968	1969	1970	1971	1972
Filadelfia	629	1018	792	594	558	858	514	535	482
Halbstadt	626	963	760	589	688	844	607	939	789

Source: records provided by the Administration of Fernheim and Neuland Colonies.

further compounded by the nature of the precipitation. The rainfall usually comes in heavy showers with risk of floods. Since the area receives only small amounts of frontal precipitation so that cloud-covered skies and cooler temperatures are absent, the effectiveness of the rainfall is decreased. After a heavy shower the temperature climbs rapidly again with an associated return to high rates of evaporation.

A more crucial variable than overall precipitation in the Chaco is the amount that falls during the growing season. It is important that most crops be planted at the beginning of the rainy season (October–November) to avoid the danger of frost in the fall. In the Chaco Central frost occurs in about half the years. More important, however, if the planting is delayed, the crop may not receive the required moisture during the maturation period. Yet because of the high rate of evaporation the soils dry out fast and ploughing or cultivation can take place only for two to three days after the rainfall.

In Figure 9.3, we can see the tremendous variation in the monthly precipitation over an 18-year time span. The minimum precipitation for January 2.1 cm and the maximum 22 cm. A similar size spread occurred in February.

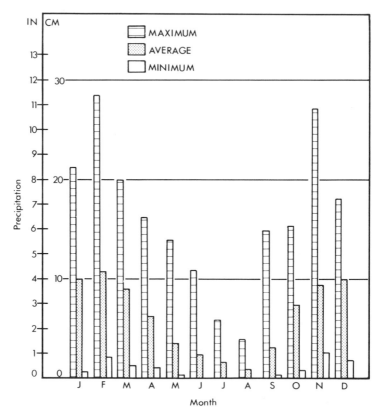

Figure 9.3   Precipitation 1932–50, Blumengard, Menno.

If we look at the planting months of October and November, again large differences are brought out. The coefficient of variation for the monthly data would be substantially larger than the coefficient of variation for the yearly data. The former is far more crucial in the planning of which crop to plant and it defines more accurately the precipitation risk for food production endeavours in the Chaco. This uncertainty is a major cause of worry. For the native Indians and most Paraguayans it is accepted as a cruel reality of life. The Mennonites on the other hand try to reduce the risk, if not with the help of technology then with prayer. Many religious gatherings have been held over the years with the specific objective of praying for rain, as observed by one of us during seven years of living in the colonies.

The spatial variation of average precipitation in the Chaco varies from about 130 cm near the Paraguay River to only 50 cm at the Bolivian border, a distance of 650 km (Fig. 9.2). The precipitation contours in the Chaco run nearly parallel to the Andes. The Mennonite settlements are located within the 75–90 cm isohyet. The spatial variation from year to year can be quite large despite the similarity in the averages. Table 9.1 gives the yearly average for two stations in the Mennonite colonies only 50 km apart, and close to the same average annual precipitation.

If we take the lower amount as the reference value, the percentage variation between these two stations, in the years 1956–72, comes to: 37, 10, 4, 24, 9, 7, 1, 28, 0, 5, 4, 0, 22, 1, 18, 75 and 63 respectively. A monthly comparison between these two stations reveals even greater variations. For the 1971–2 growing season, for example, the following percentage differences were observed: 8, 58, 37, 47, 34, 173, 20, 107, 25, 175, 300 and 430 from July to June respectively.

In drier subtropical and tropical regions the problem of moisture hinges especially upon the ratio of precipitation to evapotranspiration and rapid runoff after storms. The Chaco is no exception. Because of the high temperatures and the clear, relatively dry air, evaporation is high. As can be seen in Table 9.2, the mean maximum temperatures in the area range from 25.3 °C to 35.7 °C. Evaporation rates are especially light in the summer months when the relative humidity is only around 50%. Each month evaporation is substantially greater than precipitation and the total evaporation is nearly three times the actual precipitation (Table 9.2). With such a negative moisture balance, methods of agricultural practice that conserve moisture become very important.

In sum, the Chaco, though having relatively fertile soils and favourable topographic features, has rather unfavourable moisture conditions. It is this that has made the Chaco seem marginal for the native Indians in the past and more recently, for the Paraguayan, Bolivian and Argentinian settlement attempts. Yet, as already stated, in 1926 the first group of Mennonite settlers arrived and set up a settlement deep in the interior of the Paraguayan Chaco Boreal.

Table 9.2 Comparative weather data Paraguay Chaco region, Mariscal Estigarribia; average data for 1940–50.

	Temperature (°C) max.	Temperature (°C) min.	Rainfall (mm)	Evaporation (mm)	Relative humidity (%)
January	35.7	22.0	114.1	182.4	53.8
February	34.6	22.0	108.3	145.6	60.1
March	32.4	20.0	96.2	133.0	64.1
April	30.2	17.5	64.8	121.0	64.9
May	27.6	15.8	35.5	123.8	67.5
June	25.3	13.9	21.6	109.6	66.7
July	25.9	13.4	12.8	155.7	58.6
August	29.3	15.0	10.5	226.9	47.8
September	31.1	16.8	22.7	227.2	47.6
October	32.6	18.7	90.7	205.5	50.4
November	34.0	19.9	111.2	174.9	52.9
December	35.4	21.1	77.9	196.5	52.0
Total			766.3	2002.1	

Source: Bradford *et al.* (1955, p. 11).

Chaco Mennonite settlement

Today there are three Mennonite agricultural settlements in the Paraguayan Chaco approximately 400 km north-west of the capital city of Asuncion. They are: Menno, founded in 1926 with a present population of 6000; Fernheim, founded in 1930 with 2700; and Neuland, founded in 1947 with 1000 (Fig. 9.2). In addition to these 10 000 immigrants there are a few hundred Paraguayans and approximately 12 000 Indians (see Hecht 1980), the latter attracted there over the past 50 years by the prospects of food and employment provided by the three Mennonite colonies. However, a sense of the increase in demand to feed people can be seen from the fact that the Indian subsistence economy, before the Mennonites arrived, supported only an estimated 300 people (Hack 1976, p. 1). Complete success in feeding all the people there has not come. From 1975 to 1978, in the Indian communities near the Mennonites, 314 deaths out of 655 still were directly or indirectly related to undernourishment (Indianer-Beratungs-Behoerde 1979, Table 10).

The cultural background of each of the Chaco settlements is a colonisation epic in itself. All three originated in Russia. The Menno Colony forebearers left Russia in 1874 and settled in Canada in the Prairie provinces of Manitoba and Saskatchewan. They left Canada, after World War I, because of federal and provincial government efforts to regulate their schools and to compel them to substitute English for the German language. The Menno colonists chose the Paraguayan Chaco as a place to settle, not because of its ideal agricultural possibilities but because it offered them the political and religious freedom they were seeking.

The Fernheim and Neuland colonists came to the Chaco from Russia after

World Wars I and II as refugees and displaced persons respectively. They were socially and culturally more progressive than the Menno colonists. They settled in the Chaco because of limited alternatives. Their first preference would have been to go to Canada, but like most countries its immigration doors were closed at the time. Paraguay extended to Fernheim and Neuland the same generous privileges it offered Menno.

These privileges included complete religious freedom, the right to establish and to maintain their own school system and to conduct them in the German language; exemption from military service and from taking the oath in courts of justice; the right of all Mennonites to immigrate regardless of the state of their physical or mental health; and a 10-year exemption from payment of any taxes. Without the guarantee of these privileges, no Mennonites would have chosen to settle in Paraguay, much less in the isolated and inhospitable Chaco.

Some description of the isolated location of the three Mennonite colonies may help the reader understand why these colonists had extraordinary economic difficulties during the first three decades, notably in getting farm products to market. Paraguay is a land-locked country. Colonists entering the country had to travel a 1600 km winding journey up the Parana River from Buenos Aires to Asuncion, the Paraguay capital. From there they transferred to smaller river boats for another 520 km trip north on the Paraguay River. Thence, they took a narrow-gauge railroad inland to the west for 145 km, followed by an additional 90 km by wagon, ox cart or on foot to the respective settlement areas (Fig. 9.2).

When the colonists arrived, there were no roads. They had to cut their first trails and fill in swampy places to move with their wagon cargoes. There was the frustration of having to wait for land surveys so that each family would know where to erect houses and farm buildings. And even after the colonists had mastered the art of growing surplus food crops in the Chaco's unpredictable climate and unfamiliar soils, the geographical isolation and the lack of transportation created great difficulties in marketing farm products.

The Fernheim Colony

In this chapter the Fernheim settlement, established in 1930 with 1500 immigrants, is chosen for detailed analysis of food production through time. Moreover, we shall direct attention initially to the special human aspects of the colonising process, as an essential prelude to understanding how it affects coping with environmental risk.

It should be noted that the Fernheim colonists were deeply disappointed with their land, their isolation, and impoverished economic circumstances. They were extremely discouraged about their prospects. Many asked themselves whether their situation was an improvement over revolutionary Russia.

In Russia they had lost their religious and political freedom. Their homes were destroyed and they were often forced to flee for their lives. In their new Chaco wilderness homes they had complete religious, political and economic freedom but few means with which to enjoy it. However, their choice being made, they had to live with it.

The Fernheimers did bring those essentially invisible and non-material aspects of European culture that largely account for the survival of all the Mennonites in the Chaco. These need to be discussed. A basic asset is their religious philosophy of life which includes an awareness of and a sense of dependence upon God as the source of their strength and hope for their future. They were sustained in their difficult early Chaco years by the Biblical stories of the Children of Israel wandering in the desert from Egypt to Canaan; by the difficulties of the early Christians; and indeed the centuries of persecution of their own forefathers in Europe prior to their settlements in Russia.

At the same time, the Fernheimers brought with them a century of collective experience with the technology of the industrial revolution. They came from the most progressive group of Mennonites in Russia, where communities had developed industrially as well as agriculturally throughout the latter 19th and early 20th centuries. One-third of the Mennonite capital investment in Russia had been devoted to industrial activities. The milling industry and the manufacture of agricultural machinery were two of the major economic activities in which many of the Fernheimers were formerly engaged. In addition, there were many who had commercial businesses of their own. Others were well educated and engaged in one or the other of the professions.

The Mennonites in Russia had their own school system which in addition to the elementary schools included high schools, business colleges and teacher-training colleges. Likewise, they had their own welfare systems for looking after the indigent, the widows and orphans and their own general and mental hospitals. And, of special interest relative to hazards, they had an extensive system of mutual aid, fire and store insurance societies.

This heritage of highly developed social, economic and religious organisations, once adapted to the crude frontier conditions of the Paraguayan Chaco, spelled the difference between colonisation success and failure. In that regard one may cite the contrasting experience of the Menno Colony during its first decade: a more conservative group without extensive co-operative organisations. The story of more than 25 other immigrant settlement efforts in Paraguay also shows that efficient and thorough colony organisation made the difference in determining success or failure (Fretz 1962), including resilience in the face of natural hazards.

Already on the ship going to Paraguay the Fernheim colonists manifested their aptitude for systematic and detailed organisation by determining how many villages would be laid out, and how many of the 1481 members would reside in each village. In addition, a 'Schulze' or mayor of each village and an

'Oberschulze' or colony governor were chosen. That provided a working structure for the new colony prior to arrival in Paraguay.

The colony formed a co-operative to which every family head was required to belong. All buying and selling was to be done through this co-operative. Individuals had accounts at the colony co-operative which were credited and debited whenever goods were sold to or bought from the co-operative. Very little cash ever changed hands during the early decades. The colony co-operative served both as a bank and an effective regulator of consumer spending. Individual colonists could only buy and sell at the colony-owned stores, and the co-operative stocked only necessary items. This prevented people from spending on non-essentials.

In Russia the Fernheimers were acquainted with high standards of living and they aspired to provide the basis for similar facilities in Paraguay. A school system was immediately set up on the Russian model; at first village elementary schools and after a few years a centralised secondary school followed by a teacher-training school. In the Fernheim colony a hospital was established, initially staffed by doctors imported for short periods of time from the United States and, or Germany. Provision was made for the care of the indigent, aged and orphans. Roads were built from colony to colony and village to village. All of these public or community services were paid out of earnings from the colony co-operative. This was of course a method of funding colony services in place of levying taxes, and was much less painful.

It was this effective colony organisation to meet economic, social and religious needs on the part of Fernheim which served as a model for the more conservative and older colony of Menno which had lacked co-operative organisation. It brought the strong commitment to individual ownership and enterprise which had worked well in Canada. But that was ineffective to the point of ruination under the severe economic conditions of the Paraguayan Chaco. It is interesting to note that the native Indians of the Chaco also had a communal economic system of sharing fortune and this may be a prerequisite for adapting to hazardous environments.

By means of co-operation the Fernheim Colony could move its agricultural produce in bulk to the rail head, thence on a three-day riverboat trip to Asuncion. A colony-employed representative resided permanently in Asuncion to serve as buyer and seller, and to negotiate economically and politically with public or private agencies. It would have been impossible for each of the colony farmers to market his own products or purchase his own needs in any other way. Because the colony operated as a collective it had real bargaining power when it came to negotiate for the marketing and purchasing of economic goods and, in time, for securing commercial air service from Asuncion to the Chaco.

As we turn to questions of habitat uncertainty and hazard, we must not ignore this sense of an independent, well organised and innovative human group. They were and are not immune to natural disaster, nor to the strains of harsh conditions. But there is a profound gulf between their experience of these problems and other groups in the region – as indeed much of the harsher Tropics. Moreover, they remind us of the danger of stereotypes in such circumstances. On the one hand we have an intensely religious, communal society engaged primarily in work on commercial agriculture. On the other, they are carrying this out in a remote marginal tropical area otherwise identified with unimproved subsistence economies. How well they have done, compared to the native Indians which are settled and practising agriculture but with a subsistence mentality, can be seen from their success in 1975, a specially dry year. The Mennonites were able to harvest a crop which was still 48% of the 1974 crop year, a good year. The Indians on the other hand were only able to harvest 25% of the cotton production of the previous year (Regehr 1979, p. 332). The difference was probably made by dry farming methods, ploughing and cultivation (when needed), a success mentality, and having the stamina as well as the motive power when it is absolutely essential. A giant agricultural step backward could not be avoided by the Mennonites, but at least it did not turn into near total collapse as was the case for the marginal Indian farmers. The successful economic growth of the three Chaco colonies was the primary reason for the construction in the early 1960s of the trans-Chaco road from Asuncion to the colonies and to the Bolivian border. At present the hope still is that eventually the road will become a part of the Pan American Highway.

Production variation in relation to climatic and technological conditions

As mentioned previously, one of the main problems the Mennonites encountered was the great variation in the environmental milieu. It determined to a large extent the fluctuating output of agricultural products (Table 9.3). Cotton, for instance, varied from 327 kg/ha to 866 kg/ha between 1955 and 1975, with particularly bad years in 1962 and 1973. The other cash crop, castor beans, varied even more, from 327 kg to 1161 kg/ha. But the most extreme variations occurred in the food crops of peanuts, beans, sorghum and wheat. For the production of peanuts for instance, per hectare production ranged from 109 kg to 1186 kg, and was seemingly unrelated to area (Fig. 9.4). That of beans varied from 139 kg to 997 kg, sorghum from 451 to 2068 kg, and wheat (in the period it was planted) from 150 kg to 549 kg/ha. No wonder the Mennonites saw the 'writing on the wall' for wheat, and ceased production in 1970.

But the data should not only be looked at in its absolute sense. Burton *et al.* (1978) in their pioneering work on hazards define a *major* drought in Tanzania as one that 'diminishes crop yields – by as much as 30%' and a *severe* drought as one that would 'cause a loss of crop and animal production of about 8%'. Using their criteria we find that on two of the 21 years cotton, a

Table 9.3   Agricultural output of Mennonite farms, 1955–75.

			Production (kg/ha)			
Year	cotton	peanuts	beans	sorghum	wheat	Ricinus (castor beans)
1955	472.67	109.54	250.65	1095.88	—	—
1956	565.28	890.84	672.83	1353.65	—	—
1957	521.20	559.74	412.21	1267.67	—	—
1958	570.52	450.12	286.87	1080.18	500.00	—
1959	778.31	836.43	324.51	1256.47	476.66	—
1960	611.02	941.50	333.38	1459.18	549.90	—
1961	606.03	806.49	511.33	1279.12	374.30	727.32
1962	327.44	398.70	334.45	540.78	422.53	368.48
1963	827.03	965.62	524.39	1414.54	266.12	853.87
1964	475.13	411.23	503.59	1374.03	187.33	643.54
1965	704.85	1156.59	594.34	1531.33	150.09	645.64
1966	601.57	929.31	477.56	1678.59	383.87	1131.63
1967	866.67	235.12	419.00	1565.87	173.75	625.00
1968	600.52	1122.70	997.94	1454.13	375.00	1161.23
1969	445.31	612.09	343.84	867.03	460.00	343.43
1970	686.49	555.48	335.12	901.14	—	400.40
1971	787.66	1125.92	433.17	2068.50	—	773.14
1972	645.41	669.65	324.37	880.73	—	634.72
1973	344.28	585.89	139.79	451.47	—	370.50
1974	(459.86)	1186.35	485.52	1767.46	—	717.61
1975	454.06	358.80	273.09	852.56	—	327.51

Source: Fernheim Colony Administration provided hectareage and total production figures.

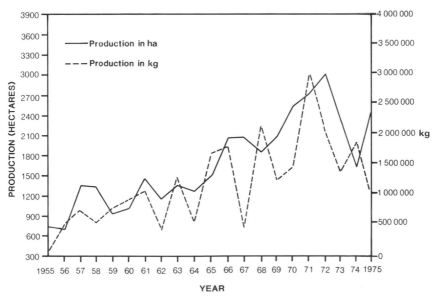

Figure 9.4   Peanut production.

hardy crop, produced 30% less than the average – a 'major drought'. Peanut production on the other hand being more susceptible to drought, was below this mark on six out of 21 years. Beans and sorghum production declined by 30% from the average in four out of 21 years, wheat in three out of 12 years and castor beans five out of 15. What the data suggest is that in about one out of four years major drought conditions exist in the Chaco. On the other hand, using the severe drought condition definition, we would find nearly *every second to third crop year* in the Chaco falls in this category.

How far output is related to the climatic (specifically precipitation) factors and to technological factors can be shown by a simple correlation analysis between average annual production figures and available climatic and technological data (Table 9.4). As can be seen the correlation between cotton and yearly rainfall is nearly zero, and with the amount of rainfall during the seeding season of October and November is negative -0.12. However, the relationship to the amount of rainfall during the growing season of January and February is significant with a value of 0.46. Peanuts had a similar relationship at 0.49. Thus the importance of rainfall in the growing season of January and February appears far greater than the amount in total or the amount during the seeding season. For sorghum, the relationship between the amount of rainfall during the growing season and the final production per hectare is especially strong, ($r = 0.69$). Beans production presents a different picture in that production per hectare is inversely related to the amount of yearly rainfall. It seems that, as the overall rainfall increases, the amount of production of beans per hectare decreases. The relation is not, however, statistically significant. Also, beans do not show a very strong dependence on the amount of rainfall during the growing season. From this one might assume that beans should flourish in the Chaco, especially in drier years. But on the

Table 9.4   Correlation coefficients of yields for selected crops as a function of climatic and technological variables (see text for details).

		Production (kg/ha)		
	cotton	peanuts	beans	sorghum
Climatic				
yearly rainfall	0.07	0.25	−0.22	0.02
seeding season[1]	−0.12	0.05	0.15	0.14
growing season[2]	0.46[3]	0.49[3]	0.23	0.69[3]
Technological conditions				
tractors	0.28	0.30	0.28	0.26
cultivators	0.27	0.21	0.23	0.23
ploughs	0.29	0.29	0.25	0.28
disc	0.26	0.25	0.22	0.24
seeders	0.22	0.18	0.13	0.16
trailers	0.28	0.28	0.24	0.29

Source: data provided by Fernheim colony administration 1955–75.
[1]Defined as rainfall for the months of October and November,
[2]defined as rainfall for the months of January and February,
[3]significant at $\alpha = 0.05$.

whole the data show the strong correlation between a short rainy season and production. It is for this reason why it is so crucial for agriculturalists in agriculturally hazardous areas to know when to plant and have the means of getting the ground ready for planting in a short time. It is all important to have good motive power and personnel available to do this. Unfortunately many people in many developing countries have neither.

The second part of Table 9.4 presents an interesting relationship between the production of the four crops and technological conditions in the colony. Here the numbers of tractors, cultivators, ploughs, discs, seeders and trailers, as measures of technological application, are related to crop production. All seem positively related and of the same order of magnitude, approximately 0.25. One could conclude from this that 'technology' is able to account for 5–10% of the increase in the production per area over the time period considered. But it probably has its limits. In talking to the Oberschulze, Mr Hildebrand found he was concerned about over capital investment in machinery in the colony (interview 10 Jan. 1980).

What the data however do not tell us is how much more land the farmer is able to cultivate with the machines, a very important way of consolidating his subsistence level. But a note of caution should be inserted here. In January 1980 I saw substantial evidence of sand erosion. Because of the need for larger fields in mechanised production, the fine soils are more easily exposed on a large scale allowing for substantial sand-dune migration over the fields, stopped only temporarily by fences and other hindrances. One cannot help but be reminded of Johnson's (1977) idea that deserts (desertification) may in part be man-made.

In summary, the relatively poor association between total rainfall and crop production is typical of climatically marginal areas. Far more important is the amount of rainfall during the growing season. If that is unreliable or is reduced for some reason, then production is low. However, if rainfall problems were to encourage supplementary irrigation during the growing season, that might stabilise production at a higher and more consistent level than the Mennonites have been able to attain until now. In general however, technological improvements, though they increase overall levels of production, do not improve its reliability.

Production decisions and the environmental and economic decision-making milieu

Because of the unpredictable Chaco climatic conditions, the decision a farmer has to make at the beginning of each new crop year as to which crop to plant and how much, is an agonising one. There is some need to rotate crops, but selection is flexible enough to reflect information as to which crop will give the best return.

Table 9.5 Correlation coefficients of area planted in various crops as a function of the previous year's crop price and yield.

Crop selection and price variation[1]

	cotton	peanuts	beans	sorghum	wheat	castor beans	guaranis/cattle
			(ha v. guaranis/kg)				
cotton	-0.72[2]						
peanuts		0.91[2]					
beans			nd				
sorghum				0.79[2]			
wheat					0.41		
castor beans						-0.45	
buffel grass							0.89[2]

Crop selection and production variation[1]

	cotton	peanuts	beans	sorghum	wheat	castor beans
			(ha v. kg/ha)			
cotton	-0.46					
peanuts		0.37				
beans			-0.09			
sorghum				0.03		
wheat					0.28	
castor beans						0.41

[1] Price and production values are taken from the previous year,
[2] significant at $\alpha = 0.05$ level;
nd, no data.

In Table 9.5 the number of hectares that the farmers in Fernheim devoted to a particular crop is related to the price in previous years. For sorghum, peanuts, buffel grass and cotton the correlation is statistically significant. For castor beans and wheat the picture is less certain. Castor beans even have a negative correlation, which suggests that, as the price for castor beans increased, the amount of land devoted to it decreases. The same holds true for cotton. It is an oddity which might be explained by the overall decrease, at least until 1972, of castor beans and cotton in the total economy of the Chaco settlement. Nearly all new improved land is now devoted to the planting of buffel grass, imported from Texas. It is an excellent feed for cattle, does relatively well on bush soils of the Chaco, and has good recuperative power after an extended drought.

The relationship between hectares planted and the production conditions in the previous years is far less certain than those between hectares and price (Table 9.5). To some extent one would expect this. Farmers can do little to anticipate the climatic conditions, though to a large extent these may determine production. Hence it is difficult for their decisions to take this into consideration, except by minimising the overall climatic effect as seen in the abandonment of wheat cultivation and selection of improved pasture on which the impact of climate is not so great.

Primary products processing industries

Major evidence of the successful battle with an adverse climatic condition and isolated geographical location is the way in which Fernheim and the other Chaco colonies have had the confidence to develop agriculturally related industries.

Very early in Fernheim's history an oil-extracting industrial plant was built to produce oils from peanuts, cotton seed and castor beans. These oils provide an important substance for domestic use and a cash commodity for export. Processing in the colony obviously reduces bulk, which in turn economises shipping costs. In 1951 Filadelfia also had three *palo santo* extracting plants. Palo santo is a native Chaco wood which, when chipped and boiled under pressure, yields a resin which is sold for use in perfumes and for various chemical and pharmaceutical purposes.

A large cheese and butter factory, equipped with modern machinery, provides a market for farmer's milk. These processed products are marketed in Asuncion where they have been taken since 1962 by large semi-trailer trucks. The adaptability of buffel grass to variation in moisture conditions is probably the most important factor in the growth of this industry.

As an indication of the degree to which this colony, in spite of its geographical isolation, has developed technologically, a summary of industrial activities needs to be given. Perhaps most important is the colony's electricity generating plant. This facility has contributed in a major way to making life reasonably comfortable and comparatively modern. In addition to industrial power, it provides for domestic appliances such as electric refrigerators, which 85% of the colony families now enjoy. This alone has allowed a mammoth advance in the area of food preservation and diets, previously a serious problem because of the long hot season.

The colony also has a tannery, a shoe factory, a metal foundry, two tile and brick yards, a telephone service, furniture factory, machine repair shops, a blacksmith and tinsmiths. The three Chaco colonies jointly maintain a large agricultural experiment station which has been a boon to all Chaco farmers and thus to the colony economy.

Evidence of emerging economic stability

Demographic, educational and economic matters (Table 9.6) speak objectively of a relatively successful human adaptation to an inhospitable geographic environment. By means of a combination of human determination, technological experimentation, cultural adaptation seasoned with a religious faith and a socioethnic identity, the Mennonites in the Chaco have demonstrated that permanent settlements and a relatively high standard of living are possible.

The chart showing the population trends of the three Chaco Mennonite populations and the Indian population in the central Chaco (Fig. 9.5) area reveals that only the Neuland Colony has had a steady decline in the course of its 25-year existence. Menno, the oldest and most conservative colony, has experienced the most steady and most rapid growth. This is due to a high birth rate and a low death rate on the one hand, and a relatively low emigration

Table 9.6 Summary of demographic, educational and agricultural statistics for a Mennonite colony, 1933–73.

	1933	1938	1943	1948	1953	1958	1963	1968	1973
inhabitants	2 078	1 330	1 717	2 222	2 486	2 500	2 591	2 702	2 810
villages	18	19	19	21	21	20	23	23	23
farms	369	221	217	261	264	258	293	292	286
families	412	280	328	402	449	463	523	546	607
marriages	26	13	14	25	16	31	29	17	20
births	90	91	70	84	99	78	90	78	60
deaths	31	10	5	18	6	19	7	10	13
arrived	—	92	61	73	79	48	13	48	47
left	76	50	8	73	150	131	51	40	123
elem. schools	13	13	15	19	19	17	14	14	14
pupils	337	169	328	586	504	374	402	357	409
high school students	45	29	31	81	134 (est.)	104	136	169	

Fernheim domestic animal census

horses	90	541	874	1434	1691	1575	1779	1642	1415
cattle	1 871	2 770	5 177	11 362	9218	10 690	12 079	17 352	18 414
pigs	467	323	677	475	575	392	294	206	370
chickens	8 246	6 262	8 514	10 402	13 903	20 163	32 781	46 898	—

Fernheim appliances and implements

farm wagons	102	226	215	245	326	305	323	276	269
buggies	—	22	97	197	259	325	329	302	323
ploughs	337	230	282	296	459	514	571	441	382
harrows	302	181	168	170	238	296	336	299	276
cultivators	325	213	256	322	509	589	648	557	516
planters	—	41	96	128	189	290	321	302	240
tractors	0	0	0	0	5	9	31	47	71
trucks	0	1	1	13	16	24	33	53	15
radios	0	6	12	15	20	63	135	244	420
refrigerators	0	0	0	0	2	17	115	240	517

Source: raw data provided by Fernheim Colony Administration.

loss. Fernheim shows a modest population increase over a 45-year period because of its steady high birth rate. The number of people leaving the colony each year exceeded the number arriving in all but a few years between 1950 and 1975. Most of those leaving migrated either to Germany or to Canada, in large part to join close relatives and friends.

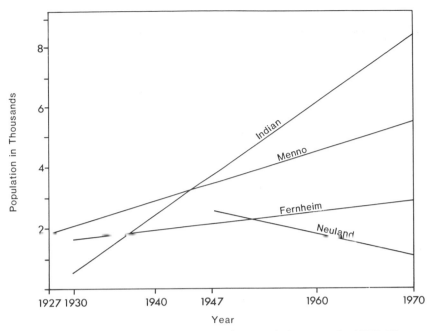

Figure 9.5   Chaco Indian and Mennonite population growth, 1927–72.

Conclusions

The settlement of marginal environments, especially for agriculturalists in climatically hazardous areas, is and will always be associated with large economic and societal risk factors. The attempts of the Mennonites to establish permanent agricultural settlements in one such region of the world – the Chaco – has shown this. However, from this experience one can tentatively conclude that with the ability to specialise in agricultural endeavours suitable to the environment, in this case the growing of grasses better adapted to the environmental milieu than the crops attempted at the initial period of settlement, settlements may not only become more viable, but even prosperous. Even some indigenous economies do benefit (*Mennoblatt* 1980, p. 6). One might suggest that environmentally sensitive milieus are vulnerable when crop production strives to meet all needs and especially needs acquired in less hazardous regions. One solution seems to be economic integration of such areas with other crop-producing regions, allowing specialisation to take place. Then, environmentally sensitive regions of the world, such as the Gran Chaco, might nevertheless make a significant contribution to the overall capacity to produce food to meet ever-growing world demand.

References

Borgstrom, G. 1973. *The food and people dilemma*. North Scituate, Mass.: Duxbury Press.

Bradford, W. E., F. R. Fisher, F. R. Romita and T. S. Darrow 1955. *The Paraguayan Chaco*. US Operations Mission to Paraguay, Asuncion.

Buenstorf, J. 1971. Tanningewinnung und Landerschliessung im argentinischen Gran Chaco. *Geog. Z.* **59**, 177–204.

Burton, I., R. W. Kates and G. F. White 1978. *The environment as hazard*. New York: Oxford University Press.

De Leuw, Cather and Company of Canada 1969. *Feasibility report on the Ruta-Trans-Chaco*. Consultant report presented to Exemo Senor Ministro, Gral. de Div. Marcial Samaniego, Ministerio de Obras Publicas y Communicaciones, Asuncion, Paraguay on 21 March 1969 Ottawa: De Leuw, Cather.

Fretz, J. W. 1953. *Pilgrims in Paraguay*. Scottsdale, Pa.: Herald.

Fretz, J. W. 1962. *Immigrant group settlements in Paraguay*. North Newton, Kansas: Bethel College.

Hack, H. 1976. *Indianer und Mennoniten im Paraguayischen Chaco*. Amsterdam: Center for Latin American Research and Documentation.

Hecht, A. 1975. The agricultural economy of the Mennonite settlers in Paraguay. *Growth and Change* **6**(4), 14–23.

Hecht, A. 1980. Relationships and tensions between Mennonites and Indians in the Paraguayan Chaco. In *Mennonite images*, H. Loewen (ed.), Winnipeg: Hyperion Press. 165–76.

Indianer-Beratungs-Behoerde 1979. *Jahresbericht* 15 Februar. Filadelfia, Chaco.

Johnson, D. L. 1977. The human dimensions of desertification. *Econ. Geog.* **53**, 317–21.

Krause, A. M. 1952. *Mennonite settlement in the Paraguayan Chaco*. Chicago: Dept Geog., Res. Pap., no. 25.

Mennoblatt 16 January 1977, 4.

Mennoblatt 1 October 1980, 6.

Pincus, J. 1969. *The economy of Paraguay*. New York: Praeger.

Regehr, W. 1969. *Die lebensraumliche Situation der Indianer im paraguayischen Chaco*. Basel: Geographisch-Ethnologischen Gesellschaft.

Shannahan, E. W. 1927. *South America*. New York: Methuen.

Unruh, R. H. 1973. *Experimental farm report*. Filadelfia, Fernheim Colony, Chaco, Paraguay, January.

10 *Climatic hazards and agricultural development: some aspects of the problem in the Indo-Pakistan subcontinent*

KENNETH HEWITT

Introduction

Few subjects have received more intense and sustained scrutiny in the Indo-Pakistan subcontinent than economic development. Food and agriculture are among the foremost topics discussed. There is also a large body of work on the region's weather systems, especially the south-west monsoon. This chapter draws mainly upon material that is already available. The sources are, however, scattered. It seems useful to bring them together for an assessment of climatic hazards, as they relate to agricultural development and the sources of food insecurity.

A straightforward review of the record and forms of recent weather damages will be given. However, in attempting to define the significance of these events we shall range more widely than occasions of destructive weather and the immediate features of agriculture that it affects. An important theme to emerge is the way certain entrenched assumptions about the region serve to distort and obscure the roots of these problems. Area specialists may be aware of the fallacies involved, or of casually lumping the region with the so-called Third World. If so, their insights are often absent from not only popular opinion but the statements of governments and international agencies.

Thus, for many observers, the Indo-Pakistan subcontinent is identified before anything else with chronic inability to feed its people and the recurrent threat of famine. Such notions have a foundation in fact, and weather risks are major ingredients of the problem. Yet overemphasis upon these matters, especially as a sort of Malthusian equation between population, undernourishment and backwardness, lead to serious misconceptions of the food picture, how it comes to be as it is, and the role of weather in it. Part of the problem is the practice of working at the level of national, and comparative international, statistics on GNP, population, calorific intake and so forth. It tends, at best, to oversimplify geographic and social complexities. Yet even at so broad a level agriculture, its performance in recent decades and the sources of its failings hardly support the usual stereotype. That, in turn, has profound implications for how we interpret weather risks.

The overall status of agriculture and food supply

In 1980 the subcontinent, if we include Bangladesh, Sri Lanka and the small Himalayan states contained about 883.4 million persons (Population Reference Bureau Inc. 1980). That is more than twice the number when the British withdrew in 1947. Barring major calamity the rates of increase, though diminishing, should put the population at over 1200 million by the year 2000.

Here is the world's second largest concentration of demand for food grains to be directly consumed by humans; second, that is, to China. Demographic statistics are a very crude way to define the food picture and wellbeing of civil societies. Yet, if people consume mainly vegetable matter, there is a fair correlation between numbers of mouths and baseline food requirements. In the subcontinent, food supply for a large fraction of people does lie close to the nutritional minimum. All but a small fraction of food need is met internally from crops. Even in years of seemingly massive foreign assistance of late, the region has produced 85–90% of the food consumed, or has used the aid to build food stocks. According to some estimates, losses of stored food to vermin exceed imports considerably.

In good years, the subcontinent produces about one-seventh of the world cereal crop. Although that is to meet the needs of one-fifth of the world's population, it should be remembered that many of the largest producers of grain, notably the United States and western Europe use much of their supplies for animal feed. On the most favourable conversion, that reduces the number of mouths a given amount of grain will feed to between one-seventh and one-tenth.

Cereal production in the region includes almost 30% of the rice and 10% of the wheat in the world. Rice is the dominant crop, but wheat production alone is twice that of Canada and roughly equal to China's. Much of the world's millet and sorghum is grown here, along with substantial crops of various vegetables and fruits.

As with so much of the tropical and subtropical world, the subcontinent has experienced that seemingly paradoxical development for nations with a mainly agricultural population; the need to import food in most years. The condition arose several decades ago and is commonly attributed to population growth. Apart from the inadequacy of that as an explanation, we must note that the subcontinent is an exporter of substantial amounts of cash-crop products. Examples include the huge exports of tea from Sri Lanka and India, jute from Bangladesh and India, cotton from India and Pakistan. Sugar cane is an important item in some areas. India is North America's largest supplier of nut products and certain condiments, while exports of various tropical fruits such as mangoes and lychees continue to grow. These crops compete with food crops for some of the best agricultural lands. They require irrigation water, fertiliser and other ingredients of high production. They are often the most attractive sectors for agricultural investment and have been well favoured by government price supports. Yet, if cash crops syphon off potential food-producing resources, they are the main source of foreign earnings. To date those earnings have been integral to agricultural modernisation. It is another reminder of the actual complexity of the relations between food need and agricultural development.

Average diet is widely thought to be inadequate. Even allowing for the exaggerated role given to animal protein by Western nutritional science, there is little doubt that a good fraction of the people in the region should, and would like to, eat better. There are chronic shortages in some parts of society throughout the region and stubborn pockets of severe malnutrition. The common impression of 'wall-to-wall' hunger is, however, quite misconceived. Meanwhile, despite rapid population growth, economic problems and natural calamity, there has been a general improvement in diet in the past two decades. It records mainly the expansion of agricultural output which, though propped up by imports and emergency food assistance, has on the average exceeded population growth. This is a large factor in declining death rates.

Overall, the ability of the region to feed most of its vast numbers in most years, and to raise food production faster than population, suggests a fair performance by the agricultural sector. The exceptional concentrations of humanity here over more than three millenia, and in a series of the most sophisticated agrarian civilisations, seems to indicate a generally favourable habitat and an agricultural base of some enduring robustness. Today, if crop yields are often lower than in some comparable environments elsewhere, in technical terms at least, that leaves a potential for further large increases in productivity. This is the view of Revelle and Lakshminarayana (1975, also Revelle 1976). Rafiq (1971) has shown that under favourable management the crop yields of the Indus Plains are already far above the average and they compare with the best agriculture elsewhere.

Yet these features have to be set against an equally impressive record of frequent small and occasional catastrophic failures of food production. Most have been directly related to weather fluctuations. From time to time some millions of folk have died in great famines. A dozen are recorded for the past 1000 years, four in the past 100 years (Bhatia 1967). Recently, the overall growth in food output has been punctuated by several disastrous shortfalls. Again, weather has usually been the immediate problem. Its importance is reflected not only in crop failures but also in the extraordinary surges of production in years of widespread good weather.

Another factor in our acute awareness of the region's food problem is, of course, the constant attention it has received from the international community; an attention deriving as much from Western political, military and commercial interest as concern for the plight of the underfed. More than any other country, India has been taken as the barometer of food sufficiency and modernisation of agriculture outside the communist world. As James Mellor noted (1976), how India has performed correlates well with swings of optimism and pessimism about the world food picture. Before turning to the weather hazards we need to review recent agricultural performance in the region.

The agricultural record since 1947

Following some initial turmoil and recession after departure of the British, food production has shown a general increase throughout the region. In India since 1950 and Pakistan since 1955 it has risen, on the average, slightly faster than population (Mellor 1976).

In the initial phase of development, roughly to the beginning of the 1960s, growth was slow and largely based upon increasing the cultivated area and intensifying traditional farming methods. Throughout the 1950s this enabled India to increase food production about 2.8% a year (Sen 1976). In Pakistan, however, the average for that decade has been put at only 1.3% (Papanek 1967). On the other hand, in the late 1950s, Pakistan plunged more fully into a programme of modernisation. It involved the installation of great numbers of tube wells and some colossal irrigation and power projects associated with the Indus Waters Treaty (Michel 1967, Hasan 1976, Gotsch 1976).

Between 1960 and 1965, Pakistan's production grew 3.8% per annum. Many came to expect that the country would soon be self-sufficient in food. In India, however, the early 1960s show some slowing in the growth rate and uncertainty about how agriculture would develop. Overall, growth averaged 2.0% a year and lagged behind population. Only in the Punjab did agriculture share Pakistan's surge of growth. This area averaged a 5.5% annual growth from 1952 to 1962, with wheat production rising at 6.7%. But the low overall rate would colour world opinion about food prospects for the rest of the decade.

Pessimistic views were further supported by the catastrophic shortfalls associated with drought in 1966–7 and 1972 (see below). But as Hutchinson (1972, p. 132) argued even then, things were not as bad as they seemed. These weather-related failures and the uncertainties of the early 1960s masked what was, for India, a phase of transition to widespread modernisation (see Mellor 1976). Since the mid-1960s, overall food production has risen a handsome 3.5% a year. In Pakistan, the period 1965–9 showed a 17% increase for all crops and 70% for wheat. India's wheat production rose more than 100% in the same period.

In the 1970s Pakistan was again doing less well in growth. Some argue persuasively that this stemmed from social and political problems that developed through overemphasis upon agriculture and related development while other needs went unheeded (Frankel & von Vorys 1972, Stevens *et al*.

1976). In India, however, the decade of the 1970s was again one in which production rose ahead of population. Some disastrous shortfalls in drought years were compensated by equally astonishing surges of production in the years between. One can cite various events behind this. The dissemination of new high-yielding strains of wheat and rice is important. But such specifics of agricultural technique are of secondary significance compared to social and economic shifts. These have been necessary to change practices, and especially to encourage and ensure that a growing fraction of production would go to market. The latter, in turn, has depended upon the growth of reliable demand, especially among urban wage-earning populations. Agricultural performance ultimately becomes a function of the overall economic picture.

The subcontinent's progress over this period may seem poor compared to that of certain small national units such as South Korea or Israel. It comes off very badly in comparison with countries having a developed industrial base such as Japan. But the tendency of some analysts to make these compari sons simply on the basis of agricultural potentialities obscures major differences in the circumstances for development.

Agriculture is not an isolated system. Agriculture in the subcontinent is not an isolated element. Even less so is the problem of hunger. Our assessments must have some regard for the presence of perhaps the greatest diversity of habitats, forms of cultivation and cultures over any comparable agricultural area. We need some sense of historical as well as geographical complexities (cf. Ch. 5). A society does not recover in a hurry from over a century of colonial rule and a much longer period of turbulent struggles for power. The inertia of a thoroughly developed imperial system, the vestiges of its shaping hand, its values oriented to a European world view – not least the instabilities of states whose composition and geography are themselves largely a colonial legacy – create extraordinary problems.

We should recall that hunger was a constant threat under British rule too. The 19th century, high point of European influence, was a period of unusual recurrence of famine. The British blamed local 'backwardness'. Others have blamed the imperial system and its priorities (Bhatia 1967). Whatever, it was not at all a new issue with independence. Moreover, in the last decades of British rule, agriculture was largely allowed to stagnate. There was a growing demand for cash crops, presumably to help Europe's ailing economies. But the dream of some colonial administrators – that India should be able to feed herself adequately and with food to spare for export – was a fast-receding possibility. Finally, imperial rule culminated in the demands and dislocations of World War II. These included, in 1943–4, the worst famine of the century. And so, what some have championed as one of the most enlightened, even desirable, colonial systems left behind it an ailing situation in food and agriculture. Indeed, a region that for long had been, under normal circumstances, a net food exporter was left with a chronic food deficit.

A more crucial comparison, perhaps, is with China, usually perceived as doing much better than India, at least in feeding its people. In that case, however, we have a drastic political and social revolution oriented to the uplift of the rural masses. There seems little doubt that the general result has been a substantial improvement in the material lot of the majority. In national food-producing performance, however, it is debatable whether China has done much better than India. Of late, there is growing evidence that it also has not solved the problem of severe crop failures in adverse weather.

Finally, our perspective can be distorted by those who usually report on these matters: experts in technical improvement and high production agriculture who mainly agonise over the distance between their management models and actual performance. Yet a full and fair assessment of the region's agriculture suggests to me that it has done more than its difficulties might warrant. The general picture is one of steadily expanding per-capita food production due to socioeconomic and technical transformation. The new nations have generally done better here, as in industrialisation, than under direct European control, and from an unfavourable and still dependent position in the global economy. That they have failed to do as much as they could depends largely upon struggles outside of farming and its weather relations. Meanwhile, large year-to-year fluctuations in food producing, imposed by weather, continue to occur. The new nations have not had better climates than the British!

Adverse weather and agricultural performance

For the subcontinent as a whole, floods and droughts are overwhelmingly the largest dangers to food production. Nevertheless, the details of weather impacts on farming have the same diversity as the many habitats, crops and agricultural systems involved. First let us develop some awareness of this range of weather hazards.

Maritime storms, especially tropical cyclones, are a risk for all coastal communities. The numbers and density of people exposed to these storms, notably in the Bay of Bengal (Naqvi 1960), is exceeded only on the shores of the East and South China Seas. From Gujarat on the Arabian Sea to the east coast of Bangladesh, one of the densest rural populations in the world forms an almost continuous belt. There are also numerous large- and medium-sized cities (see White 1974a, Figs 30–3).

The extent of the risk is recognisable in a series of major disasters in recent years. The cyclone that struck Bengal in 1970 is one of the worst typhoon disasters on record. In addition to the enormous loss of life, the storm and coastal floods destroyed some $(US) 63 million in crops and 280 000 head of cattle, while almost wiping out many fishing communities, along with perhaps 65% of the coastal fishery resource (Frank & Hussain 1971).

On average, about three severe cyclones in every two years do damage to some part of the low-lying coasts of the Bay of Bengal (Burton *et al*. 1978, p. 4). India's worst cyclone disaster of the century occurred in 1977 when 20 000 people died along the coast of Andhra Pradesh.

Severe hail, wind and tornadic storms affect most of the subcontinent. Some of the largest hailstones and hailstorm damages in the world have been reported from here. In 1978 alone, three tornado disasters were reported: one in Orissa, one on the outskirts of Delhi, and another in West Bengal. It is a simple matter of spatial probability that such hazards mostly occur in rural areas and affect agricultural activity (Hewitt & Burton 1971, p. 46).

In the north-west and the mountain zones, frost is a serious problem, especially towards the limits of the areas with a second, winter cropping season. Adverse weather in the mountains is also associated with widespread landslide losses. Since some parts of the Himalayan front ranges, the Assam hills, Western Ghats and Sri Lanka include intense farming of steep slopes, local agricultural losses can be high. The same areas have a long history of accelerated erosion associated with farming and grazing (Hewitt 1975b). Landsliding is commonly a part of the worst deterioration that one sees, though more severe when aggravated by storms, earthquakes and the aftermath of drought (Hewitt 1975, 1976, 1977). Landslide disasters associated with storms in 1977 and 1978 were reported from the tea-growing areas of Sri Lanka, and in Assam and Kerala.

The rivers draining the Himalayan ranges have a history of devastating floods from the bursting of landslide and glacier dams, their frequency having some relation to secular climatic variations (Hewitt 1968a, Ch. 16; 1968b, 1982). Those from the 1841 and 1856 landslide dambursts on the Upper Indus irreversibly damaged thousands of once-fertile hectares along that river. The 1929 Shyok ice damburst caused losses of crops and animals along the whole of the main stem of the Indus.

In the drier areas, desiccating winds and dust storms are hazards (e.g. Joshi 1969). Chronic dust palls in the atmosphere have been cited as a possible long-term danger to agricultural production in the north-west (Bryson & Baerreis 1967). The process of desertification observed by many in the semi-arid and subhumid parts of the subcontinent tends to be accelerated during adverse weather (Hewitt 1977, UN 1978). In the irrigated areas of the Indo-Gangetic Plains, where waterlogging and salinisation are threats to agriculture, adverse weather, especially drought, aggravates the problem.

Among other hazards that are brought on or aggravated by certain types of weather conditions, we may add insect infestations, including locust plagues, blights, and increased soil erosion. Nor is the region any longer immune to the climate-related risks of urban-industrialism. Around such rapidly industrialising cities as Lahore in Pakistan, there have already been episodes of severe photochemical smogs related to weather. These are reported to do great damage in surrounding orchards and high-production areas of cereal and sugar cane cultivation (Government of Pakistan 1973, Hewitt 1975b).

Something of the diversity of risks for agriculture should be apparent from this short survey. They also create the possibility of compounded losses in some years. Tornadic storms and hail can be associated with both cyclonic storms and a severe burst of monsoon, as are floods and wind damage. Areas frequently appearing as the worst hit by food shortages in major droughts often have these other problems as added stresses. Rajasthan, with a severe desertification problem and areas of chronic undernourishment, or Bengal, with its great floods and coastal storms, are examples.

Nevertheless, in terms of the overall picture for national and regional possibilities of major food dislocation it is rainfall that emerges as the decisive indicator. And if precipitation is the single most important item, it is in turn largely dependent upon a single great weather system, the south-west monsoon.

Drought and flood

In part, the role of rainfall reflects a general feature of the lowland tropics where moisture supply rather than temperature is the main constraint upon plant growth. It is apparent that, on the whole, monsoon lands have been historically most favourable for the development of agriculture, much more so than the perennially humid equatorial lowlands. As noted before, in south and east Asia, the combination of monsoonal rains and exotic river flow from humid mountains has long provided environments that sustain massive populations.

Bumper harvests in the subcontinent are associated with abundant monsoon rains, well distributed in space and time. Danger exists in large or untimely departures above as well as below average precipitation. To be sure, the meaning of 'too much' or 'too little' varies. It is an oversimplification to say that the best weather is always closest to statistically derived averages. Nevertheless, year-to-year swings in food production generally follow those of rainfall.

In terms of rainfall itself, about 80% of the subcontinent is chronically drought-prone, while most of the heavily peopled humid and riverine lands of the northern, eastern and coastal zones suffer damaging floods somewhere in most years. The worst crop failures are associated with widespread drought. However, large flood losses occur more often and may be a greater overall drain on agricultural wealth (Table 10.1). That actual famine occurs more rarely after floods can be attributed to greater than average yields outside the flooded areas, as a response to higher moisture supply, including in the agriculturally more marginal areas. Within the damaged areas, there are the possibilities of crop recovery, of replanting and/or a more favourable winter cropping season.

Great weather-related crop failures are not purely a thing of the past. Modernisation of crop-growing itself is unlikely to prevent them. One estimate for India in the 1960s puts annual average flood losses at $(US) 160 million (Ramachandra & Thakur 1974). Crop losses are said to account for about 75% of this. However, in 1968 alone these authors report a $400

Table 10.1 Some short-term fluctuations in agricultural performance of India–Pakistan and related climatic events.

1944	excessive rains and floods, 2–4 million died in famine
1948	floods destroyed c. 0.4 million ha crops ($7.5 million estimated losses[1]) in West Pakistan
1969	good crop weather over most of subcontinent, good harvests
1950	floods destroyed 0.3 million ha crops ($7 million) in West Pakistan, and 42 000 head of cattle
1954	good crop weather over most of subcontinent
1955	floods destroyed c. 0.4 million ha crops ($8 million) in West Pakistan, 42 000 head of cattle lost
1956	West Pakistan 71 699 km^2 devastated by floods, c. 0.8 million ha of crops lost ($7.9 million)
1957–8	drought, poor harvests
1961–2	generally good weather, good harvest
1964–5	excellent weather, good harvest
1966–7	catastrophic drought, 10% drop in harvests, approx. 20% US wheat crop to India 1966 and 1967
1965–8	70% increase in wheat harvests of Pakistan
1968	good weather, 28% jump in India's total food grain harvest, 'the Green Revolution had arrived' (Mellor 1976)
1970–1	good weather, good harvests
1971	Bangladesh War, agriculture disrupted, millions of refugees to be fed
1972	severe floods in Pakistan
1972–3	series of severe droughts, precipitous decline in harvests combined with Soviet grain purchases and 'oil crisis' create bleak picture; over 1 million died in famine
1974	world fertiliser shortage; foreign exchange bill for oil doubles; devastating floods in Pakistan
1975	good weather generally, good harvests in India where food reserve increased to 100 million tonnes; large jump in India's industrial fertiliser capacity; but NE India catastrophic floods, $300 million damages in Bolan in August and September
1976	catastrophic floods in Pakistan destroy 0.8 million ha crops, 12 000 head of cattle; cotton production drops by half
1979	India, widespread floods during violent monsoon rains, estimated $100 million damages, autumn rice crop severely affected

[1] Estimates in parentheses for Pakistan by Anwar (nd).

million loss, including $300 million in crops and 270 000 head of cattle. In 1975 floods were said to have destroyed $300 million in Bihar alone.

In the 1950s flood losses in (West) Pakistan were estimated to exceed $10 million annually, with crop losses ranging between 65% and 80% (Anwar nd). In the Indus Valley floods of 1950 nearly 42 000 head of cattle were lost, and 37 000 in 1955 again. Average loss of cattle in floods was estimated to be equivalent to about $(US) 900 000 annually (Anwar nd). More than a million homes were destroyed by floods in this period. The August 1974 floods, concentrated in Punjab and Sind, left some $30 million in damages. Various local reports in my files indicate some $22.7 million in crop losses for Punjab alone. There, nearly 4 million ha were affected, including 1.4 million ha under field crops.

It is, however, major droughts that continue to pose the greatest threat of human misery. The drought-related crop failures of 1967 and 1968 had the potential to bring about the worst famine in the subcontinent's history. That they did not do so must be attributed to rather unusual political and economic conditions affecting world grain supplies.

In India, there was a 19% fall in grain production in 1966–7 from the previous crop season. Grain stocks were soon used up, leaving few reserves when drought and poor crops recurred in the following year. Massive famine was averted by the shipping, on fairly favourable terms, of United States' grain equivalent to about 15% of annual consumption over two years. But the following year, grain production in India rose an enormous 28% in all-time high level, and continued to rise for the next three years. The prophesies of imminent catastrophe were silenced.

However, in 1972–3 drought again afflicted southern and northwestern areas of the subcontinent. This time world conditions were also unusual but very different. A major human disaster was in progress in the Sahel (see Ch. 5). But more directly significant were bad harvests in the Soviet Union and China. Both were looking for grain on world markets at the same time as India and Pakistan. The price of wheat rose sharply in most countries (see Ch. 12). The Soviet Union could easily outbid India for the largest source: United States grain. A variety of economic pressures made the USA ready to sell to the highest bidder (Morgan 1979, Ch. 5). Other factors compounding the situation included the events leading up to the Arab oil embargo of 1973, and climbing oil prices. India was facing a doubling of its oil import costs between 1973 and 1974, even if no change in volume occurred. According to Saroop (1974), that would constitute a jump from a 26% share of foreign earnings to 50%. Meanwhile, there was a worldwide fertiliser shortage. The subcontinent itself was embroiled in another bitter conflict between India and Pakistan that led to the creation of Bangladesh. It is said that over a million persons died of starvation during the drought. Human institutions that could have been used to avert famine were turning out to be no more reliable than the monsoon.

The vagaries of the south-west monsoon

Over most of the region, more than three-quarters of the rainfall derives from the southwesterly or summer monsoon (Tsuchiya 1971, Fig. 2; Domros 1970). The importance of this seasonal precipitation for agriculture lies especially in the fact that, on an annual basis, nearly all of the region suffers from a net water deficit (Subramanyan 1956). According to Kayane (1971) only a narrow zone of the high Himalaya exhibits a perennial water surplus. A broader zone of the Himalaya, most of Bangladesh and southwestern Sri Lanka experience some years of moisture surplus, some of deficit. But the rest of the subcontinent has a persistent annual deficit. Except near rivers and lakes and in wells, there is at best a small carry over of moisture availability from year to year. As far as soil moisture is concerned there is essentially no carry over. For most of the subcontinent potential evapotranspiration, estimated using Thornthwaite's system (which is most likely to underestimate it) exceeds precipitation by more than 200 mm (Kayane 1971, Fig. 7).

Yoshino (1971a, p. 4) has described the precipitation of Monsoon Asia as being 'strongly characterised . . . by its seasonality, interannual variability, torrential behaviour and sharp regionality'. It is fair to say that those characteristics are seen in their most extreme degree in the summer monsoon of India. On the whole, it generously waters lands that might otherwise be largely desert in these latitudes. But its benefits are repeatedly offset by its large year-to-year fluctuations. There is an extensive literature on the system and the mechanisms whereby it transfers equatorial air and huge quantities of moisture from the Indian Ocean over the subcontinent (Flohn 1957, Lockwood 1965, Yoshino 1971b). In recent years attention has turned especially to the relations, or teleconnections, between the behaviour of the southwesterly monsoon and the general picture of atmospheric and ocean-surface conditions over a vast area from the southern Indian Ocean to Siberia and embracing most of the Pacific Ocean (Yoshino 1971b). Here, however, we shall confine attention to the interannual variability of rainfall over the subcontinent.

A sense of the moisture problem for agriculture can be grasped at once from the region's rainfall records, which include many stations with more than a century of observations. While the year-to-year fluctuations are certainly the most remarkable and most immediately relevant to crop production, it has been shown that appreciable secular fluctuations occur too (Khan 1960, Naqvi 1960, Raman & Krishiyan 1960).

Mizukoshi (1971) has provided another way of describing the variability of the weather situation, relating to climatic classification. Using the concept of the 'year climate', he has examined the frequency with which annual data fall within given Köppen classes of climate. He found that very little of the subcontinent lies uniformly within a single class, and most of it is, in his terms, 'transitional' in climate. That is to say, the year climate occurring most frequently, i.e. the one that would appear on a standard Köppen climate map, does not exceed in occurrence the next year climate in more than 30% of the years. And he found that the transition zone between areas with 100% A and B climates is about 2000 km broad here. Moreover, throughout much of the heavily populated northern plains, year climates representative of at least three classes, including A, B and C types, occur.

So long as food production barely matches demand, such secular changes, especially the possibility of runs of dry years, are significant not only to the occurrence of series of bad harvests. They represent a serious issue for the levels of investment in government grain purchases and storage facilities needed to avert famine – or the political and economic costs of periodic requests for emergency food aid.

The variability of the monsoon is not merely temporal. Geographically extensive coincidence of conditions, or of values close to station averages, are relatively rare. There are large year-to-year changes in the spatial mosaic of precipitation, timing of the monsoon and related conditions such as cloudiness.

Some years ago Ramdas (1949), summarised the spatial and temporal variations in monsoonal precipitation for the period 1875–1950. His data serve to demonstrate the scope of the problem for agriculture and reliable food supplies. He defined 'flood' or 'drought' as the occurrence of precipitation twice the mean deviation above or below station averages for some 32 locations scattered over the region. He found that we can expect, on average, a subcontinent-wide drought once in 20 years, and a monsoon of equally widespread 'flood' rains in about the same interval. For comparison he noted that a general occurrence of 'normal' rains throughout the region might be expected once in 10 years. Drought occurred in one or more provinces almost 4 years in every 20, and flood in nearly 7 years out of 20. In other words, widespread favourable conditions could barely be anticipated in one year out of two! He also found that areas with more marginal rainfall – Baluchistan, Sind, Uttar Pradesh – were also most prone to flood and drought years.

It should be noted that some areas are not dependent upon the monsoon, or are cushioned in various ways against its variations. In the far north-west, in Pakistan, precipitation derives largely from westerly depressions in the winter half of the year. The monsoon rarely penetrates the area. There is, however, a substantial risk of both flood and drought here. At the southeastern tip of India and in Sri Lanka, the southeasterly, or winter, monsoon is a source of moisture. The variability of precipitation from this system is much smaller than for the summer monsoon. Then there are extensive, irrigated lands which depend on the monsoon only indirectly or not at all. In Pakistan, 70% of whose agriculture depends upon irrigation, a large fraction of water supply derives from snow and ice melt in the Himalayan ranges; snowfall is an important source other than the monsoon. Incidentally, food production by winter cropping, which depends mainly upon irrigation, has been expanding at twice the rate of production in the monsoon season (Gavan & Dixon 1975).

A particular problem for agriculture is, however, that much of the high-production area cushioned against failure of the monsoon or drought, is greatly at risk from floods. These are the well watered coastal areas, and the riverine plains with abundant groundwater resources and/or surface irrigation systems tapping flow from humid mountains.

Finally, in the drier areas we must also note basic divisions between irrigated and rain-fed agriculture (cf. Morgan 1978, Ch. 2). There are differences in the threat of crop failure from given weather variations. There are even greater differences in the relative attention given to their development. The rain-fed areas and relatively drought-resistant crops grown there – as indeed, the rangelands where goats, sheep and cattle are raised – have received virtually no attention from development programmes or modern assistance. Most are suffering from either over-use and rapid environmental deterioration, or are being abandoned (see Hewitt 1976). It is these areas that support the worst fears of students of environmental damages (Eckholm 1976). Yet, if they are not seen as suited to modernisation, they may well be valuable for cushioning against excessive rain and flood damage elsewhere, while their crops, though low in yields, are relatively drought-resistant. Meanwhile, the human misery of famine is all too evident in these areas. The squatters crowding into cities tend to come from them, as their means of life disappears without sign of concern or thought for its replacement.

Agricultural development, risk and famine

The range and severity of weather hazards is clear. Their interpretation with respect to agricultural performance and food sufficiency is much less so. A careful examination of such a regional phenomenon as the monsoons and their ecological implications is surely a fundamental concern of the geographer or anyone interested in the foundation of material life. That is not the same as treating climate as decisive in famine or feast. It is a major constraint upon the margins of security and flexibility of a society's food policies. Neither for past nor likely future populations has the monsoon absolutely prevented societies from growing and storing enough food to cope with even the worst years. The question does arise, however, why the entirely likely vagaries of this weather system seem to have influenced food policies so little. Having reviewed the evidence of weather-related damages, we must return to the questions of their significance.

I would first like to dispose of the two extremes of assessment. The first is the 'Doomsday' view of the subcontinent as a near hopeless case on the brink of uncontrollable, if not total, famine; second is a projected state in which natural hazards and disasters would be more or less eliminated. Even expert commentary often leaves one or other of these as a dominant impression. The media do so regularly with their images of starving children or ritual applauding of some transfer of food-producing technology. The position taken here is that the 'doomsday' picture is most unlikely, at least in any of the terms we have been considering; and the other extreme of complete safety is impossible.

One can envisage war in the subcontinent, or globally, so disrupting food systems as to produce 'worst-case' famine. An adverse shift in climate, perhaps due to human atmospheric modifications, could badly affect growth in productivity and sharpen year-to-year fluctuations. Just possibly, it might reduce overall food output despite continuing investment in agricultural expansion (cf. Ch. 12). The most probable result of that would be intensification of the scale and severity of malnutrition in the poorest segment of society. Average life expectancy might decrease again; deaths in periodic famines comparable to 1974 or, perhaps, 1942–3 would increase.

The epidemic spread of plant diseases among the new high-yielding crops is an even greater cause for concern and would lead to similar consequences. However, the most likely threat to existing agricultural gains and future growth would be a deep economic recession in the region. That is both a recurrent phenomenon of quasi-capitalist economies and the more severe for food supply when agriculture becomes increasingly oriented to marketable surplus.

Whether the region could survive such developments without great social disorder and perhaps revolution or regional war are questions that, on the most pessimistic view, lead back to the 'worst-case' speculation. They are, however, complex and by no means certain in their outcome. An increasingly dictatorial and ruthless trend for the maintainence of social order, despite hunger and poverty, is equally possible.

Not only are these larger threats for the most part tangential to weather hazards; they require us to recognise powerful, organised, social and political conditions at work here. But the 'doomsday' view, it seems to me, emerges from an image of these nations as a sort of featureless, structureless mass. They are uniformly described by gross statistics of population, calorific intake and monetary wealth. Their qualities are lost in a soup of supposed 'ignorance, backwardness, poverty'. Their fate is extrapolated from an equally inaccurate, undifferentiated image of past catastrophes as total collapses of society. All of this has, of course, a sturdy background in that peculiar, self-congratulatory form of Western analysis that Edward Said cogently discussed as 'imaginative geography' (Said 1978, Ch. 2). It neither values nor tells us about the internal operation and arrangements, the struggles and goals of these peoples themselves. It leaves one quite mystified as to how they keep going at all! To sustain nearly a thousand million folk largely from internal resources while having any kind of economic growth and political activity might seem to require some fairly effective systems of organisation.

On the other hand, the region's agriculture is not and cannot conceivably become safe from repeated local failures or, over a decade or two, from occasional catastrophic losses in adverse weather. That has been the record so far. That is the record virtually everywhere else, and everywhere that has adopted a similar course of intensified food producing (cf. Chs 3, 4 & 12). At the same time, we have seen that the international system is by no means sufficiently reliable to prevent hunger and starvation as and when these disasters deplete total food stocks in the region or on world markets. There is, and is likely to remain, a strong probability of some famine, bringing intensified hunger or starvation to as much as 10% of the people in the region at any one time, unless much more is done to prepare directly for such eventualities. But it is exactly here, as well as in the rapidity of food production growth, that entirely possible human actions could profoundly alter the significance of weather risks. It is here that matters of substance can be discussed rather than the mythology of the two extreme views considered above.

Now, despite various successes, there is a sense that action in keeping with the scale of human misery involved in hunger and natural disaster has not occurred. The general growth of agricultural production has not met these problems. If anything, weather losses and the plight of the poorer, poorly fed fraction of people have worsened. And, as we have seen, that cannot be attributed to numbers of mouths growing faster than food production.

On balance, the technical literature is optimistic about the biophysical capacity of the region to increase food output greatly. Even the economic requirements of a more mechanised intensive agriculture, and related infrastructure are not remarkable compared to some other expenditures. Meanwhile the Indian Constitution, for example, commits its governments to work for the *right* of everyone to adequate means of life and health. And while the circumstances that enabled famine to be averted in 1967 and 1968 were unusual, that the task could be accomplished at all is evidence of global and internal capabilities to produce, store and distribute food on an unprecedented scale. Finally, the specific problems of food production, hunger and famine have been recognised and spoken of seriously for three decades not only by scholars or technical experts inside and outside the region, but by its governments.

However, we must recognise a certain distance beween humanitarian feeling or political salesmanship on the one hand, and the actual economic, social and political conditions governing development and food supply. That in turn places a certain distance between weather losses or agricultural growth and the plight of the hungry or famine-stricken. If growing millions of the hungry were truly the outstanding factor in agriculture, we would have seen a much greater surge in food production, rather than a trend slightly exceeding population growth. Again we find the predilections of the dominant view of hazards clouding the issue (cf. Ch. 1). There are those who seem to assume that the goal of agricultural development in 'underdeveloped' countries is to feed their hungry. And if they are failing, it is assumed to be because of the natural habitat or ignorance. Instead, there is merely a small moral nightmare lurking behind what others have called 'the facts of life'!

As has often been observed, the hungry are generally poor. It is the poor who for the most part suffer starvation and death in famines. But the relation between their need and economic development can be tenuous indeed. Excepting a few agencies of government and charitable organisations, the key institutions in the food system have *only* economic criteria and incentives to regulate their affairs. In the West it is an article of faith that these are the most viable incentives. As a result, however, the enterprises that provide agricultural equipment, fuel and chemicals, the food marketing corporations, the farm lobby, and the institutions financing food-related developments, are generally far removed in their concerns from the problem of poverty or famine. As for the Indian farmer, his predicament is hardly different in certain basic respects from his North American counterpart. His initiative, hard work and foresight – or lack of them – can hardly be predicated upon the existence of hunger or threat of famine. He is most likely to see these as simply another risk for his operation.

Instead, the economics of food development tend to move in the opposite direction. An example will illustrate this. In the Punjab, where grain production in India and Pakistan has increased the most, a flourishing industry is now that of battery-produced eggs and chicken meat, partly if not wholly grain fed. It is a lucrative enterprise serving the large industrial labour force and wealthy urban middle class of the region, its bakeries, the many restaurants, and growing numbers of supermarkets. The state and major businesses are involved in the development as well as small landowners and entrepreneurs. An important link in the chain is with the multinationals of the chick-breeding industry. From such enterprise comes an excellent addition to the diet of wage- and salary-earning urbanites. One might, however, see it as the tip-of-the-iceberg that massively threatens the hungry, the ones who do not have the means to take advantage of these sorts of developments. We have already noted how in North America or western Europe several times the grain and fodder is required to feed a quarter of the population of the subcontinent – a direct consequence of diets high in animal protein. Hence, any such development in India and Pakistan bids fair to swallow up the most optimistic projections for food production. Yet we also know that the incentives and economic rewards of this kind of food system appear much greater than plant-product agriculture, least of all to feed the poor.

American and other food assistance has proved a mixed blessing. It is an open question whether food insecurity and famine in India since 1953 owes more to the monsoon than to the United States' Public Law 480. This law was designed to regularise the government disposal of surplus American production to needy and friendly nations abroad on favourable terms. It has been championed as a great humanitarian act. And in the years immediately before 1953 American food certainly did save millions from starvation, not merely in Asia but in war-torn Europe. But for the USA the motivations were not only humanitarian even from the beginning.

First, there was an American agriculture incapable, it seemed, of stable, profitable performance without massive government intervention. This paid farmers to limit production and still guaranteed to buy the surplus they regularly produced beyond what the market would bear. 'Dumping' that grain abroad had become the principal policy to avoid a recurrence of agriculture's part in the Great Crash. But secondly, there was the Cold War. In it, American grain could assist friendly but unstable governments abroad and sugar the pill of military alliance and political manipulation. Grain is an important weapon in the Cold War.

Public Law 480 can only be humanitarian in areas incapable of feeding themselves, in the short run at least. There is a widely held belief that that is so. There is also a growing admission that it need not have been so, and that PL 480, among other geopolitical interventions in the food economy, has profoundly affected production agriculture and food policies in areas such as the subcontinent. It may have served to endanger food security more effectively than the miracle grains and Western-financed or international agricultural-research stations have helped it. It seems fair to say that governments in the subcontinent *chose* to depend upon food imports and emergency assistance as the least painful option. They have preferred to define the fundamental problem behind malnutrition and famine as 'overpopulation'. They do not blame it on failure to raise food production at higher rates or prepare for recurrent shortfalls due to weather. The population thesis is, of course, a widespread interpretation. Innumerable writings by Western geographers and others use data from, and especially photographs of, crowds in Indian cities, listless knots of beggars or squatters, and underfed children – as the graphic evidence of 'too many mouths'. (I would say here only that to think in that way is to have an uninformed if not romantic view of the social and economic realities behind poverty, the flight to the cities and, indeed, the circumstances that lead families carefully to limit or not limit the numbers of their children. George 1976, Ch. 2 is a useful place to start exploring this issue.) Whatever the truth of the 'population problem', in the several decades involved, numbers have never exceeded entirely feasible levels of food production to provide food security throughout the region.

Had India or Pakistan chosen the sort of policy on food grains evidenced by Italy's enormously successful 'wheat fight' after 1925, or Japan's in the early 1930s, they could certainly have found the resources of land, labour and capital to achieve food security years ago. If the overall problems were greater in the subcontinent than for Italy under Mussolini or Imperial Japan, they were far less insuperable than, say, those of China. Instead, however, agricultural reform and diversion of investment on a scale sufficient to bring reasonable food security has not happened. Rather, industrialisation and the demands of the better-off urban sector have been the favourite children of economic development and social uplift. Governments have generally perceived military threats to be far greater than those of malnutrition or drought, to judge from the relative outlay to deal with each of these (SIPRI 1975, Ch. 8).

There is nothing unusual about this situation. It is commonplace in many states, past and present. Nor has the international community or its wealthier states failed to encourage it, except in rhetoric. If the subcontinent has been spending as much as 20% of GNP on military means, much of this has gone to purchase arms abroad. The wealthy nations have also sold more in this way than of ploughs and medicines. The international system supports developments that require industrial technology. It serves to promote urbanisation and commercial enterprise. The bulk of the exchanges of knowledge and wealth largely exclude anyone not involved in these. Emergency food assistance is perhaps a special case. But it is arguable how far or how often this has been truly humanitarian and how far an instrument of attempted political influence and stabilisation (Wallenstein 1976). Meanwhile, just as the wealthier and more powerful sectors of a given state tend to shift the risks and hardships of enterprise to the poorer and less influential, so there is some reason to believe that the same happens within the international system between stronger and weaker states (George 1979).

How far one is comfortable with or wishes to pursue such views will vary with one's preoccupations. But they need a voice in a subject so often treated in mechanical, malthusian terms: as an equation of resources and population; as a struggle between rational management and unforeseen natural calamity or social 'backwardness'.

It seems, therefore, if we were to borrow Walter Firey's terminology for the conditions governing resource development, that food sufficiency in the sub-continent is 'ecologically possible' and 'culturally acceptable' (Firey 1960). But it continues to fall outside 'economic feasibility', at least for the poorest few tens of millions of folk. For them, economic priorities or organisation do not coincide with the requirements of food security. To be sure, at this level of abstraction, one could argue that cultural and economic conditions are not distinguishable. If government, businesses, finance and international sponsorship yield to pressures that preclude solving an entirely soluble matter of irreducible human need, that adds up to a moral and ideological decision too. However, when we ask about the behaviour of specific actors within the situation, they seem less avoidably constrained by what is economically most favourable to them. Only if government and/or business are willing to remove food sufficiency from competitive enterprise can one hope to see agricultural development seriously reducing hunger and threat of death by starvation without large social changes.

In conclusion, then, we must reiterate the important distance that exists between the fact of climatic hazard and disaster, and their impact upon the responsibilities of human societies in the region. In virtually no case should the losses from weather, or hunger that can go with them, be interpreted as a raw expression of imbalance between population and natural resources, brought to a head by weather uncertainty. As Bhatia (1967) puts it, that is the kind of famine that only applies 'under primitive and medieval conditions of economic life'. He is at pains not merely to show that today's India is far removed from those conditions, but that they do not describe the nature of famines he has examined there over the past 125 years. For him the critical issue is, therefore, those conditions preventing people from being fed, and of the institutions failing to provide against famine, or even aggravating it. Specifically this bears upon the way in which 'instead of absolute want, famine under modern conditions, has come to signify a sharp and abrupt rise in food prices which renders food beyond the reach of the poor who suffer starvation' (ibid. p. 1).

The same theme can be discovered in James Mellor's work in relation to agricultural development when he says that 'Many people in the developed countries still do not understand that the demand for food in developing countries is not rigidly linked to the laws of human biology. For countries such as India, the demand is in large part the product of policies determining the choice of development strategy and the rate of employment growth and hence the fraction of total income in the hands of the poor' (1976, p. 159).

Equally, the form and level of risks from nature are a function not merely of spontaneous natural events but of human development.

References

Abelson, P. H. (ed.) 1975. *Food; politics, economics, nutrition and research: a special* Science *compendium*. Washington, DC: Am Assoc. Adv. Sci.

Anwar, A. A. (nd). Effects of floods on the economy of West Pakistan. *Pakistan Geogl J.*, 75–88.

Basu, S. *et al.* (eds) 1958. *Monsoons of the world: a symposium*. New Delhi: Hindi Union Press.

Bhatia, B. M. 1967. *Famines in India, 1860–1965*, 2nd edn. New Delhi.

Bryson, R. A. and D. A. Baerreis 1967. Possibilities of major climatic modifications and their implications: northwest India. *Bull. Am. Meteorol Soc.* **68**, 3, 136.

Burton, J., R. W. Kates and G. F. White 1978. *The environment as hazard*. New York: Oxford University Press.

Domros, M. 1970. A rainfall atlas of the Indo-Pakistan subcontinent based on rainy days. In Schweinfurth *et al.* (1970).

Eckholm, E. P. 1976. *Losing ground: environmental stress and world food prospects*. New York: Norton.

Firey, W. 1960. *Man, mind and land: a theory of resource use*. Glencoe, Ill.: Free Press.

Flohn, H. 1957. Large scale aspects of the 'summer monsoon' in South and East Asia. *J. Meteorol Soc. Japan* 75th anniv. vol., 180–6.

Frank, M. L. and S. A. Hussain 1971. The deadliest cyclone in history. *Bull. Am. Meteorol Soc.* **52**, 438–44.

Frankel, F. R. and K. von Vorys 1972. *The political challenge of the green revolution: shifting patterns of peasant participation in India and Pakistan*. Center for Int. Studs Policy Memo. no. 38, Princeton Univ.

Gavan, J. D. and J. A. Dixon 1975. India: a perspective on the food situation. In Abelson (1975, pp. 49–57).

George, S. 1976. *How the other half dies: the real reasons for world hunger*. Harmondsworth: Penguin.

George, S. 1979. The risk shifters. *New Internationalist*, 10–13.

Gotsch, C. H. 1976. Relationships between technology, prices, and income distribution in Pakistani agriculture: some observations on the green revolution. In Stevens *et al.* (1976, pp. 242–66).

Government of Pakistan 1973. *Human environment in Pakistan: problems, prospects and proposals*. Rep. Comm. on Human Environ., Ministry of Science and Technology, Islamabad.

Hasan, P. 1976. Agricultural growth and planning in the 1960's. West Pakistan. In Stevens *et al.* (1976, pp. 233–41).

Hewitt, K. 1968a. *Geomorphology of mountain regions of the Upper Indus Basin*. Unpubl. PhD thesis, London Univ.

Hewitt, K. 1968b. Records of natural damming and related events in the Upper Indus Basin. *Indus: J. Water Power Devel. Auth. Pakistan* **10**. no. 4.

Hewitt, K. 1975a. Perspective on natural hazards and disasters in the northern areas. *Dawn Magazine*, 12 January, Karachi, 1–3.

Hewitt, K. (ed.) 1975b. *National seminar on ecology, environmental protection and afforestation; proceedings*. Ministry of Urban Planning, Government of Pakistan, Islamabad.

Hewitt, K. 1976. Earthquake hazards in the mountains. *Nat. Hist.* **LXXXV**, no. 5, 30–7.

Hewitt, K. 1977. Desertification, development and the 'Admirals' of Manchar Lake, Pakistan. *Econ. Geog.* **53**, no. 6, 358–63.

Hewitt, K. 1982. Natural dams and outburst floods of the Karakoram Himalaya. *Hydrol Sci. J.* **27**, 266–7.

Hewitt, K. and I. Burton 1971. *The hazardousness of a place: a regional ecology of damaging events*. Toronto Univ., Dept. Geog. Res. Publn no. 6.

Hutchinson, J. B. 1972. *Farming and food supply: the interdependence of countryside and town*. Cambridge: Cambridge University Press.

Joshi, K. L. 1969. Problems of desert agriculture in Punjab Haryana and West Rajasthan. *Science and Culture* **35**, no. 10, October, Calcutta, 550–3.

Kayane, I. 1971. Hydrological regions in monsoon Asia. In Yoshino (1971b, pp. 287–300).

Khan, M. L. 1960. Recent pluviometric changes in the arid and semi-arid zones of West Pakistan. *Pakistan Geogr. Rev.* **15**, no. 1.

Lockwood, J. G. 1965. The Indian monsoon – a review. *Weather* **20**, 2–8.

Hopper, D. 1976. The development of agriculture in developing countries. *Scient. Am.* **235**(3), 196–205.

Mellor, J. W. 1976. The agriculture of India. *Scient. Am.* **235**(3), 154–63.

Michel, A. A. 1967. *The Indus Rivers: a study of the effects of partition*. New Haven, Conn.: Yale University Press.

Mizukoshi, M. 1971. Regional divisions of monsoon Asia by Koppen's classifications of climate. In Yoshino (1971b, pp. 259–74).

Morgan, D. 1979. *Merchants of grain*. Harmondsworth: Penguin.

Morgan, W. B. 1978. *Agriculture in the Third World: a spatial analysis*. Boulder, Colo.: Westview Press.

Naqvi, S. N. 1960. Storm waves in the Bay of Bengal. *Proc. 4th Pan-Indian Ocean Science Congr.*, Karachi.

Naqvi, S. N. 1969. Coefficient of variability of monsoon rainfall in India and Pakistan. *Pakistan Geogl Rev.* **4**(2), 7–17.

Papanek, G. F. 1967. *Pakistan's development, social goals and private incentives*. Cambridge, Mass.: Harvard University Press.

Population Reference Bureau Inc. 1980. *1980 world population data sheet*. Washington, DC.

Rafiq, C. M. 1971. Crop ecological zones on the Indus Plains. *Pakistan Geogl Rev.*, July, 38–42.

Ramachandra, R. and S. G. Thakur 1974. India and the Ganga floodplains. In White (1974b, Ch. 5. pp. 36–42).

Raman, P. K. and A. Krishiyan 1960. Runs of dry and wet spells during southwest monsoon and onset of monsoon along the west coast of India. *Indian J. Meteorol. Geophys.* **11**, 105–116.

Ramdas, L. A. 1949. Rainfall in India: a brief review. *Indian J. Agric. Sci.* **29**, 1–19.

Revelle, R. 1976. The resources available for agriculture. *Scient. Am.* **235**(3), 164–77.

Revelle, R. and V. Lakshminarayana 1975. The Ganges water machine. In Abelson (1975).

Said, E. 1978. *Orientalism*. New York: Random House.

Saroop, V. 1974. India: paying for oil. *Middle East International* no. 34, April, 15–16.

Scheinfurth, V., H. Flohn and M. Domros 1970. *Studies in the climatology of South Asia*. Wiesbaden: Franz Steiner.

Sen, S. 1976. *A richer harvest: new horizons for developing countries*. New York: Orbis.

SIPRI 1975. *The arms trade with the Third World*. Stockholm Int. Peace Res. Inst. New York: Holmes & Meier.

Stevens, R. D., H. Alavi and P. J. Bertocci (eds) 1976. *Rural developments in Bangladesh and Pakistan*. East-West Center, Honolulu: Hawaii University Press.

Subramanyan, V. P. 1956. Droughts and aridity in India: a climatic study. In *Proc. Symp. Meteorol and Hydrol Asps Droughts and Floods in India, Indian Meteorol Dept.*, New Delhi. S. Basu (ed.), 171–7.

Tsuchiya, I. 1971. Fluctuations in rainfall in Southwest Asia – equatorial Pacific and low and middle latitude accumulations in the southern hemisphere. In Yoshino (1971b, pp. 217–39).

UN (United Nations) 1978. *Desertification: its causes and consequences*. Oxford: Pergamon Press.

Wallenstein, P. 1976. Scarce goods as political weapons: the case of food. *J. Peace Res.* **13**(4).

White, A. U. 1974a. Global summary of human response to natural hazards: tropical cyclones. In White (1974b, Ch. 30, pp. 255–64).

White, G. F. (ed.) 1974b. *Natural hazards: local, national, global*. New York: Oxford University Press.

Yoshimura, M. 1971. Regionality of secular variations in precipitation over Monsoon Asia and its relation to general circulation. In Yoshino (1971b, pp. 195–216).

Yoshino, M. M. 1971a. Water balance problems in monsoon Asia from the viewpoint of climatology. In Yoshino (1971b, pp. 3–26).

Yoshino, M. M. (ed.) 1971b. *Water balance of monsoon Asia*. Hawaii Univ., Honolulu.

11 *Wheat yields and weather hazards in the Soviet Union*

IHOR STEBELSKY

The Soviet Union grows more wheat than any other country in the world. Although the present Soviet wheat production satisfies her domestic needs, recent disastrous harvests have led to huge covert purchases abroad. In some years these have drained global reserves and shocked the world wheat market. The record Soviet purchase of 1972, nicknamed in popular press as the 'Great Grain Robbery', was negotiated separately under a cloak of secrecy with private US grain dealers in order to benefit from US subsidised low prices. Ultimately the US Department of Agriculture estimated that the Soviet purchases in 1972 totalled 28 million tonnes and, when this knowledge became public, grain prices soared (see US Department of Agriculture 1974, pp. 14–16; Johnson 1974, pp. 48–9). As world demand for food continues to grow, and as the grain reserves continue to remain as low as they have been during the past decade, the fluctuations in Soviet wheat yields may assume global significance. Future shortfalls may prod the Soviet Union to purchase even larger quantities of grain, depriving poorer countries of needed grain imports (see Brown 1974, p. 70; Mesarovic & Pestel 1974, p. 19).

Why should the world's largest wheat producer experience such erratic yields? It is a significant grain exporter one year and a major importer the next. To what extent does the problem derive from weather hazards, and in what ways are managerial and political variables involved? The answers to these questions are fundamental to a better understanding of wheat yields and weather hazards in the Soviet Union.

Wheat ecology and weather hazards

Wheat is the most important crop grown in the Soviet Union. Occupying some 60 million ha or nearly 30% of the Soviet cropland, wheat accounts for about one-half of all the Soviet grain reaped. Of the grain harvested 84% is for direct human consumption. Although both spring and winter wheat are grown in large quantities, spring wheat occupies about two and one-half times more area than the fall-sown wheat. However, the yields of the latter are higher, thus making the production ratio of spring to winter wheat 2:1 (*USSR agriculture atlas* 1974, p. 46).

Spring wheat is grown widely in the Soviet Union (Fig. 11.1). Extending in a broad but tapering sweep from west to east, the area sown to spring wheat is

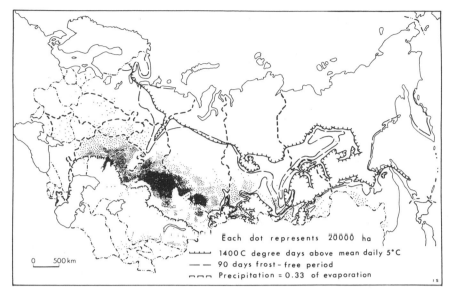

Figure 11.1   Spring-wheat area of the Soviet Union, 1965.

limited in the north by cold and in the south by drought. As a biological heat requirement, spring wheat needs 1400 to 1700 C degree days of accumulated temperature above 5 °C and 90–120 frost-free days, depending on the variety grown (Sinitsina *et al.* 1975, p. 43; Berlyand & Kryuchev 1967, p. 71).

Upon closer scrutiny, the distribution pattern reveals other, more specific limiting factors. West of the Volga spring wheat cannot easily compete with more valuable crops. Even in the more northerly areas, where crop competition is less intense and there is sufficient heat and an adequate growing season, spring wheat is not grown widely. It does poorly on the acidic podzols. In western Siberia extensive swamps and poor soils confine spring wheat to the settled zone along the Trans-Siberian Railway. Only in eastern Siberia is the spring wheat area closely defined by the limit of 90 frost-free days. There are local, exceptionally early varieties developed to mature within a period of 70 frost-free days (Ivanov 1975, p. 8).

The southern margin of the main spring wheat area is closely defined by drought. This margin coincides with the semi-desert, where the average annual potential evaporation exceeds the average annual precipitation by about three times (*Atlas sel'skogo khozyaystva SSSR* 1960, pp. 46–7). Here and there, some rivers have extended wheat-growing into drier regions. In the Transcaucasus and in Soviet Central Asia a small quantity of spring wheat is grown in early summer on lands that are sparsely irrigated. In elevated foot-hills the crop depends upon a very scanty and uncertain spring precipitation (Mints 1969, pp. 130–69).

For any given year, however, climatic limits are related to weather hazards that occur in greater frequency and greater severity near the margins. Because the young sprouts of spring wheat can tolerate frost down to $-8\ ^\circ$C, dangerous late spring frosts are not a threat, except in Siberia. But spring frosts may reduce yields and, more rarely, destroy the crop, depending on terrain, anywhere from 1 to 5 years in 10 (Sinitsina *et al*. 1975 pp. 124–6). Early autumn frosts, however, are more widespread. At -1 to $-2\ ^\circ$C frost can damage the flower and at -2 to $-4\ ^\circ$C it can damage the ripening kernel. Indeed, the exposure of flowers to $-3\ ^\circ$C and ripening kernels to $-5\ ^\circ$C may destroy the entire crop (Rudnev 1964, pp. 150, 190). The chance of such frost damage in the European north and western Siberia ranges from 2 to 3 years in 10, but in eastern Siberia, where the growing season is shorter, the risk increases to 4 years in 10. Even south of these marginal zones in the main spring wheat area of European Russia, astride the Volga early autumn frost damage may occur once every 10 years. The main spring wheat area in Kazakhstan may suffer from such frost 1 to 2 years in 10 (Sinitsina *et al*. 1975, p. 130).

As the risk of autumn frost decreases to the south, the risk of drought looms larger. The chance of drought, with yields of spring wheat reduced by more than 25% from the mean, in the Kazakh spring wheat region varies from 10% in the north to 60% in the south. Along the Volga the frequency of drought increases from north-west to south-east: 5% near Moscow, 10% near Kazan, 20% near Kuybyshev, 40% near Volgograd and thence rising steeply to the south-east (ibid. p. 142).

The most hazardous weather condition leading to severe drought is the so-called *sukhovey* (Lydolph 1964). This hot dry air associated with an anti-cyclone can cause rapid wilting and damage to grain. The probability of spring wheat suffering from *sukhovey* increases southwards from 2 years in 10 in western Siberia to 7 years in 10 in the dry steppes of Kazakhstan. Similarly the incidence of damage from a *sukhovey* along the Volga increases from 2 years in 10 near Ulyanovsk to 6 years in 10 near Volgograd (*Atlas sel'skogo khozyaystva SSSR* 1960, p. 41); Sinitsina *et al*. 1975, p. 155).

Winter wheat, by contrast, has a growing cycle that makes better use of autumn rains and spring thaw. With yields nearly twice as high as those of spring wheat, the fall-sown wheat has been promoted to displace spring wheat wherever possible. Although it needs as much heat as spring wheat (1400–1500 C degree days accumulated during its growing season, depending on variety), it must endure winters that may be fatal if temperature near the ground drops to $-18\ ^\circ$C (Berlyand & Kryuchev 1967, pp. 38, 44). Snow will provide some protection from cold air temperatures. But at $-40\ ^\circ$C snow cover of at least 30 cm is needed, a mean depth seldom achieved by the end of January in the spring wheat belt of western Siberia and northern Kazakhstan (*Atlas sel'skogo khozyaystva SSSR* 1960, p. 43). Consequently, the harsh continental winters, where the average annual minimum temperatures drop below $-35\ ^\circ$C (ibid., p. 9), restrict winter wheat to areas west of the Ural Mountains and south of the Aral Sea (Fig. 11.2).

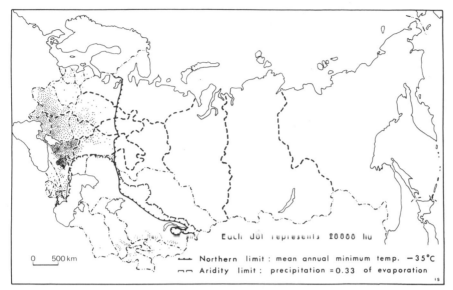

Each dot represents 20000 ha

0   500 km

Northern limit : mean annual minimum temp. −35°C

Aridity limit : precipitation = 0.33 of evaporation

Figure 11.2   Winter-wheat area of the Soviet Union, 1965.

Meanwhile, in those regions where the minimum temperatures are not extreme, weather conditions may lead to sizeable crop losses. In northern European Russia, prolonged deep snow cover following a mild moist autumn will cause the grown plants to respire excessively, lose their stored-up food supply and, before the onset of spring growth, succumb to rot or fungus (Prutskov 1976, pp. 82–3).

By contrast, a dry autumn may preclude winter wheat from acquiring sufficient cold hardiness. Wind currents, guided by topography and vegetation, will remove snow cover from some parts of the field, exposing the crop to winter kill. During occasional thaws, particularly common in the west, reduced snow cover may expose the crop, and ice may form on the surface damaging winter wheat.

Wet snowfall under semi-thaw conditions will form an icy crust that can lead to winter kill. The formation of such crusts is common in European Russia. In the central part, extending between Kiev and Moscow, it occurs in more than 7 years in 10 (Sinitsina *et al*. 1975, p. 95).

In the spring, winter wheat may suffer either from overabundance of water or from lack of it. In the European north-west, water may inundate entire fields after the thaw. Prolonged inundation of plants can thin out the stand of winter wheat, and the entire crop may be destroyed if water (at 5 °C) covers the plants for more than 26 days (ibid. p. 96).

In the south-east, winter wheat may also be damaged by the *sukhovey*. In southern Ukraine winter wheat suffers from the *sukhovey* 1 to 2 years in 10. Along the Don and Kuban rivers the frequency increases to 2 to 3 years in 10, and south and east of Volgograd the incidence of damage is even greater (*Atlas sel'skogo khozyaystva SSSR* 1960, p. 41).

In the Transcaucasus and Soviet Central Asia winter wheat is grown either on irrigated land in rotation with a summer crop such as cotton, or in elevated foothills where the crop depends on seasonal winter rains. In either case the moisture supply is uncertain and may be robbed by frequent and severe hot dry winds (Babushkin 1957).

Adverse weather conditions often lead to increased pest and weed infestations. In the European north-west, late spring and cool moist summer weather will inhibit timely ripening of grain and encourage the infestation of spring wheat with swedish fly (Nettevich 1976, pp. 126–9). In the drought-prone areas fields repeatedly sown to wheat without clean fallowing face increased competition from weeds (Shul'meyster 1975, p. 44).

Such weather hazards and their associated effects have contributed to wide fluctuations in wheat yields for the Soviet Union. A brief survey of a century of records suggests that variations of 10 to 20% from the mean have been normal. For the country as a whole, grain yields 45% below normal have been recorded, and some regions have experienced calamities where only 25% of the norm has been harvested (Selyanimov 1958, pp. 22–3).

Political and managerial trends

Important as climate is, we must also recognise that political events and farm management have had profound effects on yields, harvests and ultimately the supply of grain for human consumption. Of course, this does not apply only to the Soviet period. In a survey spanning one millenium of Russian history, W. A. Dando identified 121 years of famine and 100 years of hunger, an average of one famine or hunger year out of every five (Dando 1976, p. 221). Usually, these events were localised and involved both a bad harvest and a political constraint that expressed itself in food shortages for the populace. In the first seven centuries examined by Dando, the frequent human causes included wars, banditry, civil disruption or armed repression. Famines in the 17th through 19th centuries were conditioned by a combination of high rural densities, poor transportation and serfdom or post-emancipation rural poverty (Stebelsky 1972).

In the Soviet period, however, famines have been associated with political repression of peasantry and forced collectivisation. Although the famine of 1919–23 was brought about, in part, by the civil war, the great famine of 1932–4 was entirely politically induced. Food was ruthlessly extracted from the farmers to supply grain for export, the war chest and industrial workers, and to drive a reluctant peasantry, which was considered to suffer from over-population anyway, into collective farms (Fisher 1927, Dalrymple 1964). Reimposition of collectivisation in 1946–7 had a similar effect.

De-Stalinisation and *detente* brought with its policies more favourable to the peasantry. Khrushchev's commitment to improve the diet and living standards of the Soviet population led to a number of changes. Agriculture was assigned a higher level of priority. More funds were allocated to it, and higher government purchase prices were offered to improve incentives. Organisational reforms and ambitious programmes to increase agricultural production were introduced. When shortfalls occurred, the government negotiated sizeable grain imports to prevent massive livestock slaughter or famine. Following the poor wheat harvest of 1963 the Soviet Union imported an unprecedented 3 million tonnes of wheat, and from 1964 through 1966 imports rose to 6 or 7 million tonnes annually to replenish the losses. Thereafter imports declined until the poor harvest of 1969 (see Vneshnyaya Torgovlya SSSR 1967, p. 113; 1969, p. 44; 1971, p. 46). However, the war chest (emergency supplies kept in underground storage bins near major cities in case of nuclear attack) remained untouched. For example, *The International Herald—Tribune* (2–3 Oct. 1976) reported that such bins had been confirmed from satellite photography around 36 cities, with an estimated capacity of 2 million tonnes. Associated warehouses were said to hold another 4–6 million tonnes. The report speculated that more underground bins may exist, but that these have not yet been spotted.

Soviet agricultural programmes had a profound impact on wheat production and wheat yields. Until 1958 the main thrust was to increase wheat production by increasing sown area (for details see Jackson 1959, 1962, 1963). Under Stalin, wheat was extended into dry marginal areas east of the Volga and into the non-chernozem zone of central and northern European Russia. Fertiliser and manure were lacking, and in their place a grass-field crop rotation was encouraged. This expansion encountered considerable difficulties, resulting in rather low and fluctuating yields (Table 11.1).

Khrushchev's virgin lands programme (1955–8) more than doubled the sown area of spring wheat east of the Urals by ploughing the land to its limits. Although Khrushchev and his advisers were aware that wide fluctuations in yields could be expected in the east, they were willing to take the risk. It was hoped that poor yields in one part of the country would be compensated by a better harvest in another and the net result, more wheat. In the later years of the programme (1959–63) increases in spring wheat area could come only from reducing fallow, a practice that led to lower yields and accelerated erosion. This is also said to have been a large factor in the eventual political demise of Khrushchev.

The new leadership, under Brezhnev and Kosygin, assumed a cautious agricultural policy and directed even more investments into the farming sector. Realising that the limits to expanding Soviet ploughland had long been reached, and that reclamation of swamps or deserts is very costly, their goal was to raise yields of all crops, including wheat. For this purpose the agricultural sector was supplied with much more mineral fertilisers, herbicides, insecticides and dispensing equipment for such products. Even extensive

Table 11.1 Wheat areas, yields and harvests in the Soviet Union.

Year	Spring wheat SA	yield	MD	Winter wheat SA	yield	MD	All wheat harvest
1945	15.9	4.8		9.0	6.3		13.4
1946		4.2			5.4		12.5
1947		6.3			7.5		17.4
1948		4.4			11.3		24.3
1949		5.7			7.8		23.6
1945–9 mean		5.1	14.6		7.7	19.8	
1950	26.0	7.6		12.5	9.1		31.1
1951		5.7			10.9		32.4
1952		6.9			13.8		43.8
1953	30.5	7.0		17.8	11.1		41.3
1954	33.6	8.3		15.7	9.3		42.4
1950–4 mean		7.1	9.5		10.8	12.2	
1955	42.2	5.3		18.3	13.5		47.3
1956	49.1	10.7		12.9	11.6		67.4
1957	50.5	6.1		18.5	14.7		58.1
1958	48.4	9.7		18.2	16.2		76.6
1959	45.6	9.4		17.4	15.2		69.1
1955–9 mean		8.2	24.8		14.2	9.6	
1960	48.3	9.5		12.1	15.1		64.3
1961	45.7	8.2		17.3	16.9		66.5
1962	49.3	8.2		18.1	16.8		70.8
1963	48.2	5.9		16.4	12.9		49.7
1964	48.9	9.9		19.0	13.8		74.4
1960–4 mean		8.3	12.9		15.1	9.3	
1965	50.4	5.5		19.8	16.1		59.7
1966	50.2	12.0		19.8	20.4		100.5
1967	47.3	8.9		19.7	17.8		70.4
1968	48.2	12.2		19.0	18.3		93.4
1969	52.0	10.1		14.4	18.9		79.9
1965–9 mean		9.7	20.9		18.3	5.9	
1970	46.7	12.3		18.5	22.8		99.7
1971	43.3	11.8		20.7	23.1		98.8
1972	43.5	13.0		15.0	19.6		86.0
1973	44.8	13.5		18.3	27.0		109.8
1974	41.1	9.5		18.6	24.0		83.9
1970–4 mean		12.0	9.5		23.3	7.6	

Note: SA, sown area in million hectares;
yield, in quintals per hectare;
MD, mean deviation of yields within each 5-year period from the 5-year mean yield,
expressed as per cent of the 5-year mean yield;
harvest, in million tonnes.

drainage, irrigation and other land improvement schemes have been encouraged (see Bush 1974, Jackson 1970, Karcz 1970, Nove 1970). All these inputs have resulted in significant increases in the winter-wheat yield. Moreover, the provision of a guaranteed supply of moisture in dry areas by means of irrigation has reduced the severity of fluctuations in the winter-wheat yield.

In the dry farming regions of Kazakhstan, measures were taken to apply better management techniques. The area sown to spring wheat was reduced slightly and some fallow was reintroduced. Blade cultivators were made available in large quantities to make stubble-mulch fallowing possible. Regular crop rotations were planned (Ivanov 1975, pp. 5–6). These practices, together with systematic application of herbicides, have resulted in higher, though not significantly more stable, spring-wheat yields (Table 11.1).

Regional assessment of yield improvement

In assessing yield improvement, it is not easy to separate managerial and political variables from weather hazards. Data pertaining to crop production inputs and practices at the farm level are lacking. Even at the regional and national level no data are published to indicate which inputs reach the cropland and in what quantities, nor at what rate they are employed for various crops.

One simple way of separating out the influence of weather from that of technological progress is to smooth out the trend in yields over time by means of regression analysis. Darell E. McCloud employed regression trend curves assuming they would represent, over a span of 40 years or more, technological progress. Year-to-year fluctuation of observed yields above or below the trend line were assumed to reflect favourable or unfavourable weather conditions (Hinckley 1976, App. B). A similar, though simpler, technique will be employed to assess the trends in wheat yields in the Soviet Union, and to differentiate between the human inputs and weather hazards, contributing to the observed trends. Clearly these are simplifying assumptions that may not be valid in all years, since managerial and technological inputs also fluctuate from year to year. However, though different policies pursued by Stalin, Khruschev and Brezhnev obviously had different effects on wheat yields, the overall trend in the past three decades has been that of more intensive application of modern technology and improved production. A regional assessment of yield improvement will be carried out to gain some insights into the relationships between wheat yields and weather hazards.

Methodology   From the available spring- and winter-wheat yields published for the Soviet Union, its constituent union republics and economic regions, a set of consecutive annual data were selected; the period involved is since the mid-1950s. Scattered observations from earlier years were omitted in order to avoid statistical bias from years that may not have been typical for that period. For the republics the data spanned 18 years (1956–73), but for the large economic regions only data for 1958 and 1960 through 1973 were included. Thirteen republics were represented as separate units. The remaining Russia and Ukraine were subdivided into 10 and 3 economic regions respectively. Altogether 26 areas were distinguished in the Soviet Union.*

For each republic or economic region the annual spring and winter wheat yields were plotted on a histogram. Since the period represented 18 years or less, it was decided that a straight line regression should suffice. Thus, for each region, a regression line was plotted and the mean yield, the regression coefficient (representing the slope of the line) and the correlation coefficient were computed (Table 11.2). Finally, each of the three indices describing the spring and winter wheat yields were mapped for visual interpretation.

Of the three indices, the mean yield should summarise the spring- and winter-wheat performance levels in the past two decades; the regression coefficient should reveal the average annual rate of change in quintals (100 kg) per hectare per year; and the correlation coefficient should indicate the extent to which yields have been steadily increasing or, in other words, the stability of yields through time. Assuming that throughout this period there was no consistent climatic change, the last index may serve as a very rough estimate of the degree to which human inputs rather than weather explain the variation in yields.

Mean wheat yields   The distribution of mean wheat yields corresponds, in the first instance, to natural conditions for growing wheat and, in the second instance, to levels of technology. Highest spring-wheat yields (Fig. 11.3) of 15 q/ha or more were encountered in western Ukraine, where climate is best and especially in Estonia, where the rates of fertiliser application are among the highest in the Union. A medium range of yields (8–11 q/ha) was observed in the main spring wheat region east of the Volga. Lowest spring-wheat yields (less than 5 q/ha) were found in the desert and foothill republics of Azerbaydzhan, Uzbekistan and Tadzhikistan.

Winter wheat (Fig. 11.4) boasted better yields generally and especially in the southern zone, where it could make better use of moisture accumulated during autumn and winter. The best yields (in excess of 20 q/ha) were recorded in Ukraine and Moldavia. They exceed local spring-wheat yields by 7–12 q/ha, the widest margin in the Union, thus encouraging the recent elimination of spring-sown wheat in the area. The second best yields were registered in the adjoining North Caucasus and central black earth regions (18–19 q/ha) and only then in the Baltic republics (16–18 q/ha). Winter-wheat yield of the southern regions outranked those of the Baltic republics because, reportedly, all these areas now apply mineral fertilisers to high-

---

* Since yield data are not published for oblasts in the RSFSR, it was not possible to establish the precise yields in Kaliningrad Oblast that, along with Lithuania, Latvia and Estonia, comprise the Baltic Economic Region. In order to avoid a blank area for Kaliningrad Oblast (where wheat is obviously grown), it was decided to assign to it the same values as the ones registered in the adjacent Lithuanian SSR. Raw yield data for the calculations of the indices presented in Table 11.2 were compiled from official Soviet statistical yearbooks for USSR, RSFSR and Ukrainian SSR.

Table 11.2   Wheat yields in the Soviet Union, 1956–73.

	Spring wheat				Winter wheat			
	SA	X̄	b	r	SA	X̄	b	r
USSR	48 670	9.8	0.27	0.60	17 637	17.6	0.60	0.82
RSFSR	30 686				8 154			
North-west	106	8.7	0.60	0.88	39	11.1	0.39	0.72
Centre	510	11.1	0.82	0.89	1 007	12.7	0.72	0.86
Volga-Vyatka	687	10.4	0.63	0.79	172	12.1	0.46	0.64
Central chernozem	495	14.4	0.73	0.75	1 248	17.9	0.64	0.58
Volga	8 118	11.2	0.30	0.52	1 057	15.1	0.36	0.39
North Caucasus	239	11.7	0.41	0.45	4 549	19.7	0.44	0.48
Ural	6 831	11.5	0.40	0.59	31	12.6	0.67	0.69
Western Siberia	9 762	10.4	0.43	0.52	0			
Eastern Siberia	3 320	11.5	0.29	0.57	0			
Far East	613	8.5	0.30	0.56	0			
Ukrainian SSR	148				6 317			
Donets-Dnieper	115	12.8	0.50	0.55	2 475	22.2	0.76	0.64
South-west	26	15.0	0.75	0.90	2 201	21.7	0.95	0.85
South	7	10.6	−0.28	−0.42	1 640	22.2	1.02	0.83
Baltic	43				238			
Estonian SSR	11	16.2	0.94	0.88	15	17.6	0.98	0.91
Latvian SSR	24	13.7	1.01	0.92	57	16.7	1.17	0.88
Lithuanian SSR	4	14.4	1.14	0.84	116	16.2	1.30	0.91
Kaliningrad O.[1]	4	nd	nd	nd	50	nd	nd	nd
Belorussian SSR	34	12.0	1.08	0.85	209	13.2	0.85	0.91
Moldavian SSR	4	10.8	0.06	0.07	340	20.1	1.04	0.70
Transcaucasus	39				710			
Georgian SSR	7	6.3	0.01	0.04	160	12.3	0.49	0.78
Azerbaydzhan SSR	4	4.5	0.01	0.07	444	10.3	0.34	0.77
Armenian SSR	28	7.2	0.05	0.21	106	12.2	0.49	0.83
Kazakh SSR	17 395	8.4	0.16	0.31	786	10.7	0.29	0.53
Central Asia	325				932			
Uzbek SSR	163	4.7	0.15	0.61	454	5.6	0.07	0.23
Kirgiz SSR	92	8.2	0.32	0.72	238	13.7	0.77	0.87
Tadzhik SSR	57	4.8	0.13	0.62	194	5.7	0.07	0.42
Turkmen SSR	13	6.1	−0.04	−0.14	46	7.0	0.19	0.54

Note: SA, sown area, in thousand hectares, 1960–70 mean;
  X̄, mean wheat yield, in quintals per hectare;
  b, regression coefficient, in quintals per hectare per year;
  r, correlation coefficient;
  nd, no data; mapped same as for Lithuanian SSR;
[1]Sown areas of Kaliningrad O. are included both in the Baltic and the RSFSR subtotals.

yielding varieties of winter wheat (Prutskov 1976, pp. 229–31). In addition, the southern regions also benefit from better natural conditions for winter wheat than for spring wheat.

Medium yields of winter wheat (11–12 q/ha) and a small yield advantage over spring wheat (1–2 q/ha) were encountered in the less significant wheat areas of European Russia and in southern Kazakhstan. The Transcaucasian republics and the mountainous Kirgiz SSR of Soviet Central Asia also

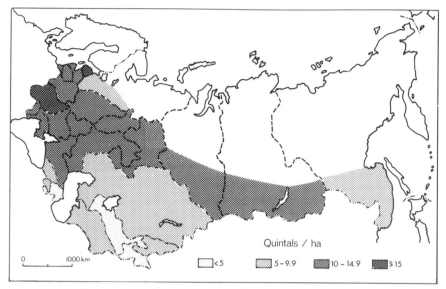

Figure 11.3   Spring-wheat yields in the Soviet Union.

recorded medium mean yields, but these exceeded their spring-wheat yields by considerably higher margins (5–6 q/ha). Apparently, in these southern mountainous areas, winter wheat derives considerable advantage over spring wheat from winter precipitation.

In the remaining central Asian republics winter-wheat yields were low (6–7 q/ha) and only slightly more advantageous than spring-wheat yields. Appar-

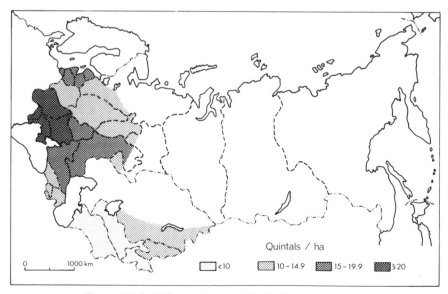

Figure 11.4   Winter-wheat yields in the Soviet Union.

ently the natural conditions for growing winter wheat here are more difficult – less winter rain in the foothills or less secure water supply for irrigating the crop.

Yield increases   Wheat yield increases, measured by means of the regression coefficient, represent the mean annual yield increase in quintals per hectare. In general, winter-wheat yields increased twice as fast as spring-wheat yields.

Although the patterns of yield increases generally resembled those of mean yields, some subtle differences were observed. The highest spring-wheat yield increase (Fig. 11.5) occurred not only in the Baltic republics but also in Belorussia and the central region. This was so even though some of the highest mean yields were recorded in the former, and yields only slightly above average in the latter. In the meantime, the high-yielding south-west region and the slightly lower-yielding central chernozem region attained only moderately high increases. These were almost comparable to those attained in the north-west with its below average yields. Apparently, spring wheat in Belorussia and the central region must have benefited either from direct or, more likely, indirect fertiliser application in rotation with flax, potatoes and sugar beets. It should be noted, however, that technical crops in these regions, such as flax, potatoes and sugar beets, have always enjoyed higher priorities for fertiliser application. In the past, when less fertiliser was available, grain would not be fertilised but the higher value crops would benefit from it.

The main spring-wheat growing regions have experienced average or less than average yield increases. Drought-prone Kazakhstan clearly exhibits very slow progress, even below the performance of the mountainous Kirgiz SSR.

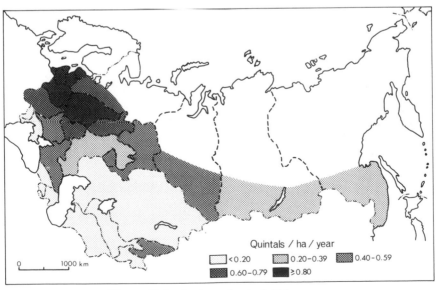

Figure 11.5   Spring-wheat yield increases.

Indeed, until 1965 Kazakhstan and the adjoining parts of western Siberia suffered from declining yields. Improper soil management techniques in a dry environment are to blame including the lack of stubble-mulch fallowing (Dando 1970, p. 235).

The lowest increase occurred in the remaining central Asian republics and in the Transcaucasus – the very regions where all effort had been lavished on valuable technical or horticultural crops! Moreover, little or no progress in spring-wheat yields occurred in Moldavia and the south where, in the last few years, spring sown wheat had been discontinued. The fact that here spring wheat bears a 10–20% greater risk from drought than winter wheat (*Atlas sel'skogo khozyaystva SSSR* 1960, p. 41) probably contributed to the abandonment of spring wheat in preference for winter wheat or for other, more profitable heat-loving crops.

The winter-wheat yield increases (Fig. 11.6) did not coincide with regional yield levels, either. On the whole, yield increases in the Baltic republics slightly exceeded those of the Ukraine and Moldavia. Belorussia and the central region exceeded the rates of yield increases in Donets-Dnieper and central chernozem regions, respectively, even though the former pair had considerably lower yields than the latter. As in the case of spring wheat, farms in the European non-chernozem zone – at least as far as Moscow – appear to have lavished more care and resources on winter wheat than in any other region except, perhaps, Moldavia and Ukraine.

To the north and east progress in yield increases had been below average. Even in North Caucasus, one of the best winter-wheat growing regions, yield

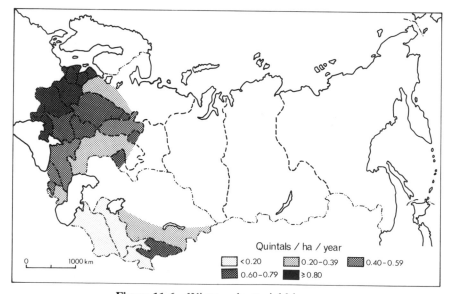

Figure 11.6 Winter-wheat yield increases.

increases have been low. Of the three Transcaucasian republics, Azerbaydzhan – relying most heavily on irrigation – had the *lowest* yield increases. The
use of fertiliser on irrigated wheat in this area could double or even triple the
yields (Mints 1966, p. 173).

The lowest winter-wheat yield increases of all occurred in the irrigation-
dependent republics of Central Asia. Except for the mountainous Kirgizstan,
which enjoyed respectable yield improvements, the performance in southern
Kazakhstan was poor and in the remaining republics abysmal. Apparently
winter-wheat yields had been neglected in the Tadzhik, Turkmen and Uzbek
Republics.

Yield stability   The degree to which yields improve steadily from year to year
– in short, yield stability – can be measured by the correlation coefficient. This
measure of yield stability should indicate, approximately, the extent to which
technology explains the variability of wheat yields in different regions. At the
same time, it should be remembered that the larger the region the more
internal compensation between good and poor yields may occur in any one
year, and hence the coefficient may tend to overstate the role of technology
and underestimate the vagaries of weather.

The highest stability of spring-wheat yields ($r = 0.84$) was observed in the
European west and north-west, where the incidence of drought is lowest (Fig.
11.7). This, combined with the highest rates of yield increases, reflects a
steadily increasing commitment of technology to improve spring-wheat yields
in the area (Nettevich 1976, p. 3–4).

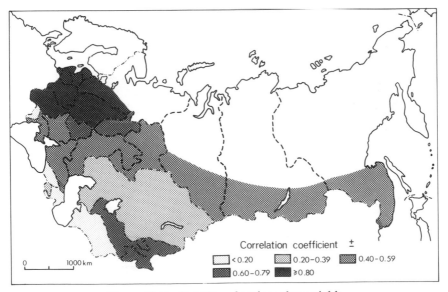

Figure 11.7   Stability of spring-wheat yields.

Soviet Central Asia also registered above-average yield stability. That reflected, in part, the region's dependence on irrigation. However, its poor performance in yield increases would suggest a consistent technological lag, notably neglect of the use of fertiliser, in the production of spring wheat.

The main spring-wheat regions east of the Volga had average stability, but the drought-zone Kazakhstan indicated below average stability. Weather and managerial problems combined to explain the variability of yields in this region.

Low and below-average values were also observed in the southern areas where little spring wheat is grown today or has been abandoned altogether. Although such figures may be considered statistically anomalous because of the small quantities of spring wheat grown in Moldavia, Transcaucasus and the Turkmen Republic, they do reflect the hazard that drought poses to spring wheat in those areas.

The stability of winter-wheat yields (Fig. 11.8) generally surpassed spring wheat in most areas where both crops were grown. Clearly, winter yield improvement had been most successful in the west where fertilisers, applied to wheat, proved their effectiveness in the most humid western part of the country.

The long-term implications of these patterns are clear: as long as the Soviet Union continues to depend on the dry farming of wheat east of the Volga, the yields and harvests will remain erratic and improve slowly. Yet the need to grow wheat and moisture-loving high-energy feed grains and technical crops west of the Volga rules out the possibility of major shifts in wheat area to less hazardous places.

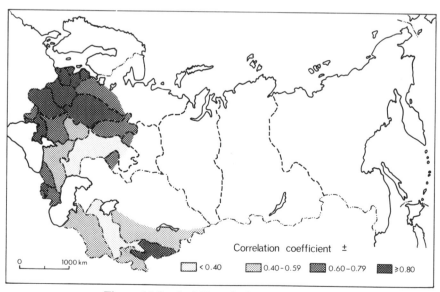

Figure 11.8   Stability of winter-wheat yields.

Perhaps higher-yielding wheat could be concentrated on smaller, better areas in the east. But the development of productive wheat varieties for Siberia and Kazakhstan is difficult. Cold-hardy and early-maturing varieties of wheat are relatively low yielders because their long stalks would lodge from a heavy head. The high-yielding dwarf varieties lack cold hardiness and are not suitable for the region. However, there are hopes that within five years a hardy winter-wheat variety will be available for use in western Siberia.* Curtains of corn left standing through the winter are expected to generate sufficient snow cover for the crop. These measures, however, are still experimental. At present it seems that only the widespread adoption of sprinkler irrigation, expensive though it is, will offer greater stability to Soviet wheat yields. Few Soviet planners consider their storage capacity adequate. A greater storage capacity is essential to eliminate losses during bumper crops or to reduce calls for massive imports (Trisvyatskiy 1975, pp. 35–6).

* P. P. Vavilov, the rector of Moscow Timiryazev Agricultural Academy, told me in an interview given in his office (Moscow, 2 Oct. 1976) that the famous wheat breeder, V. N. Remeslo, is on the threshold of developing a very hardy winter wheat that should be ready for field use within five years.

Acknowledgements

Research on the analysis of grain yields was funded by a grant from Canada Council.

References

Atlas sel'skogo khozyaystva SSSR 1960. Moscow: GUGK.

Babushkin, L. N. 1957. O klimaticheskoy kharakteristike letney vozdushnoy zasukhi i sukhoveyev v khlopkovoy zone Uzbekistana. In *Sukhovei: ikh proiskhozhdeniye i bor'ba s nimi*, B. L. Dzerdzeevskiy (ed.), 59–64, Izdatel'stvo Akademii Nauk SSSR, Moscow.

Brown, L. B. 1974. *By bread alone*. New York: Praeger.

Berlyand, S. S., and B. D. Kryuchev 1967. *Rastenievodstvo*. Moscow: Kolos.

Bush, K. 1974. *Soviet agriculture: ten years under new management*. Radio Liberty Res. Pap., Munich.

Dando, W. A. 1976. Man-made famines: some geographical insights from an exploratory study of a millennium of Russian famines. *Ecol. Food Nutrit.* **4**(4), 219–34.

Dando, W. A. 1970. *Grain or dust; a study of the Soviet New Lands Program, 1954—1963*. Unpubl. PhD dissertation, Dept. of Geography, Univ. Minnesota.

Dalrymple, D. G. 1964. The Soviet famine of 1932–1934. *Soviet Studies* **15**(3), 250–84.

Fisher, H. H. 1927. *The famine in Soviet Russia, 1919—1923*. New York: Macmillan.

Hinckley, A. D. (ed.) 1976. *Impact of climatic fluctuations on major North American food crops*. Washington, DC: Institute of Ecology.

Ivanov, P. K. 1975a. Biologicheskiye osobennosti i urozhay. In *Vysokiye urozhai yarovoy pshenitsy*, V. A. Ivanov (ed.), 8–20. Moscow: Kolos.

Ivanov, V. A. 1975b. Vvedeniye. In *Vysokiye urozhai yarovoy pshenitsy*, V. A. Ivanov (ed.) 3–7. Moscow: Kolos.

Jackson, W. A. D. 1959. The Russian non-chernozem wheat base. *Ann. Assoc. Am. Geogs* **49**(2), 97–109.

Jackson, W. A. D. 1962. The Virgin and Idle Lands Program reappraised. *Ann. Assoc. Am. Geogs* **52**(1), 69–79.

Jackson, W. A. D. 1963. The Soviet approach to the good earth: myth and reality. In *Soviet Agricultural and Peasant Affairs*, R. D. Laird (ed.), 171–85. Lawrence: University of Kansas Press.

Jackson, W. A. D. 1970. Wanted: an effective land use policy and improved reclamation. *Slavic Review* **29**(3), 411–16.

Johnson, G. 1974. Soviet agriculture and world trade in farm products. In *Prospects for agricultural trade with the USSR*, 43–50. US Dept of Agriculture, Economic Research Service, Washington, DC.

Karcz, J. F. 1970. Some major persisting problems in Soviet agriculture. *Slavic Review* **29**(3), 417–26.

Lydolph, P. E. 1964. The Russian Sukhovey. *Ann. Assoc. Am. Geogs* **54**(3), 291–309.

Mesarovic, M. and E. Pestel 1974. *Mankind at the turning point: the second report to the Club of Rome*. New York: Dutton.

Mints, A. A. (ed.) 1966. *Geografiya khozyaystva respublik Zakavkaz'ya*. Moscow: Nauka.

Mints, A. A. (ed.) 1969. *Srednyaya Aziya*. Moscow: Mysl'.

Nettevich, E. D. 1976. *Yarovaya pshenitsa v nechernozemnoy zone*. Moscow: Rossel'khozizdat.

Nove, A. 1970. Soviet agriculture under Brezhnev. *Slavic Review* **29**(3), 379–410.

Prutskov, F. M. 1976. *Ozimaya Pshenitsa*, 2nd edn. Moscow: Kolos.

Rudnev, G. V. 1964. *Agrometeorologiya*. Leningrad: Gidrometeoizdat.

Shul'meyster, K. G. 1975. *Bor'ba s zasukhoy i urozhay*. Moscow: Kolos.

Sinitsina, N. I., I. A. Gol'tsberg and E. A. Strunnikov 1975. *Agroklimatologiya*. Leningrad: Gidrometeoizdat.

Selyaninov, G. T. 1958. Proiskhozhdeniye i dinamika zasukh. In *Zasukhi v SSSR*, A. I. Rudenko (ed.). Leningrad: Gidrometeoizdat.

Stebelsky, I. 1972. Rural poverty and environmental deterioration in the central Russian black earth region before revolution. In *International geography, 1972*, W. P. Adams and F. M. Helleiner (eds), vol. 1, 450–52. Toronto: University of Toronto Press.

Trisvyatskiy, L. A. 1975. *Khranenie zerna*. 4th edn. Moscow: Kolos.

US Department of Agriculture 1974. *The agricultural situation in the Soviet Union: review of 1973 and outlook for 1974*. USDA Economic Research Service, Washington, DC.

USSR agriculture atlas 1974. Washington, DC: Central Intelligence Agency.

Vneshnyaya Torgovlya SSSR. 1967. *Statisticheckiy sbornik 1918–1966*. Moscow: Vneshtorgizdat.

Vneshnyaya Torgovlya SSSR za 1968 god. 1969. *Statischeskii obzor*. Moscow: Vneshtorgizdat.

Vneshnyaya Torgovlya SSSR za 1970 god. 1971. *Statisticheckii obzor*. Moscow: Vneshtorgizdat.

12 Climatic hazards and Canadian wheat trade

GORDON McKAY

Trade is dependent on co-existent surpluses and deficiencies. The century-old Canadian wheat trade is based on the surplus production of the Prairies and the global market environment. The trade has enabled Canada to prosper, and changes therein have affected Canada dramatically. The variability in supply and demand is highly dependent on climate. Periods of favourable weather and drought have been associated with prosperity and disaster to the western plains.

In recent times, in particular 1972, climate has demonstrated that the wheat trade, and through it the economy and even our way of life are critically affected by regional climatic hazards. Technology, social and economic programmes have helped to mitigate the effects of this hazard by a cushioning process. But the blows remain, and the aggregated effects may be greater because of increasing interdependencies, investments and obligations.

Wheat production is determined by the availability of suitable lands, technology, economics, markets, cultural and social attitude and climate.Wheat is the favoured export staple because of its qualities as a food, for storage and transportation, and in milling and baking. It is also cultivated because of its hardy nature, and the ease with which it may be grown and handled. Because of its hardiness, it is often grown in climatically marginal areas, the warmer, more humid areas being reserved for higher-yielding crops such as rice and maize.

In the Canadian context wheat is grown extensively in the Prairie provinces near the northern limit of economic agriculture. At the time of Confederation, Ontario wheat supplied the national need. The opening of the Prairies to grain farming enabled Canada to reap the benefits of world export, while helping to foster the ties that bind a nation. The first prairie wheat, 313 hl, was shipped to Toronto in 1876. In 1877 shipments were made to Britain. By 1891 the production had risen to 15 million hl, reaching 198 in the 1928 bumper year; 290 in 1966, and 314 (Prairies 303) in 1976. However, production has not always been reliable. Climatic variability is a major factor, but production reflects market opportunity as well as climate. Yield per hectare provides a better indication of the effects of climate. Yet this too is not an ideal indicator, since yield figures are usually on the basis of harvested (not planted) hectares. In addition, they reflect the abandonment of lands of low productivity.

Popular conceptions of climatic hazard to agriculture include the return of

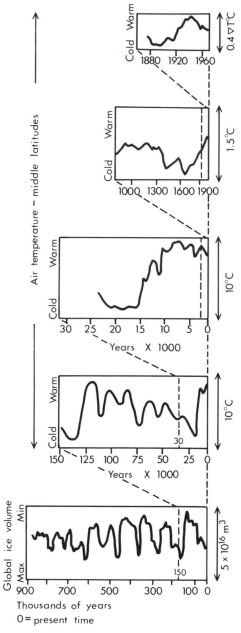

Figure 12.1 Climatic change on different timescales.

an 'ice age', global warming, or a much more variable climate. Careful investigation of these issues indicates that increased variablity is the most valid and relevant one for present-day agriculture (Fig. 12.1).

Agriculture and its development involves time spans ranging from a day to about half a century. Most agricultural decisions bearing directly upon crop production are seasonal in nature. The purchase of equipment relates to periods of about 10 years, and that of land to perhaps 50 years at the extreme. But the tendency towards glaciation, or the warming of the atmosphere due to man's influence, relate to much greater time spans. They involve trend lines that are not readily discernible because of the much greater variability in climate due to other causes. Furthermore, agriculture is concerned with detail that is not apparent in the general trends. The farmer is closely dependent upon when the rains occur during the growing season, and whether the lands are sufficiently dry for field work at seeding, cultivation and harvest times.

Cooler climate

Society may react in distinctive ways, for example through migration. Nevertheless, it will be useful to review the possible significance of long-term climatic shifts when confronted by adverse climatic trends. There are many examples, of course, where people remain in areas near the limits of climatic thresholds of crop production. This is illustrated by Icelandic agriculture which is menaced each time the sea ice from Denmark Strait moves in on the island. Again, for Canadian frontier agriculture a slow cooling would further increase the hazard of crop loss since this too is practised in a marginal area.

With a cooling trend, wheat farmers near the northern limit for wheat must shift to other crops, such as barley or rape, that will mature with a shorter growing season. A 1 °C drop in mean annual temperature would probably be accompanied by a 9- to 15-day reduction in the length of the growing season. Such a reduction could prove critical for wheat production for which the season is just adequate in many northerly and more continental areas. It would not seriously affect barley production.

Cool climates are generally more humid than average. Winter snows accumulate over longer periods, soils do not dry out quickly in spring, and drying weather is less probable at harvest time. The best wheat lands have lacustrine soils that are poorly drained, and with wet weather their use may be constrained. During the wet 1950s many Prairie farmers had to wait to harvest their crops until their wet fields froze.

Warmer climate

Should the climate warm, the effects would be beneficial for frontier agriculture, but not necessarily beneficial for Canadian wheat production. Hot dry years on the Prairies have been the most disastrous for wheat production. Warm climates in the past have been related to drought, grasshoppers and soil erosion. The continental interior was considered to be more arid during the climatic optimum (8000–5000 BP), and this type of climate was evident in the 1860s, the 1890s and the 1930s (see also Warrick, p. 67). Although the warmer climate would favour the northward extension of agriculture, here the full climatic advantage would be severely constrained by lack of suitable soils.

Greater climatic variability

A more variable climate is the more probable source of the more urgent agricultural risks. Climatic history shows that, while the last century was highly variable, the past 15 years had been unusually stable. The recurrence of periods of cool–wet or hot–dry climate is inevitable, and so too must be some major impacts on wheat production.

The yield per hectare of Canadian wheat has been highly variable throughout history. Crop–weather history shows this variability to be closely correlated with climate. Diaries for the Red River settlement disclose failure due to drought in 1820. The seed had been obtained from Minnesota in 1819. Oats and barley were a complete failure in 1867, and in 1868 an appeal for aid was sent to Canada, England and the United States. But in 1869, the wheat was 1.8 m tall, and during the wet 1870s there was great optimism due to 'breaking of the sod and planting causing eastern rainfall to migrate to the western plains'. Droughty weather returned in the 1880s and pioneers returned eastwards brokenhearted (Fig. 12.2).

This sequence of wet and dry, hot and cold climate continued on through the 1930s (Figs 12.3 & 4). In 1937 the average Saskatchewan wheat yield was a very poor 2.3 hl/ha. Since 1962, yields have been relatively good, culminating in a bumper 1976 crop, with an estimated yield of 28.3 hl/ha. This improvement also coincides with the more extensive use of fertilisers and weed sprays.

Risk and technology

The question we must now ask is whether new technology has insulated us from climatic variability. The land originally had its natural fertility and soil quality. As this has been exploited by agriculture, other things being equal, the crop yields should diminish with time. That problem seems to have been more than compensated by the introduction of new technology. Included in the new technology are practices to conserve soil fertility and soil moisture. The time for maturation of wheat has been reduced by about 25 days compared to early Prairie agriculture. Farmers then were also unable to respond as rapidly to adverse weather as with today's mechanisation. And, in particular, the use of nitrogen fertilisers and short-stemmed wheat is considered to be the greatest factor improving production. Herbicides became essential in

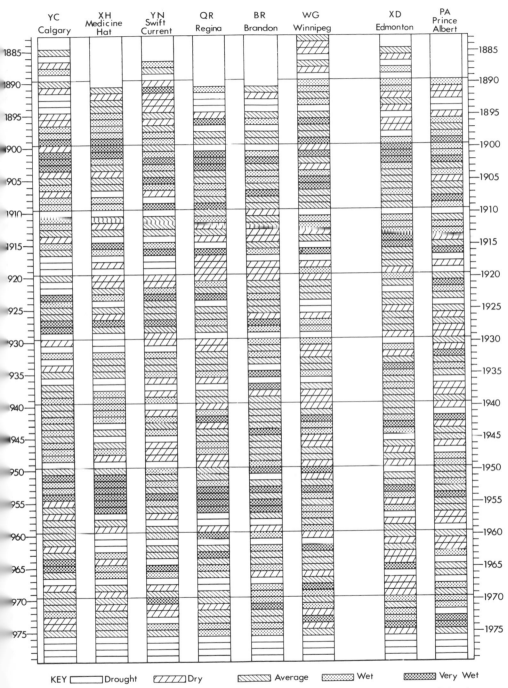

Figure 12.2 Agricultural weather in the Canadian Prairies based upon precipitation records. The categories are percentiles: drought, less than 25%; dry, 25–40%; average, 40–60%; wet, 60–75%; very wet, 75–100%.

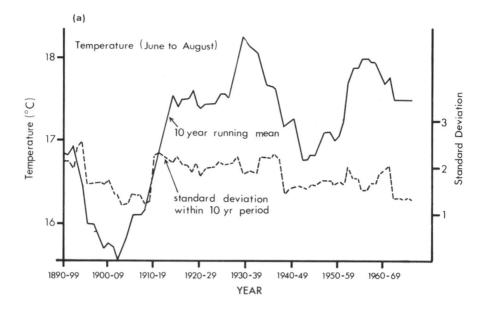

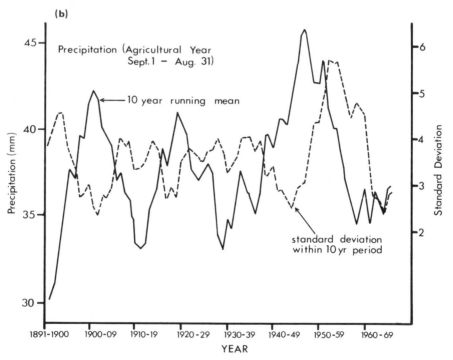

Figure 12.3 (a) Crop season temperature for Regina, Saskatchewan, 10-year running mean, 1890–1969; (b) crop season precipitation for Regina, Saskatchewan 10-year running mean, 1891–1969.

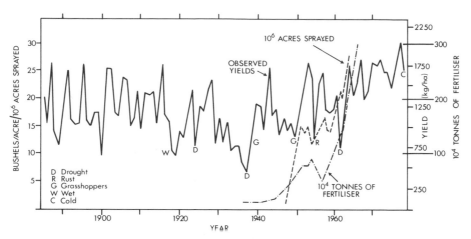

Figure 12.4 Wheat yield in the Canadian Prairies and some risk-related factors.

response to the weed problem that evolved with the development of Prairie agriculture. But as these innovations have become widespread, the climate too has been especially favourable to agriculture. A parallel analysis by McQuigg (1974), for example, showed the stable US maize production from 1956 to 1973 to be the result of an anomalously favourable climate.

There is a need to separate out the effects of climate and technology in order to assess the hazard potential of future climatic variability. Crop–weather models have been used for this purpose, using climatic data and standardising estimates to 1973 technology. It has been shown that production losses over 25% are still probable in disastrous years like the 1930s, with Canada's short growing season (1937 was not analysed in this study) (Hinckley 1976). In brief, technology is improving the overall production levels, but climate variability still causes major fluctuations about the trend line. According to Hinckley (1976) 'a future recurrence of certain past climate fluctuations or weather sequences in US and Canadian food-producing regions, would indeed have a significant impact on North American food production'.

Trade

Trade is based, albeit in complex ways, on supply and demand. The capabilities of technology to increase supplies are repealed by increasing demand. One of the extraordinary features of the second half of this century is the way North America has become virtually the world's granary. In 1973–4 Canadian and United States grain exports accounted for 86% of the total trade, Canada's share being 13%. For the foreseeable future Canada will be able to meet its own national requirements. The supply concern is one of meeting export and assistance commitments. Since there is a tendency to

.write long-term trade pacts, climatic variability necessitates that these be entered into with caution.

The global demand for wheat is also climate-related. Adverse weather and changing attitudes in 1972 caused a large disappearance of wheat, the USSR purchasing the equivalent of a quarter of the US annual crop. While wheat reserves tumbled to emergency-level lows, prices trebled on the Canadian market (Figs. 12.5 & 6).

Bumper crops replenished granaries in 1976, but it is generally accepted that the recurrence of large surpluses cannot be depended on. A future major regional drought in any agricultural area is likely to produce further substantial increases in prices of food stuffs and general inflationary pressures. As noted by Berman (1976) 'price stability in the US depends largely on fortuitous developments of the world's weather'.

Although the world production in 1972 was not seriously in deficit, a major regional imbalance of supply and demand existed. The imbalance created a scrambling for supplies. We can expect that this will be repeated in the future as a response to the scale of droughts and the evolving interdependence between countries.

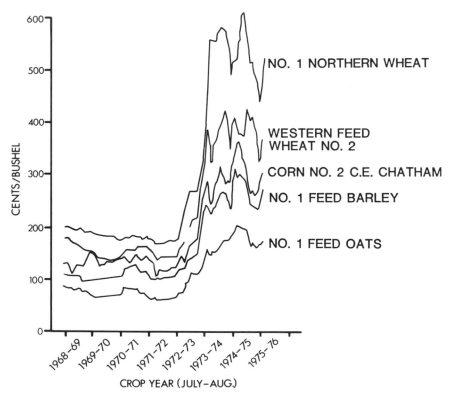

Figure 12.5   Monthly grain prices at Thunder Bay, Ontario, 1968–76 (after Canada Agriculture 1975).

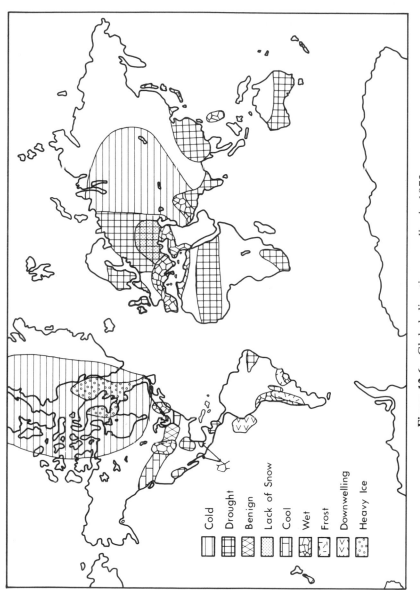

Figure 12.6 Global climatic anomalies in 1972.

Cold
Drought
Benign
Lack of Snow
Cool
Wet
Frost
Downwelling
Heavy Ice

Conclusions

Climatic fluctuations are the major cause of year-to-year variability in Canadian wheat production. Although wheat is a hardy crop, it is grown in Canada very close to the northern limits for economic agriculture. There it is exposed to two major risks: drought and the occurrence of too short a growing season. These risks are always present, and time series show that the level of risk varies with time.

Canada's wheat industry has grown with a view to export. National requirements for wheat can be readily met; the concern is to optimise the position in world markets for the benefit of Canadians and to be able to meet obligations to purchasers and for assistance. This requires planning for variable demand as well as supply.

Surpluses have previously caused deflated prices. Government price stabilisation schemes, such as land banks, have failed to provide price stability and have added to the inflationary effects of regional droughts. The nature of the production and marketing system precludes the development of a significant storage buffer, and therefore leaves nations vulnerable to shortages due to adverse regional climatic anomalies.

With widespread drought such as prevailed in the early and mid-1970s over western North America, and adverse climate in China and Australia, the pertinence of climatic variability as a hazard and catalyst for the Canadian wheat trade is of continuing significance, despite advanced technology and controls.

References

Berman, L. 1976. A new case for that old, ever normal granary. *Fortune,* April, 96–9, 170–4, 176.

Canada Agriculture 1975. *Situation outlook '75.* Canadian Agricultural Outlook Conf. Proc., Ottawa.

Hinckley, A. D. (ed.) 1976. *Impact of climatic fluctuation on major North American food crops.* Washington DC: Institute of Ecology.

McKay, G. A. and T. R. Allsopp 1977. *Climate and climatic variability.* Canadian Committee on Agrometeorology Proc.

McQuigg, J. D. 1974. *Climatic variability and the world food situation,* 3–7. Environmental Data Service, US Dept of Commerce.

National Science Foundation 1974. *The report of the* ad hoc *panel on the present interglacial.* Interdepartmental Committee for Atmospheric Sciences. Federal Council for Science and Technology, ICAS 18B-Fy75.

Sergent, J. P. 1976. Le temps change, cycle ou accident? *Science et Vie* **708**, septembre, 14–20.

World Meteorological Organisation 1969. *Meteorological factors affecting the epidemiology of wheat rusts.* Tech. note no. 99.

Part III
ALTERNATIVE FRAMEWORKS

13 *On the poverty of theory: natural hazards research in context*

MICHAEL WATTS

From the specific form of material production arises a specific
relation of men to nature.

Karl Marx (1967)

We must take seriously Vico's great observation that men
make their own history, that what they can know is what
they have made, and [to] extend it to geography.

Edward Said (1978)

For too long the ruling classes have attributed to 'Nature' . . .
the inequalities and sufferings for which the organisation of
society is responsible.

Sebastiano Timpanaro (1975)

I have quite deliberately chosen as a title for this chapter a recent book by
Edward Thompson (1978) whose substantive interests must seem, at first
glance, far removed from the geographic study of natural hazards. Thompson's polemical treatise is in fact part of a volatile debate in British historiography (see Anderson 1980) which specifically raises problems surrounding
the nature and place of fact in intellectual enquiry, the appropriate concepts
for the understanding of social and historical processes and the distinctive
object of historical knowledge. As such *The poverty of theory* is a work of
epistemology which emphasises that our knowledge is critically shaped by the
preoccupations we bring to it, that we interpret the world within the limits of a
historically conditioned imaginative vision, and that theory and concepts cannot therefore be taken for granted. It is precisely this series of questions that
constitute the starting point for my evaluation of natural hazards research. I
wish to suggest that in a critical examination of this work we should broaden
our horizons and begin with the epistemology and concepts of society and
nature; that is with the broad problematic into which hazards must be situated. I argue that hazard theory has been framed by concepts and assumptions which carry a historically specific view of nature, society and man and
hence, by extension, of the relations between them. This colours the entire
corpus of hazards work. In trying to provide such a critical elaboration I wish
to place the content of this volume into the wider body of social theory of
which geographers have all too frequently been parochially disinterested.

In delimiting natural hazards research I pay special attention to work with a cross-cultural bent and particularly those studies which address hazard occurrence, genesis and effect in the Third World. In doing so I necessarily engage the enormous volume of work in the cognate field of human–cultural ecology since, especially over the past five years, there has been much theoretical interchange. While I appreciate that the work on hazards in the less developed countries hardly constitutes the entire body of hazards research, the issues I raise are entirely apposite and relevant to the field as a whole. Indeed, Kates' (1971) human ecological perspective and White's (1974) questionnaire methodology have been applied *grosso modo* in First and Third Worlds alike.

In the light of my agenda, this chapter has five major sections. The first examines the epistemological and conceptual underpinnings of man–nature relations in general; the second analyses the critical concept of adaptation as a motif pervading both hazard and cultural ecological research. The third section specifically investigates geographic hazards work in light of my theoretical concerns, particularly the prevalence of cybernetic views of social systems and the individual rationality approach to hazard behaviour. The fourth proposes an alternative materialist epistemology and theory with special attention to the dual foci of labour (social relations of production) and intersubjective meanings in the society–nature relation. And finally, part five is an empirical case study which attempts to apply these materialist postulates to the drought hazard among peasants in northern Nigeria.

Epistemology and the human–environment problematic

A proper starting point for the study of environmental hazards is the epistemology and conception of nature itself (see Golledge 1979). A great deal of the conceptual and theoretical questions posed by the natural hazard paradigm emerge from the broad epistemological context in which such work is ultimately grounded. This should come as no surprise because, as Gregory Bateson pointed out long ago, epistemological premises which predicate all intellectual labour are notoriously sticky and colour all theoretical practice. I shall examine three authors – Anthony Wilden, Andrew Sayer and Karl Marx – whose work is of great practical significance in understanding the relevance of epistemology for both a critical evaluation of hazards work and also for situating such work into the wider realm of contemporary social theory. I cannot hope to do justice to the enormity of this task; but I would like to raise *explicitly* what is at best only implicit in much of what passes as hazard research, namely the manner in which we know and the reliability of 'environmental knowledge', the nature of the object(s) of knowledge and the social situation under which knowledge and the object of knowledge is produced. All this is to say that we cannot take for granted the relationship between people and nature, between knowing subjects and objects of study or between theory and fact.

I should like to begin with the work of Anthony Wilden (1972) and in particular his observation, following Whitehead, that much of social science is still living on the intellectual capital accumulated from the 17th century. It was, of course, precisely during this period when 'nature' became materially and ideologically commoditised, an object of control and domination (Leiss 1974, Merchant 1980). Coeval with the transformation of nature and science was a fundamental restructuring of social relations emerging from new forms of commodity production, in short from a nascent capitalism. Wilden sees the use of a Newtonian–Cartesian science – of the world as constituted by self-regulated closed systems – as rapidly imported into the mainstream of biological and social science where it still resides and flourishes. In his own words:

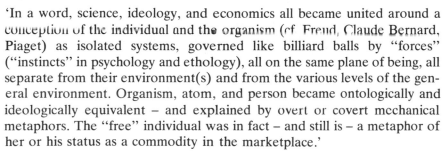

'In a word, science, ideology, and economics all became united around a conception of the individual and the organism (cf Freud, Claude Bernard, Piaget) as isolated systems, governed like billiard balls by "forces" ("instincts" in psychology and ethology), all on the same plane of being, all separate from their environment(s) and from the various levels of the general environment. Organism, atom, and person became ontologically and ideologically equivalent – and explained by overt or covert mechanical metaphors. The "free" individual was in fact – and still is – a metaphor of her or his status as a commodity in the marketplace.'

(Wilden 1979, p. 77).

For Wilden epistemology is principally a question of distinction, of, as he puts it, 'where you draw the line'; accordingly, the line drawn, for instance, between 'organism' or 'human' and the 'environment', is one such epistemological distinction. In this case it has arisen in part from the solipsism of Descartes, but like all lines it is a necessary fiction. This type of punctuation or boundary distinction is essential in a methodological sense, but such imaginary or socially constituted oppositions (a) become real for those who employ them and (b) can serve inappropriate and often exploitative ends. Of course Wilden cannot lay claim to this insight since it was William Blake who observed over 150 years ago that 'Nature hath no outline but Imagination has'. As Blake understood so well, these epistemological issues should not be taken lightly, but unfortunately few geographers read 'The Marriage of Heaven and Hell'.

Sayer (1980) in a brilliant contribution does, however, start precisely from this epistemological juncture. He posits that geographers have in fact had little to say on these subjects largely because a positivist science sees 'such vague subjects as the essential character of people and nature ... as "metaphysical" and/or meaningless or at least irrelevant' (1980, p. 20). The naïve, empiricist view of nature as a constellation of physical 'facts', unambiguously observable and unified through a positivist deductive method, welded together the entire body of social and natural sciences. To the extent that geographers took a stance on what were seen to be metaphysical issues, the belief in a neutral observation language led in a *de facto* way to the recognition of a commonsense epistemology as the basis for all knowledge. In this way, parochial knowledge was based on taken-for-granted assumptions, eternal verities which remained largely unexamined. Burgess (1976) has rightly suggested that the failure explicitly to address or problematise fundamental categories such as nature or the individual in geographical discourse has resulted in an extraordinary eclectism. The people–nature debate accordingly oscillated between idealism and crude materialism, between determinism and possibilism, and between 'a naturalisation of humanity and a humanisation of Nature' (see Smith 1979, Smith & O'Keefe 1980).

Why, then, would heady discourses be pertinent to a discussion of the merits of hazard research? In short I would like to suggest that, following Sayer, we must recognise the essential and necessary unity of society and nature and that 'to start in the conventional manner with such a separation followed by a listing of interactions would be to prejudice every other aspect of the exposition' (Sayer 1980, p. 22). Properly defined, nature is internally differentiated and the subject matter of human ecology is accordingly *inner*actions with nature (Sayer 1979), what Wilden (1972, p. 220) calls 'messages-in-circuit'. At this point Wilden and Sayer come together, for this internal differentiation perspective leads inexorably to a discussion of *inner-action* shared between humans and nature and those which are particular to humans; where, in other words, one draws the line. These epistemological lines are controversial (Timpanaro 1975) and in geographic work some fundamental attributes of social life are misrepresented. Deterministic conceptions of people and nature reduce humans to objects in which their role as subjects and agents of history, as conscious, active and intentional producers of social relations and material conditions, is irrevocably lost. While much of recent cultural human ecological or hazard work has moved beyond a crude determinism or possibilism, the question of epistemological assumptions remain. I shall argue that such endeavours nevertheless posed the people–nature relation in a manner which partially misrepresents human life. Specifically I believe that much conventional work rests on building blocks inherited from biology and cybernetics. This ecosystemic approach, broadly defined, blurs and obfuscates the character of inneractions and erodes the irreducibly social character of human life to atomised individuals or organisms – albeit rational decision makers or Simonian satisficers – whose status is roughly synonymous with that of a top carnivore. This biological lineage can, I shall argue, be identified through the critical role which the concept of *adaptation* holds in most human cultural ecological work.

Adaptation as a frame of reference

In this section, I would like to make two basic arguments with respect to the general body of environmental research of which hazards is specifically part.

Although geographic work on hazards has often been seen as a separate realm of enquiry associated with decision-making models (see Burton *et al.* 1978), it is clearly aligned with the phalanx of work which broadly falls under the title of human–cultural ecology or ecological anthropology. This kinship has developed as geographic hazards work embraced cross-cultural and Third World subject matter (Kirkby 1974). My first point is that, even in diachronic analyses, people and nature are seen as discrete entities – culture and environment – in which the latter is seen as limiting, non-dynamic and generally stable. Anderson (1973, p. 203) has commented on this division in light of the functionalist bias in human ecology, a point to which I will return later:

'The structural-functionalist approach and its dominant strategy of analysis encourage the treatment of ecology (generally meaning "environment") as a discrete component among other institutional components. Thus most ethnographies or problem-oriented studies begin with a chapter on the physical environment – the gross natural setting of the sociocultural investigation. Since the contents of the chapter are seldom referred to subsequently, we infer that such information is viewed as a backdrop, discretely separated from the primary components of the study.'

In spite of the claims of Winterhalder (1980), who has rightly pointed out that this conception of nature can be improved by increasingly sophisticated description of the environment – spatial heterogeneity, patchiness, temporal patterns, resilience, stability and so on – by positing a static polarity, the direction of subsequent analysis is inevitably limited. What emerges is a rather mechanical, billiard-board view of the world in which individuals, organisms, populations and critical environmental variables interact or interface. What is lacking conversely is (lumped together in the category 'culture' or 'man') the highly complex *social production of material life*.

The second point, which follows logically from the first, is that the pattern of interaction is conceived along neo-Darwinian lines (see Alland 1975, Durham 1976, Vayda & McCay 1975). This is made most explicit in the early work of Vayda and Rappaport (1967) when they suggest that societies can be conceptually treated like any other biological population in a web of ecosystemic relations. The character of 'man–environment interactions' is then seen through the particular biological optic of adaptation. Once again Rappaport (1977) makes this clear when he talks of human society as one form of living system; like all living systems, processes of adaptation – or adaptive structure – inhere within them. In his own words, 'I take the term adaptation to refer to the processes by which living systems maintain homeostasis in the face of both short-term environmental fluctuations and, by transforming their own structures, through long-term nonreversing changing in the composition and structure of their environments as well' (Rappaport 1979, p. 145). It is at this point that the intellectual conduit between biology and systems theory becomes clear. Ecological anthropology in particular has adopted a cybernetic view of adaptive process in social life. Specifically, social systems are seen as *general purpose systems* whose goal is nothing more than survival; that is, they can be conceived as a class of 'existential games' in which there is no way of using winnings ("payoff") for any purpose other than continuing the game for as long as possible' (Pask 1968, p. 7). From the perspective of human–environment relations, the specific form of interaction follows the general model of Slobodkin and Rappaport (1974) on orderly adaptive structure which possesses fundamental organisational and temporal characteristics: 'successful evolution requires the maintenance of flexibility in the response to environmental perturbation and that this flexibility must be maintained in the most parsimonious way. The parsimony argument is that organisms must not make an excessive or unnecessary commitment in responding to perturbation, but at the same time the deeper responses must be ready to take over to the degree that the superficial responses are ineffective' (Slobodkin & Rappaport 1974, p. 198). At the instant of perturbation a series of responses is triggered which can be ordered in terms of activation time and commitment of resources. The graduation of responses with respect to time also orders them in terms of depth of commitment. As a theoretical focus, then, adaptation became cybernetic, organised and hierarchical since 'all biological and evolving systems . . . consist of complex cybernetic networks' (Bateson 1972, p. 13).

An advantage of adaptation so defined is that it allows one to talk sensibly of dysfunction or maladaptation, which has been a major shortcoming of cultural ecology. Rappaport (1977), of course, sees maladaptation as those factors internal to systems which interfere with their homeostatic responses. They reduce survival chances since they constitute impediments to an efficient and parsimonious response to stress or environmental hazards. In light of the structural qualities of adaptation, maladaptation can, then, be seen as a class of pathologies or anomalies in the hierarchical and cybernetic functioning of all living systems. Response may be too slow or too rapid, systems may be overcentralised ('hypercoherent') or oversegregated; subsystems may come to capture ('usurp') high-order systems; the autarky of subcomponents may be eroded (see Flannery 1972). In short, what Bateson takes to be the fulcrum about which successful adaptation revolves, namely flexibility, has been in various ways structurally inhibited.

All this has taken us a long way from the early cultural–human ecology of 'human niches', adaptive radiation, and human ecological succession. This I would suggest was inevitable if only because the early simplistic ecological models were obviously incapable of handling societies in transition, where formerly autarkic systems were being incorporated into a global economy. At any rate the work by Morren (see ch. 15) and Waddell (1975) on response systems, and of Vayda (1974, 1976) and Rappaport (1977) on purportedly maladaptive systems, has clearly deepened our understanding of transactions between societies and their environments. Indeed, Vayda and McCay (1975) have advocated a hazards research approach to the study of human ecology which for the first time explicitly weds cultural ecology with natural hazards through the concept of adaptation. Emphasising its similarity to Darwinian selection theory and its stress of the efficacy of responses, this new hazard focus avoids the obvious pitfalls of a theory which is preoccupied with energy as the critical interface.

In spite of the obvious advances of the 'new ecology' (Robson 1978, Orlove 1980, Rappaport 1979), it is clear that new difficulties have emerged as anthropologists and geographers move away from relatively isolated communities to the study of social groups in transition. These problems are, I believe, derived directly from a theoretical starting point which sees society as a type of self-regulating, self-organizing living system isomorphic with nature itself. '[This] theoretical practice might be called "ecology fetishism". Nothing cultural is what it seems; everything is mystified as a natural fact which has the ostensible virtue of being basic . . . Marriage becomes an interchange of genetic materials . . . society a population of human organisms and cannibalism a subsistence activity' (Sahlins 1976, p. 88). This is not the place to enter into a protracted critique of new developments in human–environment relations, but I should like to raise two criticisms which are of signal importance, not least for the study of hazards. First, the cultural ecological model is functionalist in the sense that institutions and behaviours emerge as rational; their utilitarian purpose is to fulfil prescribed functions with regard to the maintenance of populations in a human ecological niche, that is to say with *survival*. Persistence, then, was a measure of adaptation. This, however, raises some tricky questions. Not only does a purely utilitarian view of social life deny culture – anthropology loses its object as Sahlins (1976, p. 90) puts it – but in the process adaptation becomes teleological. In other words, adaptive processes are framed by their survival function; they are defined in terms of their results. If this is not the case, the central problematic becomes either uninteresting or simply a truism. 'To say that a society functions is a truism but to say that everything in a society functions is an absurdity' (Levi-Strauss 1963, p. 13). This adaptive–cybernetic view of functional and self-regulated living systems leaves two sorts of residues; first, something vastly more simple than the actual 'adaptive processes' could account for the phenomenon under study (Bergmann 1975). And secondly, systems (including social systems) need not be cybernetic in order to be systems.

'Systems need not be cybernetic in order to be systems. Cybernetic systems are specific in that they are managed and regulated hierarchically. The systems to which I refer, and which I think are the normal case for human social systems that are not self-conscious entities, are those in which there are numerous processes and tendencies that are basically contradictory to one another. There are, of course, numerous limits that are never exceeded, but for reasons that have nothing to do with any regulatory procedure with respect to those limits.'

(Friedmann 1979, p. 259).

The second criticism pertains less to the theoretical poverty of functionalism and adaptation in social systems, than its ideological basis. This raises the spectre of the conception of mind and man (Friedmann 1979). Sahlins (1976, p. 90) for instance noted that ecological studies displace the notion of mind from the realm of humanity to the ecosystem. This is clearest in the work of Bateson (1972, 1978) for whom 'the individual mind is immanent but not only in the body' (1975, p. 436). Mind is a regulated totality organised as a central hierarchy from the lowest life forms to ecosystems that constitute the universe. This Hegelian view is, of course, embodied in the orderly adaptive structure which inheres in all living systems. Rappaport and Bateson in particular see mind as a type of metaphor and homology for their adaptive framework; control hierarchies, therefore, consist of graduated regulators, the more abstract regulators occupying a critical role in social systems. This is why abstract, non-specific 'commands' such as religion are critical for the adaptive context of social systems (Rappaport 1979).

In transcending the mundane to the ethereal realms of mind it seems we have drifted still further from hazards, but I am arguing that it actually strikes to the very core of the concerns of this volume. Let me simply raise three concerns that reflect the centrality of these views in hazards research. First, to the extent that systems do not work in the face of hazards or stress, i.e. they are *not* adaptive, it is simply because regulatory hierarchies are mixed up or non-orderly. In the parlance of the cultural/human ecologist, there is 'hyper-coherence' (overcentralisation) or 'usurpation' (lower-order goals take over high-order regulators), and so on. This is a function of industrialism, of technology or errors in thinking, and of 'attitudes in occidental culture' (Bateson 1972, Rappaport 1977), and hence a new value system is required. But the nature of the socioeconomic system is rarely addressed. Secondly, nature and ecosystems are seen as well regulated sets of interlocking programmes, messages and energy flows with which man, and particularly primitive man, is and was one. Anthropological work illustrates that human practice interdigitated with the cybernetic principle of the larger ecosystem, a regulation somehow grasped through religion. But with the evolution of more complex societies nature is somehow contradicted; the age of Rousseau is superseded by an industrial ideology which is intrinsically maladaptive. Our civilisation, with its linear purposive thinking, contradicts the self-maintaining, circular nature of the ecosystem (Bateson 1972). And thirdly, the structure of human activity – hence of the conception of 'man' – assumes a characteristically cybernetic form; culture becomes, as Sahlins (1976, p. 90) puts it, the self-mediation of nature; it is simply a systematically governed form of human response. This is clear in Bateson's favourite illustration of man–nature interaction: 'Consider, a man felling a tree with an axe. Each stroke of the axe is modified or corrected, according to the shape of the cut face of the tree left by the previous stroke. The self-corrective (i.e. mental) process is brought about by a total system, tree–eyes–brain–muscles–axe–stroke–tree; and it is this total system that has the characteristics of immanent mind' (Bateson 1972, p. 317).

What, then, is the significance of these derivations? I believe that they under-write much of hazards research in geography and other disciplines and that they are in a fundamental sense highly problematic. In short, maladaptation, or the inabilitiy to accommodate hazards, is not simply a question of hierar-chical control systems which are there but misused, or quite literally messed up. Equally adaptation is not only or even primarily a question of values or ideology in which change is a programme based on control, rules, principles and regulation rather than socioeconomic structures. And not least, man–nature relations are not *a priori* cybernetic; to return to the motif of Bateson, humans never simply chop wood. Rather humans enter into a specific relation with the wood 'in terms of a meaningful project whose finality gov-erns the terms of the reciprocal interaction between man and tree' (Sahlins 1976, p. 91). This is for Sahlins a cultural project, a symbolic order of inter-subjective meanings, in which nature is harnessed in the service of culture. But it is above all *social* and it necessitates material *production;* as Marx put it, animals collect but only humans produce 'through the appropriation of nature by the individual within and through the mediation of a definite form of society' (Schmidt 1972, p. 68). But this production is not simply survival, for societies survive in a *specific, historically determinate way;* they reproduce themselves, albeit as systems, but also as certain kinds of men, women, classes and groups, not as organisms or aggregates thereof. Friedmann (1979) is very probably correct in seeing the cybernetic vision as ideological, wholly approp-riate to our context of industrial and bureaucratic capitalism.

I would like to suggest that the cybernetic–adaptive systems perspective is the legacy from which the human ecology of hazards also suffers; it has defined the man–nature problematic for much of this work in a manner which leaves it open to the criticisms I have just levelled. There is a sense in which social systems, however, have never been adaptive; that the assumption of *a priori* cybernetic regulation may be appropriate for individual human organ-isms but *not* for social systems which are accumulative, contradictory and unstable. In the following section, I will examine briefly how hazards research has attempted to deal with these unique qualities of social systems.

Hazards in context

Roughly thirty years ago, largely under the auspices of Gilbert White, a field of geographic natural hazards research was conceived. Initially directed to the amelioration of flood-control problems in the United States, the project has expanded to include a plethora of 'natural' and man-made hazards and the collective wisdom has been drawn together in two major works by White (1974) and Burton *et al.* (1978). This is not the place to rehearse many of the well founded criticisms of this work (Torry 1979, Waddell 1977, O'Keefe & Wisner 1975). Suffice it to say that many of the forays into cross-cultural investigation were especially parochial; the rigid and, on reflection, extraordinarily naïve questionnaire design (White 1974, pp. 6–10) which provided the foundation for International Geographical Union sponsored research in the less developed countries was characteristic of the crude scientism, the ethnocentrism and the atheoretical basis of the hazard project as originally conceived. As is clear in retrospect, these field studies were ahistoric, insensitive to culturally varied indigenous adaptive strategies, largely ignorant of the huge body of relevant work on disaster theory in sociology and anthropology, flawed by the absence of any discussion of the political–economic context of hazard occurrence and genesis, and in the final analysis having little credibility in light of the frequent banality and triviality of many of the research findings (Waddell 1977).

The theoretical and conceptual poverty of the last decade's work emerges, I think, from two epistemological tendencies. The first pertains to the conception of the human–environment transactions, that is the status of nature and its transformation through human practice. And the second is the invocation of rationality as the peculiar optic through which individual and social behaviours are brought into focus. Put differently, it is the undisciplined conceptions of the nature of individual and society, which of course strikes to the very heart of all social theory, that has acted as a fetter on the past three decade's labours. And yet as much as it is firmly embedded in social science proper, hazards research has operated with a rather simple human ecological model (Kates 1971), loosely cybernetic in form, which purports to explain the widespread irrationality of exposure and response to environmental perturbations. Ironically, the Kates–White–Burton paradigm is predicated on an assumption of individual purposeful rationality expressed through a tripartite cybernetic structure: (a) hazard perception, (b) recognition of alternatives–adjustments, (c) choice of response. As Walker (1979, p. 113) has put it, however, this model is manifestly inadequate to explain human behaviour and a strategic diversion is constructed around it. Responses to hazards are arbitrarily categorised as purposeful and non-purposeful, with the latter further subdivided into incidental, cultural and biological adaptations; the theoretical significance of this taxonomy is far from clear, however. Following Herbert Simon, individual behaviour is seen as boundedly rational in which human agents, circumscribed by imperfect knowledge, perceive and act upon the world. Faulty perception and inappropriate psychological propensities (for example, the gambler's fallacy) are given analytic priority in the explanation of ineffective hazard response.

On balance, this human ecology model vacillates between individual and social causes of behavioural irrationality. Much of the work demonstrates unequivocally that social context and political economy mediate individual perception. Yet in spite of the recognition by Kates, White and others of the strategic import of social causality, they have no social theory capable of addressing social process, organisation or change. To return to the epistemological motif of our earlier discussion, the social and individual side of the human–environment equation seems to waver inconclusively between two positions. The first, based on a sharp disjuncture between humans and their physical environment, sees society as aggregates of individual decision makers in a fashion which enables Chinese communes and US corporations to be juxtaposed 'with little sense of the profound differences between modes of social organization' (Walker 1979, p. 113). There is a sense in which, in this view, individuals are atoms, society is irreducibly individuated and structureless, and hazard theory emerges as a none too sophisticated type of Linnean taxonomy. As Smith and O'Keefe comment, 'This dualism does not surpass the subject–object distinction of nature and society and so reduces scientific inquiry to an examination of two forms whose essential natures are given. More frequently, disaster vulnerability is analysed as if nature is neutral so that the environment is hazardous only when it "intersects with people" ' (Smith & O'Keefe 1980, p. 37). Maladaptation in society, to the extent it is discussed at all, simply becomes a type of cybernetic malfunction, mistaken perception, imperfect knowledge, or inflexible decision making apparatuses.

The second approach – characteristic of more recent work on Third World communities in hazardous environments – collapses internal into external nature. This is clearest in the synthesis between anthropology and geography (see Morren's chapters in this volume) which explicitly employs the adaptation problematic discussed earlier. Vayda and McCay (1975) advocate a hazards research approach emphasising a similarity to Darwinian selection theory and particularly the efficacy of adjustments; that is, with emphasis on factors important to the response of the system to stress, rather than on those relating to its cause. In many respects the very best of the recent work on hazard exposure in Third World societies has emerged from this synthesis (Waddell 1975). The increasingly sophisticated attention to ethnoscience and people's knowledge as the basis for hazard response (Richards 1978, Wisner 1981); the recognition that the 'closure' of autarkic communities has been progressively eroded by their incorporation into global market systems, which has important implications for the loss of regulatory autonomy in relation to the physical environment (Clarke 1977); and the emphasis on constraint rather than choice in hazardous environments, on the loss of social or individual flexibility and on distortions in the temporal order of decision making (Grossman 1979) – have all vastly strengthened the brittle theoretical basis of much early work. Not least in this regard has been the renewed attention to the unit of analysis in response systems, the temporal sequencing of adaptive responses, the importance of the sociocultural context and the admittedly ill specified 'external system', the long-term resiliency of social systems (Holling 1973), and on intellectual movement away from the preoccupation with energy relations and material flows (Vayda & McCay 1975).

And yet in spite of these advances, the new hazards work suffers from the limitations of much ecological anthropology (the 'new functionalism' as it is sometimes called), the epistemological and theoretical problems of which I have already discussed. In fact, what is most exciting in this work is precisely that which threatens to break out of the rigid adaptation or human ecological framework; take Clarke's work for instance, 'As society and economy are enlarged in the course of development, as communities trade autarky for access to a wider range of goods and services, new and coarser patterns of resource evaluation and selection replace old, finer patterns. Specialisation replaces diversity; economic risk is added to natural risk' (Clarke 1977, p. 384). The foci for Clarke are essentially political–economic, highlighting the subsumption of local production systems, largely through exchange and commodity relations, into a global economy. And I believe that this provides the groundwork for another approach to human ecology. Put differently, I would like to suggest that the forces and social relations of production constitute the unique starting point for human adaptation which is the appropriation and transformation of nature into material means of social reproduction. This process is both social and cultural and it reflects the relationships to and participation in the production process. For our purposes, this does not delegitimise the study of Melanesian carrying capacities or hazard responses in Botswana, but situates these questions in a new context:

> 'Nevertheless, it is important not to allow an empiricist concern for operationalization to eliminate a consideration of fundamental issues of political economic analysis. From this latter perspective, the production focus dovetails directly with problems of access to and/or control over the means of production in a given society; and, most importantly, how the total product of that society is allocated among various groups within its population. With the exception of certain simple band or tribal societies, this kind of inquiry inevitably leads into a study of the political power structure and social ranking or stratification'. (Cook 1975, p. 41).

Labour, nature and social reproduction

In Marxist scholarship, nature as somehow separate from society has no meaning. This is not simply to suggest that nature is mediated through and related to social activity, but rather that, in both historical and practical senses, nature resides at the locus of all human practice. People rely on nature for the fulfillment of basic needs; that is to say, the first premise of all human history is the production of material life which always involves a relation between producers and nature, what Marx calls the labour process. There is, then, an irreducible unity between society and nature that is differentiated from within. The socially active producer '[c]onfronts the material of nature as one of her own forces. He sets in motion arms and legs, heads and hands, the natural forces of his [sic] body, in order to appropriate the material of nature in a form suitable for his own needs. By thus acting through this motion on the nature which is outside him and changing it, he at the same time changes his own nature' (Marx 1967, p. 177). With this 'metabolic' view of man and nature (Schmidt 1971, pp. 76–7) Marx introduced a new understanding of the relation between what had been conventionally seen as a static polarity. The content of this metabolism is that 'nature is humanized while men are naturalised' (Schmidt 1971, p. 78) in historically determined forms. The whole of nature is socially mediated as society is simultaneously mediated through nature as a component of total reality. As Alfred Schmidt observed in a book on the concept of nature by Marx, 'Labor power, that "material of nature transferred to a human organism," acts on the materials of nature which are outside man; it is therefore through nature that nature is transformed. Men incorporate their own essential forces into natural objects which have undergone human labor. Through the same process, natural things gain a new social quality as use-values, increasing in richness in the course of history' (Schmidt 1971, p. 78). Nature, then, is historically unified through the labour process.

In contradistinction to human ecology, which has tended either to human-ise nature or naturalise man, a materialist perspective on society and nature is dialectical and internally related (Ollman 1974). I would like to suggest that Marx's metabolic metaphor provides a richer conceptual frame for both human–cultural ecologists and specifically for the study of hazards. Following Sayer (1980), this involves two critical concepts: (a) labour and (b) intersub-jectivity. With regard to the former, labour can be seen as the intentional and active transformation of nature for survival; that is, the motion of man on nature produces use-values for consumption. But labour is more than a simple change in the form of matter; it is a process in which man and nature partici-pates, in which humans 'start, regulate and control the material re-actions between selves and nature' (Marx 1967, p. 177); in which by acting on the external world and changing it, man changes his own nature. At the same time, the transformation of nature can only work with its given materials; human practice cannot transcend the laws of ecology, only the form in which these laws express themselves. It is, rather, the social structure which 'deter-mines the form in which men are subjected to these [natural] laws, their mode of production, their field of application, and the degree to which they can be understood and made socially useful' (Marx, in Schmidt 1971, p. 98). While nature can only be ruled in accordance with its own laws, the labour process which transforms it is social in several important respects. First, labour pre-supposes understanding of nature's mechanisms and this knowledge is clearly neither innate nor given but is socially acquired; as Sayer (1980, p. 29) observes, knowledge required from the appropriation of nature is never unmediated reflexion but 'always uses means of production in the form of existing knowledge'. And secondly, as Marx (in Bottomore & Rubel 1963, p. 155) himself noted, 'In the process of production, human beings do not only enter into a relation with Nature. They produce only by working together in a specific manner and by reciprocally exchanging their activities. In order to produce, they enter into definite connections and relations with one another, and only within these social connections and relations does their connection with Nature, i.e. production, take place'.

In the abstract, then, labour is the active and effective relation between society and nature; labour is transformative and social but in its historic mission it also changes the social relations themselves. Labour as the relation between people and nature is, however, historical in two senses: first, we must ask what kind of labour, or labourer, or labour process? There is no historical inevitability why interaction with nature is mediated through slave or serf or wage relations. But in any given period, the metabolism of humans and nature is locked into an historically determinate structure of social relations (Sayer 1980). And secondly, this metabolism is historical in the same sense that it is not voluntarist, for 'Men make their own history, but they do not make it just as they please . . . but under circumstances directly encountered, given and transmitted from the past' (Marx 1972, p. 10). In laying stress on human agency, on history, on the non-teleological quality of social systems and on the structured social relations, a materialist perspective clearly does not simply translate into Carl Sauer's notion of 'man as an ecological dominate' which is such a strong thread in the weft of contemporary human ecology.

The second concept raised by Sayer, and which I shall only touch upon very superficially, is intersubjectivity. Precisely because human life is irreducibly social, interaction within society is meaningful; that is, 'the social is grounded in the production, negotiation and use of intersubjective meanings' (Sayer 1980, p. 22). As knowing subjects, then, we all operate on the basis of understanding; human action is *constituted* by intersubjective meanings. Though they need be neither correct nor coherent, these meanings are bound up with language, action and institutions; in short, with the practices and material constitution of society. Meanings are, as Taylor (1971) observed, essentially modes of social relation. While this raises a host of germane questions on the relations between knowing subjects, between theory and society, and so on, I simply want to point out that the conception of the relation between society and nature can be constitutive and reflective of prevailing social relations. This is, of course, precisely the point made by Sahlins and Friedmann in their critiques of the ecosystemic view of adaptation.

What, then, is the significance of the materialist perspective for adaptation and the study of hazards? A focus on labour as the embodiment of the people–nature relation affirms the critical importance of social context. But in particular circumstances labour is refracted through the prism of *specific* social relations of production:

'The manner of appropriation of Nature, i.e. the form of our metabolism with Nature, is determined by the social relations, chiefly to do with ownership and control, and these forms of appropriation have the effect of reproducing those social relations. The separation of workers from the means of production means that their appropriation of Nature is governed by the interests of capitalists, and in turn this serves to reproduce the workers as wage-labourers because it does not give them the control of the means of production to enable them to become anything else, and it reproduces the capitalists as the owners and controllers of production. Therefore there is a necessary relation between the form of appropriation of Nature and the social relations of production'

(Sayer 1980, p. 29).

It is critical, however, that we move beyond the social relations of production *per se;* in conjunction with the forces of production – that is the totality of the technical conditions of reproduction – these social relations constitute a mode of production. Each mode contains within it certain contradictions and tension, which emerge from the labour process and which provide the basis for the social reproduction of the entire society. In other words, labour is one moment in what Friedmann (1976) calls a total system of reproduction. Among an African peasantry this would involve the reproduction of the productive (agricultural) cycle, the reproduction of the productive cell (the household), and its social relations of production (see Meillassoux 1981). Godelier has posited the importance of a dynamic conception of the conditions of social reproduction which is entirely congruent with our discussion of labour and intersubjectivity:

'Chaque niveau d'organisation sociale a des effets spécifiques sur le fonctionnement et le reproduction de l'ensemble de la société et par voie de conséquence sur les rapports de l'homme avec la nature ... – c'est seulement en tenant compte du jeu spécifique de tous les niveaux du fonctionnement d'un système économique et social que l'on peut découvrir la logique du contenu et des formes des divers modes de réprésentation, des diverses formes de perception de l'environnement' (Godelier 1974, p. 124).

Accordingly, for Godelier adaptation 'désigne avant tout la logique interne de l'exploitation des ressources et les conditions de reproduction de ce mode d'exploitation'. This definition implies that adaptive processes are (a) not uniquely constrained by nature but also by the social relations of production and (b) often have a contradictory character which emerges from the labour process itself. Robson (1978, p. 326) is correct when she argues that, if adaptation is to designate a compatibility between society and nature, these mechanisms must have specific social forms and be elaborated in terms of the conditions of social reproduction of society. If environmental relations are, then, instances of the labour process, hazards can (as I shall argue in the following section) be seen as moments or crises in the system of social reproduction.

Drought and the simple reproduction squeeze: a case study in northern Nigeria

Odious images of Islam have an embarrassingly longstanding lineage in the West. It is, then, entirely appropriate that Roder and Dupree (1974), in a study of drought among Hausa peasants in Muslim northern Nigeria, should discover that farmers see themselves at the mercy of the elements and in the hands of God. In their own didactic words, 'They know that drought can come again in any year and that its occurrence cannot be predicted . . . When faced with drought or other natural disasters . . . their chief response is to pray to God' (Roder & Dupree 1974, p. 118). Rather than an invocation of the fatalistic hand of Islam – of peasant irrationality derived from the ideological hegemony of religion – I shall argue that the starting point must be the labour process and the knowledge and intersubjective meanings which emerge from the social basis of labour. In short, the optic through which hazards – and in this case drought – are examined is that of the social relations of production specifically in a peasant society in transition. In the case of northern Nigeria, I shall endeavour to show that the articulation of a precapitalist mode of production with a global capitalist system, largely under the aegis of the colonial state, explains the changing character of peasant production and in particular the current vulnerability of rural producers to environmental hazards *for which they are conceptually prepared*. It is precisely the inability of some peasants to respond – in other words, to reproduce themselves – under conditions of environmental risk that characterises the transformation of the social relations of production in Hausaland. In this sense one can quite legitimately talk of structural maladaptation in peasant society in northern Nigeria.

Historical perspective By the close of the 18th century, what is now northern Nigeria consisted of a largely Islamised population in terms of its norms and values, whose rulers were also Muslim but whose legitimacy as a dynasty was based on an ancient pre-Islamic *iskoki* belief system. From these social and political tensions, emerged the Jihad or Holy War of 1804, led by a revolutionary cadre – the *jama'a* – committed to the overthrow of an old *sarauta* system. The Holy War heralded a new form of political organisation (the emirate system) and a larger unified polity (the Sokoto Caliphate) which welded together 30 emirates covering 388 485 km². The Caliphate survived for almost 100 years from the accession of Usman dan Fodio as Amir-al-muminin at Gudu in 1804 to the death of Sultan Ahmadu at the hands of the British colonial forces at Burmi in 1903.

The basic unit of production in the 19th century was the household, perhaps embracing sons, clients and slaves in an extended domestic structure in which the householder organised production and distribution and paid taxation. Households were often subsumed in communities controlled through the agency of village heads whose responsibility extended to land sales and village adjudication. A proportion of the peasant surplus was expropriated by a ruling class in the form of either labour, grain, or cash. The office holders had tenure over 'fiefs' given by the Emir, though they usually resided on private estates worked by slave, client and hired labour; they could also demand corvée labour from villages within their territorial jurisdiction. Slave labour, though crucial to the functioning of the large estates operated by the ruling class, was not a dominant characteristic of the productive system. Craft production and petty commodity production generally, emanating from within the household structure, was, conversely, a widespread phenomenon throughout Hausaland. The state controlled the means of coercion, provided protection for the peasantry and travelling merchants, organised large-scale labour projects and acted as a guarantor in times of needs. Within this tributary formation, peasant security in the face of a hazardous climatic environment was secured through a network of horizontal and vertical relationships and reciprocities which were embedded in the social relations of production.

A necessary historical starting point in light of this brief resumé of social relations in the Sokoto Caliphate is the recognition that extreme climatic variability, particularly drought, is and was an intrinsic part of nature in northern Nigeria and indeed throughout the semi-arid Sahelian desert edge. The recursivity of drought – and hence of the possibility of famine – is reflected in the historical landscape of Hausaland which is littered with references to drought and the great famines (*babban yunwa*) of the past. The dialectic of feast and famine or drought and flood is a recurrent motif in Hausa society and it occupies a significant cognitive position in the collective mentalité. Not only is there a complex and subtle lexicon which pertains to rainfall variability, but this same climatic content is embodied in the most significant cultural and artistic forms such as praise epithets, folktales, fables and historical anecdote.

In light of the recursiveness of rainfall and harvest variability, it is to be expected that rural communities were in some sense geared to environmental risk. Take the following comment from Raynault (1975) describing 19th-century Nigerian Hausaland:

'Faced with precarious natural conditions indigenous society was able to place into operation a series of practices, individual and collective, which permitted it a margin of security . . . traditional techniques of storage permitted grain to be stored for relatively long periods . . . which made possible the constitution of reserves . . . after the harvest the seed destined to be planted the next year as well as the quantity of grain necessary for the subsistence of the group during the planting season were placed by the clan head in a large granary which could not be opened until after the first rains'.

The relation between the labour process and drought extended, then, beyond the sophistry of Hausa agronomy which included sorghum–millet intercropping, moisture conservation techniques, and the exploitation of ecologically varied micro-environments into the social realm. In particular, the social relations of production defined the socioeconomic context of hazard occurrence and notably the possibility of drought-induced food shortage. The emphasis on the role of kinship and descent grouping generally was one way in which risks were diffused and collective security instituted. Among the non-Muslim Hausa the descent group referred to as the clan segment functioned precisely to this end; '[The segment] has but one function: when the grain stores of one household are exhausted, its head may borrow grain from another [segment] household and repay that grain at harvest without interest' (Faulkingham 1971, p. 123). At an ideological level, the redistributive ethic was reiterated through a Muslim dogma which saw gift-giving as obligatory for the rich and the office-holders. At another level, other formal institutional mechanisms incumbent upon the ruling élite served to free resources from the rich to the peasantry. The communal work group was a case in point in which foodstuffs were released during the critical pre-harvest period. A rather more elaborate instance was the institution of *sarkin noma* (lit. king of farming), who was elected by virtue of his capacity to produce in excess of 1000 bundles of grain. In essence, it was an attenuated variant of the North American 'potlatch' in which prestige accrued through the ceremonial distribution of resources. The office of *sarkin noma* entailed on the one hand a redistribution of foodstuffs through the harvest festival and on the other it was 'the ultimate defense against famine: when the grain in any gida is exhausted, the residents may obtain an interest free loan of grain from the S. noma's bins, to be repaid at harvest' (Faulkingham 1971, p. 81).

In a society predicated upon an absolute hierarchical segmentation between rulers and ruled, it is hardly surprising that the upper echelons of political authority in 19th-century Hausaland were expected to act as the ultimate buffers for the village-level redistributive operations. The responsibilities and obligations of the village heads were quite clear in this respect and, when their capabilities were over-ridden in cases of extreme seasonal hardship, the next level of the hierarchy (the fief holder) was activated. In Katsina Emirate, for example, the district heads often kept grain at several centres throughout their district and frequently in villages where they may have acted as patron to a number of clients. These graduated responses terminated with the state structure itself which used the grain tythe for central granaries for organised redistribution during famine periods.

The pre-capitalist form of the labour process among Hausa peasantries in relation to drought has much in common with what Thompson (1971) calls the moral economy of the poor. Scott (1976) has in fact suggested that moral economy is in fact characteristic of peasant communities generally which are organised around the problem of risk, security and the guarantee of a margin of security. Scott calls this margin a subsistence ethic which can be seen as a general proclivity towards risk aversion in agriculture ('safety first'), a tendency towards mutual support ('the norm of reciprocity') and an expectation of minimum state support ('the moral economy'). Put rather differently, Hausa households in the 19th century were largely engaged in the production of use-values; the simple cycle of household reproduction was in this sense a natural economy which involved a series of horizontal and vertical ties between households – rather than market relations – institutionalised in the moral economy, i.e. the realm of intersubjective meanings, norms and rules. All this is not to suggest a Rousseauian pre-capitalist nirvana, a glorified peasant life somehow optimally adapted and ultra-stable, a world of benevolent patrons and welfare-minded rulers. The Caliphate was, of course, a class society predicated on a determinate set of social relations in which surpluses were canalised from the countryside to the cities. Rather, I simply wish to suggest that some institutions, mechanisms and practices – indeed some of the most prosaic attributes of peasant society – embodied in the Sokoto Caliphate, provided a measure of security and buffered households from the worst effects of variability in rainfall and food supply. The security arrangements were grounded in and inseparable from the architecture and constitution of the social relation of production and were indeed instrumental in the reproduction of society at large.

Drought and colonialism   Colonialism in northern Nigeria was a process of incorporation in which pre-capitalist modes of production were articulated with the colonial, and ultimately the global, economy. This articulation was principally affected through the colonial triad of taxation, export commodity production and monetisation. Although colonial hegemony left peasant producers in control of the means of production and instituted minimal technological change, the process of incorporation did necessitate a transformation in the conditions of production. To the extent that pre-capitalist elements in northern Nigeria were eroded by colonial integration, the adaptive capability of Hausa communities and the margin of subsistence security accordingly changed. In the process, peasant producers – particularly the rural poor – became less capable of responding to and coping with both drought and food shortage. Traditional mechanisms and adjustments disappeared, the extension of cash cropping undermined self-sufficiency in foodstuffs, a dependence on world commodity prices (for cotton and groundnuts) amplified an already high tax burden, and households became increasingly vulnerable to environmental perturbations such as drought or harvest shortfalls. This vulnerability and marginality is highlighted in four major famines which occurred during the colonial period in 1914, 1927, 1942 and 1951. I cannot hope to do justice to the complexity of the process of colonial integration in northern Nigeria, nor its effects on the structure of peasant production, both of which are treated at great length elsewhere. Rather I will sketch some of the pertinent aspects of the changing conditions of production – particularly the extraction of surplus value and the dénouement of moral economy – and draw some tentative links to the increasing hazardousness of peasant livelihood.

The new colonial administration sought through taxation to divert as much of the surplus formerly extracted by the ruling élite to their own coffers. Taxes were reorganised but for the most part remained at the same level and in some cases revealed sharp increases to compensate for the declining revenue of the élite. More traumatic, however, was the move to collect tax in cash, not grain; effective by 1910, not only did this undermine the zakkat-based grain reserve but it determined the penetration of a generalised modern currency into indigenous economic systems. Furthermore, taxation had profound and direct implications for hunger itself. First, unlike the indigenous Hausa fiscal system, colonial taxes were regular, reasonably predictable and *rigid*. The inflexibility accordingly took no account of the realities of Hausa life: late rains, poor harvests, seasonal hunger, and a precarious environment subject to perturbations such as locust invasion or epidemics. The severity of colonial taxation contrasted sharply with an indigenous system which, though far from being innocent of extortion, made an attempt to graduate taxes according to existential circumstances. Secondly, the *timing* of tax collection assumed a colossal importance. This was especially the case throughout the principal cotton-growing areas where annual taxes were gathered prior to the cotton harvest, leaving the rural cultivator little choice but the sale of grains when prices were lowest or alternatively vulnerable to the clutches of the moneylender. And thirdly, the taxation system was inseparable from the colonial policy of the extension of commodity production and cash cropping into the countryside. It is quite clear in this respect that in northern Hausaland groundnuts were the principal tax-paying crop, which perhaps goes a long way to explaining the apparently 'irrational' behaviour of a peasantry which produced more groundnuts when the commodity price had actually fallen. More generally, of course, the 'groundnut revolution', meant a decrease in the area devoted to foodstuffs, increasing subjection to the vagaries of the world commodity market, and the ever-present threat of indebtedness at the hands of middlemen. It is precisely in this way that the nature of seasonal hunger changed in terms of both its dynamics and the predicament of those who find themselves suffering from its effects. The net result tended to be that seasonal hunger on a local or regional scale devolved into fully fledged famine, as was the case in 1913–14, and set a precedent for the colonial period generally.

Despite the commercial setback of the 1913–14 famine, the groundnut revolution picked up momentum and became emblematic of the subsequent expansion in the produce trade. Through this process of commoditisation and the increasingly important role that money came to acquire, it is hardly surprising that the new forms of indebtedness arose. This is especially so in the case of the co-evolution of the 'yan baranda' system and of the cash crop economy. The 'yan baranda' constituted the lower orders of the export crop-buying hierarchy, receiving cash advances from European firms via their buying agents. These sums were in turn lent directly to the producer who pledged his crop to the agent. The interest on such loans was frequently in the order of 100% and for the producer at least was the initial step into a cyclical debt trap. It is precisely in this manner that urban and merchant capital penetrated the countryside and it illuminates the way in which a domestic unit is drawn into an external merchant network. As Shenton and Freund so nicely put it, 'the most successful traders stood at the apex of a hierarchy of credit and clientage that rested on the shoulders of village middlemen, living in the interstices of a colonial economy dominated by the European firms' (Shenton & Freund 1978, p. 13).

The deepening involvement with commodity production and cash crops naturally impinged upon the social organisation of agricultural production itself. Claude Raynault (1975) has shown how, in the groundnut zone of Niger, this has taken the form of the dissolution of traditional estates, an escalation in land sales and the generalisation of hired farm labour. Changes in the sociology of production were coupled with the profusion of imported commodities, especially cloth, which articulated with the cycle of rapidly inflating prices for ceremonial exchanges on the one hand, and the chain of indebtedness on the other. Stresses consequently were imposed upon the corporateness of the rural world: the old responsibilities and obligations became less binding, communal work largely disappeared, and the extended family became less embracing and hence increasingly incapable of buffering individuals in crisis. In the densely settled areas, the extreme land shortages heralded larger food deficits and heightened vulnerability to seasonal changes. The household showed the first signs of fission, and collective security had lost its original meaning; social and familial solidarity appeared to be dissolving and the gift lost its original significance. The peasantry were torn from a social matrix of kin affiliation and obligation, and the existential problem of subsistence became subservient to marketing behaviour. In short, the social nature of the subsistence system and the qualities of the moral economy were severely ruptured. Reciprocity and solidarity, and hence the nature of inequality, itself had changed.

The general point I wish to make is that post-1903 the margin of security for the Hausa peasantry came under siege. The colonial administration, only too aware of the dangers of overconcentration on cash-crop commodities, a heavy tax burden and the spectre of starvation, tended to be in the final analysis ambivalent or to overestimate the resiliency of the peasantry. The outcome was, in contrast to the previous century, that Hausaland suffered from three major famines in 1913–14, 1927 (1931 in much of Niger) and 1942, and whose occurrence reflected an increasingly artificial character in the sense that climatic variability became less crucial in the actual genesis of food shortage. This artificiality reached its apotheosis during the early 1940s with a famine whose structural properties bore a striking resemblance to the Bengal famine of 1943.

The point that I wish to emphasise is that colonialism broke the cycle of reproduction of peasant households. The reproduction of the Hausa farming family became contingent upon the continued production of export commodities; as Bernstein (1978) put it, the reproduction of the conditions of commodity production became 'internalised' in the household reproduction cycle. The necessity for cash ensured a greater devotion to cash crops, especially during periods of low export prices and an inevitable participation on the part of the rural poor in the merchant-credit system. Falling export prices were experienced by households as a deterioration in the terms of exchange which meant either a reduction in levels of consumption or an intensification of commodity production, or both. This has been referred to as 'the simple reproduction squeeze' (Bernstein 1978, p. 63) and is one facet of what Scott called the 'margin of subsistence security'. As ever larger areas were devoted to cash crop production at the expense of foodstuffs – and this was especially pernicious for the rural poor in closely settled areas who were cultivating small holdings and experienced severe labour constraints – the reproduction squeeze deepened and both hunger and indebtedness assume increasing importance:

> 'The more commodity relations and acquisition of a cash income become conditions of reproduction, then shortfalls in production and/or income can lead to a cycle of indebtedness. Studies of peasant economy in a number of capitalist social formations have demonstrated the phenomena of "starvation rents" (the payment by poorer peasants of higher than average rents to secure a plot of land for minimal reproduction needs), and of peasants selling their food crop after harvest in order to meet immediate cash needs, and subsequently having to buy food at higher prices. Similar in principle to the latter is the practice of crop-mortgaging (to richer peasants, local traders or larger-scale merchant's capital) in order to acquire cash in the case of emergencies' (Bernstein 1978, p. 63).

Hausa peasant producers thus became increasingly vulnerable to even small variations in rainfall since the margin of subsistence security had been eroded. In a very real sense, then, hazards *had been redefined by the transformation in the social relations of production.* Indeed, the rural poor were vulnerable to *any* sort of perturbation and, under conditions of agricultural stagnation which were characteristic of the colonial period, northern Nigerian producers were particularly susceptible to the usual environmental variability typical of the northern savannas. The rural poor were hyper-vulnerable for they succumbed to relatively slight oscillations in harvest quality; a 'light' harvest could herald a subsistence crisis of famine proportions, particularly if prevailing export crop prices tended to be unfavourable. As one district officer noted, the Hausa peasantry lived constantly in the shadow of famine.

Hazards, adaptation and peasant differentiation   In the Hausa village (Kaita) in which I lived in 1977–8, the vast majority of households still owned their means of production, in spite of high population densities, land shortage and the changes wrought by colonialism. The absence of a landless class, nevertheless, should not obscure sharp socioeconomic differentiation within the community, the genesis and reproduction of which is precisely related to the appearance of wage labour, the use of indebtedness, and the dominant role of merchant's capital under the aegis of the colonial state. In light of this quantitative differentiation among peasants and the social relations of production which sustain it, the question is whether it makes sense to talk of adaptation to hazards.

Rain comes and goes, and Hausa farmers are acutely concerned with the concrete empirical variability in annual rainfall, and agronomic practice varies in tandem with the precise pattern of precipitation. In this sense, agricultural practice is not fixed – a sort of human ecological programme – but flexible with respect to environmental perturbations. With regard to rainfall variation, suffice to say that Kaita farmers appear to have a firm grasp of those local processes which are observable in their totality within the village territory, including an acute understanding of the immediate geographical milieu; what one might refer to as Hausa ethnoscience, to use the current parlance. In the case of drought, Kaita farmers had little comprehension of – or indeed intellectual interest in – its etiology, and a variety of elicitation techniques simply revealed a vague and ill specified association with Islamic metaphysics. On the other hand, they had a remarkable, almost visceral, grasp of the empirical consequences of rainfall deficits – or surfeits – on their crops and of the prescribed ways in which the symptoms might be treated. First, Hausa farmers rarely monocrop but plant in a polycultural fashion. Two, three or four crops (usually millet, sorghum and cowpeas) are normally planted or intercropped in each field. This diversity breeds a sort of systemic stability, for each crop has rather different requirements and tolerances to drought. Research has shown how indigenous crop mixtures are risk-averse, guaranteeing an adequate return under unpredictable and variable ecological circumstances.

Secondly, should the onset of the rains be delayed or the distribution of rainfall be patchy, there are various forms of water conservation which can be instituted. Ridging, exploitation of seasonally damp bottomlands, and variation in the intensity of manure application, are all varied in accordance with rainfall. Should replanting be necessary in the aftermath of an early drought, the spacing of plants (*gicci*) is usually widened. And thirdly, crop mixtures are not static agronomic patterns and neither is the environment perceived as homogeneous. Hausa farmers recognise and exploit several micro-environments in addition to the predominant upland (*jigawa*). In particular, the lowland (*fadama*) environment, which is permanently moist and occasionally flooded during the rainy season, is broken down into three distinct niches. The floodplain proper is used for rice and sorghum, the basin areas generally devoted to tobacco or sorghum and the riparian edge devoted principally to dry season irrigation and the cultivation of vegetables. This lowland area is of special import when rainfall fails or fluctuates. When the rains begin, the upland is usually planted with high-yielding millet and sorghum, and the floodplain devoted to rice and long-maturing sorghum. Should these early rains be followed by a drought – as is quite frequently the case about 1 year in 4 – replanting will make use of *different short-maturing cereals*. Equally in the lowland environments, replanting will take cognisance of the possibility of a shortened rainy season and therefore will usually entail the replacement of rice with the less water-demanding sorghums. The same process of selection occurs in the lowland micro-environments and, in the event of a poor cereal harvest, then increased attention will be paid to the dry season agriculture (*lambu*). In short, then, the different environments are articulated through a complex process of decision making which correlates with variability in rainfall (see Fig. 13.1).

In the same way that peasant farmers are agents in the appropriation of nature – of which drought is inextricably a part – so do they act in the face of likely or actual food shortage. By the rains following a poor harvest, stocks of grain are either low or non-existent and households are faced with the possibility of liquidating assets to cover grain purchases. Since the probability of food shortage is evident immediately after the harvest in September or October, families can begin to respond to the potential threat of dearth. Grain prices, even in normal years, exhibit a seasonal price rise during the wet season when domestic granaries are low; but, in the aftermath of a poor harvest, householders know full well that millet and sorghum prices will probably rise by 100–200%.

Peasant households in fact relate to the threat of shortage in a graduated sequence of responses which change as food availability worsens and prices inflate. Immediately after the poor harvest, householders attempt to generate income wherever possible – perhaps through wage labouring or craft activity – in order to cover future costs of grain purchase. As domestic stores diminish and food prices rise, families begin to look for support from their extended kin and friends. As extreme scarcity approaches, family units dispose of assets

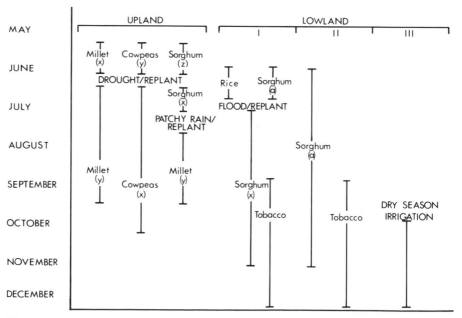

Figure 13.1   A model of farmer response to 1977 rainfall variability. The parentheses refer to crop varieties with differing maturation rates, tolerances to drought and yields.

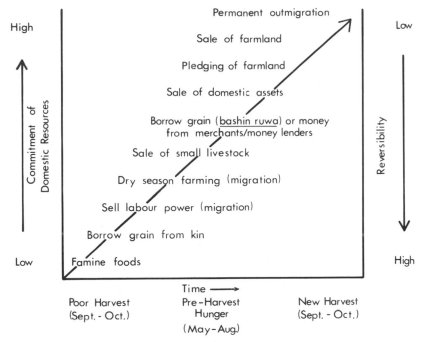

Figure 13.2 Graduated response to food shortage.

for liquidity, beginning usually with small livestock, or perhaps turn to the village trader or merchant for a loan of money or grain. Under famine conditions, starving households begin to pledge or even sell their farm holdings and, in the final analysis, resort to outmigration (see Fig. 13.2).

At an aggregate level, however, this model conveys little of the realities of drought in relation to household economy. This is precisely because the legacy of the development of capitalism in Nigeria has been to generate new patterns of interhousehold inequality. For while all households are theoretically capable of coping with various forms of stress, in practice these responses are mediated by social and economic inequality. Poor households frequently have neither the requisite seed nor the access to land to cope effectively with rainfall variability. Equally, under conditions of scarcity or poor harvests or indeed seasonal price rises in cereals, poor households are incapable of weathering economic crises. The rich households conversely have adaptive flexibility in the sense that they have access to the resources necessary to offset drought while their domestic resources enable them to maintain self-sufficiency in grain even after poor harvests. Accordingly, if one examines responses to drought-induced food shortage in Kaita village in 1973–4 certain strategies emerge (Table 13.1).

Obviously, the rural poor are largely incapable of meeting the demands of a

Table 13.1   Responses by household heads to food shortage, 1973–4.

	R	P		R	P
purchase grain	4	91	sell grain	26	
sell labour		87	buy livestock	21	
sell livestock	4	61	lend money or grain	8	
sell assets		47	buy labour power	51	
borrow from trader or merchant		39	buy farmland	6	
pledge farm		11			
sell farm		6			
migrate		5			

Note: R, rich ($n = 56$); P, poor ($n = 93$).

food crisis and are, therefore, especially vulnerable. Poor harvests and famines are thus social crises, for they are mediated by the existing social order and may actually amplify extant economic inequalities. In Kaita village during 1973–4 it was the poorer households who sold labour power, livestock and perhaps even land in a buyers' market, while the relatively well-to-do made the most of a favourable situation by purchasing cheap commodities and lending both money and grain. Clearly, then, in peasant communities, where socioeconomic differentiation is so pronounced, poor farmers, shackled by their poverty, are largely powerless to effect the sorts of changes that might mitigate the debilitating consequences of environmental hazards. *Hazard response is thus contingent upon the social context of the responding units and upon their situation in the productive process.* Drought is in an obvious sense refracted through the prism of community inequality and hence adaptation to hazard is a social process. For many households drought is experienced through constraint rather than choice.

A proper understanding of hazards requires, however, that we move beyond simple quantitative measures of inequality to the determinate structure of the social relations of production, as Sayer put it. Inequality in this sense is tied to the conditions in which wealth becomes capital; that is to the labour process itself. In this regard, Hausa peasants can be differentiated in the following fashion. First there are poor peasants unable to reproduce themselves through household production and who secure simple reproduction through the wage relation. Secondly, there are middle peasants who are sufficiently stable to reproduce themselves through family labour 'but in specific relations with other strata of the peasantry' (Bernstein 1978, p. 67). And thirdly, there is a wealthy or Kulak class capable of extended reproduction, that is accumulation and investment (largely in trade) through superior means of production and the purchase of labour power. For the rural poor the precariousness of the material and technical conditions of production, in conjunction with the pressures exerted by commodity production and the sale of labour, lends itself to a simple reproduction squeeze. The household is obviously vulnerable to failure in any of its material elements of production. But it is, of course, the constellation of social relations which bind households together and project them into the marketplace which determines the precise form of this vulnerability. I cannot hope to document these relations of production in any detail here save to say that indebtedness, the wage relation and pronounced inequality in landholding, are all critical. More pertinently, for the 20% of households who are semi-proletarianised, every wet season prior to harvest is a period of crisis in the cycle of reproduction. These households are barely capable of producing sufficient grain on their low-yielding Lilliputian farm holdings and they find themselves projected either into the local grain market when prevailing prices are seasonally inflated or into the hands of the village moneylender. Equally, the demand for cash to cover critical food consumption during the period of maximum mobilisation of agricultural labour pushes adult males into wet-season farm labouring, the effect of which is to delay the timing of, or entirely neglect, their own agricultural operations with the result that yields are pitifully low. At harvest, debts have to be repaid (often at usurious interest rates), taxes paid and household expenditures (i.e. repairs, marriage expenses) covered precisely when commodity prices tend to be lowest. The large farmers conversely withhold grains for a mid-season price rise which then finance the purchase of wage labour and investment in the highly lucrative cattle trade and, to a lesser extent, grains marketing and credit functions. The social relations of trade and production force many farmers to sell cheap and buy dear, to neglect or delay their own productive activities, and to plunge headlong into a cycle of indebtedness.

Drought hazard is, then, simply one instance of nature as contained in the metabolism of these peasant social relations. The labour process in Hausaland is complex precisely because peasant society is in transition. My historical presentation indicated how the colonial state and European merchant's capital fulfilled a contradictory function insofar as Hausa rural producers were partially transformed; there was, to use Bettleheim's felicitous phrase, both conservation and dissolution. In some respects, as new relations of production emerged, as the cycle of reproduction was commoditised, so was the moral economy distorted. That is, the relation between nature and society was itself partly transformed, a transformation encapsulated in the process of peasant differentiation. It is into these nascent capitalist relations in the countryside that hazards such as drought are deposited. In this case, drought is simply a moment in a cycle of reproduction the significance of which is related to the situation of each household in the productive process and in the nexus of social relations.

New directions

I have attempted to derive an analysis of hazards from two abstract materialist postulates which grounds the relation between nature and society – the necessary starting point for any critical elaboration of hazards – in the labour process and the irreducibly intersubjective quality of social life. In doing so I have suggested that we must be sensitive both to the status of what we take to be environmental knowledge, the manner in which our theories in a real sense partly produce the 'facts' we analyse, and the complex relationship between concepts and the material conditions from which they emerge. By examining the theoretical peculiarities of hazards research – and its sister field of human/cultural ecology – I have attempted to situate it in terms of the epistemology and conception of man–nature relations which, I believe, have inappropriately framed environmental threats and perturbations. The analysis of drought in northern Nigeria, conversely, began with the social relations of production which has to be defined historically. I argued that drought along the West African desert edge can only be understood in an historical fashion; that is, the cycle of simple household reproduction in the 19th century and its attendant moral economy in some sense coloured hazards and calamities. Drought was put in context in terms of the prevailing social and economic architecture of 19th-century Hausaland. The impact of colonialism gradually transformed the social relation of production and hence of the relation between nature and society. I would argue that with respect to drought this was given a material expression in the almost pharaoic sequence of famines between 1900 and 1960.

The evidence adduced from the contemporary village economy indicated that, in spite of a conceptual and practical preparation for drought, the social relations of interhousehold inequity constituted the necessary starting point. But this was not necessarily so in some simple quantitative sense – there are rich and poor peasants who exhibit different adaptive capabilities – but rather because differentiation emerges from the existing labour process. That the rural poor were incapable of responding adequately to drought is, of course, consistent with the cybernetic view of maladaptation. But the crucial difference is not that households suffer intrinsically from usurpation or hypercoherence, or linear thinking or bad values or inappropriate higher-order command statements; rather these pathologies, if they exist, emerge from the existing social relations of production. As Sayer observed, the man–nature relation is given form in a determinate structure of social relations of production and it is this which provides the locus for our study of drought. In Hausaland, these social relations are convoluted because they are, in some sense, in transition. But it is clearly the emergence of wage labour, or unequal exchange through trade, of expanded commodity production and of usury which defines this social field of force.

From a materialist perspective, then, an environmental crisis not only probes the darkest corners of relations, but throws into sharp relief the structure of social systems. The impact of a drought on human communities affords the social scientist a particular optic through which to view the functioning of the socioeconomic formation; indeed it was Marc Bloch who observed that as the development of a disease shows the physician the workings of the body so does a social crisis yield insight into the nature of the society so striken. In this manner, natural hazards are not simply *natural* (see quotation by Brecht, p. 7), for though a drought may be a catalyst or trigger mechanisms in the sequence of events which leads to famine conditions, the crisis itself is more a reflection of the ability of the socioeconomic system to cope with the unusual harshness of ecological conditions and their effects. To neglect this fact is to resort to a fatalism which sees disasters as 'Acts of God', placing responsibility upon nature, and in the process missing a major political point. In Nigerian Hausaland this is captured in the paradox that during the famines of the past 70 years it has been the men and women who work on the land who have perished for lack of food. Those who died were those who produced. 'The crisis created by a famine reveals the workings of the economic and social system and affords an insight into that structural violence which has the effect of denying the poorest . . . the right to feed themselves . . . The fact that . . . town dwellers can still get something to eat while the country people starve . . . is a sign of the power relation between urban and rural populations' (Spitz 1977, p. 3). This I suspect is what E. P. Thompson (1978) means when he refers to the crisis of subsistence as an 'historical category' and is clearly reflected in the comments of the Brazilian geographer Josué de Castro on Third World hazards: 'the catastrophic effects of drought and floods revealed principally the decrepit character of the prevailing agricultural structure, the shiftlessness, the improvidence and the inefficiency of the political system in force' (de Castro 1975, p. 12).

To appreciate the fact that hazard is mediated by the socioeconomic structures of the societies affected is simultaneously to recognise that 'modernisation' or 'development' has not necessarily solved the age-old problems of subsistence crises or vulnerability to environmental threats, and in some cases has actually aggravated them.

In conclusion, I would like to point out that theory, and natural hazards theory in particular, is not something ready made but, like any intellectual artefact, it has its material and ideological conditions of existence. Conventional hazards theory is also ideological in the sense that it has, to date, a sort of hegemonic role in the field which sustains historically specific views of nature, of society and of change. Ideology is ideological precisely because it presents the existing world as a litany of eternal verities. For this reason I began and conclude this essay with the observation of Timpanaro (1975, p. 17) that, all too often, prevailing power blocs attributable to nature the inequalities for which the structure of society is responsible.

Acknowledgements

In the not so distant past, this chapter was conceived as a joint effort with Mary Beth Pudup. For reasons not entirely beyond our control she was unable to participate fully but has, nonetheless, contributed significantly to the design and orientation of this chapter. As much as I would like to say she is jointly responsible for its content, she is not. The empirical work which appears here was collected as a part of a research programme (1976–8) funded by the Social Science Research Council, the National Science Foundation, the Wenner–Gren Foundation for Anthropolitical Research, and Resources for the Future. This paper is dedicated to John Berger who taught me much about seeing, to Edward Thompson for his reasoning, and to Gunnar Olsson for showing me that virtually everything is reproduction.

References

Alland, A. 1975. Adaptation. *An. Rev. Anthropol.* **4**, 59–73.

Anderson, J. N. 1973. Ecological anthropology and anthropological ecology. In *Handbook of social and cultural anthropology*, J. Honigmann (ed.), 179–239. Chicago: Rand McNally.

Anderson, P. 1980. *Arguments within English Marxism*. London: New Left Books.

Bateson, G. 1972. *Steps toward an ecology of mind*. New York: Ballantine.

Bateson, G. 1978. *Mind and nature*. New York: Ballantine.

Bergmann, F. 1975. On the inadequacies of functionalism, *Michigan Discs. in Anthropol.* **1**, 2–23.

Bernstein, H. 1978. Notes on capital and peasantry, *Rev. Afr. Polit, Econ.* no. 10, 60–73.

Bottomore, T. and M. Rubel 1963. *Selected writings in sociology and social philosophy*. Harmondsworth: Penguin.

Burgess, R. 1978. The concept of nature in geography and Marxism. *Antipode* **10**, 1–11.

Burton, I. R., Kates and G. White 1978. *Environment as hazard*. New York: Oxford University Press.

Clarke, W. 1977. The Structure of permanence. In *Subsistence and survival in the Pacific*, T. Bayliss-Smith and R. Feachem (eds), 363–84. San Francisco: Academic Press.

Cook, S. 1975. Production, ecology and economic anthropology. *Soc. Sci. Inform.* **12**, 25–52.

de Castro, J. 1975. *The geopolitics of hunger*. New York: Monthly Review Press.

Durham, W. 1976. The adaptive significance of cultural behavior. *Human Ecology* **4**, 89–121.

Faulkingham, R. 1971. *Political support in a Hausa village*. PhD dissertation, Michigan State Univ.

Flannery, K. 1972. The cultural evolution of civilization. *An. Rev. Ecol. System.* **3**, 399–426.

Freund, W. and R. Shenton. 1978. The incorporation of northern Nigeria into the world capitalist system. *Rev. Afr. Polit. Econ.* no. 13, 8–20.

Friedmann, J. 1976. Marxist theory and systems of total reproduction. *Crit. Anthropol.* no. 7, 3–16.

Friedmann, J. 1979. Hegelian ecology: between Rousseau and the world spirit. In *Social and ecological systems*, P. Burnham and R. Ellen (eds), 253–70. London: Academic Press.

Godelier, M. 1974. Considérations théoriques et critiques sur le problème des rapports entre l'homme et son environnement. *Inform. Sciences Sociales* **13**, 31–60.

Golledge, R. 1979. Reality, process and the dialectical relation between man and nature. In *Philosophy in geography*, S. Gale and G. Olsson (eds), 109–120. Dordrecht: Reidel.

Grossman, L. 1979. *Cash, cattle and coffee: the cultural ecology of development in the Highlands of Papua New Guinea*, PhD dissertation, Australian National Univ.

Holling, C. S. 1973. Resilience and stability of ecological systems. *An. Rev. Ecol. System.* **4**, 1–23.

Kates, R. W. 1971. Natural hazard in human ecological perspective: hypotheses and models. *Econ. Geog.* **47**, 438–51.

Kirkby, A. 1974. Individual and community response to rainfall variability in Oaxaca, Mexico. In White (1974, pp. 119–27).

Leiss, W. 1974 *The domination of nature*. Boston: Beacon Press.

Levi-Strauss, C. 1963. *Structural anthropology*. New York: Colophon.

Marx, K. 1967. *Capital*, New York: International.

Marx, K. 1972 *The eighteenth Brumaire of Louis Bonapart*. Moscow: Progress.

Meillassoux, C. 1981. *Maidens, meal and money*. Cambridge: Cambridge University Press.

Merchant, C. 1980. *The death of nature: women, ecology and the scientific revolution*. San Francisco: Harper & Row.

Nicolas, G. 1966. Une forme atténuée du potlatch en pays Hauss. *Cah. l'SEA* no. V.

O'Keefe, P. and B. Wisner 1975. African drought – the state of the game. In *African environment*, P. Richards (ed), 31–9. London: IAI.

Ollman, B. 1974. *Alienation: Marx's conception of man in capitalist society*. Cambridge: Cambridge University Press.

Orlove, B. 1980. Ecological anthropology. *An. Rev. Anthropol.* **9**, 235–73.

Pask, G. 1968. *Some mechanical concepts of goals, individuals, consciousness and symbolic evolution*. Paper presented at the Wenner Gren Symposium on the Effects of Conscious Purpose on Human Adaptation.

Rappaport, R. 1977. Ecology, adaptation and the ills of functionalism. *Michigan Discs Anthropol.* **2**, 138–90.

Rappaport, R. 1979. *Ecology, meaning and religion*. Richmond: North Atlantic Books.

Raynault, C. 1975. Le cas de la règion de Maradi, (Niger). In *Sécheresses et famines du Sahel*, J. Copans (ed.), vol. 2, 5–42. Paris: Maspero.

Richards, P. 1978. Community environmental knowledge in African rural development. *IDS Bull.* **10**, 28–36.

Robson, E. 1978. Utilisation du concept d'adaptation en anthropologie culturelle. *Soc. Sci. Inform.* **17**, 279–335.

Roder, W. and H. Dupree 1974. Coping with drought in a pre-Industrial, preliterate farming society. In White (1974, pp. 115–9).

Sahlins, M. 1976. *Culture and practical reason*. Chicago: University of Chicago Press.

Sayer, A. 1980. *Epistemology and regional science*. School of Social Science, Sussex Univ.

Schmidt, A. 1971. *The concept of nature in Marx*. London: New Left Books.

Scott, J. 1976. *The moral economy of the peasantry*. New Haven: Yale University Press.

Shenton, R. and W. Freund 1978. The incorporation of northern Nigeria into the world capitalist economy. *Rev. Afr. Polit. Econ.* no. 13. 8–20.

Slobodkin, L. and A. Rappaport 1974. An optimal strategy of evolution. *Q. Rev. Biol.* **49**, 181–200.

Smith, N. 1979. Geography, science and post-positivist modes of explanation. *Prog. Human Geog.* **3**, 356–83.

Smith, N. and P. O'Keefe 1980. Geography, Marx and the concept of nature. *Antipode* **12**, 30–9.

Spitz, P. 1977. *Silent violence: famine and inequality*. Geneva: UNRISD.

Taylor, C. 1971. Interpretation and the science of man. *Rev. Metaphys.* **25**, 3–51.

Thompson E. P. 1971. The moral economy of the English crowd during the eighteenth century. *Past and Present* **50**, 76–115.

Thompson, E. P. 1978. *The poverty of theory.* New York: Monthly Review.

Timpanaro, S. 1975. *On materialism.* London: New Left Books.

Torry, W. 1979. Hazards, hazes and holes: a critique of the *Environment as Hazard* and general reflections on disaster research. *Can. Geog.* **23**, 368–83.

Vayda, A. P. 1974. Warfare in ecological perspective. *An. Rev. Ecol. System.* **5**, 183–93.

Vayda, A. P. 1976. On the 'new ecology' paradigm. *Am. Anthropol.* **78**, 645–56.

Vayda, A. P. and B. McCay 1975. New directions in ecology and ecological anthropology. *An. Rev. Anthropol.* **4**, 293–306.

Vayda, A. P. and R. Rappaport 1967. Ecology, cultural and non-cultural. In *Introduction to cultural anthropology,* J. Clifton (ed.), 477–97. Boston: Houghton & Mifflin.

Waddell, E. 1975. Frost over Niugini: responses to climatic perturbations in the Central Highlands of New Guinea. *Human Ecology* **3**, 249–73.

Waddell, E. 1977. The hazards of scientism. *Human Ecology* **5**, 69–76.

Walker, R. 1979. Review of I. Burton *et al. Environment as hazard. Geog. Rev.* **69**, 113–14.

White, G. (ed.) 1974. *Natural hazards: local, national, global.* New York: Oxford University Press.

Wilden, A. 1972. *System and structure.* London: Tavistock.

Wilden, A. 1979. Ecology and ideology. In *The world as a company town,* A. Idris-Soven, E. Idris-Soven and M. K. Vaughn (eds), 73–98. The Hague: Mouton.

Winterhalder, B. 1980. Environmental analysis in human evolution and adaptation research. *Human Ecology* **8**, 135–70.

Wisner, B. 1981. *Cultural ecology and development.* Paper presented to a Special Session on Cultural Ecology, Assoc. Am. Geogs An. Conv., Los Angeles.

14 *Global disasters, a radical interpretation*

PAUL SUSMAN, PHIL O'KEEFE AND BEN WISNER

Introduction

The study of disasters is not an infant science. Examples abound of case materials, theoretical modelling and attempted global summaries. Yet, if there is a wealth of empirical data, the analytical reality behind most disaster research is hardly more conducive to a fundamental understanding of disaster than the attempts of the early physicists to explain reality in terms of four elements. Perhaps a more apposite comparison would be between the current disaster practitioners and the early medical scientists who attempted to explain disease in terms of four humours. In this chapter, we shall consider the nature of disaster in a global framework and attempt to provide a general theory of modern disaster occurrence, namely a *theory of marginalisation*.

Definitions of disaster

Involvement in disaster by international, national and academic institutions has led to a number of implicit and explicit definitions of disaster (Westgate & O'Keefe 1976a). The implicit definitions of disaster derive from the field operations of international and national organisations, particularly from relief operations, and need not concern us in this instance. The explicit definitions are those of the academic institutions and are germane to our discussion.

> The first important element to note is that disaster is an event (or series of events) which seriously disrupts normal activities (Cisin & Clark 1962).

This emphasis on normalcy highlights the need to observe *disaster as an extension of everyday life*. It also implies that an understanding of the threat of disaster is as important to the comprehension of disaster as the disaster event itself (Westgate & O'Keefe 1976b). Hewitt and Burton (1971) develop this notion of potential threat and accent disaster as a function

> both of the physical event itself and the state of human society.

This approach illustrates the second important consideration in a definition of disaster, namely the dynamic human–environment relationship. We strongly contend that to comprehend disaster thoroughly as a dynamic feature of the human–environment relationship, it is essential to see it as the extreme situation implicit in the everyday condition of given populations.

To understand the everyday condition of a population, it is necessary to consider the socioeconomic conditions in relation to physical environment. In the context of hazards, this relationship turns upon the notion of *vulnerability*. Vulnerability is the degree to which different classes in society are differentially at risk, both in terms of the probability of occurrence of an extreme physical event and the degree to which the community absorbs the effects of extreme physical events and helps different classes to recover.

It is always important to consider both the extreme physical event and the vulnerability of the population in any definition of disaster. *Without people, there can be no disaster*. And poor people are generally more vulnerable than rich ones. *Disaster* is therefore defined as *the interface between an extreme physical event and a vulnerable human population*.

Global statistics on disaster

Several major sources of data provide global statistics on disaster. These have been systematically reviewed (Baird *et al*. 1975). The best data available are from the League of Red Cross Societies and the Natural Hazards Research Group (Burton *et al*. 1968, 1978). A summary of the League of Red Cross data is available elsewhere (Westgate & O'Keefe 1976b).

The Natural Hazard Research Group has provided one of the four detailed academic data sources for global statistics. For studies of global trends in disasters the group have produced data covering the years from 1947 to 1973. Certain conventions were adopted to help improve consistency (Dworkin 1974). Disasters are defined as situations which satisfy at least one of the following conditions:

(a)   at least $1 000 000 damage, or
(b)   at least 100 dead, or
(c)   at least 100 injured.

Disasters are categorised as being large-area or small-area. Large-area disasters are defined as exceeding one $10°$ latitude by longitude square on a world map, while a small-area disaster would cover less than a $10°$ square. The data were compiled from a broad range of encyclopaedic and journalistic sources including the *New York Times index, Encyclopaedia Britannica yearbook, Collier's encyclopaedia yearbook*, the *American people's encyclopaedia yearbook* and *Keesing's contemporary archives*.

The most important tendency in the data is an increase in the occurrence of disasters over the past 50 years (Fig. 14.1). The Figure also shows the increase from 1947–73 of the large-scale disasters, that is, those disasters covering more than a 10° square on a world map and where the damage exceeds $1 million. This tendency is paralleled by an increasing loss of life per disaster. The greatest loss of life per disaster is observed in underdeveloped countries, and there are general indications that the vulnerability of these countries in particular is increasing. (Drought and famine are not included in this analysis, although recent studies indicate similar trends in these too.)

No major geological or climatological changes over the past 50 years adequately explain the rise. There is little argument about geological change, but there has been much mystifying argument about climate change, especially following the prolonged drought over the African and Asian continents (cf. Copans, Ch. 5). We may merely note that no firm conclusion can be drawn about changing climatic conditions from available evidence. Randall Baker at the Development Studies School of the University of East Anglia recently reviewed all the evidence of climatic change in Africa, and offered the Scottish judgment of 'case not proven'. Even if some long-term change were observable it would not explain the increase in disaster occurrence noted in the data (Baker 1977).

If it is accepted that there has been no major geological and climatological change in recent years, then it can be assumed that the probability of the extreme physical occurrence is relatively constant. If the probability is constant, then the explanation of the increasing numbers of disasters must be sought in conditions that increase the growing vulnerability of the population

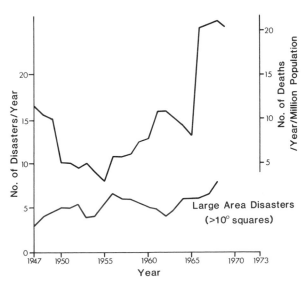

Figure 14.1 Global disasters 1947–73: 5-year moving averages (after Dworkin 1974).

to extreme physical events. In this respect our work suggests the need for some radical rethinking of the nature of 'natural' disasters.

It is known that the frequency of natural disasters is increasing especially in underdeveloped countries. Moreover, the increased vulnerability of people to extreme physical events seems intimately connected with the continuing process of underdevelopment throughout the world. As population continues to expand, and as resources continue to be controlled by a minority, the real standard of living drops for much of the world's population. As the process continues, this population is increasingly vulnerable to environmental variation. Paul Richards of the Environmental Unit in the International African Institute recently emphasised this in his introduction to *African environment: problems and perspectives*, 'just as natural processes such as lack of rainfall affect social structures,' he argued, 'so social processes such as economic "development" can affect natural systems, "causing" famine and soil erosion for example' (Richards 1975). He went on,

'In a continent where internationalities of dependency, massive international labour migration and multinational companies prevail and in a world where growth does not necessarily mean development, and development does not necessarily bring enrichment or an increase in personal happiness, the ultimate cause of environmental problems may well be traceable to the structural imbalances between rich and poor countries and we would be right

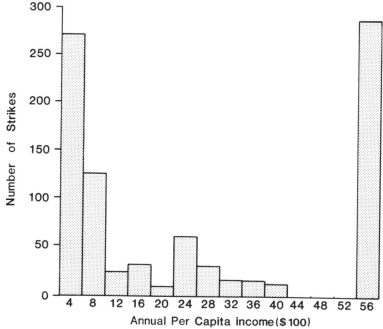

Figure 14.2   Number of disaster strikes by per capita income of disaster strike area.

to replace the term *natural* with the more appropriate term *social* or *political* disaster.'

These suggestions would strike the Guatemalan peasant as common sense. He no longer identifies the recent earthquake there as a natural event – some local inhabitants who survived are referring to the event as a 'classquake'. It is a view which reflects their broad experience.

In summary, therefore, the increasing numbers of disasters and relatively constant geographical conditions make it clear that vulnerability is increasing due to human changes, and in the largest fraction of the world's inhabited area these changes are clearly bound up with 'development' or its failure (Fig. 14.2).

Thus it is necessary for us to consider the process of underdevelopment to understand the reality of disaster vulnerability. Furthermore, to understand underdevelopment, we must recognise that it has invariably been interpreted from the standpoint of particular economic theories, and that its significance for hazards research varies greatly according to which of these theories one accepts.

Underdevelopment: a critique of the dominant Western model

It has been a commonplace of development theorists to explain underdevelopment in terms of insufficient integration of the different sectors of the underdeveloped country. Emphasis is usually placed on the lack of integration between the rural, 'traditional', or 'backward' sector and the relatively 'modern', industrialised, or capitalist sector. It is argued that if the rural sector population would adopt the correct attitudes and entrepreneurial behaviour, the problems of underdevelopment could be overcome (Myint 1958, Nurkse 1961, McClelland 1964). They note the lack of free capital movement and insufficient savings within the underdeveloped countries which contributes to a continuation of 'vicious circles' of poverty (Hodder 1973). Others point to the lack of an institutional base to provide the necessary regulatory measures, capital investment and protective tariffs to generate incentive and conditions for development (Prebisch 1964, Furtado 1971).

We can begin to grasp these issues by examining what traditional development theorists generally emphasise as the categories of problems found in underdeveloped countries and how they relate to vulnerability.

Population   The demographic structure is said to hinder the development process. It is characterised by latent unemployment in agriculture, a high proportion of dependants and a rapid growth associated with high birth rates. This reflects a pre-capitalist subsistence agriculture and its method of providing for its labour and survival needs. Added to this are lower morbidity rates due to the introduction of technologies and new medical practices accompanying the expansion of capitalism. However, before the capitalist intrusion, the overpopulation problem did not reach the magnitudes that became evident after capitalist entry. While it is clear that people in the now-underdeveloped countries did not live in a blissful state of harmony with the environment, natural balances were established. Population oscillations were of a low order. Subsequent to the establishment of capitalist relations, the population oscillations began to vary more substantially (Buchanan 1975).

The advance of capitalism has not only affected the demographic profile of the underdeveloped countries, but it has exerted great influence on their economic and geographic landscapes. One of the outstanding features of the landscape is the primate city which generally has a population about ten times larger than the next-order city. It becomes clear that the demographic structure is not an independent factor but rather is closely related to the capitalist structures imposed on the peripheral countries. As Nurkse (1961) said, 'The population explosion of Asia, due largely to the fall in death rates, reflects the *uneven* impact of Western civilization'. Thus, the very structure and population dynamics being blamed for weak performance was induced by capitalism. And this, in turn, has *increased* the vulnerability of underdeveloped populations.

Natural resources   Another characteristic of underdeveloped countries as defined by capitalist theorists is a poor endowment of natural resources and local environments. This is attributed to the interplay of the natural environment and the cultural, educational, health and nutritional deficiencies of the local working population (Viner 1963). Meier (1958) indicates that 'The present phenomenon of a low amount of resources per head is the result of either the exhaustion of resources or such a rapid growth in population that overpopulation now puts pressure on available resources'. However, poor resource endowment is another myth. The underdeveloped countries are the sites of many of the known resources of the world. What is important is the accessibility of the local populations to their own resources and their control over them. In refuting the shortage of natural resources, Higgins (1959) says 'The soil and climate of Japan did not suddenly change in the latter part of the nineteenth century when its transformation to an industrialized country began'. The literature on the cultural, educational, psychological and health factors retarding development is large. The crucial point, again, is that these factors are examined in the present without analysis of the particular historical conditions leading to them. It is interesting to note, for example, that although 'tropical medicine' is taught as a distinct body of knowledge, the endemic and epidemic diseases studied are diseases of poverty, observable in pre-capitalist Europe, rather than diseases associated with a specific location. The misuse of natural resources induced by capitalism increases the vulnerability of underdeveloped populations.

Capital   A third problem for underdeveloped countries is a constant capital shortage. It is used to explain the low level of productivity, employment and the underutilization of natural resources. 'If the capital is available for development, the capitalists or their government will soon provide the facilities for training unskilled people. . . The real bottle-necks to expansion are therefore capital and natural resources' (Lewis 1958). Why has there been this shortage and lack of investment opportunities in these countries? One answer, presented by Nurkse (1961) indicates that a lack of investment incentives rather than a lack of savings is the basic problem. He describes a circular process in which the inducement to invest is limited by the size of the market. Yet the expansion of the market is made possible by releasing money for consumption spending, which must come from the same source as investment capital for production. The circular processes are not complete systems. Reality is not a closed system. The processes must reflect a particular organisation of the economy and the space-economy. After all, how did the now-developed countries escape the circular process? The causes of the circular processes must be traced in history. This reveals important changes resulting from capitalist penetration into the underdeveloped countries. The basic problems behind the limited market is the division of labour. Without the development of complementary sectors any surplus created cannot be reinvested locally. It is consumed in luxury items and it flows out of the country directly, for example, in the form of profits to multinational corporations. It also flows out in the form of interest and amortisation payments on loans (Szentes 1971). This misuse of capital in capitalism increases the vulnerability of underdeveloped populations.

The development of underdevelopment

An alternative picture of underdevelopment is to see these problems not as its *cause*, but as *effects* of the (under)development process. From this point of view underdevelopment is indeed the expression of the successes of economic enterprise elsewhere. It seems that the paternal and self-congratulatory picture of Third World peoples prevalent in the West prevents most of us from recognising this aspect of an otherwise widely accepted philosophy of 'competition' and individualistic enterprise. However, an historical examination of Third World countries soon reveals that underdevelopment has been as much an ongoing, deepening and dynamic process as development elsewhere. Hence we speak of the 'development of underdevelopment'.

From this point of view underdevelopment is not seen as simply a contemporary condition whose solution may be found in increased investment, greater output per capita, or the many other suggestions put forth by the development theorists. The study of history reveals it to be a *process of underdevelopment* whose roots date back centuries. Underdevelopment in this sense therefore is a manifestation of the relationship between the developed capitalist countries, or centre of the world economic system, and the countries of the Third World constituting the periphery. The consequences for the underdeveloped countries have been overwhelmingly negative. These ideas have been developed especially in Lenin (1975), Luxemburg (1974), Frank (1969), Rhodes (1970), Rodney (1974), Seidman (1974), Szentes (1971). For analyses of origins in colonial and imperialist activity and of the ongoing causes in terms of the needs of the advanced capitalist countries today, one may also cite the studies of Marx (1967), Baran and Sweezy (1966), Magdoff (1967), Blaut (1975) and Amin (1974). This alternative view focuses on the interaction of external and internal factors in the genesis of underdevelopment.

External factors   Within the periphery there has been the establishment of a capitalist formation designed to serve the needs of the centre capitalist formation (Amin 1974). This penetration has led to particular economic and geographic structures within the underdeveloped countries which point to the problems of the development process. Three key problems are:

(a)   Unevenness of productivity as between sectors in terms of production per capita,
(b)   disarticulation of the economic system,
(c)   domination by foreign powers or corporations, which may perhaps be seen as the origin and result of the unevenness of production and the disarticulation of the economy (Amin 1974).

The foreign domination is easily documented (Jalée 1968). Capital flows are one example: from 1950–65 the total flows of United States capital investment to underdeveloped countries amounted to $900 million, while the flows from these countries to the United States was $25 600 million (Szentes 1971). Further, control of capital indicates domination: Morgan Guaranty Trust Company's 16 correspondent banks in Venezuela hold 55% of privately owned commercial bank resources (O'Connor 1970). These sources provide ample evidence that the peripheral countries subsidise the centre. This discussion will centre on capital investment and technology transfers as two components of the centre–periphery relationship.

   Capital investment and the transfer of technology are just two aspects of the total scenario. (It should be pointed out that technology is, for the most part *sold* and the notion of 'transfer' tends to obfuscate an important part of the international exchanges in the underdevelopment process.) The historical development of relations between the centre and periphery has reflected the changing requirements of capitalism as it expanded and changed from merchant capitalist formations through manufacturing, industrial and monopoly capitalism. From the developmental perspective, the crucial issue is whether the technologies in use contribute to the economic and spatial integration of the underdeveloped country. Does the technology provide the impetus for employment and income growth as well as for the establishment of complementary industrial linkages and service activities? Does the use of imported technology generate a sufficient surplus for domestic use or does it promote the funnelling of value produced out of the country? Evidence indicates that the flows from the periphery to the centre have increased as more technology is transferred (Amin 1974, Szentes 1971).

It is argued that the technology employed in the periphery should be designed to utilise the abundant labour supply in these countries. That is, it should be labour-intensive. In fact, the agricultural and extractive industries generally are labour-intensive but the ownership pattern of land and production facilities contributes to increasing unemployment. It further provides the framework for great income differentials between sectors and classes. This is made possible by what has been called the super-exploitation process found throughout the periphery (cf. Copans, Ch. 5). The related land tenure and ownership implications for development are clearly spelled out in a number of studies (e.g. Petras 1970, Seidman 1974, Leys 1974).

The progressive distortion of the space-economy in terms of concentration of wealth, goods and services is further explained by an examination of the type of industry that is 'transferred' to the periphery. Rather than establishing a complementary set of economic activities, the industrial activities that predominate in the periphery are consumer-good production or part production to provide the centre with lower cost production through the superexploitation of labour. 'When the advanced capitalist countries give these countries "technical assistance", they try to do it in such a way that the realization of the licenses, blueprints, standards and technical specifications, etc. given to them, the smooth operation of plants installed by them and the working and repair of the machinery and equipment, should be dependent on the deliveries of the metropolitan firms' (Szentes 1971).

By limiting the technologies employed to non-capital-good production, the periphery is forever dependent on the centre for the machinery and inputs required to produce the consumer goods or parts. Investment in consumer-good production is to the advantage of the capitalist classes in both the centre and the periphery. The turnover rate is higher than in the capital-good sector and therefore the rate of profit is higher. The individual entrepreneur benefits by this rapid turnover, as does the capitalist in the centre who is able to extract the original investment much more quickly. This, in part, explains the large flow of capital out of the periphery. Both the local entrepreneur and the international capitalist seek secure investments which are usually in the centre. (About 80% of the centre's capital flows remain within the centre itself (Szentes 1971, Amin 1974).) Furthermore, the high rate of profit permits some local reinvestment from profits without requiring further capital inputs. It is possible to control production with minimal investment. For example, out of $72 million investment in Argentina by five oil companies, the corporations only invested $18 million. Debentures raised $30 million and US government and local investment corporations supplied the rest from previously accumulated profits (O'Connor 1970).

There is also the tendency towards capital-intensive production. By increasing the capital : labour ratio, and thereby raising the organic composition of capital, the firms are able to produce greater numbers of commodities. This increase in the organic composition of capital would appear to contradict the capitalist's interests in terms of value output. However, profits are obtained in all parts of the production and distribution process. In brief, these are:

(a)   superexploitation of labour made possible by a rural sector providing value in the form of means of subsistence and reproduction;
(b)   control over circulation, distribution and sale – profits obtained through monopoly prices charged in each of these areas;
(c)   extraction of other benefits in the form of tax shelters etc.;
(d)   high interest rates on loans and payments.

   Thus, the organic composition of capital in the periphery may come to equal that in the centre. Yet it is the combination of all these factors that permits a higher profit rate in the periphery than in the centre – 20–30% profit rate in the periphery compared to 10–15% in the centre (Prof. Ann Seidman, personal communication, 1977).

   The spatial manifestations of underdevelopment are quite evident. The relative overpopulation in both the rural and urban sectors, lack of infrastructural development permitting the integration of the hinterland activities, and the concentration of capital, goods and services in the primate city, are all examples. Adoption of capitalist industrial technology creates 'strong tendencies toward the geographic concentration of productive activity' (Rosenberg 1972). In its very need for concentrated labour and access to inputs the 'transferred' technology serves to recreate, in an exaggerated form, the landscape of capitalism. It is exaggerated because of the unidirectional flow of value out of the periphery. Without reinvestment of surplus, the problems are compounded rather than alleviated. As a result of these external processes the *population of the underdeveloped areas are becoming more vulnerable*.

Internal factors   The internal structures of Third World countries reflect the ravages of their colonial history. The economic landscape discussed earlier is one aspect. Another is the disintegration of existing modes of production. Along with this is the generation of social relations oriented around capitalist production; not the type of capitalism of Europe and the United States, but rather a unique form of capitalism with its unique class structure and production organisation (Amin 1974). In Latin America, Asia and Africa there developed a stratification in society reflecting the domination by the colonial centre. The enclave sector of the peripheral country was organised to meet the needs of the foreign capitalist. It includes the mining, plantation and manufacturing sectors. There also arose a migratory urban work force whose base remained in the rural–agricultural sector. The same applies to the labour force of the mines and plantations. The rural sector contained peasants engaged in subsistence agriculture and some cash-crop production. Growing cash crops was not an 'accidental detail' (Myint 1958), nor is the phenomenon of migratory labour. They are a result of the penetration of capitalist social relations.

For example, direct colonial control of Africa resulted in the continuing extraction of raw materials and agricultural products. A variety of mechanisms were formed to 'induce' the local population to 'contribute' to the economic growth of their countries. Taxes were introduced to force the African labourers to participate in the money economy. Sources of monetary income were needed to pay taxes. Failure to pay would result in loss of land, and forced labour (Wolpe 1972, Massey 1980). Thus, the pattern that prevails to this day was implanted in the peripheral societies. Labourers were forced to leave the rural agricultural sector to work on plantations, in the extractive industries or in urban centres of manufacturing. The labour power available in the rural sector was diminished and the agricultural output was accordingly reduced. The problem in the rural sector became one of underpopulation rather than overpopulation (O'Keefe 1977, Wisner 1978a). At the same time, land redistribution programmes resulted in the alienation of land from communities to individuals. The methods of coping with environmental stress, food production and distribution of use-values were drastically reduced as a result. Ethnoscience calls for different types of social organisation, but these were not permitted by the colonial powers (Wisner et al. 1977, Watts 1978). A further factor contributing to increasing underdevelopment was the transition from producing use-values for local consumption, including a variety of food crops, to growing cash crops as the organisation of production was changed, reflecting changes in the social relations. This further reduced the ability of the population to cope with environmental stress. Nutrition suffered (O'Keefe & Wisner 1975a, Wisner 1980–81, Wisner et al. 1982). *The population became more vulnerable*.

Finally, relations between the rural sector, the enclave sector and the centre may be defined in terms of trade relations. Large trading companies and, later, oligopoly and monopoly corporations controlled, as they still control, the imports and exports of the underdeveloped countries. During the mercantile capitalist period the trading companies under monopoly charter exchanged commodities. In the modern monopoly capitalist period the element of capital goods enters the picture. Multinational corporations with a worldwide distribution and marketing network, controlling global financial sources, are in a monopoly or oligopoly situation with regard to trade and production. This complete control contributes to the *increasing vulnerability* of the underdeveloped population.

Underdevelopment is not just a contemporary phenomenon, nor is it a self-propelled process in isolation. It is an integral part of the process of development of the capitalist countries of the world. As capitalism has evolved, so has underdevelopment. As capitalist penetration reaches the furthest parts of the periphery, the ability of the local populations to be self-reliant decreases. The dynamic process promotes the disintegration of societies just as it promotes greater profit for the centre. This greater profit in the centre generates the necessity for its further expansion. According to the argument thus far, this continued expansion *will increase the vulnerability* of underdeveloped populations.

Case studies

In 1970, 225 000 were killed by cyclone and flooding in Bangladesh, and another 600 000 were made homeless. An earthquake flattened Managua, capital of Nicaragua, in 1972, killing at least 6000, injuring 20 000, and destroying nearly half of the sprawling town's housing. The recent toll in Guatemala was even greater. At least 8000 Hondurans died in the 1974 Hurricane Fifi, and throughout the early 1970s south Asia and African savanna lands suffered massive drought-related losses. Drought is thought to have contributed to the death by starvation and/or measles of about 100 000 inhabitants of the six Sahelian countries. In 1973 alone, 25 major disasters killed 110 000 people, disrupted the lives of 215 million more, and cost more than $1000 million (USAID 1976).

Guatemala: impact of the earthquake Shortly after 3 a.m. of 4 February 1976 a massive earthquake occurred in the highlands of Guatemala, leaving in its wake at least 22 000 dead, nearly 75 000 injured and over 1 million of the nation's 6 million inhabitants without shelter. The Department of Chimaltenango was hit the hardest – nearly all the homes were destroyed, and in some of its towns, more than 1 person in 10 was killed. Fourteen towns were totally destroyed, and less than 30% of all buildings remained standing in another 17 towns. Most of the damage occurred in the highland areas north and west of Guatemala City and the strip along the Montagua river valley running eastwards from the highlands to the Atlantic coast. The quake, which measured 7.5 on the Richter scale (compared to 6.3 for the 1972 earthquake in Managua, Nicaragua), spread ruin across about 9065 km^2 of the most densely populated part of the country. Two days later a second major quake, of somewhat less intensity, again sent fear through the population and destroyed additional structures already weakened by the first quake. Within the first 20 days following the quake, over 1000 aftershocks had been recorded.

Preliminary estimates indicate that by far the heaviest damage occurred to *housing*, with substantial damage also to the main highway from Guatemala City to the north-east, to the Caribbean port of Puerto Barrios, and to hospitals, health posts, school buildings and water supply systems. *The directly productive sectors of the economy suffered relatively minor damage.* At the time total reconstruction costs were estimated by the government at $ (US) 750 million, of which $210 million was likely to be in foreign exchange (Westgate & O'Keefe 1976c). The actual cost soared to $200 million. The government hoped to obtain about $270 million from external lending agencies over the next four years which would cover foreign exchange costs and provide some local cost financing.

Perhaps the most telling comment about the disaster is illustrated below:

'Some 1,200 people died and 90,000 were made homeless in Guatemala City, almost exclusively in the slum areas of the city. In this well-known fault zone the houses of the rich have been built to costly anti-earthquake specifications. Most of the poorest housing, on the other hand, is in the ravines or gorges which are highly susceptible to landslides whenever earth movements occur. The city received proportionately little aid largely because it is governed by the most radical opposition tolerated in Guatemala, the Frente Unido de la Revolucion, a social democratic coalition. Its leader Manual Colón Argueta, was shot and wounded by unknown gunmen on 29 March, the latest victim of a wave of terror attacks that has claimed 40 lives since the earthquake. One city official, Rolando Andrade Pena, was shot down two weeks after the earthquake after suggesting that homeless people should be encouraged to rebuild on unoccupied private land (*Latin America*, 9 April 1976).

In Guatemala the poorest people suffered the worst effects of the disaster.

Such cases have also been documented for drought in the Sahel (Comité Information Sahel 1974, Meillassoux 1974, Franke & Chasin 1980) and Ethiopia (Bondestan 1974, Hussein 1976). Similarly, Hurricane Fifi, which hit Honduras in September 1974, was a disaster to be understood in terms of exploitation (O'Keefe & Cherrett 1976).

Honduras: impact of Hurricane Fifi The rich fertile valleys in northern Honduras around the San Pedro Sula Valley were extensively developed by American banana companies. Heavy forest was cleared, disease was controlled, and roads and railways were constructed. 'Development' labour was attracted to the area. Problems developed from 1956, when the banana companies changed from labour-intensive to capital-intensive production. No land was available on the valley bottoms because, if it was not owned by the banana companies, it was used for large-scale irrigation. The peasants were thus forced to grub for food on poor hillslopes. The most important factor in the destruction caused by Hurricane Fifi – between 4000 to 8000 dead and losses in production and infrastructure of $350–450 million – was the deforestation which began in 1965. The river valleys on the north coast have been increasingly cleared of forest for the banana plantations of the multinational corporations, United Brands and Standard Fruit – both US owned. As a result of this economic development the Campesinos moved to cheaper land on the hills where they cleared forest to grow maize. This deforestation has led to severe erosion; the loose soil silted the rivers which flooded more frequently. Human-made factors coincided with an extreme natural event to cause destruction.

The effects of Hurricane Fifi contrast sharply with those of the tropical storm that struck Darwin, Australia, on 24 December 1974. Cyclone Tracy had windspeeds similar to Hurricane Fifi, between 230 and 250 km/h, but the loss of life in disaster impact was much less than that of Hurricane Fifi; 49 and 8000 persons respectively. Both areas are in major tropical storm zones, and both possess adequate warning facilities. Both areas received similar extensive damage and early eye-witness reports from the two areas estimated that 80% of the impact zones were severely disrupted. Why, with such parallel conditions, was the impact so much more serious in Honduras than Australia? The answer lies in the degree of vulnerability of the two societies.

The form of economic development experienced in Honduras produces underdevelopment. Underdevelopment is a process that is found particularly in the poorer countries of the world. It is a process in which societies and people suffer from change imposed and controlled from outside the community, in the interests of the outsiders. The conditions of underdevelopment make a population such as the Honduran population more vulnerable to extreme natural events such as hurricanes. The poorest people suffer the most.

Such case studies provide illuminating material but, with the powerful argument of continuing and deepening underdevelopment and its causal linkage with disaster events, we must learn from the case studies, deriving knowledge from practice, and examine this knowledge in a broader, integrative framework.

Disaster and underdevelopment

As more evidence piles up, it is clear that one must radically rethink the causal relationships involving people and nature. It is time the popular belief in the 'randomness' of disaster – the so-called 'Act of God' enshrined in the law of contract and the popular mind – is questioned. The Lisbon earthquake of 1755 was supposed to have contributed to the rejection of Divine Providence by intellectuals of the period known as the Enlightenment. They saw this as an example of sudden, uncontrollable, horrible forces unleashed 'at random'. 'Periodic catastrophes due to structural imbalances and maladaptations to the new economic system of colonialism then replaced the random disasters that characterized the nineteenth century' [our italic] (Kjekshus 1974).

The concept of vulnerability to disaster brings order out of such apparent chaos. However the 'natural' disasters confronting the enlightened today will not bring them back to an acceptance of Providence, but to a conviction that the influence of the global market reaches everywhere – into the most isolated African, Asian, Oceanic, and Latin American homes.

In this way the present revolution in thinking about disaster is related to a far wider revolution of thought about underdevelopment. What had previously been seen as a *state* out of which the poor country had to emerge is now widely seen as a continual *process* of impoverishment based on a world economy which perpetuates technological dependency and unequal exchange. A similar view is taken about the active underdevelopment of poorer classes by richer ones *within* poor countries, as well as between rich countries and poor. This process has been identified as one of *marginalisation*.

The concept of marginality was originally used to denote the plight of migrants who left rural areas to find employment opportunities in towns. The concept initially referred to the lack of adequate housing facilities that these groups faced but it was soon used to denote a general lack of facilities and socio-political access of such migrant workers (Kuitenbrouwer 1973). It was then realised that the processes of migration to cities were induced by a more serious lack of opportunities in the rural areas. The cause of this low level of 'participation' was supposed to lie in the lack of internal integration within a society. This view of marginality led to the conclusion that if marginals were helped to organise then help could be provided to them so that they could adjust and adapt better to the requirements of society (Perlman 1978).

Radically opposed to this interpretation of marginality and consequent policies, another interpretation of marginality has emerged. This interpretation emphasises that the population which was called marginal and was supposed not to be integrated within society was actually fully integrated into society as the reserve army of the unemployed and rural producers of cheap food. The condition of marginality results not from the action of the marginal group itself but from the relationship that the group has with other classes and interest groups in society (Meillassoux 1972, Wolpe 1972, Bradley 1975, LeClair 1977).

Thus the 'marginals' are those who have been either forced off the land or onto very poor or insufficient land, and who cannot find a permanent job. This is the growing class in Asia, Latin America and Africa. Those concerned serve the modern industrial groups in underdeveloped countries as cheap casual labour, or by producing cheap food for industrial workers. They also have little political power and a poor standard of living. Often they are a cultural or ethnic minority within the poor country – the nomads in the Sahel or the Mayan Indians of Guatemala. Finally, they often live in the most dangerous and unhealthy places (O'Keefe *et al.* 1976). It is no accident that a major slum in San Juan (Puerto Rico – ironically named 'La Perla') is frequently inundated by high tide; that Rio's infamous *favelas* climb slopes of alpine difficulty; that the poorest urban squatters in much of Asia live on hazardous floodplains; that those people crowded into Recifé in north-east Brazil live in, and on, the mud of the tidal estuary, living off the crabs that also inhabit the mud (de Castro 1966); or that a quarter of Kenya's population (including many of the poorest) live in that country's drought-prone 'marginal' lands (Campbell 1981). The poor are often clearly aware of their own vulnerability. Why else would the devastated slum dwellers of Guatemala City refer to the earthquake as a 'classquake'?

The poor respond to potential and actual disaster in ways that often may appear to be irrational. They overstock the land with livestock, especially goats. They clear vegetation on steep Honduran hillsides in order to farm, removing the same vegetation that holds the soil in place. They stream back to the chars of the Bay of Bengal only weeks after wind and water has swept away all signs of human life (Wisner 1978b). They have not the capital or organisational resources to provide modern adjustments. The *latter* do exist for a tiny minority in the poor countries: the few thousand rich Kenyan farmers with access to agricultural insurance against drought; the few thousand wealthy Nicaraguans and Guatemalans who are able to afford earthquake-proofed homes (Wisner *et al*. 1976).

The rich countries and rich élites within poor countries do not conspire to starve the poor, to shift them into dangerous places like Nazis shifting Jews to death camps. But it is believed that the international division of labour among rich and poor countries, and market forces within the poor underdeveloped capitalist economies of the Third World, cause the poorest of the poor to live in the most dangerous places. This is a matter of complex social allocation – both of the social surplus product (national income) and of locations within the space-economy. The issues of income distribution are entangled with the issues of 'spatial social justice'.

Population growth alone is sometimes said to be sufficient to 'explain' increased vulnerability to disaster. But of course this does not explain anything. At most, population increase is only one of the many variables which link poverty to disaster proneness. Overpopulation is a symptom, not a cause. Studies from all continents show that people limit their family size only when they are assured of certain levels of material wellbeing (Mamdani 1972, Kleinman 1980). The more uncertain a couple's life, the more likely they are to want a large family to support them. If, in the long run, such an increase in population intensifies an already serious situation of continually growing vulnerability; it is tragic.

The theory of marginalisation

Several points emerge from this discussion. First, the process of underdevelopment is intimately linked with the control and exploitation of indigenous resources by the governing élite and outside interests. The management of surplus required to maintain a peasant economy's flexibility in the face of crisis is incompatible with the expropriation of surplus value. Thus the underdevelopment process forces the peasantry into a more vulnerable position which, in turn, directs them to look for another source of livelihood in areas where security may be less and hazard more severe or to change their resource use in ways that exacerbate vulnerability.

The process of marginalisation is shown in Figure 14.3. Disaster proneness is the result of the interface of a population undergoing underdevelopment

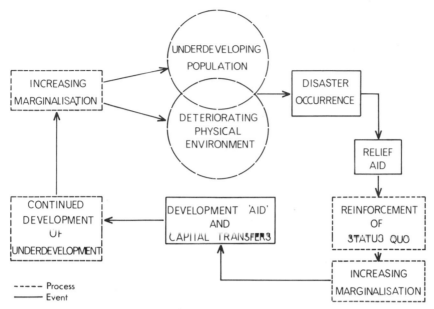

Figure 14.3 Diagram illustrating the process of marginalisation and the relationship to disaster.

and a deteriorating physical environment. The provision of relief usually reinforces the *status quo ante*, namely the process of underdevelopment that produced such vulnerability in the first place. (It should be noted that relief aid transfers parallel development 'aid' and capital transfers, i.e. relief is not altruistic; at best it is benign self-interest.) Thus, reinforcement of the *status quo* leads to further marginalisation which, through development 'aid' and capital transfers, encourage the continuation of the development of underdevelopment (Hayter 1971, Payer 1975). This exacerbates the process of increasing marginalisation that continually underdevelops a population's socioeconomic base and encourages a deterioration of the physical environment (O'Keefe & Wisner 1976, Cannon 1977). Such a casual pattern increases vulnerability to disaster.

The implications of marginalisation theory

The most important implications of marginalisation are outlined below:*

(1) Because of the continued forms of exploitation especially in the under-developed countries, disasters will increase as socioeconomic conditions

---

* In the five years since these ideas were originally drafted, international organisations such as the UNDRO and UNCHS (Habitat) as well as such NGO's as War on Want have come to accept versions of (1), (2), (4) and (5) – at least to some degree. One welcomes this, but must push on for *full* acceptance of these points *and* their translation into *practice*.

and the physical environment deteriorate (Baird *et al.* 1975, Jeffrey 1980).

(2)   The poorest classes will continue to suffer most losses (Wisner *et al.* 1976).

(3)   Relief aid, which reflects dominant interests and prevents political upheavals, generally works against the classes who suffered most in a disaster and will do so in the future disasters (O'Keefe 1975, Cannon 1977).

(4)   Disaster mitigation relying on high technology merely reinforces the conditions of underdevelopment and increases marginalisation (Westgate & O'Keefe 1976c).

(5)   The only way to reduce vulnerability is to concentrate disaster planning within development planning (O'Keefe & Conway 1975), and that development planning context must be, broadly speaking, socialist (Wisner 1979).

(6)   Because of the continued forms of exploitation, especially in underdeveloped countries, the only models for successful disaster mitigation are those conceived in the struggle against exploitation (Wisner *et al.* 1977, Wisner 1978b, Cannon 1977, Westgate & O'Keefe 1976c).

If these seem radical proposals, it is because the analysis indicates the necessity for radical proposals. Ongoing underdevelopment is placing marginal people in marginal lands. The disasters resultant from such a process are not 'Acts of God'. Quite the reverse. The poor, instead of inheriting the Earth, are being eaten up by it.

References

Amin, S. 1974. *Accumulation on a world scale.* New York: Monthly Review Press.

Baird, A., P. O'Keefe, K. Westgate and B. Wisner 1975. *Towards an explanation and reduction of disaster proneness.* Occ. Pap. no. 1, Disaster Res. Unit, Bradford Univ.

Baker, R. 1977. The Sahel – an information crisis. *Disasters* **1**, no. 1.

Baran, P., and P. Sweezy 1966. *Monopoly capital.* New York: Monthly Review Press.

Blaut, J. 1975. Models of imperialism. *Antipode* **6**(3).

Bondestan, L. 1974. People and capitalism in the north eastern lowlands of Ethiopia. *J. Mod. Afr. Studs* **12**(3).

Bradley, B. 1950. The destruction of natural economy. *Economy and Society* **4**(2).

Buchanan, K. (1975). Population and the white north. *Antipode* **6**(3).

Burton, I., R. Kates and G. White 1968. *The human ecology of extreme geophysical events.* Univ. Toronto, Dept. of Geography, Natural Hazards Res. Work. Pap. no. 1.

Burton, I., R. Kates and G. White 1978. The environment as hazard. New York: Oxford University Press.

Campbell, D. 1981. Land-use competition at the margins of the rangelands. In G. Norcliffe and T. Pinfold (eds). *Planning African Development*, Boulder, Co.: Westview.

Cannon, T. 1977. 'Natural' disasters and the Third World. In *Geography, social welfare, and underdevelopment*, N. Smith, M. Forbes and M. Kershaw (eds). J. St Andrews, Geogs Spec. Publn no. 2, St Andrews.

Cisin, I. H. and W. B. Clark 1962. The methodological challenge of disaster research. In *Man and Society in Disaster*, G. W. Baker and D. W. Chapman (eds). New York: Basic Books.

Comité Information Sahel 1974. *Qui se nourrit de la famine en Afrique?* Paris: Maspero.

de Castro, J. 1966. *Death in the Northeast*. New York: Vintage.

Dworkin, J. 1974. *Global trends in natural disaster 1947–73*. Natural Hazard Res. Work. Pap., no. 26, Colorado Univ.

Frank, A. G. 1969. *Capitalism and underdevelopment in Latin America*. New York: Monthly Review Press.

Franke, R. and B. Chasin 1980. *Seeds of famine*. Montclair, NJ: Allanheld, Osmun.

Furtado, C. 1971. *Development and underdevelopment*. Berkeley: University of California Press.

Hayter, T. 1971. *Aids on imperialism*. Harmondsworth: Penguin.

Hewitt, K. and I. Burton 1971. *The hazardousness of place: a regional ecology of damaging events*. Toronto: University of Toronto Press.

Higgins, B. 1959. *Economic development*. New York: Norton.

Hodder, B. W. 1973. *Economic development in the Tropics*. London: Methuen.

Hussein, A. M. (ed.) 1976. *Rehab: the drought and famine in Ethiopia*. London: International African Institute.

Jalée, P. 1968. *The pillage of the Third World*. New York: Monthly Review Press.

Jeffrey, S. 1980. Universalistic statement about human social behaviour. *Disasters* **4**(1).

Kjekshus, H. 1974. *Ecological control and economic development in East African history*. London: Heinemann.

Kleinman, D. 1980. *Human adaptation and population growth*. Montclair, NJ: Allanheld, Osmun.

Kuitenbrouwer, J. 1973. *On the concept and process of marginalization*. The Hague, Inst. Social Studs, Occ. Pap. no. 37.

LeClair, E. 1977. *Politics and ideology in Marxist theory*. London: New Left Books.

Lenin, V. I. 1975. *Imperialism, the highest state of capitalism*. Peking: Foreign Languages Press.

Lewis, W. A. 1958. Economic development with unlimited supplies of labour. In *The economics of underdevelopment*, A. N. Argawala and S. P. Singh. New York: Oxford University Press.

Leys, C. 1974. *Underdevelopment in Kenya*. Berkeley: University of California Press.

Luxemburg, R. 1974. *The accumulation of capital*. New York: Monthly Review Press.

Magdoff, H. 1967. *The age of imperialism*. New York: Monthly Review Press.

Mamdani, M. 1972. *The myth of population control*. New York: Monthly Review Press.

Massey, D. 1980. *International labor migration and its effects on rural development in Botswana*. PhD dissertation, Boston Univ.

Marx, K. 1967. *Capital*, vol. 1. Moscow: Progress.

McClelland, D. 1964. A psychological approach to economic development. *Econ. Dev. Cultural Change* **12**(3).

Meier, G. M. 1958. The problem of limited economic development. In *The economics of underdevelopment*, A. N. Argawala and S. P. Singh. New York: Oxford University Press.

Meillassoux, C. 1972. From reproduction to production. *Economy and Society* **1**(1).

Meillassoux, C. 1974. Development or exploitation: is the Sahel famine good business? *Rev. Afr. Polit. Econ.* **1**(1).

Myint, H. 1958. An interpretation of economic backwardness. In *The economics of underdevelopment*, A. N. Argawala and S. P. Singh. New York: Oxford University Press.

Nurske, R. 1961. *Equilibrium and growth in the world economy*. Oxford: Oxford University Press.

O'Connor, J. 1970. The meaning of economic imperialism. In Rhodes (1970).

O'Keefe, P. 1975. *Disastrous Relief*. London: War on Want.

O'Keefe, P. 1977. *Gakarara: the development of underdevelopment*. PhD dissertation, London Univ.

O'Keefe, P. and R. Cherrett 1976. *The MacNamara medicine show*. London: Christian Aid.

O'Keefe, P. and C. Conway 1975. *A survey of natural hazards in the Windward Islands*. Occ Pap. no. 14, Disaster Res. Unit. Bradford Univ.

O'Keefe. P. and B. Wisner 1975a. *The world food crisis issues* no. 1, Bradford Univ.

O'Keefe, P. and B. Wisner 1975b. African drought – the state of the game. In Richards (1975).

O'Keefe, P. and B. Wisner 1976. Underdevelopment in East Africa – a Kenyan case study. *Environment African* **2**(1&2).

O'Keefe, P., K. Westgate and B. Wisner 1976. Taking the naturalness out of natural disaster. *Nature*. **260** 15 Apr.

Payer, C. 1975. *The debt trap*. London: Penguin.

Perlman, J. 1978. *The myth of marginality*. Berkeley: University of California Press.

Petras, J. 1970. *Politics and social structure in Latin America*. New York: Monthly Review Press.

Prebisch, R. 1964. *Towards a new trade policy for development*. New York: United Nations.

Richards, P. (ed.) 1975. *African environment: problems and perspectives*. London: International African Institute.

Rhodes, R. I. 1970. *Imperialism and underdevelopment: a reader*. New York: Monthly Review Press.

Rodney, W. 1974. *How Europe underdeveloped Africa*. Dar Es-Salaam: Tanzanian Publishing House.

Rosenberg, N. 1972. Marx as a student of technology. *Monthly Review* **28**, no. 3.

Seidman, A. 1974. *Planning for development in sub-Saharan Africa*. New York: Praeger.

Sweezy, P. 1942. *The theory of capitalist development*. New York: Monthly Review Press.

Szentes, T. 1971. *The political economy of underdevelopment*. Budapest: Akademiai Kiado.

USAID 1976. Computer file printout on 'disasters'.

Viner, J. 1963. *International trade and economic development*. Oxford: Oxford University Press.

Watts, M. 1978. *Drought and underdevelopment in Hausaland, northern Nigeria*. Unpublished PhD dissertation, Michigan Univ.

Westgate, K. and P. O'Keefe 1976a. *Some definitions of disaster*. Occ. Pap. no. 4, Disaster Res. Unit, Bradford Univ.

Westgate, K. and P. O'Keefe 1976b. *Natural disasters – an intermediate text*. Bradford Univ.

Westgate, K. and P. O'Keefe 1976c. The human and social implications of earthquake risk for developing countries. *J. Admin Overseas* **4**.

Wisner, B. 1978a. *The human ecology of drought in eastern Kenya*. Unpubl. PhD dissertation, Clark University.

Wisner, B. 1978b. An appeal for a significantly comparative method in disaster research. *Disasters* **2**(1).

Wisner, B. 1979. Flood prevention and mitigation in the People's Republic of Mozambique. *Disasters* **3**(3).

Wisner, B. 1980–1. Nutritional consequences of the articulation of capitalist and non-capitalist modes of production in eastern Kenya. *Rural Africana*, nos. 8–9, winter–fall.

Wisner, B., P. O'Keefe and K. Westgate 1976. Poverty and disaster. *New Society*, 8 Sept.

Wisner, B., P. O'Keefe and K. Westgate 1977. Global systems and local disasters: the untapped power of people's science. *Disasters* **1**(1).

Wisner, B., D. Wiener and P. O'Keefe 1982. Hunger: a polemical review. *Antipode* (forthcoming).

Wolpe, H. 1972. Capitalism and cheap labour – power in South Africa. *Economy and Society* **1**(4).

15 A general approach to the identification of hazards and responses

GEORGE E. B. MORREN Jr

This chapter is a tentative approach to the natural hazards field by an ecological anthropologist. My more conventional interests are in human–environmental interactions such as subsistence, settlement pattern and the like. The development here is self-consciously naïve, much as anthropologists feel naïve in first encounters with the exotic societies they characteristically study. My immersion in the technical literature is only partial. Indeed, I have been more attracted to popular and historical writing on disasters – journalistic accounts, memorial volumes and memoirs. There is an abundance of crude data and first-person observation in these sources, that aids my 'people-oriented' approach. Yet I originally wandered into this field looking for case material to illustrate a new way of studying human–environmental interaction. Hence, while perhaps naïve, I am not without preconceptions.

I have two main concerns. The first is to develop a way to identify and describe 'realistically' the main environmental problems confronting particular groups of people. We need to emphasise that, at any given time, people face a variety of problems; that these interact in significant ways, and that we need to account for a variety of their problem characteristics. The latter include but are not limited to initiating agents or triggers such as geophysical events, and predisposing factors such as settlement patterns. They require some emphasis on group history. Economic and political 'causes' of environmental problems are frequently overlooked and, as Hewitt noted (Ch. 1), studies of hazards appear to be particularly susceptible to this kind of oversight.

In my view, the traditional distinction between 'natural' and 'man-made' disasters largely disappears. Indeed, the approach advocated here is not hazard-specific. This is consistent with the long-standing view in ecological studies that environmental problems arise, not from the environment *per se,* but from the interaction of organisms with their environment.

My second major concern is more clearly anthropological: the advocacy of more naturalistic accounts of human responses and coping devices much as I attempted in Chapter 3. It is accomplished, at least in part, through the notion of a 'process of response'. This conceptualises the relationship of responses and their properties to environmental problems and their properties. It gives special attention to the temporal dimension.

Thus, particular hazard events must be put in a social, material and historical context including other hazard events and environmental problems and responses. Indeed, I think that it is a common error to view disasters as events. Rather, they should be viewed as parts of processes with spatial, temporal and other properties (see Vayda 1974, Burton & Hewitt 1974, p. 256).

Difficulties and hazards

My initial exploratory reading of standard literature focused on drought (Morren, Ch. 3), but many of the difficulties can be extended to the general hazards field. One of the outstanding points to emerge was the obfuscation that surrounded the identification of the natural phenomenon known as drought as being the core of episodes of danger to various peoples. It is a type of mystification of the general problem field involving several features:

(1)   Only superficial attention is paid to the multitude of basic human problems that may accompany, interact with, or be initiated by natural hazard events, such as loss of livelihood, life-support, shelter, reserves and security. These problems may be recognised, but they are not studied systematically, and certainly not with the same degree of effort or research support that is devoted to, for example, weather and earthquake prediction.

One of the reasons for this misdirection and misallocation of research effort is the social structure of the field; just as in medicine, professionals make decisions affecting other professionals, or else advise politicians on the details of programmes affecting professional activity aimed at the public. The members of communities concerned only rarely have a role in shaping the outcome of professionally directed research or action programmes. Such rare instances are, however, particularly instructive. They seem to involve two possible courses of action for ordinary people, non-participation or self-organised programmes. The former is nicely illustrated by the response of many people to the US swine-flu immunisation programme of 1976. By and large, the public chose not to participate (and wisely so). The latter is exemplified by communities organising and sponsoring their own research, as in the case of the James Bay hydroelectric scheme and the Buffalo Creek flood (Stern 1976, Erikson 1976). There is something here akin to the distinction which can be drawn between intermediate technology (an engineering concept) and appropriate technology, in which the test is in the hands of the users of the technology (Jequier 1976). It is worth noting that, notwithstanding the fears of the scientific community concerning possible pernicious effects of courts of law deciding 'scientific' issues, judicial machinery in the United States and Canada has promoted greater participation of ordinary people in scientific decision making, probably to the benefit of both parties.

Also of concern are situations in which a widespread pattern of social (rather than environmental) disruption and reorganisation appears to ensue from a disaster event. For example, in some settings disasters appear to be politically destabilising, as in the earthquakes in eastern China in 1976 or Iran in 1978. Disasters have triggered pogroms and have been used by security forces as 'cover' for the pursuit of rebels.On the one hand, it is just as great a mistake to attribute the causes of such 'political disasters' to natural events (cf. Barkun 1974) as to attribute other human consequences exclusively to natural events. On the other hand, the role of disasters and other acute local problems in helping to stimulate new social and political arrangements is not to be denied.

(2)   Even less attention is paid to the ways in which ordinary people, either as individuals or members of small groups, undertake – and must undertake – to cope with these and related problems.

In part, this arises from the kinds of research strategies pursued. For one thing, survey research techniques give inaccurate results, particularly when directed at what people *intend* to do in relation to perceived hazards or prospective disaster situations. People may be adequate surrogate observers of their own and others' past experience, but are bad predictors of future behaviour. Even such useful studies as Haas and Mileti's (1977) social impact analysis of earthquake prediction has an unreal quality to the extent that a credible prediction (for some people) has been around for a long time. Thus the study sample excludes people who have already responded to the threat, e.g. by settling outside the hazard zone.

Obviously, the ideal strategy, and the most difficult one to pursue, is for trained observers to be in place starting with the 'earliest manifestations' or 'warning' phase of a particular event and continuing on through until the shape of the later recovery phases can be seen, with people's activities naturalistically described, and their effectiveness assessed. Granted the difficulty in realising this ideal, there are a number of instances in which it has been possible retroactively to recover the data involved or else to glean it from historical, ethnographic, or media sources. These materials suggest that the activities of ordinary people in a given locality during the earliest phases of a disaster can be critical, not only in relation to individual survival, rescue and the relief of suffering, but in terms of mobilising groups and of minimising permanent long-term ecological, economic and social losses. Local people and their neighbours are much more likely to know how to do this than are outsiders. They more or less know their own priorities, and are of course 'placed' to respond quickly.

(3)   On the contrary, emphasis is most commonly placed on technological solutions and on 'broad spectrum' responses sponsored by big governmental and international agencies, or other kinds of 'outsiders'. Accom-

panying this focus is a seemingly misleading picture of the costs, benefits, appropriateness and effectiveness of 'big responses'.

One very common effect of external relief is to pre-empt individual effort and local initiative; to prevent people from salvaging personal property or conserving other assets, to compete with local sources of food supplies and materials and so on. In the San Francisco earthquake and fire of 1906, the apparently illegitimate insertion of federal troops and their forcing of unselective evacuation prevented people from saving moveable belongings and from preventing or fighting fires in their dwellings and businesses. Similar problems arose in the 1980 Italian earthquake disaster. During the eruption of the volcano La Soufrère in the French Antilles, the biggest task facing security forces, including many dispatched from Europe, was that of preventing rural people from sneaking back to their homesteads to take care of livestock.

A further effect of external relief is to make some of the consequences of a disaster permanent and to exorcise local capability to deal with subsequent problems. A particularly aggravated example of this is in Erikson's (1976) description of the emergency housing provided by the US Department of Housing and Urban Development to the survivors of the Buffalo Creek (West Virginia) damburst. In addition to the actual loss of life and property, one of the most devastating consequences of the flood, according to Erikson, had been the destruction of 'community'; that is, the network of interpersonal bonds characteristic of society in small mountain hamlets. The more or less haphazard assignment of survivors to trailer camps, to say nothing of the bulldozing and burning of damaged or destroyed homes, made permanent this potentially reversible loss.

Beyond this kind of situation, descriptive literature is replete with accounts of survivors taking no action while awaiting the arrival of relief forces or else suspending their own activities upon their arrival. This is only partially explainable on the basis of either the disability or the short-run opportunism of some survivors. Rather, the most likely general factor contributing to these effects is the inappropriateness of the relief packages made available by supra-local organisations.

The kind of research emphasis I suggested under point (2) above would produce information that would be useful in designing external programmes aimed at fostering, reinforcing and supplementing individual and local initiative in an effective way. This would provide an alternative to programmes which are now known to have the opposite effect.

(4)   In the study of the causes of disasters there is an overemphasis on earth and atmospheric systems, as the immediate initiating agents, at the expense of examining the sociocultural (including political and economic) causative factors. Strongly put, I would argue a direct relationship between development (including social change and modernisation) and hazard vulnerability.

Coming fresh to this work one is struck by the way such recognition of the influence of human factors as there is assumes the form of 'blaming the victim'; for example, shifting cultivators causing erosion and landslips, over-grazing by pastoralists promoting desertification, suburbanites choosing to live in floodplains, high fertility in the Third World, and so on. Such stereotyped examples do possess the grain of truth necessary in scientific circles. A broader view would see these as frequently involving responses of ordinary people to development acts over which they had no control: the commercialisation and expansion of agriculture, urbanisation, demand for labour and the like.

I have already suggested taking a closer look at the adaptations of people at the individual and community levels as one likely way out of a muddle. Another, complementary, strategy emphasises the 'unnatural' aspects of the hazards and problems faced by people. I believe that a wide range of environmental hazards may be viewed most profitably as consequences of human activity; more specifically, as consequences of the interaction of people and their environment. I can define at least four senses in which this seems to hold:

(a) *That the hazard proceeds directly and principally from human activity.*
This situation is best exemplified by the hazards peculiar to urban–industrial living, including industrial accidents and environments affecting workers and neighbours, transportation accidents, development insults such as urban and rural relocation, economic depressions and the like. Warfare, both primitive and modern, fits in as well. Such clearly unnatural hazards point to the useful-ness of eliminating the 'natural'–'man-made' distinction because the human responses evoked in many instances are identical, and because such man-made hazards interact with natural factors in significant ways.

(b) *That the acuteness of the damaging effects is related to the magnitude of human exploitation and modification of the environment and population density.*
Rural examples are particularly relevant because their unnatural components are often masked by the prominence of natural biotic, earth and atmospheric factors involved, e.g. pests, soils, or rainfall. The most elementary develop-ment act, forest clearance, has been implicated in a wide range of hazard events – floods, the distribution of snowfall in blizzards, earthquake vulnera-bility, landslips, drought and desertification. The general tendency to overex-pand particular urban, industrial, or agricultural patterns under population or commercial pressure inevitably leads to inappropriate uses of marginal areas in ways which are irreversibly destructive to the environment and dangerous to people. Thus, inappropriate land-use patterns are often 'forced' by de-velopment contingencies, such as urban sprawl, which locate human settle-ments in floodplains or on unconsolidated landfills. Similarly, commercial development in predominantly agricultural countries forces subsistence pro-duction onto marginal lands and encourages the selection of crops and tech-

niques that contribute to nutritional hazards of different degrees of extremity; crop failure and famine or unvaried starch diets and chronic undernutrition.

(c) *That development tends to foster dependency and specialisation on the part of individuals and communities, reducing their ability to respond effectively, or narrowing the range of normal environmental variability with which they are able to cope on their own.*

The first part of this assertion relates to the consequences of inappropriate disaster relief discussed above. The second part can be supported using 'drought' as an example. In all areas of the world that receive any rainfall at all the amount of rain that actually falls varies from year to year. The average annual rainfall, however, has little meaning to people who have lived in an area for a long time. They must be more or less adapted to extreme conditions if they are to survive. Whether they be hunter–gatherers, pastoralists, agriculturists, or whatever, success is based upon their possession and control of a range of options in dealing with changes in water ability. Development aimed at increasing yields is typically based on the mid-range of normal variability rather than on the extremes. Thus programmes that sedentise pastoralists by improving local water supplies (often at the same time that the most desirable part of their range is converted to plant agriculture) create the inevitable risk of drought and famine. Similarly, rainfall farmers in an urban–industrial economy who convert to irrigation have little recourse when water supplies are reallocated to users with higher political priority.

(d) *That the involvement of outside, supra-local groups may render permanent the effects of an otherwise short-duration local problem.*

The plight of refugees or 'permanent evacuees', such as the Buffalo Creek survivors, was referred to earlier. It is a general phenomenon to the extent that a return to a semblance of a 'normal' pre-disaster state is prevented or inhibited by official relief and restoration efforts. Similar effects have been attributed to the provision of inappropriate food aid in disasters such as the Guatemala earthquake of 1976 (Riding 1977) or the killing frosts in the New Guinea Highlands of 1972 (Waddell 1975). In the Guatemala case, the infusion of large quantities of North American grain reduced the market for available locally produced foodstuffs and did more economic damage to farmers than the earthquake itself. In the New Guinea case, relief efforts may have permanently disrupted extensive patterns of intergroup relations.

Recent work in the hazards field has begun to redress the overemphasis on natural factors (e.g. White 1974; Burton *et al.* 1978) although many of the questions I raise here remain to be investigated systematically. Some advances have been fostered, and at the same time obscured by 'creative partisanship' (e.g. Waddell 1977, White 1978).

In summary, as well as identifying environment problems and hazards more realistically, we must also redirect our focus on responses. This must be in such a way as to permit us to relate their characteristics to the characteristics of problems. An approach being developed with respect to a wide range of biological and anthropological problems, that of 'response processes', is well suited to this task.

The features of response processes

The term that is basic to any discussion of the response process approach is Gregory Bateson's concept, *flexibility*. He defines flexibility as 'uncommitted potentiality for change' (1972b, p. 497). For Bateson, and for others who have employed this approach, such as Slobodkin (1968) and Vayda and McCay (1975), a particularly significant *cost* of responding to a problem is the loss of flexibility, i.e. diminished ability to cope with other problems. The economics of flexibility is not the same as the economics of energy, or of money, or of resources in which costs are merely subtractive. According to Bateson, the budget of flexibility is fractionating, e.g. it is the difference between the loss of muscle mass (subtraction) and the loss of a limb (fractionation *and* subtraction). In other words, the flexibility concept is concerned with quality more than quantity. In addition, it requires a temporal dimension. In an adaptive unit subjected to change subtraction becomes fractionation when the quality of some vital property changes and/or when the rate at which change proceeds is relatively rapid.

Thus, responding adaptively to hazards (or changes in critical environmental features of any sort) involves not only using faculties to cope with the immediate situation but also leaving other faculties in reserve for coping with future problems. Gains or losses of flexibility involve qualitative changes in other system properties, including what Holling and Goldberg (1971) refer to as the 'domain of stability' and 'resilience'. Flexibility (and other qualitative properties) cannot be defined rigorously beyond the statement of these general points except in *particular* systems. In the language of philosophy, it is a 'primitive term'. The earliest users of the concept (Bateson and Slobodkin) used it in the field of evolutionary biology. In particular, Slobodkin attempted to lend it greater specificity in postulating a progressive loss of flexibility as organisms attempted to adapt first at the behavioural level, then at the physiological level, and then at the genetic level, with learning, acclimatisation and selection respectively serving to restore flexibility to responses at each level (Slobodkin 1968). Vayda and McCay (1975, p. 293) have cited examples of the implicit use of the flexibility concept in other problem fields including physiology and medicine. Haddon (1970) has employed similar concepts in his analysis of alternative strategies for reducing losses involving 'rapid energy transfers' (e.g. hurricanes, projectiles, collisions, etc.). All of these efforts have emphasised that the process of adaptation and survival is continuous with an overall strategy aimed at loss reduction rather than prevention. Hence, the focus must necessarily be on the *relationship between* environmental problems that threaten survival and the actual process of responding to such changes. The response process approach embodies these assumptions and can be applied to a wide variety of situations involving problems and responses.

Scientific investigators reporting on development, environmental hazards, social change, planning and the like are often at a loss to explain the great variability to be observed between individuals and between groups subjected to seemingly similar circumstances. The field of human adaptation, of which the areas cited are subfields, is riddled with contradictions and paradoxes, both apparent and real. When presented with a potentially advantageous innovation, some people embrace it and others reject it. Some people, when subjected to a death-dealing disaster, rebound and purposefully embark on reconstruction while others sink into shock or engage in bizarre and seemingly irrational activities. Some members of flood-damaged communities rebuild in high-risk areas while others decide on their own to relocate. Some people, when subjected to a regional depression, migrate towards regions of apparent opportunity while others remain and participate in turn, a corollary of Bateson's concept of 'flexibility'.

(1)   In a parsimonious world there should be some correspondence between the characteristics of environmental problems and the characteristics of responses to them.

Of particular interest are such features of problems as their magnitude, duration and novelty, and such features of responses as their magnitude, reversibility, temporal order and persistence, as well as associated costs (Vayda & McCay 1975). The 'correspondence' specified is not a *necessary* one, except possibly in the context of long-term survival. In the shorter run there are numerous and familiar examples of responses which are, in some sense, disproportionate, in terms of both their quantitative costs and the loss of flexibility entailed for some responding units as these relate to benefits and effectiveness. Any analysis of alternatives would have to take this into account.

(2)   People, like other organisms, often respond to a new problem as if it were an old problem (Slobodkin 1968, p. 196) and, hence, respond to a variety of problems in an essentially similar way, or use the same responses for different problems.

This feature of responses is one of the factors tending to confound the first 'principle' stated above and, perhaps, it represents another form of parsimony. In his analysis of Enga (Papua New Guinea) responses to the risk of killing frosts Eric Waddell (1975; Ch. 2 above) describes a temporal sequence of responses including patterns of hazard mitigation, risk spreading and, under the most extreme circumstances, refuging. The higher-level responses are essentially similar to Enga responses to defeat in traditional warfare, and were also characteristic responses of New Guinea populations to clashes with aliens in the novel early contact situation. Another example is the common response of farmers in places such as Britain and the United States to both low commodity prices and poor growing conditions. Characteristically, they respond to either problem by making more extensive plantings in the following year.

An obvious operational problem in connection with this and other features is that of *identity* of problems and of responses. The example of modern farmers presented above might be restated to say that farmers respond to a 'bad year' by expanding existing activities, thus blurring the distinctiveness of the problems. Similarly, one might speak of responding to regional or local scarcity of a vital resource by establishing areally integrating networks or grids. One would then have to argue the essential identity of electrical grids, trade relationships, highway systems, water works and similarly functioning infrastructure. Identity is necessarily an artifact of the taxonomy used to classify problems or responses.

(3)   Responding minimally at the onset of a problem prevents overcommitment of resources and faculties in the face of uncertainty concerning such problem characteristics as duration and magnitude.

Manifestations of this feature frequently involve conflicts and paradoxes which are difficult for ordinary people, public leaders and scientists to resolve. Ordinary people often appear to be conservative, reluctant to abandon place and property to fate, with a strong commitment to the maintenance of the *status quo* (which also strongly influences post-disaster behaviour and sentiment). The distribution of individual experience, preparedness, and authority in small groups and communities is patchy. In the earliest phases of a process many people prefer to bide their time and implicitly to resist external and impersonal authority or to select their own mix of small adjustments, perhaps in concert with kin, friends and neighbours. At this level, individual action can strongly influence the effectiveness of responses, especially in situations where timeliness is an issue. Examples include such sudden onset or emergency situations as earthquakes, building fires, marine disasters, or potential highway accidents, where survival often depends upon the behaviour of one or two prepared and purposeful individuals who serve to organise and guide the behaviour of others close by. In such instances, 'taking charge' may consist merely of the issuance of a timely warning or a few directions. These can initiate separation of some of the exposed people from an amplifying hazard, people who might otherwise continue on their existing course of action or inaction to the point of panic and catastrophe.

Political leaders responsible for higher-level responses are similarly caught between the possible need for timely action and public inertia, on the one hand, and the long-term maintenance of the authority of their offices, on the other. The latter corresponds to one of the costs of making an 'inappropriate' decision. Officials are constantly and inevitably subjected to the charge of either inaction and not acting quickly enough *or* acting precipitously and unnecessarily. Scientists involved in the development of diagnostic and warning techniques aimed at triggering responses are in a similar bind. The chance that an attempted 'cure' will be worse than the 'disease' is a real one. The universal mode of reducing this kind of cost is to defer as long as possible those responses which may have irreversible consequences.

(4) Related to the foregoing is the principle that the cause (or causes) of entry into one phase of the response process need not be the same as the cause (or causes) of escalation to other phases of the process (Vayda 1974).

Just as responses may be temporally ordered, so too problems and other contingencies may be ordered in time. Typically, such post-disaster problems as loss of shelter, loss of livelihood and life support, and infectious disease, occur in acute form at different times after onset. In his study of warfare in the New Guinea highlands Vayda (1974) found that, while lower-level raiding and skirmishing might be triggered by a desire for revenge, the decisions to escalate to higher levels of armed conflict might occur when earlier activity revealed weakness on the part of the enemy.

(5) Similarly, escalation from phase to phase is not inevitable once a process of response is initiated, but rather escalation may depend upon the persistence of problems initiating the process or its later phases, or on the strength of mechanisms resisting escalation, as well as on the effectiveness of existing responses.

Good general examples of anti-escalatory mechanisms include so-called peasant conservatism in the face of outside agents of socioeconomic change, and the policy of some nations, such as post-revolutionary China (and the United States at the time of the San Francisco earthquake) to reject offers of disaster relief tendered by other nations. Maris (1975) believes that a 'conservative impulse' in the face of changes of many sorts has great generality.

(6) Reversibility of response processes, involving the restoration of flexibility (a return to a facsimile of a 'normal' condition or level of response), while not inevitable, is also a typical feature of response processes.

A good example of the restoration of flexibility, indeed one involving behaviour which appears paradoxical to some experts (see (10) below), is the propensity of people to return to the site of an experienced disaster and attempt to replicate the old life-style which may itself have contributed to the disaster or its impact in the first instance. After a flood, people rebuild in the floodplain. One of the most famous photographs of the 1906 San Francisco earthquake and fire shows a family sitting down at the dinner table in the out-of-doors with the ruins of the city smouldering in the background.

There are also counter-examples of the failure of restoration, involving the permanent (irreversible) loss of flexibility. Erikson's (1976) analysis of the consequences of a federal emergency shelter programme for the survivors of Buffalo Creek was cited earlier. An example familiar to anthropologists concerns the effects of contact on formerly isolated and self-sufficient primitive populations. Moorehead (1968) rightly describes it as a 'fatal impact' involving the irrevocable penetration of a social, political and economic capsule and very high mortality. Typically, tribal peoples, such as the group I worked with in New Guinea (Morren 1977), lost first their political sovereignty as part of the process administrators referred to as 'pacification' and then, more gradually, their economic self-sufficiency. The concomitant of this has been growing dependency, with the people concerned on their way to real or cultural extinction and/or peasantry. Waddell's (1975) description of the irreversible consequences of disaster relief for a New Guinea population is, according to some observers, generalisable to modern developing nations too (Waddell 1977, Hall 1975).

(7) Escalation and de-escalation from phase to phase may involve shifts in the *unit* of response, as from individual to groups of various kinds and degrees of inclusiveness, and back to individuals.

We should, according to Vayda and McCay (1975) be interested in how hazards are responded to by both groups and individuals, the unit of response being viewed as a part or dimension of the response in question. An obvious example of this kind of shift is when the efforts of individual survivors of a disaster are augmented, superseded or suppressed by the activities of outside relief workers, police, or troops under the control of a supra-local unit.

(8) A shift from a lower-level response (and unit of response) to a higher-level response (and unit of response) entails a loss of flexibility for the lower-level unit.

This corresponds to notions of dependency, previously referred to, but there is more to it than the irreversible losses implied by the concept. We noted earlier the evidence that in the course of the San Francisco earthquake and fire the illegitimate insertion of federal troops, who forced mass evacuations, prevented individuals, including householders and business people, from protecting their property and otherwise salvaging belongings. In the same disaster it has been shown that most people who were left without shelter were able to arrange emergency accommodations on their own. They were permitted to do so because it took some time for locally and nationally supported shelter programmes to be organised. It is a typical feature of higher-level responses that individuals and groups otherwise capable of coping on their own are prevented from doing so. In the absence of de-escalation, the range of normal variability with which the people can cope on their own is permanently narrowed.

(9) Higher-level responses may be more effective in dealing with environmental problems and hazards of larger (relative) magnitude than lower-level responses.

For example, a standard (historical) response to both long- and short-term local resource scarcity has been to make use of the areally integrating networks which move resources between localities. For long-term scarcity, this has involved the expansion and intensification of networks such as those cited earlier, e.g. roads, pipelines, electrical grids, etc. But an irreversible dependency and commitment is involved, entailing loss of flexibility to virtually all of the local units participating though with real gains for some as well (see Hewitt, Ch. 1).

The short-term situation may involve only the emergency consignment of commodities thought to be in short supply. This is potentially reversible, but not inevitably so. Where already extant, resource-moving networks are particularly vulnerable to damage in disasters and their restoration is the first order of business for higher-level units. Indeed being 'marooned' or cut off from the outside world, while great for Maroons,* is frequently perceived by members of urban societies as worse than sustaining casualties. The official national relief effort for San Francisco in 1906 was aimed particularly at restoring the city's function in the national economy: business, transportation, banking and the like. The post office operated throughout the conflagration!

(10) There is an apparent paradox of order and disorder created by the interplay of points (8) and (9) above, corresponding to the difficulty of assessing the balance between the real benefits and real costs of escalation from phase to phase.

According to Bateson (1972b, p. 498), it is a paradox that authorities, including planners and analysts, need consciously weigh, and it is, I assert, weighted by ordinary people often to the consternation of such authorities. Thus in the aftermath of the 1976 earthquake in eastern Turkey, which effectively destroyed most shelter in the area, government officials laboured vigorously to relocate survivors from rural to urban areas in anticipation of harsh winter conditions. On their part, many common people resisted this with equal vigour in anticipation of the loss of their livelihoods, and the fate of their livestock, which would not be able to survive without human care.

(11) There are potentially three kinds of responses involved in response processes: those which restore equilibrium by effectively dealing with the problem(s) at hand, those which restore flexibility to other responses, and those which do both.

This is a more general statement of the considerations embodied in Slobodkin's (1968) view that 'organisms respond to rapidly fluctuating features of

* A term applied in various parts of the New World to communities of runaway slaves who obviously benefited from their isolation.

their environment behaviourally and to slower fluctuations physiologically, and just as learning restores flexibility to behaviour, so does adaptation restore flexibility to physiological responses'. Equilibration is concerned with 'normal' environmental variations with which people and other organisms can cope 'routinely', whereas flexibility restoration is concerned with extreme or survival-threatening variations exceeding the capacity of equilibrating responses at a given level. The restoration of flexibility involves either a return to a facsimile of the previous equilibrium situation *or* the establishment of a new equilibrium. Elsewhere, I have argued that demographic responses restore flexibility to resource management by providing the circumstances under which intensification may occur and that, similarly, certain innovations in the sphere of resource management may restore flexibility to demographic responses in populations experiencing 'population pressure' (Little & Morren 1976, p. 26).

(12)   For individuals and groups of various kinds the ultimate response is the abandonment of group (or community) way of life, or territory.

This kind of response is triggered by some form of coercion, immediate or chronic: persecution, economic and social alienation, loss of life-support, banishment, permanent refuge from disaster, forced relocation, or a combination of such factors. It may be seemingly voluntary as with members of millenarial cults or farmers who sell their land to developers, but the wider context of such choices is, nevertheless, coercive. Minimally people find themselves in situations in which they perceive themselves to have no other alternatives, possibly excepting violence. In any event, radical changes in life-style, often irreversible, are involved.

(13)   Survival (according to Slobodkin 1968, p. 191) in its various dimensions and degrees is the true measure of the effectiveness of responses, rather than measures of efficiency or optimisation and the like.

A number of more practical tests of effectiveness of responses can also be applied: (a) the absence of escalation, because lower-level responses 'act as a bulwark' against the necessity for higher-level responses (Slobodkin 1968, p. 198); (b) the reversal of the process of response; (c) the reduction or mitigation of the intensity of a particular problem or its manifestations by a response (Morren 1977, pp. 276, 283–4); and (d) the biological state of the members of a population (or its demographic state) with respect to the problem or hazard in question (Morren 1977, pp. 276, 284).

References

Barkun, M. 1974. *Disaster and the millennium*. New Haven: Yale University Press.
Bateson, G. 1972a. The role of somatic change in evolution. In *Steps to an ecology of mind*, 346–63. New York: Ballantine.

Bateson, G. 1972b. Ecology and flexibility in urban civilization. In *Steps to an ecology of mind*, 494–504. New York: Ballantine.

Burton, I. and K. Hewitt 1974. Ecological dimensions of environmental hazards. In *Human ecology*, F. Sargent (ed.), 253–83. Amsterdam: North-Holland.

Burton, I., R. Kates and G. White 1978. *The environment as hazard*. New York: Oxford University Press.

Erikson, K. 1976. *Everything in its path: destruction of community in the Buffalo Creek flood*. New York: Simon & Schuster.

Feit, H. A. 1978. *The future of hunters within nation states; and the theory and practice of anthropologists*. Paper presented at the Conf. on Hunters and Gatherers, Paris, 27–30 June 1978.

Haas, J. E. and D. S. Mileti 1977. *The Socioeconomic impact of earthquake prediction*. Boulder, Col., Inst. Behavioral Science, Colorado Univ.

Haddon, W. L. 1970. On the escape of tigers: an ecologic note. *Technol. Rev.* **72**(7).

Hall, N. 1975. The myth of the natural disaster. *The Ecologist* **5**(10), 368–71.

Holling, C. S, and M. A. Goldberg 1971. Ecology and planning. *J. Am. Inst. Planners* **37**, 221–30.

Little, M. A. and G. E. B. Morren 1976. *Ecology, energetics and human variability* Dubuque, Iowa: Brown.

Jequier, N. 1976. The major policy issues. In *Appropriate technology: problems and promises*, N. Jequier, ed., 16–112. Paris: OECD.

Maris, P. 1975. *Loss and change*. Garden City, NY: Anchor.

Moorehead, A. 1968. *The fatal impact: an account of the invasion of the South Pacific 1767–1840*. Harmondsworth: Penguin.

Morren, G. E. B. 1977. From hunting to herding: pigs and the control of energy in montane New Guinea. In *Subsistence and survival: rural ecology in the Pacific*, T. Bayliss-Smith and R. Feachem (eds), 273–315. London: Academic Press.

Morren, G. E. B. Jr 1981. A small footnote to the 'big walk': environment and change among the Miyanmin of Papua New Guinea. *Oceania* **52**, 39–65.

Richardson, B. 1975. *Strangers devour the land*. New York: Knopf.

Riding, A. 1977. US food aid seen hurting Guatemala. *NY Times*, 6 November 1977, 53.

Slobodkin, L. B. 1968. Toward a predictive theory of evolution. In *Population biology and evolution*, R. C. Lewontin (ed.), 187–205. Syracuse: Syracuse University Press.

Stern, G. 1976. *The Buffalo Creek Disaster*. New York: Random House.

Vayda, A. P. 1971. Phases in the process of war and peace among the Marings of New Guinea. *Oceania* **42**, 1–24.

Vayda, A. P. 1974. Warfare in ecological perspective. *Ann. Rev. Ecol. System.* **5**, 183–93.

Vayda, A. P. and B. McCay 1975. New directions in ecology and ecological anthropology. *Ann. Rev. Anthrop.* **4**, 293–306.

Waddell, E. 1975. How the Enga cope with frost: responses to climatic perturbations in the Central Highlands of New Guinea. *Human Ecology* **3**.

Waddell, E. 1977. The hazards of scientism: a review article. *Human Ecology* **5**(1), 69–76.

White, G. (ed.) 1974. *Natural hazards: local, national, global*. New York: Oxford University Press.

White, G. 1978. Comment on Waddell: 'The hazards of scientism.' *Human Ecology* **6**.

Wisner, B., K. Westgate and P. O'Keefe 1976. Poverty and disaster. *New Society*, 9 September, 546–48.

Author index

Subject index